Freedom of Information Reform in China

I0124458

Freedom of Information (FOI) in China is often perceived as a recent and intriguing phenomenon. This book presents a more complex and detailed understanding of the evolution of FOI in China, using information flow analysis to explore the gradual development of government receptivity to FOI in an information environment through time. The book argues that it is necessary to reassess the widely divergent origins of FOI reform in China, and asserts that social, political and legal factors should have central roles in understanding the development of FOI in China. The book uses information flow analysis to find that FOI reform in China formed part of a much longer process of increased transparency in the Chinese information environment, which gradually shifted from the acceptance of proactive disclosure to that of reactive disclosure. FOI thus has become a beneficiary of this gradual transformation of the Chinese information environment.

Weibing Xiao is Associate Professor of Law, Shanghai University of Political Science and Law, China. He received his Master of Laws degree from Jilin University and a PhD in Law from Tasmania University. His research focuses on freedom of information, government transparency and reuse of public sector information.

Routledge Law in Asia
Series editor: *Randall Peerenboom*

Freedom of Information Reform in China

Information flow analysis

Weibing Xiao

Routledge
Taylor & Francis Group

LONDON AND NEW YORK

First published 2012 by Routledge

2 Park Square, Milton Park, Abingdon, Oxfordshire OX14 4RN
711 Third Avenue, New York, NY 10017

Routledge is an imprint of the Taylor & Francis Group, an informa business

First issued in paperback 2017

British Library Cataloguing in Publication Data
A catalogue record for this book is available from the British Library

Library of Congress Cataloging-in-Publication Data
Xiao, Weibing.
Freedom of information reform in China / Weibing Xiao.
p. cm. -- (Routledge law in Asia)
Includes bibliographical references and index.
1. Freedom of information--China. 2. Government information--China.
3. Disclosure of information--China. 4. Law reform--China. I. Title.
KNQ2476.X53 2011
342.5108′53--dc22
2011013115

ISBN: 978-0-415-67778-3 (hbk)
ISBN: 978-1-138-48142-8 (pbk)

Typeset in Times New Roman
by Taylor & Francis Books

Contents

List of tables

Preface

Most non-Chinese scholars have approached Freedom of Information (FOI) in China as a recent, strange and intriguing phenomenon. This book uses an array of Chinese sources, interviews with Chinese officials and citizens and information flow analysis to propose a more complex and detailed understanding of the evolution of FOI in China.

The book argues that information flow, a theme to explore the gradual development of government receptivity to FOI in an information environment through time, can be used as a new explanatory model for FOI reform in a jurisdiction. China serves as an example to substantiate this argument. The origins of China's FOI legislation need to be understood within the context of improved information flow conditions resulting from multifaceted factors, including social, political, legal and economic ones. This improved information flow has constituted an enabling environment for the adoption of FOI legislation.

This book also argues that it is necessary to reassess the widely divergent origins of FOI reform in China. By applying information flow analysis, the book asserts that social, political and legal factors should be accorded central roles in understanding the development of FOI in China. Economic growth and anti-corruption efforts in the process should be allocated important but secondary roles.

This book uses information flow analysis to find that FOI reform in China formed part of a much longer process of increased transparency in the Chinese information environment, which gradually shifted from the acceptance of proactive disclosure to that of reactive disclosure. FOI thus has become a beneficiary of this gradual transformation of the Chinese information environment. This is the reason China has adopted a push model of FOI legislation stressing proactive disclosure of government information, which differs from many countries that have introduced a pull version of FOI legislation emphasizing reactive disclosure through responses to access requests.

This book maintains that existing compliance analysis focuses heavily on reactive disclosure, and thus is restricted in its application to China. It therefore utilizes a revised compliance analysis model that focuses on both proactive and reactive disclosure. The revised model incorporates findings from empirical research conducted in China, allowing a more effective and dynamic analysis of compliance issues in China. Whilst information flow analysis in this book is limited in its application to an explanation of China's FOI phenomenon, it may have wider applicability as it is a dynamic and systematic explanatory framework for FOI.

Acknowledgements

The work of writing up a book would not have been completed without the support of:

My supervisors, Professor Rick Snell and Professor Don Chalmers, who constantly supplied me with informative and useful commentaries and a friendly working environment.

My friends, Paul Hubbard, Rhys Stubbs, Professor Alasdair Roberts and Professor Gino Dal Pont, who made helpful and inspirational comments on my drafts. Mr Colin Darch and Professor Peter Underwood, who made a prepublication version of *Freedom of Information and the Developing World: The Citizen, the State and Models of Openness* available. Dr Claire Hiller, Andrea Pentecost, Louise Oxley and Morag Porteous, who helped me proofread my book and improve my expression.

The Scientific Research Foundation for the Returned Overseas Chinese Scholars, State Education Ministry, and the Leading Academic Discipline Project of Shanghai Municipal Education Commission (Project Number: J52101), which provided generous funding for completing this book.

Professor Randall Peerenboom, and Peter Sowden of Routledge, who were very supportive of this book.

My parents, Shuihua Cheng and Xiaoxing Xiao, who sponsored my long journey of study. My wife, Jing Li, who encouraged me to do PhD research abroad and then backed me throughout from every aspect.

I owe gratitude to all of them.

Abbreviations

CCDI	Central Commission for Discipline Inspection
CPC	Communist Party of China
FOI	Freedom of Information
LGNI	Leading Group on National Informatization
LGNOGA	Leading Group on National Openness in Government Affairs
NCCPC	National Congress of the Communist Party of China
NGOs	Non-Government Organizations
NPC	National People's Congress
OGA	Openness in Government Affairs
OTASP	Openness in Two Areas and Supervision by the Public
OVA	Openness in Village Affairs
SARS	Severe Acute Respiratory Syndrome
SCIO	Informatization Office of the State Council
SMS	Short Message Services
WTO	World Trade Organization

1 Introduction

China's Freedom of Information (FOI) phenomenon, which refers to the introduction of FOI legislation into mainland China in January 2007, presents a puzzle to the world, demanding explanation and understanding. To solve this puzzle, the following questions need to be clarified. What reasons are there for the adoption of FOI legislation in China? What corresponding legislative process has occurred in China? What type of FOI legislation has been adopted in China? What are the prospects for the implementation of China's FOI legislation? These questions have sparked the research informing this book.

'It's FOI, but not as we know it'.[1] That was a comment made by an English academic colleague when she spoke with Professor Rick Snell about China's (FOI) reform some years ago. Friends from different countries, including Australia, Canada, New Zealand, Indonesia, Laos, Malaysia and Nigeria, also raised doubts about the feasibility and effectiveness of FOI legislation in China. They considered Chinese FOI as a 'strange' and 'intriguing' phenomenon.[2] This phenomenon is regarded as strange because a one-party state like China has not established any of the preconditions – such as liberal democracy, the rule of law, a developed economy, media freedom and an active civil society – normally associated with the easy adoption and implementation of FOI legislation. Non-Chinese academics are further confused by the rapid uptake of FOI legislation in China. The first national FOI legislation was adopted after only five years' consideration from 2002 to 2007. Above all, non-Chinese observers[3] find it difficult to fully understand China's FOI phenomenon, as it does not fit with the view that FOI is a liberal democratic tool used to limit government power.

Two explanatory models

Accountability deficit and globalization are two common explanatory models for the diffusion of FOI reform. The former is used to explain the wave of FOI before the 1990s in longstanding liberal democracies, such as the US, Australia, New Zealand and Canada.[4] The latter model is generally used to explain the recent wave of FOI since the 1990s, especially the 2000s.[5] However, both of these explanatory models have limitations when applied to

China's FOI phenomenon. The origins of China's FOI legislation need to be understood within the context of improved information flow resulting from changed social, political, legal and economic conditions. This improved information flow has constituted an enabling environment for the adoption of FOI legislation. This book suggests using information flow analysis to better understand the adoption of FOI in China, and as an improved form of FOI analysis in general.

FOI adoption before the 1990s: a tool for solving accountability deficit

A dominant theme in the FOI literature, especially before 2000, presupposed two necessary conditions for the adoption of FOI legislation: the perception of growth of government and the development of liberal democracy.[6] However, this theme has been challenged since the wave of FOI legislation began to spread across many developing countries, including China, Mexico, India, Nepal, Chile and Indonesia, after 2000.[7]

The wave of FOI legislation before the 1990s favoured the argument that FOI was an ingredient to solve a perceived accountability deficit and enhance liberal democracy.[8] This wave involved countries with long democratic traditions.[9] While some advanced democracies, such as the UK and Germany, postponed the adoption of FOI legislation until the early 2000s, they found it increasingly difficult to 'justify not adopting' this legislation,[10] especially after the adoption had become a global movement. The fact that most affluent countries have introduced FOI legislation reinforced the notion that FOI was primarily a tool for addressing concerns about the erosion of government accountability due to an expansion of bureaucratic power[11] and domination of parliaments by the executive.[12]

FOI reform in Australia reflected this need to address an accountability deficit. The traditional methods of accountability based on parliament were inadequate after the government increased its 'impact on the lives of individuals, groups and corporations' over the post-war period.[13] Missen argued that the executive had too much power, and its 'control over information is a power in itself. Parliament must restore the balance of power and FOI will assist it'.[14] In addition, question time did not assist members of parliament in acquiring the information they needed.[15] It was found that 'many members of the Parliament feel themselves unable to fulfil their proper role as elected representatives'.[16] The accountability deficit and the commitment to liberal democracy were also the origins of FOI legislation in the US,[17] New Zealand[18] and Canada.[19]

FOI adoption after the 1990s: globalization

The accountability deficit was an effective explanatory model for the wave of countries adopting FOI legislation before the 1990s. However, FOI newcomers, such as Mexico (2002) and India (2005), have focused attention on a different set of explanatory measures. Most of the FOI adopters during the last two decades have very different political and social systems to FOI adopters before the 1990s. They have been prompted by various motives, such as fulfilment of democratic transition, elimination of corruption, protection of human rights and economic development.[20] The idea of necessary conditions for FOI reform was refuted by the diffusion of FOI legislation in newly democratic countries in the 1990s[21] and other states in the 2000s.[22]

An alternative view has been that the FOI movement is being influenced by globalization.[23] Globalization necessitates cross-national learning and emulation,[24] and drives the introduction of FOI legislation to align with international standards. For Blanton, this is evidence that globalization, rather than regional varieties, plays a key role in standardizing the concept of FOI legislation for 'more value-neutral meanings',[25] like economic growth. Yet some authors, such as Darch, Underwood and Snell, contest the uniformity, necessity or even desirability of this standardization of response.[26] Darch and Underwood state that 'the Chinese example ... possibly represents the most serious practical challenge to the idea, implicit in much of the activist literature, that freedom of information procedures are essentially nomothetic, rule-based and universal'.[27] A critique built upon Darch and Underwood's comment is developed in Chapter 6.

Non-government players: major contributors to FOI reform

The explanatory models of both accountability deficit and globalization demonstrate that demand side players, who are information receivers, are key contributors to FOI reform. While domestic players, such as the media and parliament, played significant roles in FOI reform in advanced democracies for addressing the deficit in government accountability, international players, such as the World Bank and the human rights organization Article 19, have played an increasing role in FOI reform during the last two decades to prompt the idea of a global move in the adoption of FOI legislation. FOI legislation was therefore generally adopted in the hostile circumstances, especially during the wave of FOI legislation before the 1990s,[28] which was a largely reactive response to strong pressure from demand side drivers.

Domestic non-government players: FOI adoption before the 1990s

The diffusion of FOI legislation in advanced democracies suggests that FOI reform is only likely where there is a vigorous campaign run by non-government players (the media, the opposition or public interest groups). International players were largely absent from this wave of FOI. As FOI is likely to limit the power of the executive and the bureaucracy, conventional wisdom argues that the government would be more likely to resist such reforms than introduce them. Thus, a common theme, albeit with different emphasis, occurs after the exploration of the comparative development of FOI in countries such as the US, Australia and New Zealand.[29] FOI reform in these liberal democracies generally has displayed the following three features: strong pressure from non-government players, adoption by main opposition parties and various degrees of resistance by the government and/or bureaucracy.[30] The following two points explain this.

First, the media and members of parliament were significant players on the campaign for FOI in the wave of countries adopting FOI legislation between the 1960s and the 1980s. In the US, both members of Congress and media groups played a key role in prompting the government to consider FOI law.[31] This was also the case in Australia, where the organization Freedom of Information Legislation Campaign was established in 1976 to promote FOI legislation,[32] becoming 'the primary pressure group in the campaign which was mounted with varying degrees of intensity through to the passage of the FOI Bill 1981 by the Senate in June 1981'.[33]

Furthermore, FOI reform was mainly used as an election issue, and thus the opposition became another major pressure on government to reconsider its predilection for secrecy. In Australia, Senator Evans observed that 'FOI tends to be espoused as a concept rather more passionately by oppositions out of office than by governments sitting in office'.[34] At the end of the 1972 election campaign, the opposition Australian Labor Party declared that it would adopt FOI law.[35] To meet this election promise, the Cabinet of the first Whitlam government established an Inter-Departmental Committee in 1973 to prepare FOI legislation.[36] However, the introduction of FOI legislation by the Labor Party was interrupted after Whitlam's dismissal in 1975, and this incomplete task was transferred to the incoming Liberal-National Country Party, which committed to adopt FOI legislation in its 1975 election campaign.[37]

While the FOI Bill was introduced in the Senate in 1978, it lapsed due to the 1980 federal election. About one month before the election, the Fraser government responded to the Senate Committee's Report on Freedom of Information published in 1979.[38] The FOI Bill was passed by the Senate in 1981 without the complete acceptance of significant recommendations by the Senate Committee.[39] Only the Labor Party, the opposition party at the 1982 federal election, committed to fully implementing the Senate Committee's suggestions.[40] The Australian Labor Party won the 1982 election, and delivered on its commitment rapidly, passing the first amendment to FOI legislation in October 1983.[41]

In New Zealand, the opposition also pressured the government to consider FOI legislation. Eagles and others argue that FOI 'became a political issue in New Zealand in the mid-1970s'.[42] An opposition Labor MP, Richard Prebble, introduced an FOI Bill in 1977, but 'it lapsed after the first reading'.[43] In 1981, as observed by Aitken, 'the government was under pressure from the opposition Labor Party which was intending to make freedom of information an election issue'.[44] In consequence, the National Party government immediately introduced a bill drafted by the Committee on Official Information into the House of Representatives.[45] The fact that public servants predominated in the Committee on Official Information was essential to make draft FOI legislation become friendlier toward the supply side/government, which is an information supplier.[46] This is a notable contrast to the situations in other countries, such as the US, Australia and Canada, where little attention was paid to the capacity of the supply side for FOI reform as their bureaucratic reactions were hostile or at least uninterested.[47]

FOI reform in the US, Australia and Canada[48] demonstrates that the reform was, to a large extent, 'interparty politics'[49] and required significant and active impetus from the opposition and other players on the demand side, such as the media and public interest groups. Whilst the pressure from demand side players also influenced the adoption of FOI legislation in New Zealand, the New Zealand case indicated that the receptivity of the supply side to FOI was crucial to smooth the adoption and implementation of FOI. This theme is addressed in relation to China in more detail in Chapters 3, 4, 5, 6 and 9.

International players: FOI adoption after the 1990s

Intergovernmental institutions, international non-government organizations (NGOs) and foreign governments interested in transparency issues[50] have contributed to the global FOI movement by motivating or pushing many developing states to introduce FOI legislation since the 1990s. This is a notable point of difference with the reform process between the 1960s and the 1980s in which international players were largely absent. Several intergovernmental institutions, like the Council of Europe, established a required standard on access to information in the early 2000s, which prompted its potential members to adopt FOI legislation.[51] The United Nations Educational Scientific and Cultural Organization, the United Nations Development Programme, the Organization of American States and the Pacific Islands Forum Secretariat have also assisted states in introducing FOI legislation.[52]

Some multilateral institutions, including the International Monetary Fund, required the passage of FOI legislation as a prerequisite for further funding, for example the adoption of FOI legislation in Pakistan.[53] Some international NGOs, such as Transparency International and the Carter Centre, used FOI legislation as a tool for tackling corruption.[54] NGOs, such as Article 19, the Commonwealth Human Rights Initiatives, the Carter Centre and the Open Society Justice Initiative, encouraged countries to introduce FOI legislation for protecting the right to know as a fundamental human right.[55] Foreign governments, including the US,[56] also encouraged other countries to adopt FOI legislation by funding international NGOs that collaborated with local demand side players to help catalyse local demand for government information. Cambodia serves as a case in point.[57]

Reassessment of FOI reform in China

This book argues that the wide diffusion of FOI reform in the last decade across numerous and diverse political and administrative systems may necessitate a rethink about the explanatory models used for FOI reform. In particular, domestic or local information flow conditions over time may justify a higher and more dominant explanatory role. The economic growth, globalization and anti-corruption explanations for FOI reform in China fail to sufficiently account for and identify the significant and constantly evolving changes in the social, political and legal environment. These more traditional explanatory models, in particular, obscure or downplay the importance of improved information flow, which has created an enabling environment for FOI reform in China.

FOI reform in China: missing liberal democratic elements

Liberal democratic values, processes and institutions are rarely found in China and the presence of FOI reform in the absence of these elements has caused a quandary for non-Chinese scholars. It is observed that '[t]he real paradox of [FOI] in China is its introduction into a non-democratic political system'.[58] Kolhammar also argues that 'it might seem paradoxical that a traditionally authoritarian state such as China is implementing a regulation that is giving citizens greater insight into the dealings of the state'.[59] These statements are based on the dominant argument that FOI reform should come later than other fundamental liberal democratic values, which can tolerate FOI.[60] China, in the absence of these liberal democratic elements, provides a significant and divergent case study in FOI reform.

Globalization: a follow-up to FOI reform rather than a key driver

In contrast to the claims made by Blanton and others for the integral role of globalization in FOI reform after the 1990s,[61] its role in China has been secondary in terms of importance and timing. Globalization advocates have stressed the role of emulation, international players and policy convergence in contributing to the spread of FOI reform.[62] These three factors have played a minor role in China.

First, China's FOI reform was not simply an emulation of 'better-off states'[63] or liberal democracies. Second, whilst the most recent FOI reform saw the growing involvement of external assistance, the initial role played by international players, including multilateral organizations and NGOs, was minimal in China. This contrasts with the dominant transparency efforts of international institutions that marked most of the recent FOI adopters in the Asian region.[64] However, international involvement or cooperation was important in formulating the actual content of FOI legislation in China. The EU–China Information Society Project and the China Law Centre at Yale University provided fora for international cooperation in this area.[65]

Third, policy convergence, as a result of globalization, was not a significant factor in Chinese FOI reform. Several substantive mechanisms, which are generally advocated and regarded by international players as decisive factors to promote increased transparency, such as the right of everyone to access information, a principle of maximum disclosure, a general public interest test and an independent oversight body[66] did not surface in China's FOI legislation. Indeed, the only convergence occurred on many of the non-substantive measures, such as forms of requests, partial disclosure, fees for requests, time limits and an annual report.[67] This partly explains the lukewarm and often negative reception given to the news of FOI reform in China.

China's reform is an example that can be used to support warnings against the dominant notion, which holds that 'FOI is a readily transplantable law and therefore there is little need for analysis'.[68] Globalization fails to provide a satisfactory justification for FOI reform in China. A consideration of FOI reform in China necessitates a search for improved forms of analysis capable of explaining the deviations from expected patterns. Information flow is such an improved form of analysis.

Local information flow conditions: an explanatory model

The current explanatory models of accountability deficit and globalization do not explain China's FOI phenomenon, suggesting the need for a new analytical device. Information flow is developed in this book as a possible improvement in FOI analysis. Information flow is a theme that can be used to explore the gradual development of government receptivity to FOI in the Chinese information environment through time. Information flow analysis, which focuses on a historical exploration of the shifting dynamics of the Chinese information environment resulting from social, political, legal and economic factors, has a high explanatory capability for China's FOI phenomenon.

An information flow analysis model builds on, and brings together, multiple strands from several disciplines. Information flow, including flow from the government to citizens and from citizens to government, and flow among governments, and among citizens, is a critical concept to understanding an information environment. Furthermore, as all streams of information flow are correlative, this analysis brings greater flexibility and a more dynamic understanding to the processes involved. An information environment is a complex system where all the key elements impact on, and are impacted by, other elements. Information flow analysis has some capacity to take into account this dynamic interaction. It is an analytical framework used in this book for examining the improvement of the Chinese information environment that has paved the way for FOI reform in China.

Information flow analysis is first used in this book to provide a better understanding and explanation of the changing capacity of the Chinese information environment over time to support or accommodate FOI as an important policy instrument of government. For China, the book argues, FOI has become both a beneficiary and important contributor to the transformation of the Chinese information environment assisted by a gradual improvement in information flow conditions over time. Furthermore, information flow analysis can improve existing compliance analysis by focusing on a broad, dynamic and cross-jurisdictional analysis of FOI performance. Whilst information flow analysis in this book is limited in its application to an explanation of China's FOI phenomenon, it may have wider applicability.

Reappraisal of reasons for China's FOI reform

The social, political, legal and economic context of information flow in recent Chinese history is fundamental to fully understanding the development of FOI in China. Both Chinese and non-Chinese scholars have given China's FOI a primary role in contributing to economic growth[69] and anti-corruption efforts.[70] These two driving forces are commonly used to explain the apparent paradox of China's FOI phenomenon,[71] but this book asserts that they have been over-stressed in the existing literature. Close scrutiny of the historical background to the introduction of FOI finds that the new mode of economic growth – informatization which means the modernization of China's information technology infrastructure – was used as a means of making FOI reform more politically acceptable, rather than as a primary driving force for FOI reform. Furthermore, the role of the impetus of anti-corruption measures for FOI reform should be downplayed, as the link between anti-corruption initiatives and FOI appeared late, and the access mechanism was not considered as a primary anti-corruption tool.

There are three other driving forces for China's FOI reform that should receive higher prominence. First, improved information flow lessened the level of information asymmetry in the longstanding secretive Chinese information environment, which in turn increased China's capacity to accept a form of FOI. The relaxation of the Chinese information environment prompted the Chinese government to abandon a secretive and reactive approach to information management, and instead to adopt a more transparent and proactive approach. Under this approach, FOI became a useful tool in a more open environment. Arguably, the more open environment, rather than crises such as Severe Acute Respiratory Syndrome and the Songhuajiang River contamination, created the necessity for FOI reform (see Chapter 3).[72]

Second, China's FOI reform formed part of a wider package of transparency reforms linked to a long-term democratization process. This wider transparency reform package relaxed the secretive Chinese information environment, and this in turn increased the receptivity of the Chinese government to an access mechanism. Openness practices, including Openness in Village Affairs and Openness in Government Affairs (OGA), were first introduced to develop grassroots democracy, a key political reform programme for China to gradually develop its socialist democracy.[73] OGA was extended to a higher level of socialist democracy through developing democratic means (democratic decision making, management and supervision) and democratic rights (the rights to know, freedom of expression, participate and supervise). These proactive disclosure practices, which preceded FOI, softened the secretive information environment in China. This change gradually increased the Chinese government's receptivity to FOI (see Chapter 4).

Third, three decades of administrative law reforms mellowed the secretive Chinese information environment, thus resulting in the acceptance of FOI in China. After earlier administrative law reforms had moved toward creating effective checks on government power from ex ante and procedural perspectives, the capacity to accept FOI increased. In 2004, the central government's law-based administration initiative associated with administrative law reforms further contributed to the acceptance of an access mechanism in China (see Chapter 5).

Internally generated FOI reform

The Chinese central government initiated and promoted FOI reform in China.[74] The passage of the first FOI legislation in 2007 became 'another self-revolution' of the government following the adoption of the *Administrative Permission Law 2003*.[75] This self-revolution action led to the departure of FOI reform in China from the more typical FOI reform process, creating a problem for non-Chinese academics' understanding of China's FOI phenomenon. Concern has been expressed about the feasibility of this self-revolution action. After all, the initiative in FOI reform has rarely come from the government.[76] Roberts states that '[a] natural question is why the leaders of a one-party state would *be eager to* [emphasis added] adopt a policy that is usually sold as a tool for limiting governmental power'.[77] Answers to this question require an understanding of China's FOI reform from broader and historical perspectives.

The central role played by the Communist Party of China (CPC) or the Chinese central government is analysed in Chapters 4, 5 and 7. Without this support and leadership role, China could not have achieved its historic FOI breakthrough in early 2007. There were several reasons why a particular type of FOI programme, which emphasizes information flow, was more attractive to the CPC than a pure type of FOI which is closely associated with liberal democracy. Nevertheless, despite this CPC leadership, the adoption of FOI was not universally supported throughout all layers of the Chinese government or all areas of government. The adoption of FOI in China is a rationalist story of many transparency advocates and activities taking place amid the absence of any uniform or strong opposition due to the CPC's support of a general move toward greater transparency.[78]

FOI reform was invigorated by informatization agencies in 2002 to develop the new mode of economic growth – informatization.[79] This reform was subsequently strengthened by anti-corruption agencies' endeavours to tackle corruption.[80] Other agencies, such as the State Council Information Office and the State Secrecy Bureau, also made contributions to greater transparency by improving proactive disclosure systems and classification respectively. Whilst these agencies promoted FOI to further their interests, their direct and indirect efforts assisted in generating favourable consideration of FOI reform by the central government. Their efforts are further explored in Chapters 3 to 7.

In retrospect, rather than being a completely unexpected development in China, FOI was in part a long-term policy development that was strongly supported by several key organs of the Chinese government. The feasibility of FOI reform increased with each major development in wider government information policy, practice and changing information flow between government and citizens in China.

Gradualism: the hallmark of FOI reform

Gradualism has been the hallmark of political and law reforms in China.[81] Political and legal tools like FOI have been no exception. Contrary to the external perception that FOI reform in China occurred essentially overnight or in a very limited time period from 2002 to 2007, the reform formed part of a much longer process of increased transparency. Indeed, the apparent fast tracking of formal FOI legislation at city, provincial and national levels was conditional on the Chinese government having acquired confidence from various openness practices in the last three decades. These practices included openness in village and government affairs and local FOI rule-making activities in particular, as illustrated in Chapter 7. They, together with more proactive disclosure of crisis information and administrative transparency appearing in many administrative laws, gradually reduced the level of secrecy in the Chinese information environment, developing a favourable environment for FOI.

A limited push model of FOI legislation

China's FOI legislation focuses on proactive disclosure or 'push', rather than citizen-initiated access or 'pull'.[82] The terms push and pull, supply and demand, proactive and reactive disclosure/access are used interchangeably in this book.[83] The greater focus on proactive disclosure in China's FOI legislation, which regards information requests as a last or at least secondary resort,[84] is a significant divergence from a traditional or classical version of FOI legislation. However, it should be noted that a push model of FOI legislation is emerging around the globe. A few countries, including the UK and Mexico, and several states in Australia, namely Queensland, Tasmania and New South Wales, are seeking to amend their FOI legislation by strengthening proactive disclosure.

China's push model grew out of its local conditions, including two decades of limited proactive disclosure practices and an improved information environment due to the formation of multiple paths for information flow. Other local conditions, including a dense population, vast territory and high volume of government information,[85] also contributed to the push model. However, the degree of China's push model of FOI legislation has been restricted by several factors, including a limited access mechanism, broad and vague exemptions and omission of the principle of maximum disclosure (see Chapter 8).

A revised compliance analysis model for FOI implementation

The current FOI compliance analysis model created and developed by Roberts, Snell, Darch and Underwood[86] to explain the differential performance of government compliance with FOI legislation in a jurisdiction[87] is restricted in its application to China. The model was developed largely on the experiences of FOI in advanced liberal democracies, such as Canada, Australia and New Zealand, and new democracies like South Africa. A mechanical use of the current compliance analysis to China produces a far too negative picture. Thus, without undermining the analytical integrity of the existing compliance model, the book suggests a modification of this model to provide a better explanatory framework for Chinese FOI, and to reveal the real strengths and weaknesses of China's FOI reform.

Reflection on the current compliance analysis model

The development of a compliance analysis model is 'an important step forward in a generally under-theorized field'.[88] This model has been named the Roberts–Snell model.[89] However, this model remains in an early stage of development. It analyses compliance issues from reactive disclosure and in a static way. As discussed below, this model is also ineffective in comparing FOI performance across different jurisdictions. The current compliance analysis model can be improved through the incorporation of a push and pull focus inherent in an information flow perspective.

The Roberts–Snell compliance analysis model

A prototype of the compliance analysis model was first developed by Roberts in 1998 for analysing government non-compliance with FOI legislation in Canada.[90] Snell developed this model between 1999 and 2001 by exploring government compliance and non-compliance with FOI legislation in Australia in terms of the types of information sought and information requestors.[91] However, the factor of government capacity and willingness was only implied in the Roberts–Snell compliance analysis model. Delagrave added this factor to the Roberts–Snell model in order to examine the role of a culture of openness in ensuring compliance.[92] Government and public capacity to ensure compliance was explicitly addressed by Roberts in 2006,[93] but government and public willingness was still implicitly addressed. Darch and Underwood revised the Roberts–Snell model by adding the variables of government capacity and willingness to different levels of government compliance and non-compliance.[94] They applied this revised model to analyse compliance issues in South Africa.

The Roberts–Snell compliance model assumes certain conditions for making FOI legislation operate in practice, which generally relate to both the capacity and willingness of the supply side/government and the demand side/public. The following two points explain this. First, from the supply side, the compliance analysis literature requires certain capacity, including advanced democratic institutions, a well-developed rule of law, good record keeping practices, a professional civil service and adequate resources to comply with FOI legislation.[95] However, the existing literature presupposes low willingness of the government to comply, because FOI legislation limits its power, and this encourages aggressive and often negative administration of FOI legislation.[96] The enduring adversarial nature of FOI in countries, such as Australia, is a central feature of compliance with FOI legislation. Bureaucrats often regard many requesters as their opponents who want to discredit them.[97]

Second, while strong or even aggressive input from the demand side is needed to ensure compliance, this input requires users to have a strong sense of citizenship, capacity to use government information, a free press and independent NGOs.[98] Strong capacity of players on the demand side only means that the possibility of applying for government information is high. Actual use of FOI legislation may not realize this high possibility. In addition to this capacity, the compliance analysis literature presumes strong willingness of demand side players to continue after a passionate and vigorous campaign for FOI reform. In reality, the willingness of the demand side drivers, especially the media, is constrained by many factors arising from their own issues, such as personal relationships, readership and unwillingness to undertake difficult tasks,[99] and government non-compliance practices.[100]

Assessment of the Roberts–Snell compliance analysis model

The Roberts–Snell compliance analysis model has weaknesses in analysing FOI performance in a broad, dynamic and cross-jurisdictional way, as explained in detail below. First, it only focuses on the pull/demand aspect of FOI, paying little attention to the push/supply aspect of FOI. A singular focus on the pull aspect of FOI does not help obtain a broad picture in an information environment. Second, the current model evinces a static rather than dynamic analytical framework. Information or information release, rather than information flow in an information environment, is its focus. It consequently lacks explanatory power for comparing FOI performance over time. Due to a short period of implementation of China's FOI legislation, a long-run comparison of FOI performance in China is not available at this stage. However, analysis of this short period still demonstrates that information flow in China has improved, especially the push aspect of FOI (see Chapter 9). Third, the current compliance analysis model lacks effectiveness in a dynamic comparison of the differentials of FOI performance across jurisdictions.[101]

Information flow analysis has the potential to enhance the current compliance analysis. It puts FOI into a wide information environment. This helps identify the two-directional nature of FOI – the push and pull aspects of information flow – and capture the dynamics of FOI or changes in these two aspects of FOI over time.

Concerns about implementation of FOI legislation in China

Concerns about the implementation of FOI legislation in China are related to the willingness and capability of both the supply and demand sides, as explained in detail below. First, the concern over compliance with FOI legislation in China generally arises from doubts about the Chinese government's willingness to subject itself to the normal demand side drivers of FOI, including journalists, lawyers, NGOs and citizens seeking to hold government agencies to account.[102] Further, there are concerns about China's capability to comply with its own legislation due to existing poor records management,[103] insufficient resources[104] and bureaucratic culture.[105] The worry about poor records management is justified as chaotic records management cannot ensure the availability of information for access.[106] In particular, the central government's capacity to force its subordinates to implement FOI legislation raises doubt over compliance with FOI legislation as '[t]he policy applies across the largest bureaucratic complex on the planet'.[107] In addition, the current literature, both Chinese and non-Chinese, highlights the potential unwillingness of the Chinese government to enforce FOI legislation arising out of concerns over the diminution of the central government's impetus after the change of policy objectives[108] and the nature of China's bureaucracy.[109]

Second, a focus on the demand side raises concerns about the incentives for citizens to request government information, and their capacity to act on it. Roberts states that '[i]t remains to be seen how well this policy will work ... The lack of a free press, limited political rights, and a weak judiciary also complicate matters. What good is information, after all, if you lack the capacity to act on it?'[110] There are concerns about citizens' lack of incentives to request government information, especially public information. Darch and Underwood doubt the concept of citizenship as a tool for asserting rights against the state in China, arguing that the state's relation to citizens is 'conceptualized in a way that leaves virtually no space' for claiming the access right.[111] Furthermore, there are concerns about an apparent low use of FOI legislation by Chinese journalists, primarily due to government control of the media.[112] Some authors are, moreover, sceptical of the role of Chinese courts in compelling government compliance with access requests.[113]

A revised compliance analysis model incorporating a push and pull focus

A singular focus on the problems of reactive disclosure and effective enforcement in China would be misleading. This book thus utilizes a revised compliance analysis model that focuses on the outcome of information flow resulting from a changed willingness and capability of players on both the supply and demand sides to examine compliance issues in China. The revised compliance analysis model incorporating a push and pull focus allows the application of a broad and long-run analysis. Chapters 9 and 10 apply this revised analytical model.

The current compliance analysis pays too little attention to the specifics of China's FOI reform, which is largely generated internally and focuses on the proactive disclosure duty of the government. The current compliance model is constructed on the basis that the FOI initiative rarely comes from the supply side,[114] therefore possibly undermining its persuasive power in explaining China's FOI phenomenon. The internally generated nature of FOI reform suggests incentives for the Chinese government to enforce FOI legislation. Also, the current compliance model is based on FOI legislation where reactive disclosure features prominently, and so is at odds with China's FOI legislation, which places more emphasis on proactive than reactive disclosure.

The changed willingness and capability of both the supply and demand sides have assisted in prompting government compliance with proactive disclosure in practice (see Chapter 9). In the last three decades there have been significant changes and trends that influence the Chinese government's willingness and capacity to comply with FOI legislation. A central political commitment and a number of transparency advocacy groups on the supply side have created a willingness for other government agencies to become more transparent. Furthermore, the capacity of the government to implement FOI legislation has increased due to its changed technological, political, legal, economic and civil service conditions. Also, the demand side is not the same as it was three decades ago. As noted in Chapters 9 and 10, Chinese citizens have improved their rights consciousness; media competition has increased and journalists enjoy greater freedom to publish; Chinese rights activists and lawyers are able and willing to request public information, becoming a major group of requesters to ensure government compliance; and Chinese review bodies, including administrative reconsideration agencies and courts, also aid in increasing the capacity of demand side players to redress government non-compliance with proactive disclosure requirements.

However, at this stage of implementation, there remain obstacles to compliance with reactive disclosure or the pull aspect of information flow in China. The Chinese government has typically responded with a controlling flow approach to information requests. Courts have bolstered this approach through various restrictions on FOI lawsuits, thus restricting the capacity of demand side players to request information flow from the supply side. And the use of FOI legislation by demand side players has been hamstrung by legal, political and resources constraints. The current problematic implementation of the access mechanism precludes any overly optimistic view about compliance with FOI legislation (see Chapter 10).

The need for this research

The research on China's FOI is necessary for at least two reasons. First, it affords a fuller understanding of the apparent paradox of the introduction of FOI legislation into China. The current analysis fails to provide a full and accurate account for this introduction. Some non-Chinese authors have grappled with the FOI phenomenon in China, but their explanations are limited. Roberts argues that the Chinese government recognized that FOI legislation might have helped 'improve control over a vast and unresponsive bureaucracy'.[115] Another similar explanation is that FOI was endorsed by the Chinese central government to strengthen 'bureaucratic control'.[116] This explanation cannot provide a more complete answer to the paradox of FOI legislation in China because it does not consider the influence and contribution of three decades of social, political, legal and economic reforms. Horsley's reference to 'economic and political motives' for FOI reform in China[117] is accurate to a degree.[118] However, a more extensive and systematic analysis of these motives is needed. Therefore, the existing literature should be supplemented and reconfigured to provide a more accurate analysis of the development of FOI in China.

Secondly, the concerns expressed, especially by non-Chinese observers, over the prospects of FOI implementation need to be addressed. The current compliance analysis, which focuses on reactive disclosure, is liable to misinterpret the actual dynamics of FOI reform in China. In part, it underplays the differences caused by a greater – if not almost exclusive – emphasis on proactive disclosure, and possibly overplays the weaknesses on the demand side. Further, it may overlook or attach too little significance to the slow but steady changes in social, political and legal reforms over the last three decades. Finally, the narrative about Chinese FOI, which is being generated by non-Chinese scholars, has shifted focus and study away from the internal or unique Chinese aspects of this reform process.

The aim of this research

This research seeks to analyse more thoroughly the Chinese FOI phenomenon. Its specific aims are to:

1. Better understand the adoption of FOI legislation in China. This book examines the nature and extent of the driving forces behind FOI reform in China.

2. Better elucidate the legislative process of FOI in China. This research examines the process of gradual legislative reforms leading up to the introduction of FOI legislation in China.
3. Analyse a limited push model of FOI legislation in China.
4. More effectively assess the implementation of FOI legislation in China, and evaluate the strengths and weaknesses in the enforcement process.

Note on terminology

Some terms need to be clarified. Openness in Government Affairs or OGA (*Zhengwu Gongkai*) means that government agencies proactively disclose information at their own discretion.[119]OGA was practised in China before the implementation of FOI legislation. Freedom of information (*Zhengfu Xinxi Gongkai*) refers to proactive and reactive information disclosure. Two aspects of FOI, including push/proactive disclosure and pull/reactive disclosure are discussed in this book. China's FOI legislation, titled '*Zhengfu Xinxi Gongkai Tiaoli*', in the book is translated as Freedom of Information Regulations, rather than Open Government Information Regulations which is generally used. One key reason for this translation is that the term *Zhengfu Xinxi Gongkai* was originally used to diminish the political sensitivity of FOI.[120] Another reason is that the use of the phrase Open Government Information for China's FOI has already created the wrong impression that transparency reform in China focuses on discretionary disclosure without 'the creation of enforceable legal obligations'.[121] This is because 'open government information' has been used in a pejorative sense in the Western world, the UK in particular.[122] In fact, Chinese experts, such as Zhou, argue that the Chinese term *Zhengfu Xinxi Gongkai* has been used to strengthen the government's legally binding disclosure duty[123] without the pejorative connotations. This means that the term Freedom of Information Regulations or FOI Regulations should not be regarded as a misnomer for China's legislation.

Legislation in this book is an Act or law, regulation and rule.

Chapter summaries

Chapter 1 comprises this introduction.

Chapter 2 explores the capacity and effectiveness of information flow analysis as an analytical device to further advance the current understanding of FOI in relation to China, but also possibly for other jurisdictions, and to enable comparisons.

Chapter 3 examines the influence of the improved Chinese information environment on China's capacity to accept FOI. It compares different information management approaches to crises taken by the Chinese government over time, and argues that without the improvement of the information environment, the Chinese government would have been unlikely to be receptive to FOI reform.

Chapter 4 examines the influence of a long democratization process on China's capacity to accept FOI. It argues that FOI reform in China was conditional on the dynamics of gradually upgrading openness practices associated with the democratization reform agenda.

Chapter 5 explores the influence of administrative law reforms on China's capacity to accept FOI. It argues that three decades of administrative law reforms gradually ameliorated the Chinese information environment, resulting in an acceptance of the pull aspect of FOI in China.

Chapter 6 examines the roles of two main driving forces – economic growth and anti-corruption efforts – in influencing China's capacity to accept FOI. It argues that these two forces should be accorded an important but secondary role in FOI reform, as they only have a limited and indirect influence on relaxing the secretive Chinese information environment.

Chapter 7 explores the process of gradual legislative reforms leading up to the introduction of FOI legislation in China. It shows that the FOI Regulations were a key but interim result of many increments.

Chapter 8 examines China's FOI Regulations. It argues that China has adopted a push model of FOI legislation that emphasizes proactive disclosure of government information.

Chapter 9 explores the strengths in the implementation of FOI legislation in China. It argues that the real strength of the way that FOI legislation is implemented in China is in compliance with proactive disclosure requirements.

Chapter 10 explores the weaknesses in the implementation of FOI legislation in China. It argues that while significant steps to government compliance with proactive disclosure requirements can be ensured, it is difficult to anticipate that reactive disclosure will operate effectively in China at this early stage of implementation.

Chapter 11 concludes the book.

2 Information flow as an analytical device for FOI research

This chapter explores the capacity and effectiveness of information flow analysis as an analytical device to advance the current understanding of FOI in relation to China, but also possibly for other jurisdictions, and to enable comparisons.[1] Information flow analysis is an analytical tool that can be used to explore the gradual development over time of government receptivity to FOI in the Chinese information environment. The primary objective of this chapter is to develop information flow analysis. This is a necessary first step in evolving a theory of information flow. The book argues that, for China, improved information flow resulting from enhanced social, political, legal and economic conditions has decreased the level of information asymmetry in the Chinese information environment, thus increasing government receptivity to FOI.

The reasons for developing an analytical device for FOI research

FOI is 'a generally under-theorized field'.[2] Academic analysis of FOI needs to shift its focus from 'descriptive case studies'[3] to 'comparative or theoretical analysis'[4] to better explain the divergence of FOI developments around the world. This involves three elements.

First, academic analysis of FOI is still in a very early stage of theoretical development.[5] Darch and Underwood's critique places FOI theoretical development more at the concept, rather than the mini-theory stage.[6] The rapid spread of FOI in the last decade to a diverse range of countries and political systems has outpaced the development of a critical literature and analysis to fully explain this phenomenon. FOI analysis is struggling as more and more exceptions to the general explanatory models appear. The divergence is not just at the development stage, but extends to the implementation phase. A better understanding of the divergence of FOI developments around the world necessitates the utilization of a new explanatory model.

Furthermore, China's FOI phenomenon has caused the distance between theoretical understanding and the divergence of FOI developments to become much greater than before. It is said that 'the "rhetoric of transparency" ... has been spreading as far as China in the past few decades'.[7] There is a need to add more intellectual rigour, understanding and analysis to accounts of China's FOI phenomenon. The current explanations, including economic growth, globalization and the fight against corruption, cannot fully account for this phenomenon because other social, political and legal rationales have not been taken into account. A new analytical device may bridge the gap in understanding the wide and rapid diffusion of FOI around the globe.

Second, a more effective analytical device is needed for comparative analysis of FOI, which remains at an early stage of development. The current Roberts–Snell compliance analysis model is a useful tool for comparing FOI performance, but it has limitations particularly with regard to comparisons of FOI performance between very different systems,[8] like those of Australia and China, and within jurisdictions over time.

Third, a broad and dynamic approach is essential to building better understanding of China's FOI phenomenon. Understanding of China's FOI is 'not a simple matter'[9] of comparing its FOI legislation with model FOI laws. It should be understood in a broad way and within a multifaceted context related to the changed social, political, legal and economic conditions. It also needs to be viewed from a historical or dynamic perspective. Observing and analysing changes over time is fundamental to understanding the genesis of the current push version of FOI legislation (see Chapter 8). The future of FOI reform cannot be fully realized without a sense of how local conditions have altered over time. North argues that '[h]istory matters. ... Today's and tomorrow's choices are shaped by the past'.[10] Lenin argued in 1919 that:

> The most reliable thing in a question of social science ... is not to forget the underlying historical connection, to examine every question from the standpoint of how the given phenomenon arose in history and what were the principal stages in its development, and, from the standpoint of its development, to examine what it has become today.[11]

The basis for developing information flow analysis

This book argues that information flow analysis has the potential to improve the current theoretical and comparative analysis of FOI. Its potential can be demonstrated by its application to an explanation of China's FOI. Information flow analysis builds on a diverse range of literature, especially that concerning law, public administration and economics. Information asymmetry – a term used by economists, such as Stiglitz, Akerlof and Spence, who shared the 2001 Nobel memorial prize for their analyses of markets with asymmetric information[12] – has been applied to FOI by some scholars.[13] This application has provided an important part of the foundation for information flow analysis.

FOI and information asymmetry

Information flow analysis follows on from the efforts of various scholars who have been searching for ways to better analyse and explain all aspects of FOI including adoption, implementation and performance. The Roberts–Snell compliance analysis model is an important step in this process. In particular, it has assisted the book in paying attention to the roles of both government and public capacity and willingness in influencing FOI performance. However, Snell recognizes the shortcomings of the current compliance analysis model, such as its singular focus on FOI legislation itself, and static analysis or comparison of compliance issues within jurisdictions. His work in 2006 went some distance toward overcoming the limitations of the current compliance analysis model.[14] He developed a simplified model of information asymmetry to compare the differentials in FOI performance between Australia and New Zealand over time.[15]

The application of the theory of information asymmetry to FOI has led to the idea of information flow analysis. First, the concept of information asymmetry provides a benchmark to compare changes in the level of information asymmetry in a particular jurisdiction over time.[16] It can also be used as an effective measure to capture the different levels of information asymmetry across jurisdictions.[17] However, the current comparison from an information asymmetry perspective is largely descriptive. It has less power to explain the reasons for the different levels of information asymmetry. An analytical tool, like information flow analysis, which focuses on information relationships in an information environment, can improve this explanatory capacity. Improved information flow between government and citizens resulting from social, political, legal and economic factors can shift a system from a closed or highly asymmetrical information environment to an open or less asymmetrical one in the long run.[18]

Second, the link between the development of FOI and a broad information environment has been explicitly or implicitly addressed in existing scholarly work.[19] This has contributed to this book by recognizing that an analysis of an information environment is relevant to an understanding of FOI reform.[20] The concept of an information environment has promising analytical potential for FOI scholars. This concept has shifted FOI analysis from a narrow and technical focus on the process of FOI requests to a wider multi-dimensional inquiry into the dynamics of information relationships and information flows between citizens and government. However, this potential has not been fully exploited.

FOI and information flow

The linkage between FOI and concepts such as information asymmetry and information flow has been shifted to a higher level by public administration scholars, especially Taylor.[21] Taylor observes that information flow in a political system has been largely ignored by schools of public administration.[22] He has repeatedly called for more research on information flow or 'information relationships'[23] in an information environment or 'information polity' which refers to 'a political system made comprehensible by the information that flows, or fails to flow'[24] in and around government. Taylor has limited his information flow analysis to new questions in relation to public administration.[25] However, this analysis has the potential to encourage an understanding of questions related to other research areas, including FOI. In particular, Taylor's focus on information relationships encapsulates a key, although often implicit, focus of FOI analysis, namely the political and power dimensions of who can access government information and under what conditions. Taylor's analysis meshes with Roberts' concerns over who actually benefits from that access.[26]

Information flow has not been considered a key factor in FOI reform in much of the FOI literature. Exceptions include the work of Roberts and Snell, which has been incorporated into a series of influential government reports,[27] all of which have focused to one degree or another on concerns about flow of information in the information age.[28] The absence of information flow from FOI discourse is not surprising as the common usage of the concept of an information age from the late 1980s took place after the development of most of the key features of the dominant FOI analysis. Accountability deficit has sufficed to explain the wave of adoption of FOI legislation between the 1960s and the 1980s. However, the degree and type of information flow in a polity is a key factor that can influence government receptivity to FOI in an information environment.

Information flow analysis

Information flow analysis can assist in a better understanding and explanation of the changing capacity over time of the Chinese information environment to accommodate FOI as an important policy instrument of government. This analysis indicates that information flow in terms of its patterns and conditions could be a useful focus for FOI research. This contrasts with most FOI literature, in which the concept of information tends to be used in a relatively static and physical way.[29] Information flow, including flow of information from the government to citizens and from citizens to government, and flow among governments and among citizens, is crucial to an information environment.[30] There are four streams of information flows in an information environment:

- Information flow within the supply side/government.
- Information flow within the demand side/the public.
- Push/supply/proactive disclosure: the supply side proactively discloses information to the demand side.
- Pull/demand/reactive disclosure: the demand side requests information from the supply side.

These four streams of information flow are correlative. The closure or liberalization of one stream of information flow has an impact on others. This involves three elements. First, the liberalization of information flow within the government or society can pave the way for new or renewed information flow between government and society. Second, the acceptance of the push aspect of information flow can help create an enabling environment for the acceptance of the pull aspect of information flow, and vice versa. Third, the acceptance of the pull aspect may facilitate information flow within public administration, as the government is under pressure to shift the current static and government-oriented information management approach to a more dynamic and user-oriented one.[31]

Information flow analysis can incorporate a supply and demand variable. The government represents the supply side, and the public or a citizen represents the demand side. Whilst the terms supply and demand have been commonly used by Marshall and other economists for market analysis,[32] they have begun appearing in FOI forums and literature.[33] It should be recognized that either government or citizens can play both roles of supplying and demanding information in a specific situation. However, the analysis in this book follows a general assumption that government supplies information, and citizens demand information. Arguably, the willingness and capability of the supply and demand sides are two factors that determine the effectiveness of information flow in an information environment. The use of these economic terms helps differentiate the capacity of key players, the government and the public, in an information environment. It focuses discussion on the government's capacity in terms of records management and civil service, and on the capacity of information receivers to use, distribute and analyse the information received. The use of these economic terms also assists in differentiating the roles of various government players who are willing to supply or prompt other agencies to supply information, and the roles of non-government players who are inclined to demand and utilize information (see Chapters 9 and 10).

The level of information asymmetry or secrecy which features in an information environment can be identified by examining information flow resulting from the shifting dynamics of social, political, legal and economic conditions. A particular jurisdiction may at one stage have an information environment marked by a high level of information asymmetry resulting from one stream of information flow. This environment indicates that supply and demand side players have low willingness and capacity to share information, thus presenting little opportunity for increasing government receptivity to FOI. At a later stage, the state may have an information environment characterized by a decreasing level of information asymmetry arising from multiple streams of information flow. In such an ameliorated information environment, both supply and demand side players have increased their willingness and capability to share information, thereby making FOI first a beneficiary of, and then a contributor to the transformation of an information environment. China serves as a case in point.

High utility of information flow analysis

An approach to FOI using information flow analysis offers an explanatory device for systematically understanding the development, implementation and future prospects of FOI. It may also improve existing compliance analysis, and have comparative utility to track FOI developments over time.

An effective tool for explaining the divergence of FOI developments

Information flow is a useful analytical tool for explaining the divergence of FOI developments, as illustrated in the following way. First, it is able to capture the change of government receptivity to FOI in a state. In a secretive or highly asymmetrical information environment, where the degree of information flow is low, the capacity to accept FOI is weak, especially for FOI reform dominated by supply side players. Whilst strong pressure from the demand side made it possible for the adoption of FOI between the 1960s and the 1980s, the effectiveness of FOI legislation was constrained due to a hostile attitude held by the supply side. However, in an enhanced information environment, where information flow has become a matter of routine, or information relationships have become important to the state, the compatibility of FOI with the environment is improved and the adversarial nature of FOI is lessened. Most of the current literature identifies FOI as a largely independent policy initiative, and thus omits a multifaceted analysis of the dynamic transformation of one jurisdiction's information environment.

Second, information flow analysis offers a useful analytical framework and a tool for comparisons of FOI legislation in a macro way (see Chapter 8). The current comparisons of FOI laws are largely undertaken in a micro way, focusing on the differences in detailed or black-letter clauses related to scope, time limits, exemptions and external review mechanisms. Information flow analysis provides a tool for comparing FOI laws from a macro perspective. Such a macro perspective assists in identifying two models of FOI legislation: push and pull, or 'version 1.0' and 'version 2.0'.[34]

Information flow analysis helps reposition the importance of access requests in improving information flow in a wide information environment. It has been gradually acknowledged that access requests should be accorded a less important role in FOI legislation, and the role of proactive disclosure in contributing to information flow should increase.[35] As a result, a push model of FOI legislation has begun to be favoured around the world (see Chapter 8).

Third, information flow analysis may improve the application of the Roberts–Snell compliance analysis model to compliance analysis in China. The current compliance analysis model can be improved by combining a push and pull focus to better understand compliance issues in China. While information flow is treated at this stage as a subcomponent of the Roberts–Snell compliance analysis model, information flow analysis has the potential to become an independent framework for FOI analysis in the future, as it can help examine compliance issues in a broad and dynamic way.

The Chinese case indicates that information flow could be a useful measure of the effectiveness of FOI legislation in a jurisdiction. If FOI legislation has no, or a limited, role in improving information flow, it is pointless or at least flawed. From this point of view, international non-government organizations, such as Article 19, may have oversold their model of FOI legislation,[36] largely neglecting the building of an FOI newcomer's capacity to implement FOI legislation.[37] Furthermore, information flow analysis suggests that generally an administrative approach to the implementation of FOI legislation is superior to a legalistic approach[38] in contributing to information flow in an information environment. Greater willingness of the government to share information with the public can be found in the administrative, rather than legalistic approach.

Information flow analysis will be more effective if objective measurements can be developed and consistently applied across jurisdictions. Some organizations, such as the Organization for Economic Co-operation and Development and the Carter Centre, are developing detailed elements or indicators to measure the implementation of FOI laws.[39] Their work in progress can be improved if they utilize information flow as a key tool for developing these indicators.

An effective measure for comparative studies of FOI

Information flow analysis can contribute to the development of comparative FOI studies. It has great flexibility to interpret what information flow occurs within a particular time period, and to capture the direction and type of information flow change over time, thus helping improve the current largely descriptive and chronological comparative studies of FOI.[40] For liberal democracies, such as Australia and Germany, the affordability of the expensive access mechanism or pull aspect of FOI became a major concern. FOI reform in Germany suggests that accountability deficit was not a sufficient condition for FOI reform. It postponed the adoption of FOI law until 2005.[41] Bennett therefore argues that accountability deficit is only a necessary condition for FOI reform in advanced democracies.[42] A key reason for this significant delay may have been the long duration of a highly asymmetrical and pre-Internet information environment, which resulted in high costs associated with access to information.[43] These costs can only be reduced in an improved information environment by shifting the focus from the pull aspect to the push aspect of FOI.

Furthermore, information flow analysis can aid cross-jurisdictional comparisons by comparing the different development paths of FOI among jurisdictions. Information flow analysis helps identify two aspects of FOI: push and pull. The development path in China follows the path of push to pull. The push aspect of FOI, which is the major discourse in China, is a less problematic approach for China than the pull aspect. The gradual transformation of the Chinese information environment has provided a receptive space for the push aspect, but the pull aspect was muted or not acceptable until the adoption of FOI Regulations.

In contrast, most FOI adopters, such as the US and Australia, follow a path of pull to push. The pull to push path is appropriate for a reform agenda vigorously driven by demand side players. However, the push to pull path suits the FOI initiative from the government, through gradually developing an enabling environment for FOI reform. Both the paths of pull to push and push to pull have the objective of improving information flow in an information environment.

This section indicates that information flow analysis is different from top-down or bottom-up analysis which focuses on the direction of FOI reform. Information flow analysis is capable of explaining FOI development over time, but neither top-down nor bottom-up analysis has this capability. Furthermore, information flow analysis does not singularly focus on FOI legislation itself. It can be used to analyse either top-down or bottom-up direction of FOI reform. Arguably, the key to understand any type of FOI reform is the lessening of difficulties with government receptivity to reactive disclosure through improving other relatively easier accepted streams of information flow.

Limitations of the application of information flow analysis

Whilst information flow analysis has great potential to facilitate a move away from largely 'descriptive case studies',[44] and to improve current theoretical and comparative analysis of FOI, its use remains tentative. There are at least three reasons for this. First, terminology borrowed from different disciplines to build the analytical framework of information flow may be criticized as ad hoc and lacking in organic cohesion. Indeed, the reasons for selecting and matching these components or modules are linked to the availability of certain literature.

Second, information flow analysis is limited by the conceptual uncertainty around FOI. FOI is used interchangeably in the literature with other terms, including transparency, open government, openness, access to information and freedom of expression.[45] The differences and meanings of these terms have lacked 'serious debate'.[46] Information flow analysis calls on scholars to view FOI as a particular form of information flow, and to start addressing and assessing the exact relationship between loosely related terminology, in order to confront the conceptual uncertainties of FOI. To date, most of the analysis about FOI is cast in static, rather than dynamic terms; it must enter new conceptual territory.

Third, while information flow analysis allows more focus on information relationships in an information environment, this book mainly focuses on FOI, rather than other positive and negative information management regimes linked with FOI, such as archives, internet censorship, government secrecy, spin doctors, privacy, whistle blowing and public access to private sector information. All these information management regimes can be subsets or modules of a wider academic discipline – information law, which could examine information relationships or information flows between different players in an information environment.

Conclusion

This chapter presents information flow analysis as a means of better understanding and explaining the changing capacity of the Chinese information environment to accommodate FOI. It argues that information flow in an information environment is a useful analytical device for better understanding FOI reform in China. Closer examination finds that FOI was first a beneficiary of the transformation of the Chinese information environment, but that it is now moving toward being a contributor to this transformation. The rest of the book applies information flow analysis to examine the origins of the adoption of FOI legislation in China and the prospects for its implementation.

The analytical tool of information flow is a dynamic and systematic explanatory framework for future FOI theoretical and comparative analysis. It may have wider applicability, as demonstrated by some parts of the book. FOI scholars should focus more on FOI from an information flow perspective, in order to examine the acceptance of FOI in an information environment and the role of FOI in contributing to the environment.

3 The improved information environment as a rationale for FOI reform in China

This chapter examines the influence of the improved Chinese information environment on China's capacity to accept FOI. It utilizes information flow in a crisis as a key lens through which to demonstrate the changing capacity of the Chinese information environment to accommodate FOI. The reasons for choosing this are the following. Any change in crisis information management makes a significant difference to the social order. Crises are also generally considered, albeit wrongly, as a direct motive for FOI reform in China. This chapter compares different information management approaches taken by the Chinese government over time. It argues that without the improvement of the Chinese information environment due to the formation of multiple paths for information flow, the Chinese government would have been unlikely to have been receptive to FOI reform. In the previous highly asymmetrical Chinese information environment, information flow was very limited, and a secretive and reactive information management approach was favoured. FOI was incompatible with this environment. However, the Chinese information environment is now far less asymmetrical, as information has flowed in multiple paths, and so a more proactive disclosure approach is preferred. FOI was a beneficiary of this ameliorated information environment, and has helped create further conditions for reducing information asymmetries between citizens and the state.

Limited information flow in the Chinese environment of the past

In the restricted Chinese information environment of the past, a secretive and reactive approach to crises dominated for a long period of time. The intent of the Chinese government was to maintain social stability in China.[1] The incompatibility of FOI with this form of information management proved a major obstacle to Chinese FOI reform. Information flow was very restricted due to social or cultural factors. A highly asymmetrical information environment with limited and very controlled information flow supported a secretive and reactive approach to crises. This created a hostile, if not incompatible, environment for transparency reform. Thus, there needed to be significant information environment changes and adaptations to the FOI process in order to give FOI reform a workable foothold in the Chinese information environment.

Information flow within government: reporting good, rather than bad news

Chinese government officials began the process of 'reporting good, rather than bad news' (*Bao Xi Bu Bao You*)[2] to deal with crises, indicating a reluctance to share information. The reporting of good rather than bad news has been embedded in Chinese society[3] with its roots in Confucianism. Confucius said that anyone working in the bureaucracy should speak prudently to avoid accusation.[4] He argued that the more one said the more one would be defeated (*Duo Kou Duo Bai*).[5] These aphorisms were generally ingrained in many Chinese government officials.[6] Current officials have also learnt from Deng's warning on 'saying less and doing more'[7] to avoid criticism or expose their fallibility and incapacity, but neglected the original purpose of the warning, which was for reducing formalism, a form of bureaucratism.[8]

The reporting of good rather than bad news was strengthened by government officials' capacity to control information flow.[9] The highly hierarchical and scattered nature of bureaucracies resulted in government agencies' extreme monopoly on crisis information. Officials considered that most bad news could be concealed effectively.[10] A widely known case is the mine water leakage disaster in Nandan in 2001, when one of the leaders struck his chest as a gesture of a 100 per cent guarantee that it would not be made public.[11] This showed a restriction on information flow within public administration.

Information flow among citizens: limited threats to social stability by rumours

In the past, the flow of crisis information among citizens was limited, as personal communication via word of mouth appeared to be the only way to share crisis information. The majority of people were thus kept in ignorance of crises. Whilst the lack of reliable information from the government made room for the spread of rumours or unverified explanations for crises,[12] threats to social stability by rumours were limited. Although rumours can prompt social panic and destabilize society,[13] the pace and distance of rumour transmission was constrained by the personal communication method. Furthermore, an effective filter role[14] played by the traditional news media prevented mass communication from becoming a tool for spreading crisis information and rumours.

Information flow from the government to society: a paternalistic approach

The paternalistic approach, which concealed crisis information from its citizens, was justified by the perception of Chinese government officials about the low psychological endurance of the masses.[15] The fear was that informed masses could hold different ideas, express disagreement with each other and live in a state of panic during crises, which could in turn destabilize society. Ruling people by concealment or through parent officials (*Fumu Guan*)[16] was an idea embedded in the governing philosophy of the rulers throughout 2000 years of China's imperial history. Confucius said that 'the common people may be made to follow, but may not be made to know' (*Min Ke Shi You Zhi, Bu Ke Shi Zhi Zhi*).[17] Lao Zi, the founder of Daoism,[18] also said that '[t]he ancient followers of Tao did not use it to increase knowledge, but rather to preserve simplicity. People are difficult to govern when there is too much knowledge. Whoever rules a country by furthering knowledge is that nation's curse … '[19] Shu opposed the disclosure of criminal law by Chan Zi in the Zheng Kingdom in BC 536 in China, stating that the masses would argue about the meaning of the terms set out in the law if they knew them.[20] Many examples can be used to illustrate this cultural influence. The crisis of the Songhuajiang River contamination in 2005 is a recent and widely known case in point.[21]

As a result, Chinese government officials generally processed a crisis before or without any information disclosure,[22] as they held that only the conceal-ment of crisis information could contain public panic and maintain social stability.[23] According to the officials, the involvement of journalists added trouble to an already bad situation.[24]

Furthermore, the government's capacity to control information flow in the pre-Internet age was strong. It was able to suppress information by enforcing constraints on the traditional news media, which were previously the single channel for the public to obtain information. News reports were guided by the principle of 'the news, old news or no news' (*Xinwen, Jiuwen, Buwen*),[25] first mentioned by Chairman Mao in 1957. The principle means that the release of some news should be timely, but the release of other news should be postponed or even deliberately ignored.[26] This became a key principle for the Chinese Party media to produce news reports.[27] The reporting of many crises which occurred before the early 2000s, such as the Tonghai earthquake, the Tangshan earthquake and the epidemic of Hepatitis A virus in Shanghai, followed this principle.[28]

Thus, the capacity to accept FOI in the highly asymmetrical or secretive information environment was weak. This was due to the low willingness of the government to share crisis information with its citizens and a strong cap-ability to control flow of crisis information. There was a direct and serious incompatibility between any form of FOI and the secretive crisis information management process coupled with the issues of regime stability and survivability.

Improved information flow in the Chinese information environment of the present

The incompatibility of FOI with the macro information environment has les-sened since the early 2000s. The secretive and reactive approach has been challenged by an improved information environment where information flow is more frequent. New media have not only created difficulties for the government to conceal crisis information, but facilitated the flow of crisis information within the demand side, such as media, citizens and civil society. New media have also increased rumours in circulation and their pace of distribution, and in turn increased threats to social order by rumours. These factors have triggered a reassessment of the efficiency and desirability of a secretive and reactive approach. Thus, guidance of public opinion, which is an approach to involve the government in the improved information environment or the emergent Chinese 'network society'[29] to retain the power of agenda setting,[30] has risen to the top of the political agenda. This has increased the government's willingness and capacity to share information with the demand side.

Information flow among government: improved by e-government projects

Informatization programmes, especially e-government[31] projects, have increased the flow of information in public administration. The previously hostile information environment for transparency reform has begun to move to a direction that can encourage an increase in information flow. The development of informatization, a new mode of developing China's economy, can be traced to the 1980s, when the Chinese government conducted the office automation project among all government agencies.[32] The starting point of a series of incremental information infrastructure initiatives was the launch of the 'Three Golden Projects'[33] in late 1993. Another eight e-government projects that cover a wide range of government functions have been initiated in China since these original projects.[34] The Government Online Project was formally launched in China in 1999, presenting the opportunity for greater information flow.[35]

Whilst the improvement of information flow within the supply side does not directly increase the prospects of transparency reform, the rising information flow in public administration remains a relevant shift. This has partially prevented lower levels of government agencies from taking advantage of their previous extreme monopoly on crisis information as the hierarchical and scattered nature of bureaucracies has been diminished.[36] The increasing information sharing among government agencies advanced by e-government projects has also increased the central government's capacity to release more reliable information to the public.

Information flow among citizens: improved by new media

New media, such as the Internet and cell phones, have been widely used by Chinese citizens, as shown by Table 3.1, increasing citizens' capacity to communicate directly with one another. This emergent interactive information network[37] has challenged the traditional secretive and reactive information

Table 3.1 The use of the Internet and cell phone in China

Use of the Internet	1997	2007
Number of users of the Internet	620,000	210 million
Internet penetration rate	0.1 per cent	16 per cent
Bulletin Board System	Nil	1.3 million
Blogs	Nil	47 million
Annual growth rate of netizens	About 20 per cent	
USE OF CELL PHONE	**2000**	**2007**
Number of cell phones	0.14 billion	0.55 billion
Penetration rate of cell phones	6.77 per cent	41.6 per cent
Number of Short Message Services (SMS) messages	15 billion (2001)	592.1 billion

Sources: China Internet Network Information Centre; The Ministry of Industry and Information Technology

management approach. New media have also assisted rumour and information transmission, potentially increasing the threat to social stability. Enhanced information flow among citizens has prompted the Chinese government to become more transparent and proactive, thus opening up the possibility of experimenting with the push aspect of FOI or proactive disclosure.

New media have enabled citizens to share agenda setting power with traditional media

New media have made it possible for ordinary citizens to become citizen journalists, giving a relatively free and convenient platform for citizens to share crisis information, even without flow of crisis information from the government. New media have assisted Chinese citizens to overcome technical and financial obstacles to produce news reports,[38] enabling almost anyone to become a comparatively independent media source. This guarantees the dissemination of those articles that cannot be published by the traditional media. The article that exposed the mine water leakage disaster in Nandan was first published on the electronic media, *People's Daily* Online, rather than the newspaper, *People's Daily*.[39] In the 2008 Sichuan earthquake, the first live video was recorded by a cell phone and posted to the Internet by a university student within ten minutes of the quake and eight minutes prior to the official announcement.[40]

The government has encountered technological difficulties in controlling information flow efficiently. Internet censorship exists in China,[41] but it 'cannot keep up with the spread of information',[42] and so it has become 'increasingly difficult for the government to regulate what information is accessed'.[43] Some officials confess that 'we can prevent one journalist from reporting bad news, but we cannot prevent all journalists from doing so; or even if we can require all journalists not to report bad news, we are still incapable of asking all netizens not to expose it'.[44] This indicates that in an improved information environment where information flows in multiple ways, it is difficult for the government to censor information.[45]

As a result, ordinary citizens also have the power to set agendas that were previously tightly controlled by government news media. Now, they are information consumers and creators. Thus, the 'interactive audience' supersedes 'the mass audience' coupled with the mass media.[46] All cell phone users and netizens or Internet users have the capacity to set the agenda for others, diminishing the government's monopoly on agenda setting. The emergency of a decentralized agenda setting power has challenged the secretive and reactive approach. The Severe Acute Respiratory Syndrome (SARS) crisis provides a good example.[47] Chinese citizens used cell phones to forward messages about an unknown fatal flu at a time when they could not obtain reliable information from the traditional media and the government.[48] SMS messages aided them to overcome the influence of the agenda set by China Central Television, which reported heavily on the Iraq War at the time of the crisis.[49]

The strong public concern finally attracted the attention of the central government. After 20 April 2003, it required all levels of government to 'report information on SARS accurately, honestly, and in a timely manner'.[50] The central government warned that harsh punishment would be imposed for any delay or concealment, as proved by the fact that the Minister of the Health Ministry and Mayor of Beijing were dismissed for their concealment of information on SARS patients.[51] In an improved information environment where alternative information sources, such as citizen journalists, can provide reliable crisis information to the general public, government officials will pay huge financial and public-trust costs for concealing information. This has prompted the Chinese government to become more transparent and proactive in dealing with crises.

New media have increased threats to social stability by rumours

New media have increased threats to social stability by rumours or unverified explanation for crises. This has prompted the Chinese government to become more transparent and proactive in order to diminish the negative impact of rumours. New media have advanced the pace and distance of rumour transmission within the demand side.[52] Wang asserts that in the information era, a rumour already travels around half of the earth when the truth still remains unknown.[53] There is a vast difference between 1000 users of new media and more than 200 million users.[54] When so many users interact with others via the Internet or SMS, many unexpected things occur. Thus, late or reactive disclosure of crisis information will provide an opportunity for rumours to spread quickly and influence public opinion at first due to the primacy effect, which means that 'the message presented first exerts a disproportionate impact on an individual's opinion'.[55]

Furthermore, new media via varied real-time communication tools[56] have allowed rumours to spread much more extensively, as they combine personal communication with mass communication. In the past, rumours could have only spread via personal communication, but this is not the case now. Mass communication, another feature of new media,[57] is used nowadays to transmit rumours, and so rumours can appear in 'the collective mind'.[58] In addition, new media are based on personal communication.[59] They consequently have a higher rate of receipt, readership[60] and participation than traditional media.[61]

Rising threats to society by rumours in the improved information environment have forced the Chinese government to abandon its old information management approach. It now recognizes that rumours can be transformed and denied with reliable information release (*Yaoyan Zhi Yu Gongkai*), rather than the converse.[62]

Information flow among citizens: precondition for the push aspect of FOI

China's capacity to support the push aspect of FOI has increased due to the following three factors. First, increasing information flow among citizens has created difficulties for the Chinese government to conceal information. The secretive and reactive approach is outdated and should be changed. Second, the government has increased its willingness to share crisis information with the public. It has recognized the importance of guiding public opinion or setting agendas for others. Third, the capability of the government to actively disseminate information to the demand side has been strengthened by the launch of spokesperson systems and government websites.

Increasing willingness to proactively disclose information

The Chinese government wants to retain the power to guide public opinion. This has increased its receptivity to the push aspect of FOI. The secretive and reactive approach has resulted in the government losing the power to set agendas for others. Whilst it is possible for the government to regain the initiative of agenda setting, the price will be high.[63] Therefore, guidance of public opinion has been regarded as an important measure to assist the Chinese government in improving its governance capability.[64] This view calls for more proactive disclosure to retain the power of agenda setting. The Chinese government cannot guide public opinion if it persists in the secretive and reactive approach in the improved information environment.[65] President Hu thus has urged the Party media to actively set the agenda for others to respond to crises.[66] Wu Cai, the former Director of the State Council Information Office, has called on government officials to alter their mindset of concealing information to manage crises.[67] Yangwu Ou, the Deputy Director of the State Council Informatization Office and a member involved in drafting FOI legislation, said in an FOI seminar that 'information disclosure has the role of ruling out rumours and guiding public opinion. Others are keen to take full advantage of this mechanism. Why does the government not want to do this?'[68] This comment by Ou is significant because it indicates that only a more transparent and proactive approach can help the Chinese government to adapt to the improved Chinese information environment.

Some Chinese scholars observe that crises, especially the 2003 SARS crisis, accelerated the legislative process of FOI in China.[69] However, this book argues that the way the public responded to crises by using information technology to share crisis information has changed in recent years. This encouraged the government to reconsider its approach to crisis information management. FOI then became a more useful tool in a more open environment. Arguably, it is a more open environment, rather than the crises, that created the necessity for FOI reform. The Chinese government recognized that it would be in its interest to become more transparent and active in managing crises.

The rising willingness for more proactive crisis information disclosure has reversed the previous concern about a low psychological endurance of the public, and helped smooth the adoption of FOI legislation in China. Zhou argues that if Chinese political leaders had not considered that information release benefited social stability, the current extent of FOI reform would have been difficult to achieve.[70] Political leaders have shifted their views about the relationship between information disclosure and social stability from mutually exclusive toward mutually inclusive. Article 6 of China's FOI Regulations, in particular, reflects this changed view. This Article requires government agencies to release accurate information in order to rectify any false or incomplete information that has affected or may affect social stability, and that has disturbed or may disturb social management order.[71]

Increasing capability to proactively disclose information

The Chinese government has not only recognized the importance of proactive disclosure, but has improved its proactive disclosure systems since the early 2000s. The government has revised and adopted several specific laws and regulations to legislate on proactive disclosure of crisis information. These measures have increased the government's capability to share information with the public, thus preparing the ground for the Chinese government to consider a push model of FOI legislation (see Chapter 8). There are three key features to this increased capability.

First, many government agencies have established the spokesperson system since 2003. This has provided a basis for the Chinese government to legislate on proactive disclosure. The State Council Information Office has pursued the establishment and improvement of news briefing and spokesperson systems as its central task in recent years.[72] This made slow progress until the SARS crisis, which accelerated the progress.[73] The former director of the State Council Information Office argues that spokespersons, who are the guides of the Chinese and foreign media outlets to report on China, play a vital role in promoting government information release.[74] As a result, press conferences are laid down in China's FOI legislation as an important way to actively disclose government information.[75] Zhou argues that this arrangement is unreasonable since other countries' FOI laws rarely list press conferences as a formal way to disclose government information.[76] However, his argument underestimates the need for the government to retain and build upon its capacity to set agendas. The legitimization of press conferences in the FOI Regulations fits within a proactive approach to information management.

Second, many government agencies have launched official websites to increase information flow. The Government Online Project was initiated in early 1999 by more than 40 ministerial level agencies.[77] This project prompted most government agencies to launch their own official websites, as shown in Table 3.2.[78] More importantly, the central government launched its official web portal in late 2005. The number of Chinese government websites with the domain name gov.cn has increased, rising to 28,575 in 2007, about 20 times as many as that of 1999 (1470).[79] The central government has also determined to use government websites as the priority platform for actively distributing information.[80]

Third, many specific laws and regulations were adopted or revised to legislate on active distribution of crisis information. This has improved information flow in the Chinese information environment, preparing the ground for the Chinese government to accept FOI. Death tolls have been withdrawn from the list of state secrets, facilitating active disclosure of crisis information. In the past, death tolls were prohibited from disclosure as they fell into the category of state secrets.[81] This prohibition remained unchanged until the issue of the *Notice on Disclosure of Death Tolls and Related Natural Disasters Information* in 2005.[82] Since then, death tolls are allowed to be disclosed in a timely fashion. This has cleared the way for disclosure of crisis information.

The outbreak of SARS caused the State Council to introduce *Regulations on Preparedness for and Response to Emergent Public Health Hazards* in 2003. The Regulations provide a mechanism for ensuring the release of information on the emergent hazard, requiring government agencies to disclose information in a timely, accurate and comprehensive manner.[83] The *Law on the Prevention and Cure of Infectious Diseases 1989* was modified in

Table 3.2 The percentage of websites launched by government agencies

Government agencies at various levels	Year and Percentage		
	2005	2006	2008
Government agencies directly under the State Council	96.1	96.1	96.1
Government agencies at the province level	96.1	100	100
Government agencies at the county level	77.7	83.1	99.1

Source: The State Council Informatization Office

2004. It has added SARS to the second class of infectious diseases, and improved the release system by requiring national and regional health agencies to regularly release information on the epidemic situation.[84] The *Criminal Law* was also amended in 2006, to provide a maximum sentence of seven years of imprisonment for those who fail to report or falsely report accidents endangering safety.[85] These law reform initiatives have increased flow of crisis information from the government to society in China, creating a more favourable environment for the consolidation of FOI legislation.

China's FOI legislation as a beneficiary of the improved information environment

The preceding section demonstrates that information flow has improved in the Chinese information environment. This improvement has created a critical precondition for the acceptance of the push aspect of FOI, as explained in the following two points. First, the analysis of crisis information management demonstrates that it is necessary for the Chinese government to shift from a secretive and reactive information management approach to a proactive disclosure one. To achieve this shift, the institutionalization of discretionary proactive disclosure is necessary. Spokespersons and official websites are useful platforms for government agencies to proactively disclose information to the public, but this disclosure depends on government agencies' discretion.[86] Furthermore, if only official spokespersons are responsible for information disclosure, it will be insufficient to guide public opinion.[87] The Chinese government realized that it was important for all government officials to have a certain level of media literacy and awareness.[88] The desire to achieve this has necessitated the emphasis on the government's proactive disclosure duty[89] by adopting a push model of FOI legislation in China.

Second, demand side players have increased their desire for greater information flow. New media have offered Chinese citizens the opportunity to expose and share their concerns about their immediate interests, like public health, in a series of crises. Chinese citizens have also changed their information expectations as they have increased their use of new media to access information, prompting the government to supply information actively or voluntarily.[90] As a result, the Chinese government may have recognized that a push model of FOI legislation is necessary to adapt to the improved information environment.

The acceptance of the push aspect of information flow also provided an enabling or favourable environment for the acceptance of the pull aspect of FOI or reactive disclosure. Only after the government increased its desire to share information with the public, did the hostile or incompatible conditions for FOI reform lessen. Improved information flow in the Chinese information environment, together with political and legal factors as illustrated in Chapters 4 and 5 respectively, jointly resulted in the gradual shift from an emphasis on the push aspect to the pull aspect of FOI in China.

Conclusion

Improved information flow in the Chinese information environment over time was critical to accept FOI. An exploration of crisis information management shows that improved information flow caused the Chinese government to abandon a secretive and reactive approach to information management, and instead to adopt a more proactive disclosure approach. This movement has ameliorated the Chinese information environment, and thus created a more favourable environment for FOI. Therefore, the traditional accounts of economic growth and anti-corruption efforts for China's FOI reform should be downplayed due to this important, but largely unexplored factor of information flow.

4   Democratization as a rationale for FOI reform in China

This chapter examines the influence of a long-term democratization process on China's capacity to accept FOI. It argues that FOI reform in China was conditional on the dynamics of incrementally upgrading openness practices associated with the democratization reform agenda. The gradual promotion of openness practices improved information flow in the restrictive Chinese information environment, thus increasing the Chinese government's receptivity to the pull aspect of FOI. Government receptivity further increased after temporarily moving the concept of FOI away from an emphasis on media freedom, to an emphasis on information flow, including push/proactive disclosure and pull/reactive disclosure aspects of information flow. This helped abate serious concern over the incompatibility of FOI with China's Marxist-Leninist political system.

A type of FOI emphasizing information flow: an acceptable version

Chinese reformers developed effective strategies to lessen the concern about the incompatibility of FOI with China's political system. This was achieved by finding ideological and constitutional evidence to demonstrate the compatibility of a type of FOI emphasizing information flow with the Chinese political system. An important strategy was to temporarily uncouple FOI from freedom of expression. This aided the Chinese government in accepting FOI as a particular form of information flow. The changing government response to freedom of expression from 2006 also favoured a more positive reception to FOI.

Sources of the incompatibility concern

A narrow definition of FOI, closely intertwined with liberal democracy and freedom of expression, raised concern over the incompatibility of FOI with China's political system. The failure of Gorbachev's glasnost reform heightened this concern. Chinese reformers identified ideological and constitutional evidence, and uncoupled FOI from freedom of expression, at the initial stage of consideration, to lessen the incompatibility concern in the early 2000s, when FOI was still a politically sensitive term.[1]

A strong liberal democratic ethos of FOI

FOI has strong perceived links to liberal democracy. It has been used as a tool for limiting government power[2] and improving efficiency of public participation in political activities, including elections.[3] The one-party or unelected leadership of the Communist Party of China (CPC) contradicts or is in opposition to these key attributes of FOI. Furthermore, a global move toward FOI has been promoted vigorously by many international organizations which 'share a commitment to Western liberal values',[4] like the organization known as Article 19, which campaigns for freedom of expression. This organization took its name from Article 19 of the *Universal Declaration of Human Rights*, which states that '[e]veryone has the right to freedom of opinion and expression; this right includes freedom to hold opinions without interference and to seek, receive and impart information and ideas through any media and regardless of frontiers'.[5] Many other international human rights instruments, such as the *International Covenant on Civil and Political Rights* and the *American Convention on Human Rights* were modelled on Article 19.[6]

The terms 'to seek, receive' under Article 19 of the Universal Declaration of Human Rights have been interpreted as the guarantee of public access to information.[7] The United Nations Special Rapporteur on Freedom of Expression stated in 1998 that 'the right to seek, receive and impart information imposes a positive obligation on states to ensure access to information ... '.[8] The right to know also forms part of many Commonwealth countries' constitutions as part of freedom of expression.[9] National courts in Japan,[10] India[11] and Korea,[12] and the Inter-American Court of Human Rights and the European Court of Human Rights,[13] have adjudged that the right to know is protected by the clause that guarantees freedom of expression under domestic constitutions or international human rights instruments.

FOI is therefore typically considered as an adjunct of freedom of expression[14] or as being the same as freedom of expression.[15] Scholars observe that FOI and freedom of expression have been conflated so much so that they are difficult to separate.[16] This concerned Chinese reformers, at least in the initial stage of consideration of FOI reform.

The failure of Gorbachev's glasnost reform

The failure of Gorbachev's glasnost reform[17] in the former Soviet Union further raised doubts over the role of FOI in the development of socialist democracy in China,[18] thus necessitating effective strategies to lessen the concern about the incompatibility of FOI with China's political system. Gorbachev's glasnost reform agenda was seen in China as being partly responsible for the ultimate breakdown of the Soviet Union. This situation was likely in the eyes of some Chinese authorities to strengthen the incompatibility between transparency and the broad political system in China.[19]

Chen argues that the Glasnost agenda was actually a factor contributing to the postponement of transparency reform in China, which was proposed at the 13th National Congress of the CPC (NCCPC) in 1987.[20] The breakdown of the Soviet Union was also the key reason why a retrospective TV programme, entitled '*You Have the Right to Know*', did not pass the censoring process in 2002, only five years before the adoption of FOI legislation in China.[21] An overall negative impression of Gorbachev's glasnost reform highlighted political sensitivity to FOI and freedom of expression linkage, especially in the early stage of developing an FOI policy.

Strategies to lessen the incompatibility concern

Chinese reformers developed effective strategies to lessen the concern over the incompatibility of FOI with China's political system. The longstanding central political commitment to developing democracy since the late 1970s encouraged reformers to conduct FOI reform. Some support for transparency from Marx, Lenin and Mao gave Chinese reformers further confidence to introduce transparency reform during the process of democratization. In addition, Chinese reformers found support for FOI reform from the sovereignty of the people as set out in the *Constitution 1982*.[22] Thus, the development of socialist democracy, at least from an ideological or theoretical basis, made it possible for the acceptance of the pull aspect of FOI in China.[23] More importantly, the book argues that the political sensitivity of FOI was lessened after Chinese reformers opted to temporarily disconnect FOI from freedom of expression in the initial stage of FOI reform. This increased the possibility for the acceptance of a particular type of FOI that emphasizes information flow in China.

A constant political commitment to democracy: precondition for FOI reform

In the last three decades, Chinese political leaders' advocacy of democracy that emphasizes local elections and political participation presented an opportunity for China to accept FOI, a type of information flow, as part of its long-term democratization programme. Chinese political leaders have absorbed a significant lesson from the destructive impact of the Cultural Revolution (1966–76), namely the necessity to build democracy gradually.[24] The leaders, including Deng,[25] Jiang[26] and Hu,[27] have consistently stated that democracy is the goal of the CPC. The reason for taking democracy as the goal of the CPC is the recognition that '[w]ithout democracy there could be no socialism, much less socialist modernization'.[28] Democracy has been considered by Chinese leaders as a panacea for a wide range of social and political challenges, including social unrest and a broadening income gap arising from the process of modernization.[29] The CPC recognizes that democracy is the lifeblood of socialism and the state.[30] Thus, the development of socialist democracy has been a central task for the CPC since the end of the 1970s.[31]

Chinese political leaders' commitment to developing democracy has generated a favourable consideration of transparency reform. Political leaders have not considered that socialism is alien to democracy.[32]

Furthermore, the central endorsement of deliberative democracy as one form of socialist democracy[33] has arguably made FOI less incompatible with the Chinese political system. FOI is critical in developing deliberative democracy that has emerged in the last two decades to allow citizens to participate in and deliberate on public problems and solutions.[34] Information disclosure is a precondition for public participation in decision-making, which lies at the core of deliberative democracy.[35] Compared with liberal democracy, deliberative democracy is more compatible with the current Chinese political system.[36] This is the reason why Chinese political leaders have laid great stress on scientific and democratic decision-making to develop socialist democracy in recent years. Yu argues that democratic decision-making actually includes elements of deliberative democracy.[37] More importantly, in February 2006 the CPC Central Committee explicitly showed support for deliberative democracy in its policy document, *Opinions on Strengthening the Work of the Chinese People's Political Consultative Conference*.[38] The document states that electoral and deliberative democracies are two forms of socialist democracy.[39] In 2007, the *White Paper on China's Political Party System* further claimed that '[o]ne major feature of China's socialist democracy is the combination of democratic election and democratic consultation ... [and this] has extended the width and depth of socialist democracy'.[40]

Ideological support for FOI reform from leading Marxists

Some support for transparency from Marx, Lenin and Mao may have influenced the acceptance of a type of FOI that emphasizes information flow between the government and citizens to develop socialist democracy. Marx stressed the importance of openness when he discussed the experiences of the Paris Commune.[41] He said that 'the Commune did not pretend to infallibility. ... It published its doings and sayings; it initiated the public into all its shortcomings'.[42] This indicates that Marx advocated transparency.[43] Lenin recognized that transparency was a precondition for socialist democracy.[44] He stated that the new Soviet authority 'concealed nothing, it had no secrets. ... It was an authority open to all, it carried out all its functions before the eyes of the masses, was accessible to the masses ... '.[45]

The Mass Line, which refers to 'everything for the masses, reliance on the masses in everything, and from the masses, to the masses',[46] has become a domestic political foundation for transparency reform in China.[47] Both Marx and Lenin's support for transparency may have been considered disconnected with China's local conditions. The views of leading Chinese Marxists, including Chairman Mao and Premier Zhou, are more important and relevant. Mao relied on the Mass Line to support transparency. The Mass Line, a vital part of Maoism, has been considered by the CPC as its inexhaustible source of strength.[48] Transparency or flow of information is inherent in the Mass Line as it is essential for achieving the goal of 'to the masses'.[49] In 1948, Mao called on government officials to change their secretive working styles to inform the public of land reform policies in order to gain their support and implement the policies.[50]

Also for the purpose of implementing land reform policies, Enlai Zhou, the first premier of China, said that any decision or change concerning a policy, and any correct or wrong part of a policy, had to be disclosed to the masses at the appropriate time to gain their understanding and support.[51] The Mass Line became the basis for the 13th NCCPC in 1987 advocating transparency.[52] This NCCPC called on leading agencies to improve the openness of their activities and let the people know about and discuss important matters in order to carry on the fine tradition of the Mass Line, 'from the masses and to the masses'.[53]

Leading Marxists' support of transparency suggested that reformers would not make any serious political mistakes if they undertook transparency reform. However, the support of transparency from leading Marxists was only a necessary, rather than a sufficient, condition for the Chinese government to accept the role of transparency in developing socialist democracy.[54] This suggests that further support, especially through the *Constitution*, was also needed.

The sovereignty of the people: constitutional support for FOI reform

Chinese reformers found convincing evidence from the *Constitution 1982* to reject the perceived incompatibility or mutual exclusivity between FOI and a Marxism-Leninist political system. The reformers' original assertion that FOI reform was supported by the *Constitution 1982* became more acceptable and gained more support after the central endorsement of full implementation of the *Constitution* in late 2002. In a December 2002 speech commemorating the twentieth anniversary of the adoption of the *Constitution*, Hu stated that 'implementation of the rule of law first and foremost requires fully enforcement of the *Constitution*'.[55] He reiterated this announcement in a speech at the fiftieth anniversary of the National People's Congress (NPC), stating that 'ruling the state by the rule of law first needs ruling the state by the *Constitution*, [and] administration by law first requires administration by the *Constitution*'.[56]

Chinese reformers rationalized FOI primarily from the sovereignty of the people set out in the *Constitution 1982*.[57] The sovereignty of the people appears in many countries' constitutions. China's *Constitution 1982* is no exception. The *Constitution* states that all the power in China belongs to the people.[58] This means that the people are the masters of the state, which is the essence of China's socialist democracy.[59] A right to know, albeit only implied in the *Constitution 1982*,[60] is a right to aid the people to exercise the masters' role.[61]

Chinese reformers viewed FOI as a prerequisite for the exercise of several key constitutional rights related to the sovereignty of the people.[62] It has been recognized that the people's constitutional rights are not comprehensively protected without an FOI mechanism.[63] As masters of China, the people can manage the state, the economy, the culture and other public affairs through a multitude of means and forms.[64] Such management cannot function well without information availability.[65]

Chinese reformers also saw FOI as a precondition for the exercise of the right to supervise.[66] The *Constitution 1982* requires all government agencies and officials to rely on the support of the people, keep in close touch with them, heed their opinions and suggestions, accept their supervision and work hard to serve them.[67] However, the people cannot supervise government agencies and officials without knowledge concerning the operation of government work.[68]

The original disconnection of FOI with freedom of expression

While Chinese reformers asserted that FOI is a mechanism for the eventual securing of a right to freedom of expression,[69] they uncoupled FOI from freedom of expression at the initial stage of consideration. The *Constitution 1982* empowers the people to criticize and make suggestions to any government agency or official, to make complaints and charges against, or exposure of, any government agency or official for violation of the law or dereliction of duty.[70] To exercise this constitutional right, the people need a right to know. However, Chinese reformers recognized that reliance on the link between FOI and freedom of expression under the *Constitution* only encouraged more resistance to FOI reform, especially after the failure of glasnost reform in the former Soviet Union.

The temporary separation of FOI from freedom of expression is a prominent feature of FOI reform in China. This separation helped diminish the political sensitivity of FOI in China, and smoothed the way for FOI reform. Chinese reformers realized that it was inappropriate to couple FOI with the promotion of the right to freedom of expression due to the lack of *Freedom of the Press Act* and an authoritative interpretation of freedom of expression laid down in Article 35 of the *Constitution*.[71] Yet this approach to FOI is contradictory to the dominant theme in the literature, which closely entwines FOI with freedom of expression or presents each as a mutually dependent limb of the same process. The uncoupling allowed the idea of FOI to be openly discussed in China, and created a precondition for reconnecting FOI with freedom of expression at a later stage of considering FOI legislation. This reconnection increased government receptivity to FOI in China.

Grassroots democracy: an experiment in transparency

FOI reform was needed to reinforce and extend openness experiments that have served China's incremental democratization process for a long period.

These experiments reduced the concern about the incompatibility of FOI with China's political system. Grassroots democracy, a key part of socialist democracy in China, made it possible to experiment with the antecedents of FOI, including Openness in Village Affairs (OVA) and Openness in Government Affairs (OGA) at the township level. This gradually improved information flow from the government to the public, thereby increasing the capacity to accept FOI. Thus, contrary to the perception that FOI reform gained full force overnight with little warning and few antecedents, the reform was the outcome of a gradual transformation toward a pull aspect of FOI.

Openness in Village Affairs: safeguarding grassroots democracy

Grassroots democracy enabled OVA, the first openness experiment in China,[72] to be developed. OVA was a category of information flow that prepared the ground for another more significant push aspect of information flow, OGA, to be experimented with. Grassroots democracy at the village level has been promoted as a key political reform programme for China to gradually develop socialist democracy since the early 1980s.[73] It is the 'priority and breakthrough point'[74] of China's democratization and 'the most direct and broadest practice of democracy'[75] in China to date. Grassroots democracy was practised in China through the establishment of a self-government system with an emphasis on rural villagers' committees[76] to fill the gap in administering villages after the people's communes ceased in the late 1970s.[77] The *Constitution 1982* first supported the establishment of a villagers' autonomy system.[78] This system was further standardized by the *Organic Law of the Villagers' Committees (for trial) 1987*. After 10 years' trial, the Law was replaced by the *Organic Law of the Villagers' Committees 1998*, which signalled the institutionalization of grassroots democracy in rural areas.

Democratic supervision, a key democratic means to develop grassroots democracy,[79] made it possible to experiment with OVA because it was originally recognized as a tool for overseeing village officials.[80] In the early 1980s, some villages began to experiment with OVA during the establishment of a villagers' autonomy system.[81] These openness practices were first confirmed by the *Organic Law of the Villagers' Committees (for trial) 1987*, which required villagers' committees to periodically disclose income and expenditure on public affairs and public utilities.[82] Overall implementation of OVA achieved support from the central government in 1994 after the issue of the *Notice on Enhancing the Construction of Grassroots Organizations in the Rural Areas*.[83] This Notice broadened previous openness practices, requiring all villagers' committees to periodically disclose information of mutual interest to villagers.[84] The work of OVA was expanded in 1998 after the issue of the *Notice on Comprehensively Implementing Openness in Village Affairs and Democratic Management*,[85] which formed the basis of openness requirements under the *Organic Law of the Villagers' Committees 1998*. Since the adoption of this Law, OVA has been formally allowed by the law and developed in the whole country.[86] To strengthen OVA, the central government circulated another notice in 2004.[87] With strong support from the central government, the work of OVA is now widely implemented in China.[88] OVA became crucial for OGA at the township level.

Openness in Government Affairs at the township level: expanding grassroots democracy

Along with OVA, OGA at township governments has been considered as an important measure to expand grassroots democracy. The acceptance of openness experiments within government was a significant breakthrough in China, directly assisting information flow from the government to society and ameliorating the Chinese information environment surrounding FOI. OGA at the primary level was first supported by the central government in 1997 as a tool for expanding grassroots democracy.[89] At the 15th NCCPC, the national CPC congress, the political report stated that '[t]he grassroots organs of power and self-governing mass organizations in both urban and rural areas should ... keep the public informed of their political activities and financial affairs ... '.[90] The Chinese government considered that OGA at the primary level could aid in establishing closer ties between the government and the people, and implement the central policies.[91] The political report of the 17th NCCPC reiterated that OGA at the township level could bring about 'effective connection and beneficial interaction between government administration and primary-level self-governance'.[92]

However, OGA at the primary level was not strongly supported by the central government until late 2000 after the issue of the *Notice on Promoting Openness in Government Affairs around All Government Agencies at the Township Level*.[93] In 1998, the *Notice on Comprehensively Implementing Openness in Village Affairs and Democratic Management* encouraged, but did not require, government agencies at the township level to practise OGA during the period of implementing OVA.[94] However, the *Notice on Promoting Openness in Government Affairs around All Government Agencies at the Township Level* branded OGA as important to extend the scope of democracy at the grassroots level, requiring all township government agencies to focus on disclosure of the practical problems that people were most concerned about and that affected the vital interests of the people.[95]

Socialist democracy: developing by openness in government affairs at all levels

OGA at all levels of government was built upon OGA at the primary level. The promotion of OGA at all levels further improved information flow from the government to society, thus ameliorating the Chinese information environment and increasing the capacity to accept FOI. During the period when OGA operated at the township level, some government agencies at and above the county level started to disclose information concerning their administrative affairs.[96] The central government gained experiences from these practices. It issued the *Notice on Further Promoting Openness in Government Affairs* in 2005, deciding to expand these openness practices to government agencies at all levels.[97] In this Notice, the central government recognized that OGA was necessary to a broader socialist democracy,[98] not only to grassroots democracy. This is because OGA has been regarded as a prerequisite for developments in democratic means, such as democratic decision-making, management and supervision, and protection of key democratic rights, such as the rights to know, participate and supervise. The promotion of OGA from this political perspective directly brought about the acceptance of the access mechanism in China because the access mechanism is a tool for implementing all these democratic means and rights.

Openness in Government Affairs: precondition for developments in democratic means

Democratic election, decision-making, management and supervision have been recognized as four major means of developing China's socialist democracy since 1997.[99] The four democratic means, the last three in particular, laid the foundation for the extension of OGA to higher levels of government.

OGA was not considered as a tool for enhancing election processes. The processes of democratic election were promoted in China earlier than those of democratic decision-making, management and supervision. However, they were largely limited to the grassroots level, and had little opportunity to be upgraded to a higher level in the immediate future. Direct elections at the grassroots level were permitted under the *Organic Law of the Villagers' Committee 1998* and *the Organic Law of the Urban Residents Committees 1989*,[100] and established in China gradually.[101] However, direct elections are not allowed for governments at and above the township level, although some local governments have experimented with direct elections in recent years.[102] These experiments cannot be expanded and promoted to a higher level in China at present[103] as they violate the *Constitution 1982*.[104] Indeed, the Standing Committee of the NPC, China's Parliament, noted this unconstitutional event and called for the cessation of the experiment in 2001, although the impact of this call was limited.[105]

Thus, OGA was mainly considered as a tool for improving democratic decision-making, management and supervision. The political report of the 15th NCCPC in 1997 recognized the need for the exercise of democratic decision-making, management and supervision to be assisted by openness.[106] A goal for promoting OGA at the primary level was the implementation of the systems of democratic decision-making, management and supervision.[107]

Openness was originally recognized as a tool for democratic supervision.[108] The project of Openness in Two Areas and Supervision by the Public was initiated to encourage the public to supervise government officials.[109] The Chinese government in the *Notice on Comprehensively Implementing Openness in Village Affairs and Democratic Management* called for an effective use of OVA to improve supervision of village officials elected by villagers.[110] Chinese anti-corruption agencies have endeavoured to promote OGA to enhance democratic supervision since the late 1980s.[111] Thus, openness was regarded as an indispensable tool for developing democratic supervision in China.

The central political endorsement of scientific and democratic decision-making generated more favourable consideration of OGA at higher levels of government. The promotion of scientific and democratic decision-making became one of the three overarching tasks in the Hu–Wen administration after 2003.[112] The Chinese government recognized that 'correct decision-making is an important prerequisite for success in all work'.[113] It promoted democratic decision-making by increasing public participation in government legislation and by establishing many systems, such as OGA, expert consultation and appraisal, and public hearing.[114]

The focus on democratic decision-making necessitated a type of information flow like OGA.[115] The political report of the 16th NCCPC called for improving the decision-making mechanisms, requiring all decision-making agencies to establish a system of keeping the public informed to prevent arbitrary decision-making.[116] Transparency was regarded as a key part of administrative decision-making in the *Implementation Outline for pushing forward Administration by Law in an All-Round Way* issued in 2004.[117] The State Council adopted its new Working Rules in 2008, requiring it to directly hear the opinions and suggestions of grassroots people for important decisions.[118] This is the first time that the State Council listed the majority of people in political life. It is likely to help develop the deliberative politics in China, assuring a successful future for FOI.

Openness in Government Affairs: safeguarding key democratic rights

In recent years, OGA has been regarded by Chinese reformers as an important tool for safeguarding four democratic rights – the right to know, participate, freedom of expression and supervise.[119] These four democratic rights, mainly derived from the preceding four democratic means, have been used to develop socialist democracy. The connection of OGA with the right to know indicates that the central government has become receptive to the pull aspect of FOI. The Chinese government first recognized the role of OGA in safeguarding key democratic rights in 2006 under China's *11th Five-Year Plan for National Economy and Social Development*.[120] This was reiterated in 2006 under the *Resolution on Major Issues regarding the Building of a Harmonious Socialist Society*.[121]

The connection between OGA and the right to know

Previously, OGA was conducted in China without a tight connection to the right to know. This resulted in the predominant focus on proactive disclosure by government agencies. Since 2006, Chinese political leaders have shown strong support for promoting access to information so as to deepen transparency reform.[122] This support benefited the acceptance of the access mechanism and the development of the right to know in China.

The connection between OGA and the right of participation

Chinese political leaders have recognized OGA as a measure to secure the right of participation. In recent years, they have encouraged the public to participate in political affairs in an orderly way. The political report of the 16th NCCPC stated that it was essential to 'expand citizens' participation in political affairs in an orderly way, and [to] ensure that the people go in for democratic elections and decision-making, exercise democratic management and supervision according to law ... '.[123] This view was reiterated by the CPC in 2004.[124] The political report of the 17th NCCPC also called for the expansion of citizens' orderly participation in political affairs at each level and in every field.[125]

The work of OGA in China was developed to expand citizens' orderly participation in political affairs. The *White Paper on the Building of Political Democracy in China* states that:

> The Chinese government requires its subordinate departments at all levels to make their administrative affairs public as far as possible, so as to enhance the transparency of government work and guarantee the people's right to ... participate in ... the work of the government.[126]

The focus on public participation, together with democratic decision-making, indicates that the Chinese government has accepted some elements of deliberative democracy where citizens are allowed to engage in decision-making about important issues. In early 2006, Chinese political leaders endorsed deliberative democracy.[127] This served as a catalyst for a favourable consideration of OGA at a national level.

The connection between OGA and the right to freedom of expression

OGA has been regarded by Chinese political leaders as a key tool for guaranteeing freedom of expression, but this link has only been formally expressed by the central government since 2006.[128] Such a link indeed improved the central government's receptivity to FOI, thereby smoothing the way for the passage of FOI legislation. Chinese reformers initially considered that it was unsuitable for China to connect OGA with the safeguard of the right to freedom of expression.[129] Thus, at the beginning, the role of OGA in promoting the right to freedom of expression was ignored. On many occasions, Chinese reformers only addressed the role of OGA in promoting the right to know, participate and supervise.[130]

Chinese political leaders have addressed freedom of expression in recent years. The political report of the 17th NCCPC recognized the necessity to 'carry out democratic election, decision-making, management and supervision in accordance with the law to guarantee the people's rights to know, to participate, to express, and to supervise'.[131] The central endorsement of freedom of expression has significantly lessened the political sensitivity and incompatibility of FOI, which has increased China's capacity to accept the policy instrument of FOI. It has also helped Chinese reformers abandon their original assertion that FOI reform in China should not be coupled with freedom of expression.

The connection between OGA and the right to supervise

OGA has also been viewed as the protection of the right to supervise. This right, which plays a key role in promoting democratic supervision, is conferred by the *Constitution 1982*. Chinese political leaders have endeavoured to promote democratic supervision in order to guarantee the right to supervise under the *Constitution* since the 1980s. OGA has been considered as a tool for enhancing the exercise of this constitutional right.

FOI legislation: institutionalizing openness in government affairs

Compared with other countries, China's FOI Regulations were primarily utilized to institutionalize the widespread practices of OGA to serve its long-term democratization initiatives.[132] As such, the traditional argument of economic growth and anti-corruption efforts accounting for FOI reform in China should be, arguably, downplayed (see Chapter 6). The *Notice on Further Promoting Openness in Government Affairs* required the acceleration of the legislative process of OGA through the introduction of FOI Regulations.[133] Yong He, the Deputy Secretary of the Central Commission for Discipline Inspection, argues that the adoption of FOI Regulations can institutionalize OGA, mandate and standardize the operation of OGA.[134] Thus, FOI Regulations are the basic legislation in relation to OGA, and play a key role in gradually institutionalizing OGA in China.[135] The passage of the FOI Regulations signals that the work of OGA has been institutionalized.[136]

However, the FOI Regulations were not used to merely institutionalize the work of OGA; they were also used to legislate on an access mechanism. This was unprecedented in China because many government officials still considered adopting the access mechanism, the pull aspect of FOI, to be premature.[137] Some asked: 'is it possible to only legislate on proactive disclosure, and postpone the institutionalization of access to information to a later date?'[138] However, the impact of this lower level government's resistance was weak as the central government had become more receptive to the role that the pull aspect of FOI could play in China's long-term democratization process.

The central government has also called for the provision of legal guarantees for democracy in recent years. This increased the possibility of the adoption of FOI that is an indispensable part of socialist democracy. The political report of the 16th NCCPC in 2002 announced that '[w]e must concentrate on institutional improvement and ensure that socialist democracy is institutionalized and standardized and has its procedures'.[139] This was reiterated in the political report of the 17th NCCPC in 2007.[140] It has been recognized that OGA plays an indispensable role in promoting socialist democracy, and that it is necessary to institutionalize OGA through the introduction of FOI Regulations.[141]

Conclusion

Democratization increased China's capacity to accept FOI, as it played a significant role in improving information flow in the secretive Chinese information environment. Concerns surrounding the incompatibility between FOI and China's political system necessitated a particular type of FOI that emphasizes both the push and pull aspects of information flow. Furthermore, long periods of openness experiments, such as OVA and OGA, were used to serve democratization programmes. These experiments assisted information flow in the Chinese information environment, thus increasing the receptivity of the Chinese government to the access mechanism. Therefore, the traditional argument that economic growth and anti-corruption efforts were the primary rationales for China's FOI reform should be downplayed due to this important, but largely unexplored political factor, coupled with the social factors.

5 Law-based administration as a rationale for FOI reform in China

This chapter examines the influence of administrative law reforms on China's capacity to accept FOI. It explores the history of administrative law reforms, and argues that three decades of administrative law reforms gradually ameliorated the Chinese information environment, resulting in an acceptance of the pull aspect of FOI or reactive disclosure in China. It is difficult for non-Chinese academics to understand why a one-party state such as China would have adopted a tool like FOI legislation for limiting government power. The apparently acceptable explanation is that FOI legislation is used by the central government to strengthen bureaucratic control. However, this explanation is inaccurate in its downplaying of three decades of administrative law reform endeavours. While administrative law reform initiatives before the late 1990s did not create an enabling environment for the consolidation of FOI legislation, they facilitated a move of administrative law reforms toward ex ante and procedural controls of government power after the late 1990s. This move increased the capacity to accept FOI as an integral part of law-based administration.

Administration law reforms: improving information flow

The administrative law reform agenda has direct relevance to FOI reform. FOI legislation, which aims to control government power primarily from a procedural perspective, is 'logically part of administrative law'.[1] However, according to information flow analysis, the adoption of FOI legislation has been facilitated by the improvement of information flow resulting from disclosure requirements set out in other administrative laws prior to the adoption of FOI legislation. China is a case in point. Its FOI legislation originated from the reduction of asymmetry or the improvement of information flow in its longstanding secretive information environment. The reduction or improvement was contributed to by the three decades of administrative law reforms that were a part of the rule of law package after the late 1970s.

Administrative laws: improving information flow in democracies

FOI legislation has its origins in other administrative laws that helped to improve the flow of information within an information environment. In the

US, the *Federal Register Act 1935* and the *Administrative Procedure Act 1946* became two key heralds of FOI legislation to loosen a secretive information environment. The *Federal Register Act 1935* required the publication of all departmental and agency regulations that had 'general applicability and legal effect'.[2] This was the antecedent of the push aspect of information flow. The *Administrative Procedure Act 1946* extended the proactive disclosure of government regulations to other standard information in relation to administrative organization and procedures and the like.[3] It made a significant breakthrough in the pull aspect of FOI in allowing those individuals 'properly and directly concerned'[4] to access information. The drawbacks of the Act, including a number of vague exemptions, lack of general access and failure to provide judicial review of a refusal of access to information, caused the campaign for more robust access legislation.[5]

In Australia, FOI legislation was a key initiative of the New Administrative Law reform agenda that commenced in the early 1970s.[6] The reform agenda had three other key initiatives, including the Administrative Appeals Tribunal, the Ombudsman and the Administrative Decision Review, which achieved success a few years earlier than FOI. These initiatives prepared a firm foundation for the FOI initiative, primarily by obliging government agencies to provide a reasoned decision to individuals affected by government decisions.[7] This obligation was an antecedent of the pull aspect of FOI, and improved information flow within the secretive Australian information environment in the 1970s.

Administrative law reforms in China: a key part of the rule of law package

The rule of law programme opened the door to administrative law reforms that provided a firm legal foundation for the relaxation of the restrictive Chinese information environment surrounding FOI. The Chinese leadership saw the necessity for law in ruling the country after the end of the Cultural Revolution (1966–1976). Deng observed that there were no laws or legal systems for China to follow for many years, and it was necessary to rebuild the legal system,[8] which was 'severely damaged'[9] during the Cultural Revolution. Deng's efforts resolved the ideological confusion that stemmed from the Revolution, and guided China to gradually re-establish its legal system. Jiang continued Deng's policies. A major achievement under Jiang's leadership was the amendment of the *Constitution* in 1999, which required the government to rule the country in accordance with the law and to build a socialist country under the rule of law.[10] This revision made the rule of law 'the basic principle in running the country'[11] and ushered in 'a new chapter in China's efforts to promote the rule of law'.[12]

Whilst administrative law is more difficult to adopt than other laws in China, it has never been excluded from the work of rebuilding the legal system that commenced in the late 1970s. In 1986, Xijin Tao, the former deputy director of the Legislative Affairs Committee of the National People's

Congress and a major contributor to this rebuilding effort, argued that China should adopt six basic laws to re-establish its legal system.[13] Administrative law and administrative litigation law are two of the six basic laws.[14] Tao's argument made it certain that administrative law would be adopted eventually.

The promotion of the rule of law since 1999 increased the importance of the development of law-based administration that has been closely associated with administrative law reforms in recent years.[15] In China, law-based administration was accepted by the central government much earlier than the rule of law, but the importance of this administration did not increase until the promotion of the idea of becoming a country under the rule of law in 1999.[16] The Chinese government states that law-based administration is essential for the overall implementation of the rule of law[17] and lies at its core.[18] This was supported by the Chinese government in its policy document of 2004, titled *Implementation Outline for pushing forward Administration by Law in an All-Round Way*.[19]

The rule of law appears at odds with a one-party state. The existing literature, especially that authored by non-Chinese academics, has therefore dismissed the potential significance of taking the rule of law as a goal of China's political development.[20] While it will be a long process for China to realize a state where the rule of law prevails, the process has begun with an unprecedented adoption of myriad laws at national and local levels.[21]

Administrative law reforms: a firm basis for FOI legislation

A series of administrative law reforms during the last three decades provided an opportunity for the improvement in the Chinese information environment. This made FOI reform more compatible with the changed information environment. In general, developments in administrative law in China can be classified into four phases, but only the recent phase of administrative law reforms has increased the Chinese government's willingness to allow citizens affected by government decisions to access information. The recent phase of administrative law reforms provided a foundation for the acceptance of the pull aspect of FOI, especially after the incorporation of the pull aspect into a law-based administration reform package.

The early 1980s: the preliminary stage

Administrative law reforms in the early 1980s did not provide a favourable legal foundation for increasing the Chinese government's willingness to accept FOI reform. Administrative law reforms generally followed the line of controlling or limiting government power during the last three decades.[22] However, administrative law reforms in the early 1980s, a preliminary stage of the reforms, lacked respect for this principle.[23] The reforms were guided by the principle of controlling citizens,[24] and administrative laws adopted during this period had this striking feature. This controlling philosophy could not accept transparency as its key value, and so transparency played little or no role in this era of Chinese administrative law.

However, administrative law reforms, to a degree, did occur during this period. First, the principle of law-based administration was implicitly expressed under the *Constitution 1982*. The *Constitution* states that all state agencies must abide by the *Constitution* and the law, and requires all acts in violation of the *Constitution* or the law to be investigated.[25] This principle weakened the habitual behaviour of government agencies exercising their power through policies or leaders' instructions rather than laws.[26] The *Constitution* also allows citizens who have suffered losses as a result of an infringement of their civic rights by any public bodies to claim compensation pursuant to the law.[27] While the *Constitution* only implies law-based administration, it declares that government agencies must abide by the *Constitution* and the law.[28] This has become a firm direction for administrative law reforms.

Second, government power could be challenged. Administrative litigation was allowed under the *Civil Procedure Law 1982*,[29] but the scope of these suits was limited. To separate administrative cases from civil ones, the Supreme Court set up special procedures for trying administrative cases and directed courts to establish administrative tribunals after the adoption of *Regulations on Administrative Penalties for Public Security 1986*.[30] These measures prepared the ground for the introduction of the *Administrative Litigation Law*.

Arguably, the role of administrative law during this initial era of law reform was marginal and limited. It was rarely used to call to account, challenge or litigate against government activities. If this occurred, it was circumscribed and rare.[31] Ordinary citizens were generally unable to take government agencies to court except for administrative lawsuits on economic activities.[32] Thus, the Chinese government's willingness to make transparency a key value of administrative laws was weak. As a result, the focus on controlling citizens in this period of administrative law reforms made no contribution to the transformation of the longstanding secretive information environment. In other words, the capacity to accept FOI was negligible in this largely unchanged environment.

The late 1980s: the starting point

After the late 1980s, administrative law reforms shifted to placing limitations on government action. This made it possible for the improvement of the Chinese information environment and the capacity to envisage FOI by gradually accepting transparency as a key value of administrative law. The adoption of *Administrative Litigation Law 1989*, being the second phase of administrative law reforms, initiated an emphasis on controls of government power.[33]

The work of rebuilding the legal system was not completed in the 1980s, as there was no administrative law.[34] Administrative law was a new area unfamiliar to Chinese law academics and legislatures.[35] It was recommended that an Administrative Legislation Research Group should be established to draft important administrative laws.[36] The group was established in 1986 to draft a comprehensive administrative basic law, which covered any substantive aspect of this area, like the *Civil Code 1986*.[37]

However, a year later the research group announced that it was impracticable to draft such a comprehensive law at that stage.[38] It decided that the reform needed to be completed in stages.[39] After learning that the National People's Congress was being considered for the revision of the *Civil Procedure Law 1982*, experts in this group saw this as an opportunity to introduce a special administrative litigation law.[40] Ping Jiang, the director of this group, said that the adoption of procedural laws prior to substantive laws could make it easier to pass substantive laws.[41] This process adhered to China's legislative tradition.[42] Ming'an Jiang, a member of the group, said that this was compatible with the situation in China because the lack of such legislation impeded the process of a number of administrative lawsuits at that time.[43]

As a result, the *Administrative Litigation Law*, an important law checking administrative actions, became the first of a series of special administrative laws.[44] The Law was adopted on 4 April 1989, and took effect on 1 October 1990.[45] Chinese academics assert that the milestone *Administrative Litigation Law* made the rulers and the ruled equal before the law in China,[46] allowing citizens to sue the government for the first time.[47] This Law thus became the starting point of China's administrative law reform.[48] The *Administrative Litigation Law* contradicted the view that 'law [was] not a limit on the party-state'.[49] More importantly, it signalled a focus of administrative law reforms on controlling government power and regulating administrative actions.[50]

The early 1990s: controls of government power from ex post and substantive perspectives

Administrative law reforms in the early 1990s, the third phase of the reforms, focused on controls of government power from ex post and substantive perspectives. Transparency was not regarded as a core value of administrative law, and thus this phase of administrative law reforms contributed little to the improvement of information flow in the restrictive Chinese information environment. Therefore, the capacity to accept FOI remained minimal during this era.

There were two key features of administrative law reforms in the early 1990s. First, the reforms concentrated more on ex post than ex ante controls of government power.[51] This is illustrated through the establishment of the administrative supervision legal system. The *Administrative Litigation Law 1989* standardized external supervision by Chinese courts. However, its role is limited because it only provides a judicial review of the lawfulness, rather than the reasonableness, of administrative actions.[52]

Administrative reconsideration provides another remedial channel for Chinese citizens. It was first institutionalized in 1990 by *Administrative Reconsideration Regulations*, which was promoted to *Administrative Reconsideration Law* in 1999. The Law standardizes internal review by superior government agencies. It extends the protection of ordinary citizens' remedial rights by empowering an administrative reconsideration agency to review not only the lawfulness, but the reasonableness, of concrete administrative actions.[53] In addition, some abstract administrative actions are subject to administrative reconsideration.[54]

Apart from administrative lawsuit and reconsideration systems, Chinese reformers considered that specialized supervision was important to control government power. The *Audit Law*, adopted in 1995, empowers audit offices to audit revenues and expenditures of government agencies and public institutions.[55] The *Administrative Supervision Law*, adopted in 1997,[56] standardizes the supervision of government agencies and government officials by supervisory agencies, China's Ombudsmen.[57]

Second, administrative law reforms during this period focused more on controlling government power through substantive laws than procedural ones.[58] The *Administrative Litigation Law* did not set out the details of state compensation, although it allowed a person who suffered damage to claim compensation.[59] A comprehensive compensation system was established after the adoption of the *State Compensation Law 1994*. Luo said that the *State Compensation Law* 'forced the state in descending from the divine altar'[60] because there was no tradition in China that encouraged government agencies and officials to apologize for their mistakes and pay compensation. Besides, *Interim Regulations on Civil Servants* were adopted in 1993, which made it possible for China to develop public service professionalism. After 12 years of operation, the Regulations were promoted to the *Civil Servant Law*, passed in 2005. This Law comprehensively standardized personnel management in China for the first time.[61]

The initial set of administrative law reforms was supplemented by the adoption of a number of administrative laws in the early 1990s. However, the focus on ex post and substantive controls of government power during this period did not facilitate information flow that could relax the secretive Chinese information environment, and thus FOI was not prioritized during this period.

The late 1990s to now: controls of government power from ex ante and procedural perspectives

The fourth phase of administrative law reforms after the late 1990s emphasized controls of government power from ex ante[62] and procedural[63] perspectives. This directly contributed to the relaxation of the previous restrictive information environment and to the increase in China's capacity to accept FOI. In this phase of administrative law reforms, procedural due process became a key value of administrative law, and administrative transparency was regarded as a key element inherent in administrative law.

Procedural due process: a key value

Procedural due process became a key value of administrative law reforms during this period of reform, causing administrative transparency to be incorporated into a number of administrative laws adopted after the late 1990s. Hearings and information disclosure are two key parts of procedural due process derived from natural justice.[64] Hearings were first introduced into China in 1996 under the *Administrative Penalty Law*,[65] which requires government agencies to inform the aggrieved parties about their right to a public hearing before imposing serious administrative penalties.[66] Other laws, such as the *Price Law 1997* and the *Legislation Law 2000*, also set out price and law hearings respectively.[67] Hearings are now not limited to individuals who may be aggrieved by a concrete administrative action, but are extended to the general public who may be influenced by an abstract administrative action, such as law-making and decision-making. For instance, the *Administrative Permission Law 2003* requires government agencies to hold public hearings for implementing administrative permissions under law, regulation or rule.[68] The hearing requirements under a number of administrative laws have assisted information flow and relaxed the previous restrictive information environment.

Administrative transparency: inherent in administrative law

Administrative transparency has been regarded as inherent in administrative law in China since the middle 1990s.[69] Procedural due process requires administrative transparency,[70] which is central to modern administrative law[71] and has become a key guide for administrative law reforms in China.[72] This occurs in the following two areas.

First, laws and regulations must be published, and unpublished laws and regulations cannot be the basis of administrative decisions, as the *Administrative Penalty Law 1996* and the *Administrative Permission Law 2003* demonstrate.[73] The *Legislation Law 2000* standardizes the openness of legislation, but requires only a limited degree of publicizing draft laws.[74] In 2008, the Standing Committee of the NPC decided to make draft laws public in principle.[75] In the same year, the State Council also committed to publishing draft bills or administrative regulations that closely involve the interests of the people.[76] The mandatory publication of laws, regulations and rules fell into the category of the push aspect of information flow, which enhanced information flow in a way that can support FOI.

Second, government agencies are obliged to provide a full account of decisions to any person who may be aggrieved by an administrative action. This obligation has been extended to a number of administrative laws adopted since 1996. The *Administrative Penalty Law 1996* requires government agencies to notify the aggrieved parties of the facts, grounds and basis on which the decision is made, as well as the rights that the parties enjoy according to the law before making the decision to impose administrative penalties.[77] The *Administrative Permission Law 2003* requires government agencies to disclose their decision on approving administrative permission, and allows the public to access this decision.[78] The obligation to provide reasons for government decisions was a key antecedent of the pull aspect of FOI in China. It helped increase the government's receptivity to a general right to access information.

Administrative law reforms after the late 1990s, which focused on ex ante and procedural controls of government power, made it possible for the relaxation of the secretive Chinese information environment. The background of FOI, including the hearings, the publication of laws and rules and the giving of reasons for an administrative decision, facilitated information flow from the government to society. This has contributed to a significant change in the secretive Chinese information environment. The push aspect of information flow, although very limited, has become a firm basis for a general access mechanism.

FOI legislation: an integral part of law-based administration

The law-based administration reform agenda directly brought about the official acceptance of the access mechanism, the pull aspect of FOI. Administrative law reforms cannot be achieved without Chinese political leaders' agreement and commitment to building law-based administration. Law-based administration was first raised by former Premier Peng Li in 1993.[79] Political leaders first formally expressed their support for building law-based administration in the political report of the 15th National Congress of the Communist Party of China in 1997.[80] The central endorsement of law-based administration facilitated developments of administrative law in China.

2004 was a turning point for the promotion of law-based administration, which showed the official acceptance of the pull aspect of FOI in China. While the State Council issued a policy document in 1999 to implement the central support for law-based administration,[81] this document did not mention transparency. The Hu–Wen administration since 2003 was determined to take law-based administration as one of its three overarching tasks. Thus, the *Implementation Outline for Pushing Forward Administration by Law in an All-Round Way* (Implementation Outline) was published in 2004, which set the goal to realize a government under the rule of law before 2014, rather than merely law-based administration.[82] The Implementation Outline provided for the guidelines and specific targets, basic principles and requirements, as well as major tasks and measures for the overall implementation of law-based administration.

It is highly significant that this key central policy document took transparency seriously. It regarded procedural due process as a key principle of law-based administration. This was the outcome of the recent trend of administrative law reforms that have turned toward ex ante and procedural controls of government power. The Implementation Outline regarded administrative transparency as a key part of implementing procedural due process. It required government agencies to disseminate any information, subject to statutory exemptions, when undertaking administrative practices.[83] It also required government agencies to disclose information on the exercise of administrative management to the concerned parties in order to safeguard their rights to know, participate and remedy.[84]

More importantly, the Implementation Outline treated FOI legislation as an integral part of law-based administration. This treatment directly resulted in the acceptance of the pull aspect of FOI in China. To encourage the introduction of FOI legislation in China, the Implementation Outline put forward three basic requirements: government agencies should be liable to disclose government information except those involving state secrets, trade secrets or privacy; the public should have a right to access government information; and government agencies should facilitate public access.[85] The acceptance of the pull aspect of FOI caused FOI legislation to rise to the top of political agenda.

The Implementation Outline has had a great influence on administrative law reforms in China. It has set clear goals for the establishment of law-based administration, and become an enforceable working plan for the Chinese government. FOI legislation, which was adopted in 2007, was just one of the plans on the schedule.

Conclusion

The recent administrative law reform agenda, which moved toward controls of government power from ex ante and procedural perspectives, presented the opportunity to increase China's capacity to accept FOI. Administrative transparency has been incorporated into a number of administrative laws adopted since the late 1990s. This resulted in the improvement of information flow in the Chinese information environment, making FOI more compliable with this improved environment. The central government's law-based administration initiative in 2004, coupled with administrative law reforms, finally resulted in the acceptance of FOI in China. Therefore, the traditional accounts of economic growth and anti-corruption efforts for China's FOI reform should be downplayed due to this important but insufficiently recognized factor of administrative law reforms, together with the social and political factors.

6   Reassessment of economic growth and anti-corruption efforts as rationales for FOI reform in China

This chapter examines the roles of the two main driving forces – economic growth and anti-corruption efforts – in influencing China's capacity to accept FOI. It argues that these two forces should be accorded an important but secondary role in FOI reform, as they only have a limited and indirect influence on relaxing the secretive Chinese information environment. It is thus necessary to reassess their roles and examine further their extent and nature. FOI reform was initiated to strengthen the new mode of economic growth, that is, informatization, a term which is different from information flow and used in this book to refer to the modernization of China's information technology infrastructure. Furthermore, FOI reform was promoted to improve the efficiency of anti-corruption efforts. However, this book finds that these two driving forces have arguably been overstressed in the existing literature. This is because the social, political and legal contexts connected with FOI have been largely unexplored. The unexplored parts of the historical background to the introduction of FOI in China have also resulted in these two motives being overstated.

Reassessing economic development as a rationale for FOI

This book argues that the economic growth motive for FOI reform in China has been overstated in the existing literature.[1] This has hindered the exposure and examination of other primary driving forces, including the social, political and legal ones discussed in Chapters 3, 4 and 5. The normative view on economic growth as a driving force of FOI reform in China has presented strong evidence for non-Chinese experts[2] to rationalize China's strange and unexpected growth of FOI. However, the normative view has significant deficiencies in fully describing the actual influence of economic growth on FOI reform. Upon closer examination, this book reveals two layers of the economic growth rationale for FOI reform in China. China's FOI reform was originally a response to the revision of the *Law on the Protection of State Secrets 1988*. At a later date, Chinese reformers made FOI reform politically acceptable from the standpoint of informatization development. This effort was strengthened after the support of informatization agencies and China's accession to the World Trade Organization (WTO) in 2001.

The normative view on the economic growth motive for FOI reform in China

The following explanation for China's FOI reform is currently dominant in the FOI literature. Rather than 'moral considerations'[3] like more transparent and responsible government, it is said that 'utilitarian considerations'[4] such as economic growth led to the acceptance of FOI reform.[5] In retrospect, an alternative and more persuasive explanation for the economic growth motive or a normative view on this motive is as follows. FOI can be seen as a minor but important accompaniment on the roadmap that the Chinese leadership followed in making economic growth the central task in China.[6] Informatization has been regarded as a new and rational choice to develop the economy after the reconsideration of the direction and type of economic growth in China since the late 1990s.[7] Reuse or exploitation of government information, a vital part of developing informatization, was recognized as a priority.[8] Furthermore, FOI was considered an important method for facilitating this reuse, and therefore became part of the movement toward informatization development.[9]

The normative view, which only reflects a narrow part of the Chinese FOI story, is likely to be misleading about the origins of China's FOI reform. The economic growth impetus is important. The move toward FOI reform was boosted by its ability to reuse government information, which refers to the use of government information for commercial purposes. However, the reuse initiative can only increase the willingness of the government to share economically valuable information. It cannot motivate the government to disclose socially valuable but economically unimportant information. This means that the role of economic growth in increasing flow of general information and the capacity to accept FOI was weak. Other largely unexplored driving forces, including social, political and legal conditions, played more primary and direct roles than economic growth in contributing to the acceptance of FOI.

FOI and informatization: a casual connection

There is a casual, rather than causal, connection between informatization development and FOI. This indicates that the role of the information reuse initiative in increasing the Chinese government's willingness to share more general information with the public is not prominent or urgent. A key feature of informatization is reuse of information resources,[10] but FOI lacks a direct and strong association with information reuse. Gellman states that FOI legislation is 'insufficient to meet all public needs for government information, and it is sometimes administered indifferently by the agencies'.[11]

However, Chinese reformers originally presumed that FOI legislation would benefit reuse of government information.[12] Zhou holds the view that a key reason for the adoption of FOI legislation in China is that informatization and an information society require the reuse of government information to develop the economy.[13] He cited two examples, The *Green Paper on Public Sector Information*[14] issued by the EU Commission and the *Comprehensive Assessment of Public Information Dissemination* published by the US National Commission Libraries and Information Science[15] to support his argument. However, these two documents focused more on reusing, rather than accessing public sector information. Zhou is of the opinion that FOI legislation would be most likely to bring about the reuse of information and the development of informatization in China.[16]

Impediments to reuse from FOI legislation

Zhou's observation seems to overestimate the prospects of FOI for reuse of government information, especially when compared to the experiences in the US, Australia and the EU. FOI legislation and its implementation may not facilitate any reuse of information due to its broad exemptions, long processing time and high request fees.[17] Commercial information commonly falls within an exemption under FOI legislation, and is overprotected and overused in practice.[18] Australia serves as an example. The commercial-in-confidence exemption under Australian FOI legislation was overused in the past, and this overuse will be likely to continue in the future, especially with the ever-increasing contracting-out of government services.[19] As a result, Australian businesses have made low use of FOI legislation.[20] A former Australian Attorney-General expected that more businesses would use this legislation to access large amounts of non-confidential information with commercial value,[21] but the reality did not meet his expectation.

The key reason for the low use of FOI by Australian business is the overprotection of the release of third party information, and this has discouraged the commercial use of FOI legislation.[22] This was a response to the concerns of private bodies about the possibility of the release of sensitive commercial information supplied to the government.[23] In practice, government agencies have applied a 'mere possibility'[24] standard of proof, rather than 'reasonable expectation of damage'[25] to the commercial-in-confidence exemption. Such application has broadened the scope of this exemption.

FOI as only one positive factor for reuse

The effect of government information reuse on economic growth cannot be maximized simply by relying on FOI legislation. FOI legislation only provides a mechanism for the public to access government information; it does not set out a provision that permits the public to exploit or reuse the information sought. At least four mechanisms are needed to facilitate reuse of government information: a strong FOI law, a maximum fee limited to the cost of reproduction and dissemination, no government copyright, and no restrictions on exploitation and reuse.[26] This indicates that the role of FOI legislation in promoting reuse of government information will be limited if it does not encourage extensive access[27] or largely promote proactive disclosure.[28] The role of FOI legislation will be further constrained if other efficient mechanisms provided under other laws are lacking. In the US, the *Copyright Act* stipulates that public sector information is not protected by copyright legislation at the federal level.[29] The *Paperwork Reduction Act* prevents government agencies from conducting the four dissemination practices that impede reuse of public information.[30] These laws have a major role in facilitating reuse of government information.

Other countries do not have similar laws that encourage reuse of government information, and this hinders commercial exploitation of information. In Australia, no specific legislation regulates reuse of government information, although reuse is allowed with the permission of the Commonwealth Copyright Administration in the Attorney-General's Department.[31] Further, the charge scheme is likely to discourage businesses from using Australian FOI legislation. The Australian government may charge fees exceeding the actual cost for commercial use of government information.[32]

In the EU, the economic potential of government information may be impeded by its copyright protection, cost-recovery and competition policies.[33] While the EU has recognized the economic potential of government information, it has only partially relaxed these restrictions. The EU issued a directive to facilitate reuse.[34] However, the role of this directive is limited because it adopts a cost-recovery approach[35] that allows public bodies to charge fees, which may cover the cost of providing information and a reasonable return on investment. In addition, reuse of government information could be further constrained because this directive permits public bodies to impose conditions on reuse.

China's legal system does not facilitate reuse of government information. In order to close these loopholes, Zhou and others designed a clause in their draft FOI Regulations to prevent any restriction on reuse of government information.[36] In 2006, the State Council's legislative plan showed that one purpose of introducing FOI Regulations was for the exploitation of government information.[37] Law reformers had a high expectation of FOI legislation to facilitate reuse of government information, but the final FOI Regulations did not meet their expectations. This means that the informatization agencies partly failed to promote FOI from the perspective of informatization development. Therefore, the economic growth motive for FOI reform in China has been overstated and should be accorded a secondary role. This secondary role can also be confirmed due to the initial tactic of making FOI research politically acceptable, as discussed below.

Economic growth as a tool for making FOI research politically acceptable

The economic growth motive for FOI reform in China is more complex than it appears on the surface. The current literature neglects the origin of the first influential FOI research in China, and underestimates the impact of the political sensitivity of FOI before the early 2000s. The introduction of FOI legislation was initially a response to the modification of China's *Law on the Protection of State Secrets 1988*. The normative view does not describe this part of the historical background to China's FOI.

FOI as a response to the revision of the Law on the Protection of State Secrets

FOI originally came to the attention of Chinese academics and government officials due to the revision of the *Law on the Protection of State Secrets*.[38] This historical background has been insufficiently recognized. The State Secrecy Bureau acknowledged the positive role of FOI in enhancing the classification system.[39] It realized that the outdated *Law on the Protection of State Secrets* encouraged government officials to classify too many unnecessary state secrets, posing a risk to crucial state secrets due to scarce resources of maintaining secrecy.[40] Therefore, it is unsurprising that 'documents labelled "absolutely secret" can be found in university libraries in the United States'.[41] In view of the inefficiency and ineffectiveness of the current classification system, the State Secrecy Bureau sought consultants to assist in modifying the *Law on the Protection of State Secrets*.[42] Professor Hanhua Zhou became one of the consultants after he was told that the revision of this Law would include consideration of the relationship between maintaining secrecy and disclosing information.[43] Since then, he has continually showed interest in FOI. The involvement of law academics in the revision of the *Law on the Protection of State Secrets* presented an opportunity for Chinese scholars to do FOI research in China.

Economic growth as an initial tactic to make FOI research politically acceptable

While the involvement in the revision work of the *Law on the Protection of State Secrets* encouraged some Chinese academics to do FOI research, the topic remained politically sensitive in the late 1990s.[44] Zhou found that many citizens knew little about FOI, and media outlets reported little about this issue at that time.[45] Under such circumstances, any FOI research project would need to seek a way to be politically acceptable at first. Zhou was not an exception. He and other researchers conducted the first FOI research project in China under the auspices of the Law Institute of the Chinese Academy of Social Sciences in 1999. This project was initiated to help the State Secrecy Bureau complete one of its desirable targets: improving the efficiency of the maintenance of secrecy through the promotion of transparency work.[46] This task, however, conflicted with its core function, preservation of state secrets.[47]

However, Zhou and his research team found their research difficult as they recognized that FOI was a politically sensitive issue at that time. Hence, they called their FOI research project *Exploitation, Use and Management of*

Government Information Resources,[48] and sought to link FOI legislation with economic growth. When the development of informatization was widely accepted by the Chinese government in the late 1990s, Zhou and others took the next step of connecting FOI legislation with informatization development. This tactic reflected the reality at that time in China and made the research project politically acceptable. It demonstrates that the role of informatization development in improving flow of information, even economically valuable information, in China was indirect.

Further dividends reaped by the initial tactic

The initial tactic that made FOI research politically acceptable reaped further dividends. The Leading Group on National Informatization (LGNI), China's highest level informatization agency,[49] held a series of symposia in order to select experts for the coming Advisory Committee for State Informatization, the think tank of the LGNI. Zhou was invited to deliver a speech at one such symposium in January 2002.[50] His speech focused mainly on the relationship between informatization and FOI legislation, which attracted the attention of Jinlian Wu, a strong advocator of the new mode of economic growth and the deputy director of the Advisory Committee for State Informatization.[51] Hence, Wu recommended Zhou for membership of the future Advisory Committee.[52] As a result, Zhou was recruited to the Advisory Committee in early 2002. He was one of the few members with a legal background.[53] This platform provided him an opportunity for consultation on policies and laws in relation to national informatization. His appointment strengthened the linkage between FOI and informatization. Zhou's efforts convinced the State Council Informatization Office (SCIO) and LGNI, the national informatization agencies, of the strong connection between FOI and informatization development. Therefore, it is not surprising that the SCIO and LGNI invigorated legislation of FOI, and promoted this work in China after 2002.[54]

The LGNI published the *Guidance on Building E-Government* in July 2002.[55] The Guidance first called for the adoption of FOI legislation that was considered as a part of the legislative plan for building e-government.[56] Zhou participated in the process of drafting this document, and advised on it.[57] To implement the Guidance, the SCIO commissioned Zhou and his colleagues to draft FOI Regulations in May 2002.[58] Zhou's position and research background facilitated his involvement in the legislative process of FOI in China. This suggests that FOI in China was more a consequence of policy entrepreneurship[59] and the advocacy of key individuals than a natural outcome of the recent economic growth initiative and the move toward informatization development.

The political acceptability of the introduction of FOI legislation increased further by the accession of China to the WTO in 2001. Chinese reformers took the WTO transparency obligations[60] seriously, and used them as a tool for adding impetus to promote FOI.[61] The SCIO states that the legislation of

FOI was necessary to extend China's reform and opening up policy (*Gaige Kaifang*) that commenced in 1978, and was a measure to cherish and extend the achievement of 15 years of tough WTO accession negotiations.[62] The WTO transparency requirements directly influenced the city of Guangzhou, a Chinese economic hub, to adopt its FOI legislation.[63] The WTO transparency requirements were another economic factor that helped diminish the political sensitivity of FOI in the early 2000s, although the WTO has only required China to proactively disclose laws and policies related to trade.

Reassessing anti-corruption efforts as a rationale for FOI

Alongside economic growth, anti-corruption efforts are seen by some academics as a key driving force for the adoption of FOI legislation in many countries, including China.[64] Many Chinese and non-Chinese academics have rationalized China's FOI phenomenon from this perspective.[65] Mendel agrees with Sutton and Holsen that the motive for FOI reform in China is 'to counter the growing threat of corruption undermining their remarkable economic growth'.[66] The current literature focuses on the role of FOI in exposing, rather than preventing corruption, in China.[67] However, it was the shift of focus on corruption prevention that added impetus to accept FOI in China. Furthermore, close scrutiny of the historical background to the introduction of FOI reveals that the link between the fight against corruption and FOI appeared late, and the access mechanism was not considered as a primary tool for combating corruption. Thus, the contribution of the anti-corruption initiatives to the adoption of FOI legislation has also arguably been overstated.

The shift from fighting corruption to preventing corruption

The Communist Party of China (CPC) acknowledged the existence of corruption in China in 1982. Whilst this left open the possibility of undertaking transparency reform, no such action took place before 1987. The fight against corruption has become a recurring theme of public policy in China since 1982.[68] The CPC first recognized the existence of corruption at its 12th National Congress of the CPC (NCCPC).[69] The political report of the 16th NCCPC took the fight against corruption as a major political task.[70] Therefore, contrary to dissidents' criticism that anti-corruption trials have been used as a tool primarily for 'faction fights',[71] the CPC has taken the fight against corruption seriously since 1982. What needs to be ascertained is to what degree transparency reform has been given a role in this fight. The work of Stiglitz suggests that information asymmetries are key contributors to the high level of corruption in China.[72] The Central Commission for Discipline Inspection (CCDI), a key anti-corruption agency, has persisted in promoting Openness in Government Affairs (OGA) to combat corruption since the 13th NCCPC held in 1987.[73] Since then, the work of OGA has always accompanied China's anti-corruption initiatives.

However, it was only the shift of focus on corruption prevention that laid a foundation for the consideration of FOI legislation.[74] While the last three decades of anti-corruption efforts have achieved a certain degree of success, the fight against corruption still requires the Chinese government to continue its efforts, and also transform and improve its methods of fighting corruption by placing equal importance on corruption prevention and corruption punishment. The CPC first decided to focus on corruption prevention at its 16th NCCPC held in 2002.[75] From that date, the Chinese government has shown its determination to fight corruption from the source. It adopted measures to strengthen corruption prevention, including signing the United Nation's *Convention against Corruption* in 2003,[76] issuing an outline to establish and improve its corruption punishment and prevention system in 2005,[77] and establishing the National Corruption Prevention Bureau directly accountable to the State Council in 2007.[78] One division of the Bureau is responsible for OGA and FOI matters as well as other openness affairs.[79] This shift to corruption prevention in China after the early 2000s increased the utility of FOI.

FOI and corruption prevention

FOI, as a measure to prevent corruption, has achieved this status for two key reasons. First, FOI is a cost-effective measure compared with the high economic losses stemming from corruption. According to Hu, these losses accounted for 'an annual average of 14.5–14.9 per cent'[80] of Gross Domestic Product between 1999 and 2001. This indicates that roughly 1.4 trillion yuan (about $US175 billion) was consumed by corruption in each of those years. The likely implementation cost of FOI is dwarfed by this figure. FOI is also cost effective because it can reduce the chance or scope for corruption, saving the costs of punishing corrupt officials and improving the efficiency of allocating scarce anti-corruption resources. Therefore, compared with other countries, the Chinese government expressed little concern about the inappropriate cost of administration of FOI legislation.[81]

Second, FOI is regarded as a method to prevent corruption at the source.[82] This point is illustrated by the central government's willingness to rely on FOI legislation to disclose beneficial policies, including those for improving farmers' income or reducing farmers' burden, more effectively. Ou argues that there are many beneficial policies in China, but they are not well known to the masses[83] due to local government officials' secretive work styles. A disadvantage is that these styles have been used to serve 'selfish purposes',[84] which has created unnecessary information asymmetries between local government agencies and the masses. Two examples have been used to illustrate the necessity to make disclosure of beneficial policies more effective. One was the classification of the central government's document about the increase of farmers' income.[85] Another was the prohibition of disclosing a booklet combining the central government's policies of reducing farmers' burden.[86] Zhou stated that '[w]hat is most inconceivable is that the booklet is in no sense an illegal publication, only a compilation of the Party's rural policies'.[87]

FOI legislation is a mechanism that not only requires government agencies to actively release beneficial policies, but authorizes citizens to pressure the government to disclose these policies via access requests. FOI legislation can reduce local government officials' excessive control over many beneficial policies, aiding the central government in reducing scope for government officials to be corrupt and abusive and in saving anti-corruption resources. As Deng argues, 'if [organizational and working systems] are unsound, they may hamper the efforts of good people or indeed, in certain cases, may push them in the wrong direction'.[88] FOI legislation is a sound system, which provides the central government with a mechanism to allow greater scrutiny and transparency of lower levels of government.

The view of FOI as a tool for preventing corruption assisted FOI reform in China to gain strength and credibility. The likelihood that FOI legislation would be adopted was accordingly increased.

Reappraisal of the role of FOI as a tool for combating corruption

The current literature has overstated the anti-corruption element of the development of FOI for the following two reasons. First, the historical background to the introduction of FOI legislation shows that the link between the anti-corruption initiatives and FOI appeared late in the lead up to the first national FOI legislation in early 2007. FOI reform, an integral part of transparency reform, was promoted by Chinese anti-corruption agencies much later than other transparency practices, especially OGA, which was used to fight corruption after 1987.[89] Though it might have seemed likely that anti-corruption agencies would have promoted FOI legislation earlier than other agencies, they did not ally themselves with the informatization agencies to promote FOI legislation in China before 2004.

The political sensitivity of FOI may have hindered anti-corruption agencies from giving sufficient attention to FOI. After the issue of the *Implementation Outline for Pushing Forward Administration by Law in an All-Round Way* in March 2004,[90] the CCDI and the Leading Group on National Openness in Government Affairs (LGNOGA) began to address the importance of FOI in corruption prevention.[91] Thereafter the anti-corruption agencies advocated legislation of FOI. So it was not until 2004, when the central government called for the introduction of FOI legislation, that the anti-corruption link was accepted by the CCDI and LGNOGA, the national primary supervisory agencies. This process reduced the anti-corruption aspect of the FOI story in China.

Second, the access mechanism, which lies at the core of FOI legislation, was not promoted as a primary tool for combating corruption. Anti-corruption agencies did not promote FOI from this core concept. This created a paradox whereby FOI was regarded as a tool for exposing corruption after the fact.[92] The CCDI and LGNOGA were keen to advocate FOI primarily for institutionalizing OGA promoted by them for over two decades. Yong He, the Deputy Secretary of CCDI, considers that FOI Regulations are the basic legislation in relation to OGA, and that they can play a key role in gradually institutionalizing OGA in China.[93] Qin recalled that the LGNOGA had considered the institutionalization of OGA for many years.[94] This indicates that OGA, which focused on proactive disclosure rather than the access mechanism featuring dominantly in FOI legislation, was recognized by anti-corruption agencies as a direct tool for combating corruption. This coincided with the concern over the effectiveness of the access mechanism as an anti-corruption tool.[95]

Conclusion

The roles of economic growth and anti-corruption in the process of Chinese FOI reform were overstated, although they were important. Other factors, including social, political and legal ones are largely unexplored, but more crucial and direct than economic growth and anti-corruption rationales for the acceptance of FOI in China. Furthermore, the historical background to the introduction of FOI shows that informatization was used as a means of making FOI reform more politically acceptable, rather than as a primary driving force of FOI reform. The link between the fight against corruption and FOI appeared late, and the access mechanism was not considered as a primary tool for exposing corruption.

7 Gradual legislative process for FOI reform in China

This chapter explores the process of gradual legislative reforms leading up to the introduction of FOI legislation in China. It shows that FOI Regulations were a key but interim result of many increments, such as openness in village and government affairs, and FOI rule-making activities at both city and province levels. All these increments, which were connected with the multiple rationales discussed in the previous four chapters, helped increase information flow in the Chinese information environment. This therefore gradually enhanced the capacity to adopt the first national FOI legislation – FOI Regulations. Yet there is a paradox. On an initial survey, many inside and outside of China were caught by surprise at the apparent rapidity of Chinese FOI reform. Compared with most other countries, China experienced less internal resistance to FOI reform, and this was possible to enable the speedy introduction of FOI legislation. However, evidence suggests that the reform was part of a broad strategy of gradualism, to which the Chinese government adhered after the reform and opening-up policy that commenced in 1978.

Openness in government affairs: a firm basis for FOI legislation

Experiments in and institutionalization of OGA primarily for a long-term democratization process provided a solid foundation for the consideration of FOI legislation in China. The practices of OGA in China were first initiated by a project dealing with Openness in Two Areas and Supervision by the Public (OTASP) that commenced in the late 1980s.[1] After a decade's experimentation, OGA was formally extended to all township government agencies in 2000.[2] Five years later, OGA was officially permitted to be extended to all levels of government.[3]

The project dealing with Openness in Two Areas and Supervision by the Public

The Communist Party of China (CPC) first formally recognized the importance of openness in 1987 through the OTASP project,[4] which presented a limited opportunity for the development of OGA. The political report of the 13th National Congress of the CPC (NCCPC) in 1987 called on leading agencies to improve the openness of their activities and let the people know about and discuss important matters.[5] The OTASP project responded to the call of the 13th NCCPC to take strong action to curb corruption.[6] It included disclosure of rules and results concerning the process of administrative affairs, and acceptance of supervision from the public.[7] It was launched in Hebei Province in 1988, and shortly thereafter expanded to other provinces, including Hunan and Fujian.[8]

While the scope of the OTASP was limited, it began the process of the flow of government information in China. It also helped the Chinese government recognize the benefits of openness, including the facilitation of the fight against corruption.[9]

Openness in Government Affairs at the primary level

The OTASP project was extended to OGA at the primary level. However, the latter was not the direct result of implementation of this project, but the result of Openness in Village Affairs (OVA). The *Notice on Comprehensively Implementing Openness in Village Affairs and Democratic Management*, issued in 1998, encouraged rather than required township governments to practise OGA during the period of implementing OVA.[10] OGA at the primary level was formally supported by the central government in 2000 by the *Notice on Promoting Openness in Government Affairs around All Government Agencies at the Township Level*.[11] After several years' practice, OGA at the primary level was standardized in 2004.[12] Its standardization and expansion at the township level prepared the ground for OGA at a higher level.

OGA at the township level revealed the relaxation of the secretive Chinese information environment. It provided a catalyst for developing grassroots democracy, in addition to assisting the fight against corruption. These considerations gave force to OGA in China, increasing the prospects of greater transparency.

Openness in Government Affairs at and above the county level

OGA at higher levels of government increased the possibility and capability for the acceptance of FOI in China. During the period when OGA operated at the township level, some government agencies at and above the county level began disclosing information concerning their administrative affairs.[13] To respond to the call of the 16th NCCPC that required government agencies to disclose their affairs,[14] more local governments and state agencies began to undertake and institutionalize openness practices. These openness efforts improved information flow in the Chinese information environment, and with them increased China's capacity to support FOI.

Institutionalization of OGA by ministries

Several ministries began to legislate on their openness practices in the early 2000s. In 2003 the Ministry of Commerce institutionalized its OGA, though its scope was limited to the Ministry level rather than the administrative system across the country. The Ministry of Transport followed suit, adopting its *Interim Rules on Openness in Government Affairs* in 2004 to standardize information dissemination among transportation agencies. It prepared the ground for other ministries, such as the Ministries of Personnel, Labor and Social Securities, and Water Resources, to legislate on their OGA practices.

Institutionalization of OGA by provincial and city governments

The institutionalization of OGA was not limited to ministries. Chinese sub-national governments conducted similar rule-making activities. The Fujian government was the first provincial government to legislate on its OGA in 2001. Guangdong Province became the first province to adopt local OGA regulations in 2005,[15] elevating the status of OGA in this province. Sichuan Province followed suit in 2006. Some major cities, such as Harbin, Taiyuan and Shenzhen, also institutionalized their OGA.[16] These rule-making activities focused on the standardization of OGA, which provided models for the central government to consider proactive disclosure requirements under national FOI legislation.

Policy initiatives by other government agencies

Although other government agencies did not institutionalize OGA, they issued policy documents to develop openness practices. An example is the Ministry of Public Security. Openness in police affairs was first formally required under the *Police Law 1995*.[17] The Ministry of Public Security in 1999 issued a policy document to make laws and procedures concerning their functions public.[18] Other state agencies, including the State Administration for Industry and Commerce[19] and the State Administration of Taxation,[20] also issued policy documents to promote OGA in their own administrative systems. Whilst the Ministry of Foreign Affairs is considered a special ministry, it has exerted efforts to declassify its archives during recent years.[21] A 2006 investigation found that 31 provincial governments and 36 ministerial agencies adopted their own measures to implement OGA.[22]

Central government policy initiatives

The State Council followed this openness trend. Normative documents,[23] which are frequently used to conduct administration by government agencies, were previously prohibited from being disclosed to the public. In 2002 the General Office of the State Council decided to provide free copies of the

Gazette of the State Council, which includes many normative documents, to all public bodies and political parties.[24] The full copies of the Gazette of the State Council are now freely distributed to the public through the web portal of China.[25]

The central government formally widened these proactive disclosure practices to all levels of government in 2005.[26] In this year, the State Council joined the CPC Central Committee to jointly issue the *Notice on Further Promoting Openness in Government Affairs*.[27] The Notice required government agencies to disclose all types of information in relation to administrative management and public services unless exempted as a state secret, trade secret or individual privacy.[28] It also displayed the central government's determination to introduce national FOI legislation in China, as it called for the acceleration of the formulation of FOI Regulations and encouraged local governments to adopt FOI Rules in the interim.[29]

FOI legislation: developments at the sub-national level

China's unified and multilevel legislative system offered considerable flexibility to experiment with FOI law-making or rule-making.[30] The institutionalization of FOI was conducted at the national and local levels at the same time, but was first achieved at local and provincial levels. Sub-national FOI rule-making activities were undertaken widely with implicit and explicit support from the central government. These local legislative and implementation activities were the starting point of operating the pull aspect of information flow. They further ameliorated the Chinese information environment, thereby increasing the capacity to accommodate FOI and accelerating the introduction of national FOI legislation.

FOI legislation: developments at the city level

Chinese local governments have conducted rule-making activities related to FOI since 2002. These activities not only guaranteed the standardization of openness practices in their administrative areas, but prepared the ground for higher levels of government to consider similar rules. In China, a comparatively larger city[31] may enact local rules.[32] By the end of 2006, 17 comparatively larger cities had adopted FOI Rules, as shown in Table 7.1.

Among the 49 comparatively larger cities in China, Guangzhou was the first city to pass FOI legislation in China in November 2002. Eight cities introduced FOI legislation in 2004. Another five brought FOI Rules into their localities in 2005. Three more followed suit in 2006. Many other cities issued policy documents about FOI to boost openness in their administrative areas.[33] All these rule-making activities legislated on proactive disclosure and access to information. Implementation of FOI Rules enabled the central government to learn more about the prospects for FOI legislation to conform to China's local circumstances.

Table 7.1 FOI legislation in comparatively larger cities

City	Date passed	Date effective
Guangzhou	6 November 2002	1 January 2003
Hangzhou	15 April 2004	1 October 2004
Changchun	N/A	30 October 2004
Ningbo	28 September 2004	1 November 2004
Chengdu	4 March 2004	1 May 2004
Kunming	8 April 2004	1 May 2004
Wuhan	17 May 2004	1 July 2004
Datong	30 March 2004	1 August 2004
Anshan	23 September 2004	1 January 2005
Haikou	N/A	1 June 2005
Guiyang	25 April 2005	1 January 2006
Zhengzhou	8 July 2005	1 October 2005
Wululmuqi	26 September 2005	1 November 2005
Suzhou	25 October 2005	1 January 2006
Handan	16 May 2006	18 May 2006
Benxi	20 May 2006	1 July 2006
Shenzhen	22 September 2006	1 September 2006

Sources: Collected by the author from various government websites

However, FOI Rules were rarely used by the public. This helped the central government to realize that there would be no high use of FOI or lawsuits flowing from FOI legislation. According to Cheng, the landmark case did not occur until 2006, when Guangzhou had adopted its FOI Rules for four years.[34] Only two influential FOI lawsuits were brought in Wuhan[35] and Zhengzhou respectively.[36] No other significant FOI lawsuits were reported in other cities that adopted FOI Rules.

FOI legislation: developments at the province level

In China, local or sub-national experiments in FOI were used to serve as tests for national legislation.[37] Local FOI legislative activities may have encouraged the central government to consider a similar national policy. This explains why the State Council Legislative Affairs Office became more active in promoting the first national FOI legislation after 2006.[38] Twelve governments at the province level in mainland China had adopted FOI Rules by the end of 2006 (see Table 7.2). This provided a solid foundation for the central government to build successful national FOI legislation in China.[39]

There was a rapid uptake of FOI legislation at the province level in China. Among the 31 provincial governments in mainland China, Shanghai Special Municipality published the first FOI legislation at the province level on 20 January 2004. One special municipality and two provinces brought FOI Rules into their administrative areas in 2004. Another six provinces adopted FOI Rules in 2005. In 2006, two provinces published FOI Rules. Other provincial governments, such as Beijing, Guangxi and Ningxia, publicized draft FOI

Table 7.2 FOI legislation in provinces and special municipalities

Province	Date passed	Date effective
Shanghai	20 January 2004	01 May 2004
Chongqing	2 June 2004	01 July 2004
Hubei	18 May 2004	01 July 2004
Jilin	22 July 2004	05 September 2004
Hebei	29 March 2005	01 July 2005
Guangdong	29 July 2005	01 October 2005
Hainan	15 August 2005	01 October 2005
Shanxi	10 December 2005	1 January 2006
Liaoning	14 December 2005	1 February 2006
Heilongjiang	30 December 2005	1 April 2006
Jiangsu	07 August 2006	01 September 2006
Sichuan	12 September 2006	12 September 2006

Sources: Collected by the author from various government websites

Rules. Zhejiang also drafted similar rules, but did not make the draft version public.

At least two aspects explain the benefits of local FOI Rules to the development of equivalent legislation on a national scale. First, these provincial governments aided the central government to understand more about the compatibility of FOI legislation with the local conditions in China, especially the Shanghai FOI Rules. The Rules provided 'the most comprehensive framework' for the central government to use as a foundation.[40] More importantly, the central government scrutinized the Shanghai government's launch of 'unprecedented organizational, training and preparatory work to help ensure the effective implementation'.[41] The Shanghai Legislative Affairs Office assisted the State Council Legislative Affairs Office to arrange the legislative investigation into FOI in Shanghai in 2006.[42] Some staff members in the Shanghai Legislative Affairs Office took part in drafting the FOI Regulations.[43]

Second, implementation of local FOI rules assisted the central government to identify the potential problems of controversial definitions for government information, the diversity of agencies responsible for FOI work and the complexity of the fee structure for access requests.[44] These diverse practices necessitated the standardization of FOI work through the adoption of national FOI legislation. Third, provincial FOI practices may have strengthened the central government's belief that FOI legislation would not undermine other key interests, such as national security, privacy and trade secrets.[45] The willingness and capability to adopt national FOI legislation thus swelled.

FOI legislation: developments at the national level

The central government took the adoption of FOI legislation seriously after 2004. Informatization agencies initiated the legislation of FOI legislation in

2002.[46] Anti-corruption agencies allied themselves with this attempt after 2004.[47] Their efforts cumulatively contributed to the adoption of the FOI Regulations in early 2007.

Which to introduce first: FOI law or FOI Regulations

The Chinese government faced a choice whether to first introduce FOI law or FOI Regulations. A similar question does not arise in the common law system, where regulations are adopted after, as part of a law to provide additional detail or procedure. FOI law has advantages compared with FOI Regulations. It can create a new and enforceable access right and impose criminal sanctions against violations of disclosure requirements.[48] Chinese deputies of the National People's Congress (NPC) advocated the adoption of FOI law, submitting proposals for the enactment of FOI law to the NPC seven times between 2002 and 2006, as illustrated in Table 7.3. Chinese deputies desired FOI legislation, not to balance the power between the executive and parliament found in advanced liberal democracies, but for other local reasons, such as standardizing local FOI legislative activities and resolving the dilemma of implementation of local FOI Rules.[49]

In response to the call of many deputies, the Standing Committee of the 10th NPC in early 2003 listed FOI law in the secondary priority category of its five-year legislative plan (2003–2008).[50] This meant that the FOI law would be researched, and a review process would be initiated if appropriate.[51] However, this plan was not enforced, and FOI law is yet to be drafted. In March 2004, the Internal and Judicial Affairs Committee of the NPC recognized the need to adopt FOI law in China in order to supervise government agencies and safeguard the public's rights to know, participate and supervise.[52] It added that the State Council was drafting FOI Regulations, and that

Table 7.3 FOI proposals submitted by deputies of the National People's Congress

Deputies	Year	Session
Qi Cai and other deputies from Fujian Province	March 2002	The Fifth Session of the Ninth NPC
Suzhi Chen and other deputies from Niaoning Province	March 2002	The Fifth Session of the Ninth NPC
Zhihai Li and other deputies came from Zhejiang Province	March 2003	The First Session of the 10th NPC
Huiqiang Zhen and other deputies from Shanghai Special Municipality	March 2004	The Second Session of the 10th NPC
Zhong Yang and other deputies from Shanxi Province	March 2004	The Second Session of the 10th NPC
Zhongchuan Dai and other deputies from Fujian Province	March 2005	The Third Session of the 10th NPC
Yongqiu Zhao and other deputies from Hubei Province	March 2006	The Fourth Session of the 10th NPC

Source: The National People's Congress

FOI law would be enacted based on the experiences learnt from the implementation of the Regulations.[53] This indicates that FOI Regulations would be adopted before the adoption of FOI law.

While the adoption of FOI Regulations before law contrasts with common law legal traditions, the Chinese government elected to do so because the process is more rapid than the adoption of FOI law.[54] Furthermore, it was recognized that FOI Regulations would form an integral part of the Chinese legal system, and did not lack status because courts could take them into account as criteria to handle administrative lawsuits.[55] Thus, in China, FOI Regulations, which have basic elements similar to FOI law, have a strong impact on government activities, although they cannot override conflicting laws. In addition, introducing regulations prior to law met previous Chinese law-making practices.[56] Many administrative laws were not adopted until several years after the implementation of their related regulations,[57] such as the *Administrative Reconsideration Law 1999* and the *Civil Servant Law 2005*. Implementation of FOI Regulations helps China to gain experiences for better designing and implementing future FOI law.[58]

Informatization agencies: invigorating legislation of FOI

The Leading Group of National Informatization (LGNI) and the State Council Informatization Office (SCIO) promoted FOI from the perspective of informatization development, and initiated the legislation of FOI in China.[59] Supported by the policy document *Guidance on Building E-Government*,[60] the SCIO commissioned the Law Institute of the Chinese Academy of Social Science to draft FOI Regulations in May 2002.[61] The legislative process lasted for three months and an early draft was presented to the SCIO in August.[62] On 29 August, the SCIO held a forum with experts on this draft. On 14 September, the SCIO commissioned the State Information Centre to hold a seminar on the draft, and solicited comments and suggestions from experts and government officials. The draft was amended during October and November after negotiation with other ministries, including the Ministries of Science and Technology, and Information Industry. Then on 27 December 2002, the draft of FOI Regulations was finalized by academics and submitted to the State Council Legislative Affairs Office, the agency that assists the premier to handle legislative affairs.[63] However, the State Council Legislative Affairs Office had little passion for FOI Regulations before 2006,[64] which was understandable during this period, when local FOI rule-making activities were largely absent and the rationale of economic growth predominated over others in the FOI reform initiative.

Anti-corruption agencies: making great efforts

The national anti-corruption or supervisory agencies, the Central Commission for Discipline Inspection (CCDI) and the Leading Group on National

Openness in Government Affairs (LGNOGA), played a role in promoting FOI in China as a tool for preventing corruption from 2004.[65] Yong He, the Deputy Secretary of CCDI, first mentioned FOI in his speech at the second meeting of the LGNOGA in April 2004.[66] In March 2005, at the fourth meeting of the LGNOGA, he called for the formulation of FOI Regulations.[67] He recalled that the General Office of the LGNOGA had drafted the *Notice on Further Promoting Openness in Government Affairs*[68] in July 2004, and suggested that the formulation of FOI Regulations be accelerated.[69] This Notice, issued in March 2005,[70] accepted the need to accelerate the formulation of FOI Regulations. The following two meetings of the LGNOGA after 2005 reiterated this need.[71] The LGNOGA arranged a special discussion on FOI Regulations at its sixth meeting.[72] The involvement of the anti-corruption agencies in the legislative process for FOI was another factor that helped improve the receptivity of the central government to FOI.

The central government: commitment to adopting FOI Regulations

The State Council and the CPC Central Committee are also major contributors to the promotion of FOI in China since 2004. In March 2004, Premier Wen, in his Report on the Work of the Government at the Second Session of the 10th NPC, committed to establishing a disclosure system to make it easier for citizens to exercise their rights to know and supervise.[73] Immediately after the conclusion of this session, on 22 March 2004, the State Council issued the *Implementation Outline for Pushing Forward Administration by Law in an All-Round Way*.[74] The Outline regarded FOI legislation as part of the framework of law-based administration, and required government agencies to adopt the legislation.[75] In 2005, the central government circulated the *Notice on Further Promoting Openness in Government Affairs*, reiterating the acceleration of the formulation of FOI Regulations.[76]

In response to these calls, the State Council listed the FOI Regulations as the second priority category of its legislative plan in 2004 and 2005.[77] Since 2004, the State Council Legislative Affairs Office has joined with the SCIO to revise the draft through extensive consultation with 46 state agencies and 34 local governments and panel discussion with experts.[78] In addition, the State Council Legislative Affairs Office held the Sixth China-Germany Law Forum in 2005 to discuss legal issues concerning FOI.[79] However, FOI legislation was not an openly developed policy in China. The legislative process lacked public participation and the draft of FOI legislation was not publicized.[80] In 2006, the State Council listed the FOI Regulations as the first priority category of its legislative plan for the first time, signalling that the Regulations would be adopted within that year.[81] However, the State Council postponed the approval of the legislative plan, the adoption of the FOI Regulations in principle, until 17 January 2007.[82] Further amendments were required. The State Council published the final version of the Regulations on 24 April 2007.

Conclusion

FOI reform in China formed part of a much longer process of increased transparency. The government first gained experiences from the work of OVA. OGA followed OVA, but was trialled by township government agencies, and expanded to government agencies at both county and province levels several years later. Furthermore, many city and provincial governments adopted and implemented FOI Rules in their own localities after 2002. These sub-national OGA and FOI practices enhanced information flow in the Chinese information environment, thus increasing China's capacity to accommodate the first national FOI legislation – the FOI Regulations. The Regulations will prepare a firm foundation for the introduction of the national FOI law in the future.

The gradual legislative process for FOI demonstrates that FOI developments in China followed a push to pull path, and this indicates that China will adopt a push model of FOI legislation which emphasizes proactive disclosure.

8 China's limited push model of FOI legislation

This chapter examines China's FOI Regulations and argues that China has adopted a push model of FOI legislation that emphasizes proactive disclosure of government information. This differs from a pull model that stresses citizen-initiated access or reactive disclosure. The push model of FOI legislation, which has reduced the importance of access requests in China, grew out of two decades of limited proactive disclosure practices around the country and an improved information environment resulting from the formation of multiple paths for information flow. However, the degree of push or proactive disclosure under China's current FOI Regulations is undermined by several factors, including a limited access mechanism, broad and vague exemptions and omission of the maximum disclosure principle.

Models of FOI legislation: pull versus push

There are two factors – an improved information environment and new public management reform[1] – that have generated new possibilities and capabilities for the global shift from a pull model of FOI legislation to a push model.[2] China introduced a push model of FOI legislation, albeit as a response to two decades of limited proactive disclosure practices around the country and an improved information environment, which necessitated a subsidiary or reduced role for an access mechanism.

An emerging global trend: from a pull to a push model

Like recent FOI reform in Australian states,[3] a push model of FOI legislation that emphasizes proactive disclosure and takes access requests as a last resort[4] has emerged around the globe in recent years. An improved information environment, together with new public administration reform programmes, has prompted the push model. A pull model, albeit neatly accommodated to the pre-Internet era of public administration, therefore is now outdated. The need for FOI to respond and adapt to an information age was a major theme of Roberts's work.[5]

A pull model: emphasizing reactive disclosure

A pull model of FOI legislation was adopted by liberal democracies to solve the accountability deficit arising from a perceived growth in government power. This indicates that most FOI legislation between the 1960s and the 1980s had a strong 'antagonistic'[6] and individualized nature.[7] A pull model was the result of a compromise between key demand side players, including the media and the parliament, and the executive.[8] Globalization, promoted by international institutions such as the World Bank, has led to many recent FOI adopters favouring a pull model.

A push model: emphasizing proactive disclosure

New public management reform indicates that public administration has begun to shift from a 'government-oriented' to a citizen or 'customer-oriented' approach.[9] This has opened up the possibility for a push model of FOI legislation that emphasizes proactive disclosure or 'enabling' access.[10] Thus, the environment that surrounds FOI legislation has changed into a less 'antagonistic' one,[11] although, as noted by Roberts, government restructuring has weakened the effectiveness of FOI legislation by limiting its coverage, including the bodies and subject matter.[12]

More importantly, the significance of citizen-initiated access has been reduced in the information age,[13] requiring a push model of FOI legislation to be introduced to adapt to the changed information environment. Information flow, with the assistance of information technology, has become easier and more frequent. FOI academics, such as Snell, call for a shift from 'version 1.0' FOI focusing on reactive disclosure to 'version 2.0' emphasizing proactive disclosure.[14] Government agencies have also become more receptive to information sharing in order to adapt to an improved information environment. The US revised its FOI legislation in 1996 to accommodate the information age, changing its strong pull version to include more proactive disclosure requirements.[15] The UK FOI law sets out a publication scheme, which requires government agencies to provide information to the public routinely and proactively.[16] In Mexico, government agencies are required to publish an extensive amount of information on their websites.[17] More importantly, Australia is taking the lead in promoting a push model to become policy, especially at the sub-national level. Queensland, Tasmania and New South Wales are presently developing this model.[18]

FOI legislation in China: a limited push model

China's adoption of a push model of FOI legislation has been chiefly for domestic reasons. Three factors merit prominence for this adoption. The first is the previous two decades of Openness in Government Affairs (OGA), closely linked to a long-term democratization process. For a significant period of this democratization process, the focus has been on the capacity and the willingness of the government to share information with citizens. Proactive disclosure requirements under the FOI Regulations have provided a summary of the previous work of OGA that has focused on proactive disclosure.[19] FOI legislation has helped institutionalize the work of OGA to solve many problems, including the government's unlimited discretion to disclose information and its non legally binding disclosure duty.[20] The institutionalization of OGA can solve these problems and perpetuate the duration of OGA experiments.[21]

Second, the push model of FOI legislation in China was the outcome of an improved information environment due to the formation of multiple paths for information flow. China increased its information flow by following a push to pull path. Improving information flow within the demand side caused the Chinese government to become more proactive in releasing government information. The emphasis on proactive disclosure may be more effective than the focus on reactive disclosure in prompting government officials to abandon their longstanding secretive and reactive information management approach that has been proven outdated in the improved Chinese information environment. Furthermore, the government's capacity to proactively disclose information has increased now that government websites have been launched and spokesperson systems have been established.

Another factor also supported the adoption of the push model of FOI legislation in China. The emphasis on proactive disclosure may have reduced the workload of government agencies arising from the process of access requests due to China's huge population, vast territory and high volume of government information.[22] These unique features have required reduced importance to be placed on access requests in order to allow government agencies to exercise their core functions. This explains why several Chinese developing areas, like Hunan, are keen to adopt the push approach. The Hunan government considers that this approach can help it focus on other more urgent tasks in its locality.[23]

Whilst China's greater focus on proactive disclosure appears different from a universally accepted pull setting of FOI, the push model reflects a new approach to FOI in the information age and grew out of China's local conditions. However, China's push model of FOI legislation has been undermined by some of its key features, indicating that it is not an ideal push model as that would have no such undermining features.

A unique proactive disclosure system: evidence for a push model

China's FOI Regulations include much broader requirements for proactive disclosure than FOI laws elsewhere. They set forth minimum standards and general criteria for government agencies to determine the circumstances in which information is needed to be proactively disclosed. They also provide for other legal measures that can ensure compliance with proactive disclosure requirements. These legal measures are various means of proactive disclosure, varied locations and facilities for access, information inventory and guide requirements, time limits for publication, a reporting system and sanctions for non-compliance.

A non-exhaustive list: minimum standards and general criteria

While China's FOI Regulations were passed by the State Council in early 2007, they were not published until three months later. During these three months, there was vigorous debate about whether the Regulations should have a non-exhaustive list of the requirements for proactive disclosure.[24] The FOI Regulations eventually contained a non-exhaustive list, which sets forth general criteria for government agencies to produce their own information that is needed to be proactively disclosed, and provides for a minimum standard to oblige different government agencies to emphasize active release of varied government information. The legal design combining minimum standards with general criteria can facilitate compliance with the FOI Regulations in a practical way.

Minimum standards: for government agencies to stress

China's FOI Regulations provide a minimum set of conditions for government agencies to determine information to be proactively disclosed. Three clauses establish minimum standards in the field of making government information publicly available by listing key information that needs to be proactively disclosed. Article 10 requires government agencies at or above the county level to emphasize proactive disclosure of government information, such as information on legal documents, budgets and expenses, public health, and food and drug safety.[25] Article 11 obliges government agencies at the county level to stress disclosing additional information, such as information on land requisition and assistance to low income families.[26] Article 12 emphasizes information to be disseminated by government agencies at the township level, such as information on land use plans and the implementation of family planning policies.[27]

Four general criteria: normal guidelines for decisions by government agencies

A push model of FOI legislation calls for minimum standards, but general criteria must be established to aid government agencies in producing their own categories of information to be proactively disclosed. This is so in China. The FOI Regulations contain a general clause requiring government agencies to proactively disclose information satisfying any one of the following four general criteria:[28]

1   Information that involves the vital interests of citizens, legal persons or other organizations;

2 Information that needs to be extensively known or participated in by the general public;
3 Information that shows the structure, function and working procedures and the like concerning a government agency; or
4 Other information that must be proactively disclosed under laws, regulations and relevant rules.

This general clause sets broad standards for government agencies to justify government information subject to proactive disclosure. While the third criterion is also commonly found in a pull model of FOI legislation and the fourth criterion is only a residual criterion, the first two criteria are innovative and can encompass considerable government information. They also provide a useful analytical framework for an examination of compliance with FOI legislation.

Legal measures safeguarding proactive disclosure

The Chinese government has devised at least six legal measures to ensure compliance with proactive disclosure requirements. The first includes various means of proactive disclosure, such as government websites, press conferences and government bulletins.[29] Press conferences are understood by the Chinese government as a useful means to disseminate government information. Further, government websites are required to be the priority platform for disseminating government information,[30] thus reducing the use and importance of access requests. The central government requires government agencies to launch FOI sections, similar to electronic reading rooms, on their official websites.[31] FOI sections of the websites have become an important platform for publishing information by government agencies. They also provide other functions that can facilitate access to information, such as online searching and information requesting.

The second legal measure to ensure compliance with proactive disclosure requirements is the provision of a variety of locations and facilities for accessing proactively disclosed information.[32] More importantly, government agencies must provide all proactively disclosed information to national archives and public libraries in a timely manner.[33] This requirement goes beyond legislating state archives' previous experiments with receipt and release of current document (*Xing Xing Wenjian*) since 2000.[34] It covers all sorts of proactively disclosed information. Furthermore, the FOI Regulations have placed equal importance on libraries and archives to provide government information services to the public. The requirement for providing government information to libraries has resolved the dilemma faced by libraries, which cannot subscribe to official documents without an ISBN or ISSN.[35]

The third legal measure is the compilation and publication by government agencies of their information inventories and guides.[36] The inventory includes index, name, abstract, date of generation and other particulars of government information.[37] This not only aids requesters to formulate their requests, but assists government agencies to manage information effectively.[38] Government agencies must also compile and publish information guides and update them on a timely basis.[39] Guides include methods of cataloguing, categorizing and obtaining government information, as well as details of the relevant FOI offices' name, business address, office hours, telephone number, fax number and e-mail.[40] The requirement of information inventories and guides shows government willingness to proactively disclose information.[41] It provides the public with basic information about the documents held by the government and the methods used to arrange them.[42]

The fourth legal measure is the time limit for disseminating government information. The Regulations require proactively disclosed information to be released within 20 days of the date the information is generated or changed.[43] The time limit is rarely found in other countries' FOI legislation, and avoids an unreasonable delay of the information required to be proactively disclosed.

The fifth legal measure is a reporting or complaint mechanism. Citizens are entitled to report government failure to adhere to proactive disclosure requirements to the supervisory agencies responsible for investigating reports or complaints.[44] This mechanism gives the public an opportunity to assist the central government to discover and redress non-compliance with proactive disclosure in practice.

The final legal measure concerns administrative sanctions. Government agencies and officials are subject to administrative sanctions for failing to perform duties to disclose government information or to update categories concerning proactive disclosure, information inventories and guides on a timely basis.[45] Sanctions play an important role in ensuring compliance with proactive disclosure in practice.

A limited access mechanism

A limited information access mechanism is a factor that undermines the degree of proactive disclosure under China's FOI legislation. The access mechanism is constrained by an obscure authorization of the access right, and a potential need test. Whilst senior Chinese officials state that the FOI Regulations have been adopted to safeguard the access right,[46] the practical effect of this statement is limited.

An implied access right

While the FOI Regulations allow access to government information, they do not explicitly confer an access right. Before the passage of the Regulations, there were disputes about their ability to do so.[47] The access right was also not specially mentioned under the *Constitution 1982*.[48] As a result, there was a general consensus that the FOI Regulations were an inappropriate legal document to confer this political right, signalling that it can only be protected indirectly by the Regulations.[49] Indirect protection can constrain Chinese citizens' capacity to access general government information or compel government agencies to rectify non-compliance with proactive disclosure, as there has been much debate on whether or not the access right falls outside the scope of administrative lawsuits.

A potential need test

International best practice dictates anyone should be able to exercise the access right, whether or not they have any ground or legal interest.[50] China's FOI Regulations do not meet this aspect of best practice. The Regulations enable citizens, legal persons or other organizations to request information held by government agencies in accordance with their needs in business, daily life, research or other special needs.[51] A purpose for information sought is required, although the definition of purpose is so broad that requesters can easily meet this requirement.[52]

In terms of the concern that government agencies are likely to refuse access requests with the excuse that the information requested does not meet requesters' special needs,[53] the State Council clarifies that government agencies may refuse access requests if information sought is unrelated to the requesters' special needs.[54] Furthermore, local governments, which adopted FOI legislation prior to the central government, have changed their previous practices that did not require a purpose for access requests. The degree of proactive disclosure is therefore restricted by this retreat.

Broad and vague exemptions

The degree of proactive disclosure under the FOI Regulations has arguably been weakened by broad and vague exemptions. Whilst exemptions are a standard element of FOI legislation, exemptions under China's FOI Regulations remain less liberal than is ideal, in at least the following six aspects.

First, the scope of exemptions under the FOI Regulation is inconsistent with best practice,[55] though the Regulations ostensibly set out very limited exemptions – the main exemption clause only prevents government agencies from disclosing information concerning state secrets, trade secrets and privacy.[56] Other exemptions are stated in general in Article 8, which exempts information that may prejudice state security, public security, economic security or social stability. Much government information will remain hidden under this general exemption.[57] Moreover, whilst the FOI Regulations do not provide administrative grounds for refusing access requests, the central government considers repeated requests as administrative grounds to exercise the discretion whether or not to respond.[58]

Second, exemptions and exclusions under FOI legislation should be clearly and narrowly defined[59] to 'exclude material which does not harm legitimate interests'.[60] This is not the case in China. Exemptions and exclusions are not clearly and narrowly defined under the FOI Regulations, which prevent government agencies from disclosing any information that may be injurious to state security, public security, economic security or social stability.[61] The definition of these securities is left to government agencies, and so can easily be used to refuse access requests.

Meanwhile, state secrets, trade secrets and privacy are not well defined under the FOI Regulations and other laws.[62] Zhou argues that a broad scope for the state secret exemption will impede implementation of the FOI Regulations.[63] This is a reasonable view. The *Law on the Protection of State Secrets 1988* has not yet been revised, and the scope of state secrets remains unchanged. The longstanding culture of secrecy, although beginning to change, has impeded efforts to narrow the scope of state secrets. The definition of privacy is not 'yet addressed comprehensively in Chinese law',[64] which in turn may negatively affect the operation of the FOI Regulations. Although trade secrets are defined in Article 10 of the *Anti-trust Law 1993*,[65] it is uncertain whether or not this definition will be widened to include information in government procurements and other contracts to which the government is a party.

Third, class-based exemptions should be avoided. Again, this is not the case in China. It is argued that any FOI law should avoid sweeping 'class exemptions',[66] which exclude 'entire classes of information from access'.[67] Under China's FOI Regulations, state secrets, trade secrets and privacy are all class-based exemptions.[68]

Fourth, government agencies are prevented compulsorily from disclosing any exemption under the FOI Regulations. Discretionary rather than mandatory exemptions should be provided under FOI legislation,[69] as the former leaves the way open for government agencies to exercise their right in favour of disclosure, even though the information sought falls within an exemption provision.[70]

Fifth, although China's FOI Regulations include a harm test that features prominently in many FOI laws around the world and is advocated by FOI campaigners,[71] they envisage only a low degree of harm for exemptions concerning state security, public security, economic security or social stability. They contain the verb harm without any adverb, such as significantly or substantially, to describe the degree of injury. No harm test applies to an exemption concerning state secrets, trade secrets or privacy under the Regulations, which means these exemptions are 'class-based'.[72] Once the information sought falls into any of these categories, it is excluded from disclosure.

Sixth, China's FOI Regulations allow a special public interest test applied only to a few exemptions, rather than a general one that requires the consideration of public interest in each and every case.[73] FOI laws generally require that any exemption must be balanced against disclosure in the public interest.[74] This allows information to be released when 'public benefit in knowing the information outweighs any harm that may be caused from disclosure'.[75] In China, a public interest test is only applied specifically to exemptions of trade secrets and privacy.[76]

Government officials are likely to use these vague and broad exemption clauses to constrain the proactive disclosure degree under the FOI Regulations. These exemption clauses will shade many areas, and may become major impediments to future implementation of FOI legislation in China.

Omission of the maximum disclosure principle

The omission of the maximum disclosure principle has further diminished the proactive disclosure capacity of the Chinese FOI Regulations. It has been recognized that an ideal principle should be 'maximum disclosure'[77] and that 'disclosure is the principle, while exemption is the exception'.[78] The FOI Regulations do not set out this principle. The central government revised local FOI Rules[79] to return to a level of information disclosure that the government can accept at the present stage. While Premier Wen and other senior government officials state that the maximum disclosure principle is implied under the FOI Regulations,[80] the practical effect of this statement remains uncertain.

The omission of this principle reflects the Chinese government's pragmatic strategy during the last three decades. It appears that 'secrecy still enjoys priority during the process of information disclosure'.[81] Thus, a special principle is found under Article 8 of the FOI Regulations, which prohibits government agencies disclosing government information that may prejudice state security, public security, economic security or social stability. Article 8 is also considered by law reformers as a basic principle for guiding government agencies to disclose information.[82] This basic principle, which can encourage government officials to err on the side of secrecy, explains the lack of the maximum disclosure principle.

Conclusion

China's push model of FOI legislation was the outcome of its local causes, and this model has reduced the importance of access requests. The push model of FOI legislation reflects the push to pull development of FOI in China. Furthermore, the proactive disclosure requirements under the FOI Regulations provide a clear obligation and minimum standard for government agencies to follow, thus reducing difficulty in government compliance. However, the degree of proactive disclosure under China's FOI legislation has been constrained by a limited access mechanism, broad and poorly defined exemptions and the omission of the maximum disclosure principle. It will be necessary to relax these constraints in the future FOI law to increase the push degree.

9 Compliance with proactive disclosure requirements in practice

This chapter explores the strengths in the implementation of FOI legislation in China. It argues that the real strength of the way that FOI legislation is implemented in China is in compliance with proactive disclosure requirements. The chapter utilizes a revised compliance analysis model that incorporates a push and pull focus to identify the forces that can ensure government compliance with proactive disclosure requirements under China's FOI Regulations. It finds that government willingness and capability to comply with proactive disclosure requirements can be ensured due to a strong central political commitment and various transparency advocacy groups on the supply side. The level of compliance can increase further because active players on the demand side are willing and able to cause government agencies to rectify their non-compliance with proactive disclosure in practice. To connect the strength of FOI legislation with compliance with proactive disclosure requirements may appear excessively optimistic or simply insignificant. However, the push nature of China's FOI Regulations suggests that compliance with proactive disclosure deserves more attention. This argument does not neglect the immense obstacles or challenges concerning compliance with FOI legislation in China, as demonstrated in Chapter 10.

The supply side: willingness and capability to implement FOI legislation

A singular focus on the problems of reactive disclosure and its effective enforcement in China is misleading. This book draws attention to three decades of significant changes and trends that have influenced the willingness and capability of the Chinese government to implement and comply with FOI legislation. It argues that a central political commitment and a number of transparency advocacy groups on the supply side have caused other government agencies to become more transparent. Furthermore, the capability of the government to implement FOI legislation has increased due to changed technological, political, legal, economic and civil service conditions. The foregoing has yielded a positive result in terms of adherence to proactive disclosure requirements laid down in FOI legislation.

The supply side: willingness to implement FOI legislation

The revised compliance analysis model incorporates a focus on the supply side. This can help identify various transparency advocacy groups on the supply side. These groups have responded to the opportunities arising from FOI legislation in China in order to perform their administrative functions better. Along with a strong central political commitment, these groups have devoted resources to ensuring the enforcement of FOI legislation.

A central political commitment

The central political commitment, a major obstacle in enforcing FOI legislation, has been overcome in China,[1] although this does not necessarily mean that the central government will commit to being fully observed or subject to direct accountability. The exemptions laid down in the FOI Regulations illustrate this point well. Furthermore, the central political commitment, albeit an important factor, does not necessarily result in lower tiers of government embracing it because various factors, such as limited resources, poorly trained FOI staff and lack of cultural support for fulfilling transparency obligations, will constrain local FOI performance. The following two elements explain this central political commitment.

First, the issue of openness has been a recurring theme in each national Party congress since 1997. The 17th CPC National Congress, held in 2007, went further in pronouncing on the safeguard of freedom of expression. It also stated that 'in principle, public hearings must be held for the formulation of laws, regulations and policies that bear closely on the interests of the public'[2] to ensure scientific and democratic decision-making. Furthermore, the Party leader Hu, at a visit to *People's Daily* in June 2008, emphasized the improvement of both time efficiency and transparency in the revelation of reliable information.[3]

Second, the role of openness has been improved in the State Council's reports on the work of the government to the National People's Congress (NPC) since 2004.[4] In the government reports of 2008 and 2009 to the NPC, Premier Wen committed to increasing transparency in government to 'create conditions to enable the people to oversee the government more effectively',[5] and to 'keep them informed as to what the government is thinking and doing',[6] respectively. Premier Wen also published an article to call on government agencies to improve transparency through the implementation of the FOI Regulations and adherence to the principle that 'disclosure is the principle, while exemption is the exception',[7] despite this principle having been omitted from the Regulations.

With the support of a strong political commitment, the State Council adopted many measures to enforce the Regulations. It has revised its Working Rules to explicitly state that the promotion of Openness in Government Affairs (OGA) is one of its core working principles.[8] Furthermore, the duties of administering FOI have been allocated to the General Office of the State Council,[9] which is superior to other agencies in implementing FOI legislation due to its strong coordination role and familiarity with the process of generating, obtaining and filing government information.[10] The General Office of the State Council has authorized its Division I of Secretariat to be responsible for promoting and supervising compliance with the Regulations.[11] It has already issued two notices to aid lower tiers of government to prepare and implement the FOI Regulations.[12] Thus, China does not lack a high level of political and administrative leadership support for transparency, which is crucial for the enforcement of FOI legislation.[13]

Transparency advocacy groups on the supply side

Various transparency advocacy groups on the supply side have supported the central government to ensure compliance with FOI legislation. Doubt exists about the central government's capacity to force various levels of government to comply with FOI legislation.[14] Roberts states that '[t]he policy applies across the largest bureaucratic complex on the planet, and there are bound to be immense challenges in assuring that lower level officials pay attention to directions from distant Beijing'.[15] Though justifiable, this concern will be lessened if the many transparency advocacy groups on the supply side in China can be recognized and given consideration. While Zhou argues that two of the previous key contributors to FOI reform – the informatization and anti-corruption agencies – will be diminished or marginalized from promoting implementation,[16] this is unlikely to occur because the FOI Regulations provide clear opportunities for them to pursue their own departmental objectives. More importantly, since the adoption of FOI legislation, several other internal agencies, such as state archives and public libraries, have involved themselves in supporting transparency for improving their departmental status. Over time, their advocacy efforts are likely to benefit the operation of FOI legislation, as appears from the following.

The first form of transparency advocacy comprises informatization agencies, such as the State Council Informatization Office (SCIO) and Leading Group on National Informatization (LGNI). They are major contributors to the adoption of FOI legislation in China, whose interests in FOI will extend to areas closely related to informatization development. The SCIO ceased after the government restructure plan was approved in March 2008.[17] It was replaced by the Department of Informatization Promotion under the newly restructured Ministry of Industry and Information Technology.

Though this department may not play a similar role to that previously played by the SCIO, it will continue to give guidance on the assessment of the performance of government websites that commenced in 2005, with an emphasis on online information disclosure.[18] The assessment process will assist the implementation work by improving the proactive disclosure function set out in the FOI Regulations. Online proactive and reactive disclosure is the most important indicator in the assessment indicator system formed by the Ministry to evaluate the performance of government websites.[19] Such performance ratings can assist the central government in accomplishing the objective of using government websites as the priority platform for disseminating information.[20]

The second form of transparency advocacy consists of supervisory or anti-corruption agencies which play a role similar to Ombudsmen. They will continue to promote transparency in China from a supervisory perspective. The Leading Group on National Openness in Government Affairs (LGNOGA) now pays greater attention to implementation of the FOI Regulations. It held an introductory session about the Regulations at its seventh meeting in 2007 to prepare for the implementation of the FOI Regulations.[21] Its eighth meeting in 2008 called on state agencies to play a leading part in enforcing the Regulations.[22] In 2007, it ran an awards programme, awarding 123 agencies for excellent work on OGA,[23] in addition to selecting 63 agencies as national models of implementing OGA.[24] The LGNOGA also trialled the transparent operation of administrative power in Hebei in early 2005, and extended this transparent operation to elsewhere around the country after 2006.[25]

Along with the LGNOGA, the National Corruption Prevention Bureau is responsible for OGA and FOI matters.[26] Furthermore, the supervision agencies, being statutory agencies having the power to accept and process complaints from the public, may play a more direct role in processing individual FOI cases to ensure compliance with FOI legislation.

The third form of transparency advocacy comprises information offices. The State Council Information Office, China's publicity department, together with spokespersons and local information offices, can improve government officials' media literacy and awareness and encourage proactivity in disclosing government information. The State Council Information Office has striven for greater transparency in government in recent years. It will continue to be a major force in promoting more proactive disclosure. Its efforts have resulted in a wide establishment of spokesperson systems in China.[27] The State Council Information Office trained about 400,000 officials to improve their media literacy and awareness in 2008.[28] It has agreed to train more officials to improve government awareness of and compliance with the FOI Regulations.[29]

The fourth form of transparency advocacy consists of audit and environmental agencies. Audit agencies have used the disclosure of audit reports as a means to promote their audit work. In 2003, the National Audit Office made a commitment to promoting the disclosure of audit results. It has been the pioneer in public exposure of the problems in government, creating a series of 'audit storms'[30] since 2003. Jinhua Li, former Auditor-General of China, confessed that informing the public about audit results undoubtedly drove the Office's work.[31] The current Auditor-General continued the release of audit findings, which allayed public concern about the cessation of 'audit storms'.[32] The Office's continued efforts in publicizing audit findings are an effective way to supervise the use of public funds.

The State Environmental Protection Bureau is another agency which has supported transparency in the performance of their functions in recent years. It published *Interim Measures on Freedom of Environmental Information* on 20 April 2007, four days prior to the issue of the FOI Regulations. While the Bureau focuses on the disclosure of environmental information, its efforts help improve transparency in this area of high public interest. Yue Pan, the Deputy Minister of the Ministry of Environmental Protection, confessed that environmental protection agencies were not powerful in China.[33] The FOI Regulations therefore could better support its function.[34] Zhou argues that the promotion of transparency in environmental information and the use of public funds have made environmental protection agencies and audit offices more powerful than before.[35]

The fifth form of transparency advocacy is the State Secrecy Bureau. The Bureau has striven to revise the *Law on the Protection of State Secrets 1988* through the promotion of transparency since the late 1990s, thus indirectly facilitating the introduction of FOI legislation in China. It achieved a significant breakthrough in 2010 when the proposed revised draft of the Law was approved by the Standing Committee of the NPC. The revision of the Law is partly to align it with the FOI Regulations.[36]

The sixth form of transparency advocacy consists of archives and libraries. Archivists and librarians' increasing interest in FOI legislation can provide professional support for better records management.[37] This is likely to assist adherence to FOI legislation, as appears from the interviews with archivists and librarians in six provinces in China. State archives are willing to implement the FOI Regulations, as they consider that this is a great opportunity for them to avoid marginalization.[38] While the work of establishing reading places in state archives confronted various difficulties, many archives had done so by 1 May 2008. The State Archives Bureau is currently planning to make efforts to revise the *Archives Law 1987*, partly to further clarify and intensify its role in disclosing government information.[39] The success of this revision may also facilitate implementation of FOI legislation.

Public libraries, which have been granted equal statutory importance with state archives for receiving and releasing government information, are enthusiastic about the implementation of the FOI Regulations to improve their roles in providing information services to the public.[40] They consider government information services as an opportunity for them to reshape library services.[41] The real problem is the view of government agencies, which often hold that 'the roles of libraries are not like ours'.[42] The National Library is currently launching an online platform to help collect and search all government information released by government websites and official publications.[43] It has also called for government information to be managed more efficiently and professionally via the establishment of government printing offices, as in the US.[44] Furthermore, the Standing Committee of the 11th NPC listed *Library Law* in the secondary priority category of its five-year legislative plan from 2009 to 2013.[45] The adoption of this Law will further clarify and strengthen the role of libraries in providing government information services.

The seventh form of transparency advocacy likely to help encourage government compliance with FOI in China is local government forerunners. China has not lacked local forerunners who experiment with new policies. The first national FOI legislation was largely based on local FOI forerunners' useful experiments. Local forerunners have become important references for other government agencies to follow. In 2009, the Shanghai government committed to becoming the region with the highest transparency across the country.[46] Shanghai is an economically rich area. Its experiences may have been considered less useful and not transferable to other poorer areas.[47] Sichuan, a poor province, has showed a much stronger interest than others in preparing and implementing the FOI Regulations since the adoption of the Regulations.[48] The Sichuan case could be used to refute any future excuse of resource constraints. With the support of the central government, these local forerunners have not only accomplished the relatively successful implementation of FOI legislation in their own localities, but have the potential to encourage more local governments to follow suit.

Varied supervisory agencies, directed to anti-corruption, financial or environmental inspection, have become the major forces for the implementation of FOI legislation in China. Along with supervisory agencies, some professional agencies, including informatization agencies, state archives and public libraries, are keen to enforce FOI legislation to serve their departmental interests. The central government and these advocacy groups can pressure other government agencies to comply with FOI legislation.

The supply side: capacity to implement FOI legislation

The Chinese government's capacity to comply with FOI legislation can arguably be derived from the changed technological, political, legal, economic and civil service conditions. The ongoing development of democracy, the rule of law and the professional civil service, together with increased economic power and improved records management, has likewise created capacity to assure compliance with FOI legislation in China.

Improving technological conditions

An increasing volume of electronic records and a wide launch of government websites have improved information flow, thus facilitating compliance with FOI legislation. The following two aspects are important. First, record keeping practices in China are improving. The central informatization agencies have assisted the Chinese government in realizing the importance of information management. They circulated a document, '*Suggestions on Strengthening Exploitation and Use of Information Resources*',[49] in 2004, which stated that information resources enjoyed equal importance with energy and material resources and played an irreplaceable role in developing the economy.[50] They urged the improvement of government information management through institutionalizing the collection, register, maintenance, release and classification of government information.[51] China, a newcomer to the FOI family, also recognizes record management as indispensable to an access regime.[52] This is demonstrated by the requirement for government agencies to produce and publish information inventories and guides.[53]

It follows that records management should not be a major source of concern over compliance with FOI legislation.[54] In 2008, the General Office of the State Council circulated an interim directive to guide the compilation of FOI inventories.[55] In addition, FOI legislation has created incentives for professional record keeping agencies, including archives and libraries, to involve themselves in promoting FOI, which will improve information management in China and facilitate implementation.

Second, the launch of a wide number of government websites can help reduce the use and importance of access requests. China has an opportunity to design its FOI legislation to make full use of the advantages of information technology.[56] This has resulted in China's FOI legislation taking a push model that focuses on proactive disclosure. This push model can reduce the number of individual requests. Furthermore, government agencies have launched FOI sections, online searching and information requesting on their official websites to provide government information services in a holistic way.

Improving political conditions

The longstanding democratization efforts show that FOI legislation can be implemented in China. Many years of grassroots democracy experiments have presented the opportunity for local governments to familiarize themselves with openness. The work of OGA which emphasizes proactive disclosure has been accepted by all levels of government as an integral part of the framework of administration.[57] Thus, compliance with FOI legislation will not necessarily imply a revolution in the work practices of low levels of government. Implementation of FOI legislation for lower tiers of government is largely a project that continues and extends their previous openness practices. This will lessen the concern over the central government's capacity to force local governments to comply with the FOI Regulations.

The central government has regarded deliberative democracy as a vital form of socialist democracy since early 2006. This increased transparency in decision-making. Democratic decision-making, which lies at the core of deliberative democracy, has been considered an overarching task of the Hu–Wen Administration. This has made public consultation, by keeping the public informed or holding hearings, a common feature of significant policy decisions.[58] Significant policy changes now generally do not come as a surprise to the public, who have been informed in advance through various measures, including consultation with experts and public participation.[59]

Improving legal conditions

China's gradual strengthening of the rule of law may allay concerns over China's bureaucracy to impede compliance with FOI legislation. The rule of law has been accepted and considered by the Chinese government as a ruling principle. Furthermore, administrative law is now associated with government transparency, as the recent administrative law reforms have emphasized ex ante and procedural controls of government power. A government under the rule of law, a key part of the rule of law plan, has also become a clear goal of the Chinese government to accomplish by 2014. FOI legislation serves as a key part of achieving this long-term law reform process.

Rising economic power

China's rising economic power during the last three decades will enable the Chinese government to comply with FOI legislation, especially from the supply side perspective. China has increased its comprehensive national strength, and is not the same country as it was three decades ago. This indicates that China has the capacity to afford the necessary costs of administration of FOI legislation. Indeed, the Chinese government has few worries about the costs of implementing this legislation, even in the face of wide regional disparities in economic growth. Moreover, the high costs in processing access requests have been reduced by the Chinese government's emphasis on proactive disclosure, and the use of new technologies to release government information in a holistic way.

Improving professional civil service

Professional civil service in China has been improved in a variety of ways, which may assist the implementation of FOI legislation. The implementation may be assisted in three ways. First, an institutional framework of a personnel system has been formulated. *Interim Regulations on National Civil Servants* were adopted in 1993 to establish a personnel management system in China for the first time. These were upgraded to the *Civil Servant Law* in 2005. Other accompanying rules were also introduced to improve the personnel system in China,[60] combining to form the institutional framework of the personnel system.

Second, permanent jobs or 'iron rice bowl' (*Tie Fan Wan*) in the public service have ceased. The procedures and conditions for civil servants' resignation and dismissal were regulated in 1995 for the first time. The *Civil Servant Law 2005* further legislates on these. While only a small number of civil servants resigned or were dismissed in the past,[61] government agencies are now staffed by individuals who move in and out of government. This will likely diminish the habit of government secrecy.[62]

Third, the quality of professional personnel has increased. The three-decade pursuit of younger, more educated and professional staff has succeeded.[63]

More than 35 per cent of civil servants now have undergraduate diplomas or above.[64] Fourth, a training system has been established,[65] improving public service professionalism. The State Council Legislative Affairs Office conducted six training sessions in 2007, and trained about 3000 attendees from various government agencies for the implementation of the FOI Regulations.[66] Local governments also trained their own staff. FOI has now been included in the training courses for civil servants, indicating that all civil servants will receive FOI training in the future.[67]

The supply side: compliance with proactive disclosure in practice

Various supply side transparency advocacy groups and interested citizens, along with the central government, have become the main forces of implementing China's FOI legislation. As a result, relative success has been achieved by holding the government to the proactive disclosure requirements under FOI legislation. This compliance means that government agencies themselves implement proactive disclosure requirements without access requests serving as reminders. Government agencies have followed the fundamental criteria under the FOI Regulations to decide which information is required to be proactively disclosed. They have actively distributed the information involving the vital interests of the public so as to win public support. They have also proactively disclosed government information, which has aided public participation and improved policy outcomes. In addition, government agencies at various levels have actively released standard information about their administrative organization, function and working procedures.

Proactive disclosure of crisis information: protecting the vital interests of the demand side

The FOI Regulations prescribe four general criteria for government agencies to decide which information is required to be disclosed actively.[68] Assessment of the enforcement of these four criteria can capture the reality of government compliance with the proactive disclosure duty, especially the first three criteria. The fourth one is a residual criterion designed to cover proactive disclosure requirements under other laws and regulations. The first criterion is information that involves the vital interests of the demand side.[69] This book uses disclosure of crisis information as a key lens to explore government compliance with this criterion. It reveals that the Chinese government has proactively disclosed a wide range of crisis information since the adoption of the FOI Regulations. Release of prompt and accurate crisis information was a focus in 2008,[70] improving information flow in China. The following three aspects substantiate this statement.

First, the Chinese government has become more transparent and active than before in dealing with natural disasters. The snow crisis[71] and the Sichuan earthquake[72] provide two striking examples that contrast with the government's response to the Severe Acute Respiratory Syndrome (SARS) crisis. In the snow crisis, the government disclosed information in 'a very open way'.[73] The release of information on the Sichuan earthquake, which occurred only 12 days after the FOI Regulations took effect, was impressive and highly praised by non-Chinese observers.[74] After the earthquake, Premier Wen made the commitment that 'we will never change our transparent policy, and once there exists an epidemic, we will promise to process it in an open way'.[75] This commitment aligns the shift from a secretive and reactive approach to crisis information management toward a transparent and proactive approach.

Second, the Chinese government has become more open and active in releasing information about various mass incidents, such as the taxi strikes in Chongqing[76] and the riots in Gansu.[77] Government officials recognize that active disclosure of massive accidents is important, confessing that 'in today's Internet era, hiding things does not help',[78] and 'will only make things worse'.[79]

Third, the Chinese government has proactively disclosed information regarding public safety in a timely manner, as the rail disaster in Shandong[80] and a subway tunnel collapse in Zhejiang[81] have demonstrated. Fourth, the Chinese government has proactively disclosed information regarding public health to counter rumours, such as information concerning food safety. The crises of pork in Beijing[82] and banana contamination in Hainan[83] illustrate this active disclosure approach.

There are some negative cases, like the scandal of baby milk power contamination.[84] These cases prove that information release is important to manage crises efficiently. This scandal resulted in senior officials resigning or being dismissed for their concealment.[85] Government officials accordingly paid a high price for their concealment. After this scandal, the new leadership of the Shijiazhuang government conducted an extensive training session to improve the capability to release crisis information.[86]

Active distribution of information: encouraging public participation

The second criterion for proactive disclosure under the FOI Regulations is information that needs to be extensively known or participated in by the general public.[87] The Chinese government has undertaken unprecedented proactive disclosure practices since the passage of the FOI Regulations to facilitate wide public participation and debates. These practices did not occur coincidently with the adoption of FOI legislation, but were part of the activities to comply with FOI legislation.

Willingness to actively release environmental information

The Chinese government has actively released information on environmental impact assessment to encourage public participation. Such information disclosure was first institutionalized by *Interim Measures for Public Partici-pation in Environmental Impact Assessment 2006.*[88] It was strengthened after the adoption of the FOI Regulations, as an aim of the Regulations and one general criterion are to encourage public participation.[89] The first widely known case of environmental information release, which occurred in 2007, related to the Xiamen Paraxylene plant project.[90] Another occurred the same year, relating to a Maglev construction project in Shanghai.[91] These events were an indirect result of implementing the FOI Regulations as they occurred before the Regulations came into force. However, they have marked a sig-nificant step in releasing information on environmental impact assessment in China, and caused other government agencies to follow suit, such as Guangdong.[92]

Willingness to proactively disclose information on decision-making

Public participation has played a more valuable role in Chinese legislative processes, aiding China to develop deliberative politics. The NPC, China's top legislature, and the State Council have become more transparent in publishing draft bills or administrative regulations, especially those closely involving the interests of the general public. Apart from this, the Chinese government has become more open in key decision-making closely related to public interest. After the FOI Regulations entered into force, information on several key decisions, such as the readjustment of public holidays,[93] reforms of fuel taxa-tion and pricing mechanisms,[94] and health care,[95] was proactively disclosed by the government to let the public know and comment on it.

Furthermore, public participation in decision-making, especially rule-making, has become more convenient once many legislative affairs offices and other government agencies launched online systems for seeking public opinions on drafts of administrative regulations and rules.[96]

Proactive disclosure of standard information: facilitating public supervision

The third criterion for proactive disclosure under the FOI Regulations is standard information about government agencies' structure, functions and working procedures.[97] Government agencies had few difficulties in disclosing this category of information; its disclosure commenced before the FOI Reg-ulations were adopted. This disclosure may be viewed from the perspective of the facilitation of democratic supervision by ordinary citizens. After govern-ment agencies had proactively disclosed their number of leadership positions on official websites, Chinese netizens or Internet users had the opportunity to discover and question the pervasive and longstanding overstaffing issue. A netizen's post in November 2008 about the overstaffing problem of the Tielin government stimulated other netizens to discover similar issues in gov-ernment agencies from official websites.[98] As a result, the disclosure of the size of leadership positions sparked heated discussion on the Internet. Many called for a reduction in the number of deputy leadership positions. The central government did not ignore this increasing public opinion. It circulated a notice in January 2009 to require local governments to standardize the quotas of assistants and deputy secretary-generals.[99]

Ordinary citizens could not have known about this overstaffing issue without proactive disclosure of leading posts on the Internet. The online discussion about the overstaffing issue demonstrates that all streams of information flows are correlative. Previously, the improvement in informant flow among citizens caused the Chinese government to become more proactive in disclosing government information. Today, the improvement in proactive disclosure of government information has enhanced the capacity of Chinese citizens to use, distribute and analyse the information.

Review systems: increasing the capacity of the demand side to redress non-compliance with proactive disclosure

The increasing willingness and capability of supply side players have resulted in much government information being proactively disclosed by government agencies themselves. The level of compliance has further increased because government agencies have rectified their non-compliance with proactive disclosure requirements since active players on the demand side pressure government agencies to implement the requirements. Rights activists, legal professionals and interested citizens, who represent major players on the demand side, have the capacity to redress government non-compliance with proactive disclosure. This is because the current internal and external review systems are capable of supporting their lawsuits against this non-compliance.

The administrative reconsideration system

Administrative reconsideration has increased demand side players' capacity to call on government agencies to disclose information required to be actively released. Applications for administrative reconsideration are generally processed by legislative affairs offices. Two striking cases related to the enforcement of local FOI Rules occurred before the FOI Regulations came into effect. The first is the *Chen* case,[100] which occurred in Guangdong Province in early 2006. Chen submitted a number of applications for administrative reconsideration to prompt local government agencies to reconsider their transparency policies. The second, the *Huang* case,[101] occurred in Hubei Province. Huang filed a series of administrative reconsiderations to call on government agencies to redress their non-compliance with online information disclosure. Both Chen and Huang won their support from administrative reconsideration agencies, causing government agencies to correct their non-compliance activities.

The *Xu et al.* case[102] is a significant case that occurred after the FOI Regulations came into effect. On 26 May 2008, Yaofang Xu and 67 other villagers filed a request to the Yuyao Government in Zhejiang Province for more details about the transfer of approximately half of the total lands of their village. After receiving no response from the Yuyao Government, they applied for administrative reconsideration to the Ningbo Government, which required the Yuyao Government to handle this request pursuant to the FOI Regulations. This case won support from the administrative reconsideration agency, indicating that administrative reconsideration agencies have the capacity to help redress government non-compliance with proactive disclosure requirements.

Furthermore, a current pilot project has the capacity to intensify demand side players to rectify non-compliance with proactive disclosure. The State Council Legislative Affairs Office decided in September 2008 to experiment with a new administrative reconsideration mechanism in eight provinces, aiming to establish a more centralized, professional and impartial administrative reconsideration mechanism to process administrative reconsideration applications.[103] Administrative reconsideration committees consisting of experts, scholars and government officials were also established in these provinces. This pilot project will help process increasing administrative reconsideration applications for FOI decisions.[104]

The administrative lawsuit system

The capacity of demand side players to redress government non-compliance with proactive disclosure has increased, as Chinese courts have supported the lawsuits against non-compliance. In the *Xu* case, the court adjudged the Bureau's mute refusal illegal. This judgment was the first FOI lawsuit supported by the court after the FOI Regulations came into effect.[105] The Hubei Provincial Legislative Affairs Office issued a bulletin to inform all government agencies of this non-compliance, calling on government agencies to comply with the Regulations.[106] An official in this Office questioned 'why the agency has not disclosed the information until the masses take it to court'.[107] The bulletin has the potential to create positive effects on the enforcement of FOI legislation.

This was not the only lawsuit upheld by courts. In the *Zhou* case,[108] the government did not answer Zhou's request for a building dismantlement licence and other necessary legal documents until he initiated court action. In the *Xie* case,[109] the government did not release the documents regarding subsidies for breeding pigs to Xie until the court actively mediated in the dispute.

Along with administrative reconsideration agencies, Chinese courts have bolstered compliance with proactive disclosure requirements under the FOI Regulations. In the long run, courts will likely play a more positive role in ensuring compliance with the proactive disclosure requirements under the Regulations.

The reporting system

A reporting mechanism is preferable to an administrative lawsuit and reconsideration in systematically redressing non-compliance with proactive disclosure requirements in China.[110] Han reported several central government agencies' failure to disclose national standards to the State Council in May 2008.[111] His complaints received a response by the State Council, which called on government agencies to rectify their malpractice.[112] The Ministries of Health, and Housing and Urban–Rural Development rectified their improper disclosure practices immediately as soon as they were informed by the State Council.[113] The General Administration of Quality Supervision, Inspection and Quarantine proposed launching an online platform for collecting and searching national standards. This proposal was accepted by the State Council, and the launch is now ongoing.

Imperfections in the Chinese review system, such as a non-independent judiciary, have led to concerns over the effective enforcement of FOI legislation.[114] However, this does not mean that administrative reconsideration agencies and courts are incapable of causing government agencies to correct their non-compliance with proactive disclosure. The availability of internal and external review of government FOI decisions can have considerable influence of a cautionary nature. After all, no government agencies welcome being taken to court.[115] FOI cases are not the exception. Government officials in Shanghai state that a key reason for their better FOI performance compared with other regions is pressure from judicial review.[116] Furthermore, the reporting mechanism is a useful tool for the demand side to remind government agencies of their duty to actively release information. These review mechanisms have improved the capacity of the demand side to redress non-compliance with proactive disclosure.

The demand side: willingness to redress non-compliance with proactive disclosure

Apart from the capacity of active players on the demand side to prompt government agencies to correct their non-compliance with proactive disclosure requirements, rights activists, legal professionals and interested citizens are willing to compel government agencies to comply with proactive disclosure requirements through their access requests or complaints. This is because demand side players cannot bring government agencies which have not complied with proactive disclosure requirements to court directly. However, this indirect way has still helped enhance information flow from the government to society. The level of compliance with proactive disclosure thus has increased after the demand side input. Such input shows the dynamics of operation of FOI legislation in China.

The willingness of demand side players has come from increased rights consciousness over the last three decades. The building of the rule of law since the late 1970s has created many rights activists and legal professionals to take advantage of the FOI Regulations to ensure policy implementation and change. Demand side players either send their requests for information that is required to be proactively disclosed, or report non-compliance with proactive disclosure requirements, to supervisory agencies to redress government non-compliance with the requirements. Demand side players have also used enforcement mechanisms, including administrative reconsideration and lawsuits, to cause government agencies to reconsider refusals of information requests. Three factors explain the willingness of demand side players to increase government compliance with FOI legislation.

First, Chinese rights activists, such as Chen and Huang, have been a major force for rectifying non-compliance with proactive disclosure obligations, despite their requests often being viewed as vexatious. In Guangdong, Shuwei Chen submitted approximately 109 applications for internal and judicial review of FOI decisions between 2002 and 2007.[117] Chen's series of requests for information that is required to be proactively disclosed may have accelerated the adoption of the Shenzhen FOI Rules.[118] Huang's 16 applications for FOI inventories also caused government agencies to rectify their non-compliance with proactive disclosure of such inventories.[119]

Second, legal professionals have emerged as an important group to correct non-compliance with proactive disclosure requirements, through lawsuits, direct information requests and complaints. The request of Jianguo Xu, a Beijing lawyer, for information that is required to be proactively disclosed won support from the court and the Hubei government.[120] The report from Puzheng Han, a Hebei lawyer, to the State Council about state agencies' non-compliance with the proactive disclosure of national standards received a positive response from the State Council. This has benefited the proactive disclosure of national standards in China.[121] Another case concerned the Sichuan earthquake. Jie Cheng, an associate professor in law, sent a request dated 13 June 2008 to the State Earthquake Administration for a seismic intensity distribution map.[122] Cheng's request may have caused the State Earthquake Administration to publish the map. The State Earthquake Administration made this map public on 29 August, abandoning its initial policy that required citizens to pay for this map.[123]

Third, ordinary citizens have acted as important drivers to redress government compliance with proactive disclosure requirements for protecting their own interests. This is demonstrated by Xu and the other villagers[124] and Zhou's requests[125] for land use and house demolition, and Xie's request for documents concerning his pig farming business.[126]

Conclusion

The significant strengths for China in the implementation of FOI legislation have come from the dynamics of the supply and demand sides, in conjunction with proactive disclosure or push-emphasized legal design. On the supply side, there is a strong central political commitment and various transparency advocacy groups. This has prompted a comparatively high level of government compliance with proactive disclosure requirements.

On the demand side, rights activists, legal professionals and interested citizens have become major players in prompting government agencies to redress their non-compliance with proactive disclosure requirements. They are not only willing to force government agencies to implement the proactive disclosure duty, but capable of this due to support from internal and external review bodies. The input from demand side players has aided the level of FOI compliance.

10 Non-compliance with reactive disclosure requirements in practice

This chapter explores the weaknesses in the implementation of FOI legislation in China. It argues that while significant steps to government compliance with proactive disclosure requirements can be ensured, it is difficult to anticipate that reactive disclosure will operate effectively in China at this early stage of implementation. The government has typically responded with a controlling flow approach to requests for information that is not required to be proactively disclosed. Chinese courts have bolstered this approach through various restrictions on FOI lawsuits, thus restricting the capacity of demand side players to request information from the supply side. Furthermore, demand side players' use of FOI legislation has been limited by legal, political and resource constraints. The problematic implementation of the access mechanism or reactive disclosure depicts a negative picture of FOI developments in China, which dampens optimistism about compliance with FOI legislation. However, a totally pessimistic view of FOI developments in China is also unwarranted, as Chapter 9 demonstrates.

Low willingness from the supply side: a controlling flow approach

Since the FOI Regulations came into force, the Chinese government/supply side has taken a controlling flow approach to implement the access mechanism, reflecting the low willingness to respond to access requests. Chinese scholars, like Cheng, also hold a similar view.[1] Along with a limited capacity to comply with FOI legislation, this low willingness has prevented government agencies from fully complying with FOI legislation.

Restricting the scope of FOI legislation to limit access

Chinese government agencies have applied a controlling flow approach by restricting the scope of FOI legislation, with reference to both the bodies and the subject matter covered by the legislation.

Limiting the coverage

While no government agency is completely excluded from coverage of the FOI Regulations, some government agencies have deliberately limited this coverage. The General Office of the State Council has issued a policy docu-ment, *Several Suggestions on Implementation of the China's FOI Regulations*,[2] to the effect that the General Office of the State Council will not process any access request directly. The General Office provides a negative precedent for other agencies to follow. The General Office of the Inner-Mongolia Autono-mous Region prevents any access request, claiming that the Office has no information that needs to be accessed.[3] This claim is unreasonable as a major responsibility of the General Office is drafting, examining, verifying and cir-culating official documents, and so it should hold government information for public access. The General Office of the Inner-Mongolia Autonomous Region has not changed this claim until recently, allowing citizens to send information requests to it.[4]

Limiting the scope of government information

Setting limits on the scope of government information also reflects the Chinese government's controlling flow approach, as appears from the following six ways. First, government agencies have limited the scope of information by adopting their own FOI Rules. For example, the Commission of National Defence and Science Industry adopted FOI Interim Rules under which gov-ernment information is defined as that which can be disclosed on its website.[5] This definition is narrower than that under the FOI Regulations, and will likely impede the Commission's future compliance with the Regulations.

Second, government agencies have interpreted government information as excluding the information generated or obtained by them in the course of performing criminal enforcement or prosecution functions. It is argued that only the information generated or acquired by public security agencies under the *Law on Administrative Penalties for Public Security 2005*, not the *Crim-inal Litigation Law 1996*, falls within the subject matter of the FOI Regula-tions.[6] Information regarding criminal litigation is not subject to the FOI Regulations, as the *Lin* case indicates. Lin lodged a request dated 28 February 2007 to Shanghai Municipal Public Security Bureau for a legal document, *Rules for the Implementation of the Provisions on the Public Security Agency's Handling of Cases Involving the Crime of Injury*.[7] The Bureau replied that this document was used for criminal enforcement, rather than public administra-tion, and so the document sought fell outside the definition of government information under the Shanghai FOI Rules.[8]

Third, government agencies have limited the scope of government infor-mation to information generated or obtained after the passage of the FOI Regulations. Youjian Huang and his colleagues applied for a survey report on the restructure of a water supply company, but their request was rejected.[9] The government held that according to the principle of non-retroactivity, it was not required to disclose the information sought as it was generated before the effective date of the FOI Regulations.[10] Other government agencies have learnt from this explanation, as demonstrated by the *Li et al.* case.[11] On

10 June 2008, Zihong Li and other villagers sent a request to a township government for information concerning the operation of a public coal company, but the government only replied in oral form. The requesters then filed a lawsuit in court. During the trial, the government's defence was that the information sought was created before the FOI Regulations took effect, so that the Regulations did not apply. The government has arguably misunderstood the non-retroactivity principle. It should be applied to the time when a request is submitted, not when the information is generated or obtained.[12] However, some government officials deliberately persist with this misunderstanding.[13] The reason for this is an unwritten rule that incumbent leaders are reluctant to handle unresolved issues left by their predecessors.[14]

Fourth, government agencies have interpreted the definition of government information in a literal way. The view is that government information must meet three conditions: generated or acquired by government agencies, aimed at exercising power and performing functions, and recorded in certain forms.[15] These conditions derive from the literal meaning of government information. They have been used by government agencies to reject access requests for information that does not meet any of these conditions.

Also, government information that is not generated or acquired by government agencies is unlikely to be subject to disclosure because government agencies split hairs or quibble over small differences. For example, information compiled by government agencies does not need to be disclosed. Lian's request for some documents compiled by a police office was refused because the documents sought fell outside the category of government information generated or acquired by the police office.[16]

Moreover, government information unrelated to government responsibilities may not be subject to disclosure. Government agencies limit these responsibilities to economic and social management and public service, and thus any information requested should relate to this limitation.[17] Gang Li, the founder of the China Public Interest Litigation website, asked for information from the Shanghai government about tuition fees paid to the Shanghai National Accounting Institute for several senior figures' Executive Master of Business Administration training courses.[18] The government replied that the information sought fell outside the category of government information, as it bore no relation to government responsibilities of economic and social management and public service.

Oral information that is not stored in any form is also excluded from disclosure. In the *Su* case, the government replied to Su that it had no duty to disclose the information sought as it was communicated orally.[19] The decision gives an incentive for government officials to communicate orally, rather than in writing, in the future.

Fifth, government agencies have archived some information immediately after receiving information requests in order to preclude disclosure. This is because the *Archives Law 1987* sets a higher standard and a longer period for access to archived information, generally 30 years.[20] This practice occurred in

Shanghai.[21] In order to solve this problem, the new Shanghai FOI Rules prescribe that government agencies, when transferring government information to state archives, must inform state archives whether or not the government information transferred falls within the scope of proactive disclosure, access or non-disclosure.[22]

Sixth, to frustrate requesters, government agencies have frequently argued that the information sought does not exist. While poor information management may contribute to this, government agencies may simply employ this justification to conceal less standardized practices.[23] The revelation of these practices may embarrass government officials. Government agencies may also use this reply to conceal sensitive information,[24] and so avoid negative social impact. More seriously, government agencies may use this excuse to conceal their wrongdoing.

Using exemptions to control access

This book finds that government agencies are using internal documents, a new non-statutory exemption, and broad and vague exemptions laid down in the FOI Regulations to refuse access requests. The findings are supported by the following.

Internal documents: a non-statutory exemption

Government agencies have adopted a non-statutory exemption – internal documents – to exempt government information from access, despite this exemption not being envisaged by the FOI Regulations. Chinese law reformers have opposed writing the exemption of work secrets or internal documents into the Regulations.[25] Its omission has reduced the non-disclosure degree of the Regulations,[26] but in effect government officials have shown little respect for this omission. Internal documents generally include requests for instructions, research reports, leading officials' views and minutes.[27] It is argued that these documents need to be urgently excluded from disclosure.[28] The following three aspects explain the use of internal documents to refuse access requests.

First, requests for instructions have been claimed as internal documents that are not allowed to be disclosed. For example, Kang and other citizens asked for a letter to the Ministry of Labor for instructions concerning the methods used to count fired employees' total working years.[29] Their request was refused as the government held that the letter fell into the category of internal affairs.[30] A similar case occurred in Anhui. Yulai Yuan asked for a letter sent by the Anhui government for instructions about the laws and policies relating to the establishment of developmental zones and industrial parks.[31] His request was refused by the government, which held that the information sought fell outside the category of government information under the FOI Regulations. Internal documents have been used as an effective tool for rejecting access to information concerning requests for instructions. This has limited the role of FOI legislation in improving information flow.

Second, research reports have been considered as internal documents exempted from disclosure. The request for a survey report on the restructure of a water supply company was refused on the ground that it did not represent the government's opinion as the report only aided leaders to make decisions.[32] Government officials have also held that leading officials' views fall into the category of internal affairs, and so are excluded from disclosure.[33] Furthermore, requests for minutes have been generally refused by government agencies.[34] A reason for this is that minutes record inconsistencies in government officials' arguments.[35]

Third, there is a tendency to regard information on the process of individual petitions as internal documents. In Shanghai, Zhang repeatedly petitioned against his layoff after 2002.[36] In April 2002, a government agency and other departments jointly held a meeting about the process of Zhang's petition. Zhang's request for the minutes of this meeting in September 2007 was wrongly processed as a petition. The administrative reconsideration agency did not support his application as it held that the information sought was petition information. A similar case occurred after the FOI Regulations took effect. The General Administration of Quality Supervision, Inspection and Quarantine commissioned an expert team to investigate the quality of XGK-1400 rolling mills produced and sold by the Zhengzhou Top Company, and to produce a survey report.[37] On 17 October 2008, Qi Wang was commissioned by businesses, experts and National People's Congress deputies to lodge a request for the survey report. However, the General Administration rejected the request, ruling that the report was issued to respond to petitions for internal research. The rejection of access to information on the process of individual petitions has narrowed the scope of information set out in FOI legislation.

A broad interpretation of exemption clauses

The government has implemented a controlling flow approach through a broad interpretation of exemptions under the FOI Regulations in the following two ways. First, government agencies have broadened the exemptions under the FOI Regulations by adopting their own FOI Rules. Many government agencies, such as the Ministry of Education,[38] the National Bureau of Tax,[39] the State Archives Bureau,[40] and the Shanghai government[41] have added a deliberative process exemption to their FOI Rules. There is a tendency to exclude deliberative process information in all circumstances, even if the decision to which it refers has been made. Some authors hold that this information is not a concrete administrative action with legal effect, and so is not subject to disclosure.[42] The justification is primarily that the disclosure will not bring any public benefit, and thus its release is pointless.[43] A deliberative process exemption, a key exemption in many FOI laws, is justified as it encourages free and frank discussion and avoids public confusion.[44]

However, the following exemptions are uncommon and difficult to accept. The Commission of National Defence and Science Industry introduced an exemption that prevents its agencies from disclosing information that might be sensitive or result in negative speculation.[45] The Bureau of Intellectual Property's Interim Rules on FOI stipulated an exemption that allows its agencies not to disclose information that is unsuitable for disclosure.[46] These exemptions have narrowed the scope of information that can be potentially accessed under national FOI legislation.

Second, government agencies have broadly interpreted statutory exemptions to refuse access requests. This broad interpretation was already in place before the commencement of the FOI Regulations. The *Ren* case shows that government agencies intended to refuse access requests through the abuse of the exemption of state secrets.[47] It is arguably unreasonable to wholly refuse an access request if only part of the information sought falls within the exemption category. Another case also reveals a broad interpretation of the exemption of state secrets. After a citizen learnt that the government wished to close some inferior companies and remove inferior products, he asked for a list of the closures and recalls.[48] However, his request was refused because the information sought was marked as a confidential state secret, the lowest secrecy level laid down in the *Law on the Protection of State Secrets 1988*. It is difficult to accept that this information is a state secret.

The exemption of trade secrets has been used to include information on government procurement and other contracts to which the government is one of the parties.[49] Hu applied for an investment absorption agreement between a district government in Chongqing and a company.[50] The government refused to disclose this agreement, classifying it as a trade secret. Other cases also reflect that government agencies have used the exemption of trade secrets to protect certain information. A public transportation company's financial reports were considered as trade secrets, and thus prevented from being disclosed.[51] As a result, the requester was unable to judge whether or not the public transportation company's increase in bus fares was reasonable. Average social costs in relation to commercial residential houses were excluded from disclosure for being trade secrets.[52] There is an apparent overuse of the trade secret exemption. This overuse has exempted much government information.

The privacy exemption has also been used to refuse a request for information that had been already disclosed. Li's request to the Xuchang government for a list of the beneficiaries of subsidies for breeding pigs was refused on the ground that the information sought fell into the privacy exemption category.[53] This refusal did not adhere to the provincial government's policy document which requires government agencies to publish such a list.

Imposing procedural restrictions on access requests

Along with substantive restrictions placed on access requests, government agencies have also used procedural limits, such as requiring a purpose, setting hurdles for access, passing the buck and making perfunctory responses, to deny information access. The following substantiates these findings.

Requiring purposes for access requests

Several provincial governments, including Fujian Guizhou, Jiangsu and Zhejiang, require applicants to specify their purpose for information requests. The State Council vests discretion in government agencies to refuse access requests that have no relation to requesters' special needs.[54] It remains uncertain whether government agencies will rely on failure to specify a purpose as a ground for refusing a request. Apart from the purpose of an access request, some government agencies, like the Bureau of Foreign Currencies, also limit reuse of the government information disclosed. They require requesters to reuse the information disclosed for legal purposes.[55] The purpose requirement, which does not appear in many other FOI laws, leaves open the prospect of refusing access requests, especially those for public information.

Setting hurdles for access

Government agencies have set unreasonable hurdles to block access requests. When Zhu sent a request to the Beijing Planning Committee, he was required to provide the file number of the document sought.[56] Government agencies have also controlled access through limiting access methods. After Linxing Xu recognized that high voltage lines would go through his roof, he lodged an application to the Shanghai Municipal Environmental Protection Bureau for information concerning an environmental impact assessment report on this project.[57] The Bureau accepted Xu's request, but informed him that he was not permitted to photocopy the report, and only read it on the spot. The curb on access methods has limited the capacity of the demand side to use, distribute and analyse government information.

Passing the buck

Government agencies have used the strategy of passing the buck to postpone a reply to a request. A journalist submitted a request to the Linyi County Land Resources Bureau for information on the process of examining and approving a company's application for land use.[58] The Bureau replied that it did not hold that information, and suggested that its Xingtong Branch might hold the information, but this Branch referred him to the Hengyuan Branch because the company was under the jurisdiction of that Branch. When the journalist went to the Hengyuan Branch, he was told that this company was directly managed by the Land Resources Bureau that operated one of the county's investment absorption projects, and thus passed its responsibility back to the Bureau. As a result, the journalist did not obtain the information requested. This strategy is used to test requesters' patience, and operates as de facto blocks to accessing information.

Making perfunctory responses

Government agencies have made perfunctory responses to access requests, rarely working closely with requesters to accommodate their needs. Realizing that high voltage lines would go through the roof of his house, Wenhua Ni went to the Shanghai Municipal Planning Bureau to request drawings in relation to the construction of Yuanyun 220kV transformer station.[59] The Bureau replied to Ni, and gave him about seven drawings, but Ni could not understand the drawings and identify the sign of high voltage lines. This reply meant nothing to him. It did not add helpful context to raw data, and so caused unnecessary disputes between Ni and the government. Such perfunctory treatment reflects the dominant notion, which holds that FOI legislation only allows government agencies to provide raw information without editing or explanation.[60] Government agencies may apply this notion mechanically to reply to FOI requests.

Review systems: limiting the capacity of the demand side to request government information

The current internal and external review systems have constrained the capacity of demand side players to promote greater information flow because they have bolstered the government's controlling flow approach toward information requests. As appears from what follows, administrative reconsideration has been inappropriately used by administrative reconsideration agencies to both implicitly and explicitly uphold original decisions. In general, Chinese courts have shown a conservative attitude toward FOI lawsuits, upholding most FOI decisions made by government agencies via various procedural and substantive constraints.

The administrative reconsideration system

Administrative reconsideration, a category of internal review, is provided under the FOI Regulations to examine FOI refusals.[61] However, this type of internal review has bolstered the controlling flow approach to access requests in the following three ways. First, administrative reconsideration agencies have upheld most original decisions. According to Snell, one piece of administrative adversarialism non-compliance is that internal review upholds more than 75 per cent of original decisions.[62] This was the case in Shanghai. Within the last four years, the Shanghai Legislative Affairs Office, the administrative reconsideration agency, upheld approximately 80 per cent of denials of access.[63]

Second, administrative reconsideration agencies have used mute administrative reconsideration to object to information disclosure. Chen submitted his request to the Guangdong Province Land and Resources Bureau for information concerning a project to create farmland, but the Bureau replied that the information requested was not subject to disclosure.[64] Chen applied for administrative reconsideration to the Ministry of Land and Resources, but received no response.

Third, administrative reconsideration agencies have asserted that FOI refusals fall outside the scope of administrative reconsideration. Gao requested the minutes of a mediation meeting, but the township government provided him with inaccurate minutes.[65] Gao asked for administrative reconsideration, but the reconsideration agency stated that his request did not fall within the scope of administrative reconsideration, even the Ningbo FOI Rules empowered requesters to apply for administrative reconsideration. This argument lacks rigour now that the FOI Regulations are in effect. The Regulations, which are of higher legal status than the FOI Rules, establish a stronger legal basis for the exercise of administrative reconsideration.

The administrative lawsuit system

After the implementation of the FOI Regulations, courts processed a series of lawsuits. The results reveal that Chinese courts tend to adopt a conservative attitude toward the process of access to information that falls outside proactively disclosed categories. This attitude may assist the Chinese government to strengthen its controlling flow approach, thus limiting the capacity of demand side players to apply for government information. This conservative attitude may have resulted in concerns over Chinese courts' weak position in rectifying government non-compliance with access requests.[66]

The scope of administrative lawsuits

Courts may reject an FOI lawsuit on the ground that it does not fall within the scope of administrative lawsuits, as appears from the following. First, courts have interpreted a reviewable administrative action strictly. Chinese courts are sceptical about whether the access right is actionable, as common understanding holds that a citizen can only sue for an infringement of personal or property rights pursuant to the *Administrative Litigation Law 1989*.[67] The infringement of an access right, which is irrelevant to any infringement of personal or property rights, is thus considered not to belong to the category of cases that courts must accept.[68] Furthermore, it has been recognized that political rights, such as the access right, are excluded from the scope of a lawsuit.[69] An exception is Shanghai as noted below.

Yet, the doubt about whether the access right is actionable should not persist, as the FOI Regulations permit citizens to bring an FOI lawsuit to court.[70] This stipulation does not conflict with the *Administrative Litigation Law 1989*, which vests power in courts to accept an administrative lawsuit that may be brought pursuant to the provisions of relevant regulations.[71]

While courts in Shanghai accepted lawsuits concerning the access right after its FOI Rules took effect in 2004, courts in other cities, the

Zhengzhou City, for example, refused to accept these lawsuits, as the *Ren* case indicates. Ren sought judicial review of the government refusal of his request for information on planning and licence arrangements for installation of parking-meter mechanisms.[72] The court ruled that although Ren had a right to access the information, he could not prove that the FOI reply infringed upon his lawful rights and interests, which was one condition for the plaintiff bringing a lawsuit to court.[73] As a result, the court rejected Ren's action.

Even after implementation of the FOI Regulations, some courts hold this narrow explanation and reject FOI lawsuits. Chen submitted his application to the Beijing Municipal Public Security Bureau for information concerning the use of management service fees for raising dogs.[74] After the Bureau rejected his request, Chen took legal action against this refusal. However, the court rejected this action as the defendant was not required to reply to the requester.[75] Gao's request to a township government for information on an inappropriate transfer of resettled houses was refused.[76] He then sued the government for non-disclosure of related information, but the court ruled that his lawsuit did not fall under the *Administrative Litigation Law 1989*, and so rejected it.

Second, courts have conservatively interpreted a concrete administrative action, an administrative activity that aims at specified events or individuals and can only be carried out once. They hold that an FOI refusal has no real impact on the complainant's right and duty, and so it falls outside the scope of administrative cases.[77] This is because the Supreme Court excludes review of the exercise of a concrete administrative action that has no real impact on a citizen's right or duty.[78] This impedes the courts' ability to accept an FOI lawsuit because they hold that an FOI refusal, which is a concrete administrative action, does not infringe on a requester's right, or impose a duty.[79] Jinsong Hao lodged a request to the Shaanxi Forestry Department for information on an investigation concerning the disclosure of controversial pictures of a rare wild South China tiger.[80] The Department replied that it would disclose the information after the investigation was completed.[81] Hao was dissatisfied with this reply, and took legal action against the Department, which the court rejected as it held that the FOI reply did not have any real impact on his rights and duties.[82]

Third, courts have rejected an FOI legal action on the basis that information sought falls outside the scope of administrative lawsuits. The request of Youjian Huang and other colleagues was refused by the government.[83] The court did not accept the subsequent lawsuit on the ground that the information sought related to an enterprise's restructure, and did not fall within the scope of administrative lawsuits.[84] In this case, the court did not reject the case from the quality of being actionable, but rejected it from the category of the information sought, an enterprise's restructure, which is not reviewable. The major concern is that courts may exploit this explanation to reject contentious cases in the future.

A wrong jurisdiction

Courts have rejected an FOI lawsuit on the ground that it falls outside its jurisdiction. This reason may be used by a court to pass the responsibility to another court. Zhu submitted a request to the National Audit Office for information concerning the inappropriate use of land-use fees and the like.[85] His request was refused based on the exemption for social stability. Zhu's lawsuit in the Beijing No 1 Intermediate Court was rejected on the ground that the General Office of the National Audit Office, not the National Audit Office, was the correct defendant, and the former fell under the jurisdiction of the Xicheng District Court. Zhu insisted on taking the National Audit Office, rather than its General Office, to court as he recognized that only the former was the qualified defendant in accordance with the law.[86] The Intermediate Court received Zhu's files this time, but did not inform Zhu whether his lawsuit was accepted or rejected.[87]

Postponing the acceptance

Courts have postponed a time limit to decide whether to accept or reject an FOI lawsuit, as the *Li* case shows.[88] Li sent a request dated 16 September 2005 to the Shanghai Municipal Engineering Management Bureau for information on the roads built by loans or public funds. He received no reply from the Bureau within the set timeframe, and then sought judicial review of the decision on 19 October 2005. The court refused his claim on the ground that it only accepted a lawsuit until a government agency did not reply to a requester over 60 days.[89] Thus, the court held that Li should file after 16 November 2005. It interpreted narrowly the *Supreme Court's Explanation on Several Questions Related to the Implementation of the Administrative Litigation Law 1989*. This document also allows the court to accept a lawsuit in relation to a government agency that does not perform its statutory duty within the set timeframe under rules, like the Shanghai FOI Rules. The Rules require government agencies to provide information within 30 days maximum after receiving access requests. As Li had lodged his lawsuit after more than 30 days of his request was sent, it appears that the court could have accepted Li's lawsuit, but opted not to do so. The court may have utilized the general timeline, 60 days, to give itself more time to consider the acceptance of a contentious case.

Unfortunately, courts have kept silent on some contentious FOI refusals. This was the case for the first FOI lawsuit after the FOI Regulations came into effect in China. The previously discussed information request submitted by Youjian Huang and his colleagues may have revealed an illegal closing of the water supply company.[90] Their request was refused by the government on the ground that the information requested fell outside the scope of information required to be disclosed. Hence, Huang and his colleagues filed a lawsuit to the Chenzhou Intermediary Court, but the Court did not inform them as to whether it would accept or reject this complaint within seven days, the time limit set out in the *Administrative Litigation Law 1989*.[91] The court explained that it could not inform them, as the case was awaiting instruction from the Supreme Court.[92] The reason for this delayed response was the court's reluctance to be the first to try a contentious case. One judge confessed that the acceptance of such a contentious case needed professional knowledge as well as courage.[93]

Literally explaining the definition of government information

Courts have interpreted the definition of government information in a literal way, as appears from the following. First, they have asserted that information compiled, rather than generated or acquired by a government agency, is not subject to disclosure. This assertion was found in the *Lian* case.[94] The court rejected Lian's claim on the ground that the documents requested were compiled by the defendant to facilitate its daily work, and thus fell outside the scope of information defined under the Shanghai FOI Rules. The case reveals that compiled government information falls outside the scope of information subject to disclosure. While this case was processed before the FOI Regulations took effect, it may set a precedent for similar cases in the future.

Second, courts have maintained that oral information is excluded from disclosure. The *Su* case indicates that courts support the claim that information communicated in an oral form is not subject to disclosure.[95] Third, courts have held that information irrelevant to the exercise of government responsibilities is excluded from disclosure. In the *Su* case, the court adjudged that the information sought was related to the reform of salaries, which had no relation to economic, social management, or public service, and so was in the category of internal affairs that was not required to be disclosed.[96]

Examining purposes for access requests

Courts have used the purpose requirement under the FOI Regulations to reject FOI legal actions, especially contentious ones. The rationale is that the requester's purpose must be examined to control the abusive use of access rights.[97] Observers predict that the request for information on environmental pollution would be likely to be rejected by the court on the ground that it is irrelevant to requesters' special needs.[98] Yulai Yuan filed a lawsuit to the Hefei Intermediary Court after his request for a letter sent by the Anhui government for instructions about laws and policies was refused.[99] The court rejected this application on the basis that the information sought lacked relation to the requester's special needs.

No legal interest in the information sought

Courts have rejected an administrative lawsuit on the ground that the requester has no legal interest in the information sought. This rejection may have misunderstood the requirement under the Supreme Court's explanation, which states that only individuals who have legal interest with administrative actions are entitled to file an administrative lawsuit.[100] This sets a limit on the qualification of a plaintiff. However, the legal interest limit should be understood between the requester and the request, rather than the requester and the information sought.[101] Arguably, any government information is of interest to citizens from either a broad or narrow standard. However, the legal interest limit presents an opportunity for courts to support a narrow standard, in particular when they process contentious cases.

Unreasonable burden of proof

Courts have used the ambiguity of burden of proof to dismiss FOI legal actions, especially when reviewing FOI decisions in which officials claim that the information sought does not exist. Such claims create difficulties for courts, which must decide whether plaintiffs or defendants bear the burden of proof, and to what degree.[102] While the government/defendant bears the burden for its concrete administrative action,[103] this requirement contradicts a fundamental principle of the standard of proof; it is not a party's duty to provide evidence to support his allegation about the fact which does not exist.[104] This contradiction raises the possibility for courts to frustrate the requester or plaintiff, specifically when trying some contentious cases, as the *Dong* case indicates.[105]

The demand side: diverse interests in the use of FOI legislation

There is concern about a low use of China's FOI Regulations.[106] It is difficult to obtain an accurate picture of the use of FOI legislation at present because official statistics about the types of FOI requesters are not available. However, secondary data gathered from a wide range of sources for this research shows that the public expressed interest in access to government information for varied purposes after the FOI Regulations came into effect. This could lessen the concern about low use. However, the role of demand side players, especially journalists and lawyers, is constrained due to the government's controlling flow approach to FOI requests. Furthermore, diverse interests in the use of FOI legislation by demand side players have resulted in patchy, if not completely poor, FOI performance in terms of responses to requests.

Chinese citizens: using FOI for various purposes

Even in liberal democratic states, FOI scholars are concerned about citizens' low incentives to request government-held information, especially public information.[107] The state's relation to the citizen in China magnifies this concern due to its concept of citizenship as a tool for asserting rights against the state.[108] A valid concern must be viewed against the backdrop of the changing situation in China. Indeed Chinese citizens have increased their rights consciousness, which may have resulted in access to information that involves immediate interests.

Chinese citizens: increasing rights consciousness

Chinese citizens' rising rights consciousness, which has been stimulated by the reform and opening-up policy that commenced in the late 1970s, may benefit the use of FOI legislation.[109] Before that, citizens' individual rights were largely neglected due to greater emphasis on national and collective interests.[110] The amendment of the *Constitution* in 2004 responded to this trend, requiring the state to respect and preserve human rights.[111] The following five aspects explain Chinese citizens' growing awareness of rights.

First, rights consciousness, property rights consciousness in particular, has increased. This prompted the amendment to the *Constitution* in March 2004, which announces that 'the state protects the right of citizens to own lawfully earned income, savings, houses and other lawful property'.[112] This also resulted in the adoption of the *Property Law* in 2007, which confers on private property the same protection as state-owned assets.[113]

Second, Chinese citizens have an enhanced consciousness of personal freedom. The death of Zhigang Sun prompted three law postgraduates to jointly petition the Standing Committee of the National People's Congress to revoke the State Council's detention rules due to their unconstitutionality.[114] The State Council was pressured by this, replacing detention rules in June 2003 by new rules that change migrant detention centres into voluntary service ones.[115]

Third, Chinese citizens have armed themselves with the *Constitution* to reduce employment and gender discrimination. Many have called for a review of discriminatory employment against Hepatitis B virus carriers in recent years.[116] This may have prompted the central government to adopt a new policy document in 2005 in order to resolve this discriminatory issue.[117] Gender discrimination has also caught public attention, with a special focus on different retirement age for males and females.[118] Chinese citizens have challenged this discriminatory requirement by referring to Article 48 of the *Constitution*, which entitles males and females to equal employment rights.[119]

Fourth, Chinese citizens have sought judicial review of administrative decisions to protect their own legal rights and interests. There were only 13,006 administrative lawsuits in 1990, the first year of operation of the *Administrative Litigation Law 1989*, but 52,792 in 2006.[120] Fifth, Chinese citizens have strived for election as deputies of congresses by self-nomination to protect their interests more directly. A few citizens won election for deputies through self-nomination.[121]

Chinese citizens: primarily for information that involves their immediate interests

Interviews conducted for this book reveal that Chinese citizens have a strong interest in accessing information that involves their immediate interests. Yet, it is difficult to see a continuing motivation to use FOI legislation because the FOI Regulations have only devised a limited access mechanism that cannot become a realistic tool for solving their issues.

After the implementation of the FOI Regulations, Chinese citizens used FOI legislation for access to the following five main categories of government information, all closely related to their immediate interests. First, they applied for information to examine whether or not their interests had been violated.[122] This occurred primarily in three areas: enterprise restructure, house demolition and land use. Given China's rapid marketization and urbanization in the last three decades, this is hardly surprising. Second, Chinese citizens used the FOI Regulations to better understand their personal legal matters, such as pending criminal and civil cases.[123] Third, they filed access requests to learn more about how government agencies processed their business affairs.[124] Fourth, they asked for historical records to solve their outstanding issues with the government, such as housing takeovers before and during the Cultural Revolution.[125] FOI legislation provided an indirect opportunity for individuals aggrieved by the enforced takeovers to seek protection for their private property. Fifth, Chinese citizens requested information on their personnel files in order to claim benefits from the government.[126]

However, the preceding discussion of citizens' positive use of FOI legislation does not necessarily indicate an optimistic view. It is likely that Chinese citizens will not have steady impetus to use FOI legislation, especially when they find that the use cannot help them to solve their issues. At the present stage of implementation, there are three problems concerning citizens' use of FOI legislation. First, there exists doubt about the effectiveness of the access mechanism. In interviews, many citizens said that FOI requests did not assist in solving their problems.[127] Some citizens displayed reluctance to request government information, fearing that they would be unable to obtain the information they wanted.[128] Academics said that if they needed government information, their first course was to make full use of close relationships with government agencies, rather than sending direct access requests.[129] Second, FOI officials complained that citizens did not really need government information, but instead official responses to their outstanding problems that could not be easily provided.[130] This may lessen FOI officials' motivation for processing information requests.

Third, petitioners heavily used the access mechanism for information on various outstanding issues with the government,[131] but the outcome of this use was generally negative. The access mechanism is becoming another petition mechanism.[132] Petitioners expected that access to information regarding the process of their administrative disputes would enable the disputes to be reconsidered by government or retried in court. While petitioners have showed their special interest in access to information, they will likely lose their interest in this vehicle and discontinue using it once they find information access cannot assist them to solve their problems.

Journalists: tentative use

Chinese journalists have made tentative use of FOI legislation. Roberts argues that the effectiveness of FOI legislation in China will be limited by the lack of free press.[133] Callick opines that the chances of Chinese journalists using the FOI Regulations are 'very slim'.[134] This does not mean that Chinese journalists have not responded to FOI legislation now that media competition has increased and Chinese media groups enjoy greater freedom to publish.[135] At this stage, Chinese journalists remain concerns over the sensitivity and likelihood of access, to government information,[136] and so their use of FOI is cautious. Even though journalists apply for government information, they focus on information that is largely permitted.

After the implementation of the FOI Regulations, Chinese journalists showed interest in access to information, but they had much less interest in filing direct requests than that in reporting government non-compliance and following it up. Weak press freedom was one factor. Chinese journalists were reluctant to use FOI legislation because they had limited capacity to act on the information sought. The controlling flow approach taken by the government also resulted in low direct use of FOI legislation. Like their counterparts in Western democracies with long experience of FOI, Chinese journalists were most likely to face the problems coming from government agencies, such as long processing time, high fees, wholesale redactions and sweeping exemptions;[137] and those stemming from themselves, such as heavy reliance on personal relationships, unwillingness to undertake difficult tasks and concern about readership.[138]

Furthermore, FOI reform that emphasizes information flow rather than media reform has caused Chinese journalists to be concerned over the use of FOI legislation. Thus, they applied for government information as ordinary citizens, rather than as journalists. This undoubtedly limited their use of FOI legislation as an investigative tool.

Legal professionals: major requesters of public information

After the implementation of the FOI Regulations, Chinese legal professionals were the most frequent requesters in China. Their requests have the following four features. First, a wide range of legal professionals, such as lawyers, law academics and students, used FOI legislation to access government information. In particular, Chinese lawyers showed special interest in requesting information. Second, their requests were primarily for information in the public interest. The information sought covered a wide range of areas, such as the use of charges and public funds, and the exercise of administrative power. Third, legal professionals played an educational role in promoting information access. Professor Xixin Wang and his colleagues aimed at boosting the use of FOI legislation through their requests.[139] Hongxiang Wen, a Shenyang lawyer, said that his requests were largely for teaching ordinary citizens how to request government information.[140] Fourth, legal professionals understood how to work closely with media outlets in reporting the progress of their requests, thus bringing about a maximum propaganda effect.

Chinese legal professionals have an advantage over other groups when using FOI legislation. They have greater professional knowledge as they are likely to know which information is needed and which government agency holds the information, as well as how to use FOI legislation. They, especially lawyers, are also wealthier and more independent than other groups, and so have greater capacity and willingness to request public information. The use of FOI legislation by Chinese legal professionals is a positive response to the impetus of law-based administration for FOI reform in China, though they may use FOI legislation as part of their private commercial lawsuits. However, the use of FOI legislation by legal professionals is largely individualized. It is necessary to initiate a coalition of active FOI requesters to apply for public information in the future.

Conclusion

The prospects for effective Chinese FOI reform, simply measured by reactive disclosure or the pull aspect of FOI, appear limited in the foreseeable future. The level of non-compliance with access requests for information that is not required to be proactively disclosed is currently high. The government's controlling flow approach to manage FOI requests is bolstered by courts, as shown by the various procedural and substantive restrictions placed on FOI lawsuits. This controlling flow approach thus constrains the role that demand side players, especially journalists and lawyers, can play. Ordinary citizens have found the access mechanism an impractical and unrealistic tool for solving their problems. Journalists have been largely restricted to reporting on government non-compliance. Legal professionals have used FOI legislation in a largely individualized way. Concern over compliance issues in China is derived from this excessive focus on government non-compliance with reactive disclosure.

11 Conclusion

Information flow analysis enabling an adequate understanding of FOI reform in China

The purpose of this book is to more thoroughly analyse the Chinese FOI phenomenon. This book has used information flow analysis to examine this strange and intriguing phenomenon. It has argued that a sufficient understanding of the adoption of FOI legislation in China cannot be achieved without focusing on the capacity to accept FOI, through examining the development of local information flow over time due to changed social, political, legal and economic conditions. It has also argued that a sufficient understanding of the prospects for the implementation of FOI legislation in China cannot be achieved until equal attention is paid to both the push and pull aspects of information flow.

Information flow analysis: explaining the adoption of FOI legislation in China

Information flow analysis has been demonstrated in this book to have the power to explain the apparent paradox of the introduction of FOI legislation into China. This analysis, which focuses on the dynamic interaction between one stream of information flow (push) and another stream (pull) in an information environment, has been created and utilized in this book to examine the gradual development of China's capacity to accept FOI. The use of a new and effective explanatory model is necessary, because the explanatory models of accountability deficit, globalization, economic growth and anti-corruption have been arguably inadequate for an understanding of China's FOI phenomenon. Information flow analysis enables an adequate understanding.

By applying information flow analysis, this book has demonstrated that China gradually increased its capacity to accept FOI through the move from an emphasis on proactive disclosure to one on reactive disclosure. This capacity increased after the formation of multiple paths for information flow in the longstanding secretive Chinese information environment. Two decades of Openness in Government Affairs coupled with a long-term democratization process also improved information flow between citizens and the state, thus increasing government receptivity to an access mechanism. Moreover, the focus for administrative law reforms, which moved to ex ante and procedural controls of government power, improved information flow in the Chinese information environment. This thus raised China's capacity to accommodate FOI. In addition, economic growth and anti-corruption efforts were important rationales for increasing China's capacity to support FOI due to the advocacy of key individuals or agencies. However, these two driving forces played only a limited and indirect role in improving information flow. From this point of view, these two motives should be allocated important but secondary roles in understanding the development of FOI in China. Social, political and legal motives should be accorded central roles.

The book has argued that the gradual development of government receptivity to FOI, which began with the acceptance of proactive disclosure and then recognized the importance of reactive disclosure, resulted in China adopting a push model of FOI legislation with an emphasis on proactive disclosure. This model has accepted reactive disclosure as a basic element in improving information flow, but reduced the significance of reactive disclosure in this process.

This book has shown the explanatory power of information flow analysis for understanding the apparent paradox of the Chinese FOI phenomenon. The explanatory power has come from a dynamic and broad approach to the examination of an FOI phenomenon. This analysis has not isolated FOI from a broad information environment, or viewed FOI as a timeless phenomenon. The application of information flow analysis to the Chinese case is the first significant step in gaining a better understanding of the divergence of FOI developments around the globe.

Information flow analysis: understanding the implementation of FOI legislation in China

Apart from its capacity to explain the adoption of FOI legislation, this book has argued that information flow analysis also has the potential to improve the current compliance analysis, by moving toward a broad, dynamic and cross-jurisdictional analysis of FOI performance. The undue focus on reactive disclosure in the Roberts–Snell compliance analysis model limits its application to analysis of compliance issues in China, because the specifics of China's FOI reform, such as internally generated reform and the push model, have not been taken into account. This book has thus revised the compliance analysis model through the incorporation of the push and pull focus to allow a more effective and dynamic analysis of compliance issues in China.

By applying this revised compliance analysis model, the book has demonstrated that government willingness and capability, in conjunction with a push model of FOI legislation, can ensure a certain level of compliance with proactive disclosure requirements. This level of compliance has increased since active players on the demand side have been willing and able to redress government non-compliance with proactive disclosure via access requests. Yet the book has shown that the prospects for reactive disclosure of information that is not required to be proactively disclosed are limited in China in this early stage of implementation. A controlling flow approach to information requests has reflected the fact that government willingness to comply remains low. Furthermore, both the capacity and willingness of demand side players to use FOI legislation for information outside the scope of proactive disclosure have also been limited.

In this book, information flow analysis has been utilized to improve understanding of compliance issues in China. This analysis has indicated that the two-directional nature of FOI, the push and pull aspects of information flow, should be recognized in a compliance analysis model. Compliance with the push aspect of information flow is equally important to compliance with the pull aspect.

FOI: moving from a beneficiary to a contributor to the Chinese information environment

By applying information flow analysis, the book has demonstrated that FOI was first a beneficiary of, and then a contributor to the Chinese information environment. In order to improve the contributor role of FOI, it is necessary to upgrade the FOI Regulations to FOI law, through improving and strengthening the push nature under the Regulations. Future FOI law should move the factors undermining the push nature by explicitly authorizing an access right, deleting the purpose requirement for access requests, limiting and clarifying exemptions, and allowing a maximum disclosure principle.

Furthermore, the future of FOI reform should continue focusing on the supply side, which is the key to success in China. It is necessary to establish effective measures to sustain a constant strong central political commitment to FOI, and to maintain the interest of various transparency advocacy groups. Demand side players, both domestic and international non-government organizations, can cooperate with supply side drivers to create a more favourable environment for the implementation of FOI legislation in China. Apart from this, demand side players should also assist in improving the level of compliance in China, by focusing on rectification of non-compliance with proactive disclosure requirements. They can use this success as a tool for boosting public confidence with regard to reactive disclosure. It is also necessary to establish professional associations to provide training of potential requesters, increase public awareness of FOI and assess the degree of government compliance from a user perspective.

Conclusion

This book began with an inquiry as to whether or not China's FOI is a strange and intriguing phenomenon. By applying information flow analysis, it has argued that China's FOI is hardly strange, as it is deeply attached to social, political, legal and economic contexts of information flow in recent

Chinese history. As a beneficiary of the gradually improving Chinese information environment, FOI is now becoming a contributor to this environment. Furthermore, China's FOI is far more intriguing than is currently recognized, as it is unique and has not been sufficiently understood.

The case study of China's FOI in this book has demonstrated that information flow is an effective analytical tool for coherently examining both the adoption and implementation of FOI legislation in a jurisdiction. In the future, a better understanding as to whether FOI legislation can be adopted or implemented should not ignore its interrelation with other streams of information flow in a broad information environment. This book thus calls for more empirical research to apply and develop information flow analysis.

Notes

1 Introduction

1 R. Snell and W. Xiao (2007) 'Freedom of Information Returns to China', *Public Administration Today*, 10: 47.
2 Ibid 44.
3 Only a handful of non-Chinese, like Horsley, do not consider China's FOI as a strange phenomenon or paradox. See J. Horsley (2007a) *China Adopts First Nationwide Open Government Information Regulations*, Online. Available HTTP: <http://www.freedominfo.org/features/20070509.htm> (accessed 28 August 2007); J. Horsley (2007b) 'Toward a More Open China?' in A. Florini (ed.) *The Right to Know: Transparency for an Open World*, New York: Columbia University Press, pp.54–91.
4 C. Bennett (1997) 'Understanding Ripple Effects: The Cross-National Adoption of Policy Instruments for Bureaucratic Accountability', *Governance: An International Journal of Policy and Administration*, 10: 213.
5 T. Blanton (2002) 'The Openness Revolution: The Rise of a Global Movement for Freedom of Information', *Development Dialogue*, 1: 16.
6 Bennett, op.cit., p.213.
7 A. Roberts (2006a) *Blacked Out: Government Secrecy in the Information Age*, New York: Cambridge University Press, pp.108–109; C. Darch and P. Underwood (2009) *Freedom of Information and the Developing World: The Citizen, the State and Models of Openness*, Oxford: Chandos Publishing, pp.13–15.
8 Bennett, op.cit. p.213; Roberts argues that these two preconditions only 'capture the realities of the 1970s and 1980s'. See Roberts (2006a), op.cit., p.107.
9 The world's first FOI law was adopted in Sweden in 1766, although its influences for other FOI adopters were very limited. After the US introduced its FOI legislation in 1966, four countries in the 1970s and another five in the 1980s followed suit. Denmark, Norway, France and Netherlands adopted their FOI laws in 1970s. Australia, New Zealand, Canada, Greece and Austria adopted their FOI laws in 1980s. See R. Vleugels (2006) *Overview of FOIA Countries Worldwide – February 1 2006*, Online. Available HTTP: <http://www.statewatch.org/news/2006/feb/foia-feb-2006.pdf> (accessed 3 October 2008).
10 J. Ackerman and I. Sandoval-Ballesteros (2006) 'The Global Explosion of Freedom of Information Laws', *Administrative Law Review*, 58, 113.
11 Ibid 107–108.
12 Bennett, op.cit., p.222.
13 The Australian Attorney-General's Department (1983) *Freedom of Information Act 1982 Annual Report 1982–1983*, Canberra: The Australian Attorney-General's Department, p.1.2.2; G. Terrill (1998) 'The Rise and Decline of Freedom of

Information in Australia', in A. McDonald and G. Terrill (eds) *Open Government: Freedom of Information and Privacy*, London: Macmillan Press Ltd., p.90.

14 A. Missen (2002) 'Freedom of Information – The Australian Experience', *Freedom of Information Review*, 100: 43.

15 Ibid.

16 The Australian Senate Standing Committee on Constitutional and Legal Affairs, Parliament of Commonwealth (1979) *Freedom of Information Bill 1978, and Related Aspects of Archives Bill 1978*, Canberra: Commonwealth of Australia, p.[3.14].

17 Ackerman and Sandoval-Ballesteros, op.cit., p.116–119.

18 The New Zealand Committee on Official Information observed that one motive for FOI legislation was the concern about the extent of executive powers, arguing that '[t]he Government has a pervasive involvement in our every day national life ... [and this] circumstances give New Zealanders special reason for wanting to know what their government is doing and why'. See The New Zealand Committee on Official Information (1980) *Towards Open Government: General Report*, Online. Available HTTP: <http://www.ombudsmen.parliament.nz/imagelibrary/100168.pdf> (accessed 31 May 2008); J. Aitken (1998) 'Open Government in New Zealand', in A. McDonald and G. Terrill (eds) *Open Government: Freedom of Information and Privacy*, London: Macmillan Press Ltd., p.117.

19 R. Gillis (1998) 'Freedom of Information and Open Government in Canada', in A. McDonald and G. Terrill (eds) *Open Government: Freedom of Information and Privacy*, London: Macmillan Press Ltd., pp.143–145.

20 Roberts (2006a), op.cit., p.107–111; Blanton, op.cit., p.16; Ackerman and Sandoval-Ballesteros, op.cit., pp.92–93.

21 Roberts argues that the wave of FOI legislation sweeping newly democratic countries in the 1990s began to demonstrate that the argument about the necessary conditions for FOI reform was 'inadequate'. See Roberts (2006a), op.cit., p.108. The new democracies introduced FOI legislation as part of their fulfilment of a democratic transition, in contrast to the requirement that affluent democracy should be a precondition for FOI. See Ackerman and Sandoval-Ballesteros, op.cit., p.114.

22 Snell and Xiao, op.cit., p.45.

23 Blanton, op.cit. p.16.

24 C. Bennett. (2001) *Globalization and Access to Information Regimes*, Online. Available HTTP: <http://www.atirtf-geai.gc.ca/paper-globalisation1-e.html> (accessed 30 January 2008).

25 Blanton, op.cit. p.16.

26 Darch and Underwood, op.cit., p.172.

27 Ibid.

28 Schartum argues that 'an antagonistic relationship between government and citizens fits well with the mode of the 1950s and 1960s, when [FOI] legislation was prepared, and when legislation, to a large extent, came into existence to protect individuals from an ever stronger government'. See D. W. Schartum (2004) 'Information Access Legislation for the Future? Possibilities according to a Norwegian Experience', in G. Aichholzer and H. Burkert (eds) *Public Sector Information in the Digital Age: Between Markets, Public Management and Citizens' Rights*, Cheltenham: Edward Elgar Publishing, p.78.

29 H. Foerstel (2000) *Freedom of Information and the Right to Know: The Origins and Applications of the Freedom of Information Act*, London: Greenwood Press, pp.14–26; Terrill, op.cit., p.90; Aitken, op.cit., p.117.

30 A. Roberts (1998) *Limited Access: Assessing the Health of Canada's Freedom of Information Laws*, Online. Available HTTP: <http://www.cna-acj.ca/Client/CNA/cna.nsf/object/LimitedAccess/$file/limitedaccess.pdf> (accessed 17 November 2006);

R. Snell (2001) 'Administrative Compliance – Evaluating the Effectiveness of Freedom of Information', *Freedom of Information Review*, 93: 29; R. Snell (2002) 'FOI and the Delivery of Diminishing Returns, or How Spin-Doctors and Journalists Have Mistreated a Volatile Reform', *The Drawing Board: An Australian Review of Public Affairs*, 3: 187–203.

31 McCrann observes that '[a] major factor was no doubt the 11 years worth of publicity and pressure engendered by the Moss Subcommittee, as well as the parallel publicity and coverage by the American media'. The Moss Subcommittee was established in 1955 with strong support from Congressman Moss John. See G. E. McCrann (2007) *An Examination of the Conditions Surrounding the Passage of the 1966 US Freedom of Information Act*, Online. Available HTTP: <http://www.opengovjournal.org/article/viewArticle/995> (accessed 22 July 2009); S. Lamble (2002) 'Computer-Assisted Reporting and Freedom of Information', unpublished thesis, Queensland University, pp.100–102.

32 P. Bayne (1984) *Freedom of Information: An Analysis of the Freedom of Information Act 1982 (Cth) and a Synopsis of the Freedom of Information Act 1982 (Vic)*, Sydney: Law Book Co., p.4.

33 Ibid p.5.

34 Australian Commonwealth (1981) *Parliamentary Debates*, House of Representatives, Canberra: 8 April, p.1232 (Senator Evans).

35 G. Whitlam (1972) 'It Is Time for Leadership', speech delivered at the Blacktown Civic Centre, Sydney, 13 November.

36 The Australian Attorney-General's Department (1974) *Proposed Freedom of Information Legislation: Report of Interdepartmental Committee*, Canberra: Australian Government Publishing Service, 1.

37 G. Terrill (2000b) *Secrecy and Openness: The Federal Government from Menzies to Whitlam and Beyond*, Melbourne: Melbourne University Publishing, p.109.

38 The Australian Attorney-General's Department (1983), op.cit., p.2.7.1; The Senate Standing Committee on Constitutional and Legal Affairs, op.cit., p.3.14.

39 The Australian Attorney-General's Department (1983), op.cit., p.2.8.

40 Bayne, op.cit., p. 6; Terrill, op.cit., p.90.

41 The Australian Attorney-General's Department (1983), op.cit., p.2.7.1.

42 I. Eagles, M. Taggart and G. Liddell (1992) *Freedom of Information in New Zealand*, Auckland: Oxford University Press, p.1.

43 Ibid.

44 Aitken, op.cit., p.122.

45 Eagles, Taggart and Liddell, op.cit., p.2; Aitken, op.cit., p.122; R. Snell (2000) 'The Kiwi Paradox – A Comparison of Freedom of Information in Australia and New Zealand', *Federal Law Review*, 28: 583.

46 Eagles, Taggart, and Liddell, op.cit., p.1; Snell (2000), op.cit., p.583; R. Snell (2006) 'Freedom of Information Practices', *Agenda*, 13: 297.

47 Snell (2000), op.cit., p.578.

48 Gillis, op.cit., pp.143–145.

49 Ackerman and Sandoval-Ballesteros, op.cit., p.119.

50 Roberts (2006a), op.cit., pp.109–110.

51 Article 19 (2002) *Promoting Practical Access to Democracy: A Survey of Freedom of Information in Central and Eastern Europe*, Online. Available HTTP: <http://www.article19.org/pdfs/publications/freedom-of-information-survey-of-central-and-e.pdf> (accessed 25 February 2009).

52 K. Suominen (2003) 'Access to Information in Latin America and the Caribbean', *Comparative Media Law Journal*, 2: 33.

53 M. A. Ali (2003) *Freedom of Information in South Asia: Comparative Perspectives on Civil Society Initiative*, Online. Available HTTP: <http://www.jdhr.org/publications/papers/Mukhtar%20A%20Ali-Media%20panel-0Edited%2027.4.pdf>

(accessed 25 February 2009). However, Darch and Underwood hold a different view, arguing that there is little evidence which shows that FOI is an explicit policy of these intergovernmental and multilateral institutions. See Darch and Underwood, op.cit., p.53.

54 Roberts (2006a), op.cit., p.110.
55 The Open Society Justice Initiative (2006) *Transparency & Silence: A Survey of Access to Information Laws and Practices in 14 Countries*, Online. Available HTTP: <http://www.soros.org/resources/articles_publications/publications/trans-parency_20060928/transparency_20060928.pdf> (accessed 12 November 2006).
56 Lamble points out that the US determined to promote FOI through bilateral treaties or agreements in the 1940s. See S. Lamble (2003) 'FOI as a United States' Foreign Policy Tool: A Carrot and Stick Approach', *Freedom of Information Review*, 105: 38–41. The United State Agency for International Development now plays a similar role.
57 The United State Agency for International Development has funded Pact Cambodia to assist Cambodia to develop a policy paper on FOI since 2007.
58 P. Hubbard (2008b) *China's Regulations on Open Government Information: Challenges of Nationwide Policy Implementation*, Online. Available HTTP: <http://www.opengovjournal.org/article/viewArticle/2651> (accessed 22 July 2009).
59 J. Kolhammar (2008) *The Challenge to Implement the Open Government Information Regulation in China*, Online. Available HTTP: <http://en.chinaelections.org/newsinfo.asp?newsid=17891> (accessed 2 October 2008).
60 Bennett, op.cit., p.223.
61 Blanton, op.cit., p.16.
62 An implicit assumption by some academics is that globalization leads to policy convergence. FOI legislation has not been an exception. See Bennett, op.cit., p.213; C. Bennett (1991) 'Review Article: What Is Policy Convergence and What Causes It?' *British Journal of Political Science*, 21: 215–233.
63 Roberts predicted that one reason for other less wealthy countries to adopt FOI legislation might have been an emulation of 'better-off states'. See Roberts (2006a), op.cit., p.109.
64 Such as Pakistan and the efforts in Cambodia. Pakistan adopted its FOI legislation to respond to the call of the Asian Development Bank. See D. Banisar (2006) *Freedom of Information around the World 2006: A Global Survey of Access to Government Information Laws*, Online. Available HTTP: <http://www.freedominfo.org/documents/global_survey2006.pdf> (accessed 9 November 2006).
65 The EU–China Information Society Project is a 4-year cooperation project between the Chinese government and the EU (2005–2009). Access to government information is its important part. The China Law Centre at Yale University did not directly contribute to the first national FOI legislation in China. However, it has been involved in legislative processes of local FOI Rules, such as Guangzhou and Shanghai. J. Horsley (2009) 'Weibing's Draft for Comments' (6 May).
66 The Open Society Justice Initiative, op.cit., p.89; Article 19 (1999) *Right to Know: Principles on Freedom of Information Legislation*, Online. Available HTTP: <http://www.article19.org/pdfs/standards/righttoknow.pdf> (accessed 1 July 2007).
67 *Freedom of Information Regulations 2007*. Arts 20, 22, 27, 31.
68 R. Snell (2005) 'Using Comparative Studies to Improve Freedom of Information Analysis: Insights from Australia, Canada and New Zealand', paper presented at Sixth National and Second International Congress on the Right to Information, Mexico, 8–11 November.
69 H. H. Zhou (ed.) (2003) *Zhengfu xinxi gongkai tiaoli zhuanjia jianyigao [Academic Draft of FOI Regulations]*, Beijing: China Legal Publishing House, pp.19–20; M. J. Zhang (2003) *Kaifang de zhengfu: zhengfu xinxi gongkai falv zhidu yanjiu*

[Open Government: Research on FOI Laws], Beijing: China Law Press, pp.212–213; Blanton, op.cit., p.16.

70 Z. Q. Zhao (2001) 'Zhengwu gongkai fanfubai lunyao [Discussion of Anti-Corruption through Openness in Government Affairs]', *Theory and Modernisation*, 6: 54; Roberts (2006a), op.cit.,p.110; Blanton, op.cit.,p.16.

71 Darch and Underwood, op.cit.,p.171; Blanton, op.cit.,p.16; G. Sutton and S. Holsen (2006) *China Progresses Information Access and Data Protection Laws*, Online. Available HTTP: <http://www.opengovjournal.org/article/view/621/482> (accessed 22 July 2009).

72 Some Chinese scholars observe that after the SARS crisis, the legislative process of FOI was accelerated. Professor Hanhua Zhou, a key member of drafting China's FOI legislation, held this view when he was interviewed by a newspaper reporter of *China Youth Daily*. See Y. J. Wang (2007) 'Zhengfu xinxi gongkai tiaoli shinian pobing [The Breakthrough of Legislating on FOI after a Decade]'. *China Youth Daily*, 25 April, p.3. Datong Li, a Chinese Journalist, also held the similar view. See D. T. Li. (2007) *An End to Exclusivity*, Online. Available HTTP: <http://www.opendemocracy.net/node/4585> (accessed 7 March 2009). Darch and Underwood agreed with Li on this. See Darch and Underwood, op.cit., p.178.

73 The CPC Central Committee (2000) *Communiqué of the Fifth Plenary Session of the 15th CPC Central Committee*, Online. Available HTTP: <http://cpc.people. com.cn/GB/64162/64168/64568/65404/4429268.html> (accessed 9 January 2011).

74 H. H. Zhou (2007d) 'Woguo tuixing xinxi gongkai zhidu de yiyi yu tedian [Significance and Features of Introducing FOI Legislation in China]', *China Today Forum*, 6: 30.

75 W. P. Wen (2008) *Chinese Scholars Hail Government Information Transparency Regulations*, Online. Available HTTP: <http://en.chinaelections.org/newsinfo.asp? newsid=17678> (accessed 2 October 2008).

76 Blanton, op.cit., p.7; Ackerman and Sandoval-Ballesteros, op.cit., p.121. Snell would argue that New Zealand was a particular and important exception to this assertion. See Snell (2000), op.cit., p.583.

77 A. Roberts (2008) *Freedom of Information: From Millions to Billions*, Online. Available HTTP: <http://www.sunshineweek.org/sunshineweek/roberts08> (accessed 2 October 2008).

78 H. H. Zhou (2008a) Speech delivered at Seminar on the Challenges and Possibilities for Government Information Disclosure, Beijing, 25 June. Horsley states that 'the primary motivating force is domestic dynamics'. See Horsley (2007b), op.cit., p.54.

79 The State Council Informatization Office (2002) *Zhengfu xinxi gongkai tiaoli (cao an) qicao shuoming [Explanation Memorandum of the Draft of FOI Regulations 2002]*, Beijing: The State Council Informatization Office, p.23.

80 Y. He (2004) 'The Speech of Yong He at the Second Meeting of the Leading Group on National Openness in Government Affairs', speech delivered at Beijing, 29 April.

81 Gradualism refers to the belief that changes occur, or ought to occur, slowly in the form of gradual steps. The gradual approach is a key element of Dengism that is a series of political and economic ideologies first developed by Chinese political leader Xiaoping Deng. This theory was written into the CPC's *Party Constitution* and the preface of the *Constitution* in 1999. See X. P. Deng (1994a) *Deng Xiaoping wenxuan (dier juan)[Selected Works of Xiaoping Deng (Volume II)]*, 2nd edn, Beijing: People's Press, p.168; X. P. Deng (1994b) *Deng Xiaoping wenxuan (disan juan)[Selected Works of Xiaoping Deng (Volume III)]*, 2nd edn, Beijing: People's Press, p.285.

82 The use of the term push and pull to differentiate models of FOI legislation comes from the work of Kubicek and Paterson. See H. Kubicek (2004) 'Third-Generation

Freedom of Information in the Context of E-Government: The Case of Bremen, Germany', in G. Aichholzer and H. Burkert (eds) *Public Sector Information in the Digital Age: Between Markets, Public Management and Citizens' Rights*, Cheltenham: Edward Elgar Publishing, p.280; M. Paterson (2005) *Freedom of Information and Privacy in Australia*, Sydney: LexisNexis Butterworths, p.498. There is a common use of the terms pull and push in Australia, led by the FOI Independent Review Panel chaired by David Solomon. See The FOI Independent Review Panel (2008) *The Right to Information: Reviewing Queensland's Freedom of Information Act*, Online. Available HTTP: <http://www.foireview.qld.gov.au/documents_for_download/FOI-review-report-10062008.pdf> (accessed 9 January 2011). The discussion paper of Queensland's FOI legislation also agreed on the use of this term. See The FOI Independent Review Panel (2009) *Enhanced Open and Accountable Government: Review of the Freedom of Information Act 1992*, Online. Available HTTP: <http://www.foireview.qld.gov.au/FOIDiscussionpaper240108.pdf> (accessed 9 January 2011).

83 The economic terms supply and demand developed by Marshall for market analysis are used here to help form a clear description of the situation of information flow from the government to the public. Supply and demand are two ways of information flow. The supply side refers to the government which controls and releases information, and the demand side refers to the public which receives information. See A. Marshall (1920) *Principles of Economics*, 8th edn, London: Macmillan and Co., pp.323–503.

84 The FOI Independent Review Panel, op.cit; Tasmanian Department of Justice, op.cit.

85 X. S. Yang (2007) 'Subsidiary Report on Learning FOI Regulations', speech delivered at Conference on Learning FOI Regulations, Beijing, 17 May.

86 Darch and Underwood, op.cit., p.119.

87 Snell (2006), op.cit., p.298.

88 C. Darch and P. Underwood (2005) 'Freedom of Information Legislation, State Compliance and the Discourse of Knowledge: The South African Experience', *International Information and Library Review*, 37: 80.

89 Ibid.

90 Roberts (1998), op.cit. In 2002, Roberts developed government non-compliance or bureaucratic resistance and classified it into two categories: formal and informal ones. See A. Roberts (2002) 'New Strategies for Enforcement of the *Access to Information Act*', *Queen's Law Journal*, 27: 650–659; A. Roberts (2006b) 'Dashed Expectations: Governmental Adaptation to Transparency Rules', in C. Hood and D. Heald (eds) *Transparency: The Key to Better Governance?* Oxford: Oxford University Press, pp.109–117. Other scholars, such as Pasquier and Vileneuve, also established a typology to observe bureaucratic resistance to FOI legislation. See M. Pasquier and J. P. Vileneuve (2006) 'The Totally Transparent Administration: Radical Change or Bureaucratic Illusion?', paper presented at Conference on Public Managers under Pressure between Politics, Professionalism and Civil Society, Milan, 6 September.

91 R. Snell (1999) 'Administrative Compliance and Freedom of Information in Three Jurisdictions: Australia, Canada and New Zealand', paper presented at Conference on Freedom of Information: One Year on, Dublin, 23 April; Snell (2001), op.cit; Snell (2002), op.cit.

92 A. Delagrave (2001) *Creating a Culture of Openness & Transparency*, Online. Available HTTP: <http://www.atirtf-geai.gc.ca/speeches/london01-e.html> (accessed 18 August 2009).

93 Roberts (2006), op.cit., pp.107–123.

94 Darch and Underwood (2009), op.cit., p.119.

95 Roberts (2006), op.cit., pp.107–116.

96 The information asymmetry theory developed by Nobel Prize winners like Stiglitz can be used to illustrate this agency problem. Stiglitz argues that 'even seemingly public-spirited public servants often engage in secrecy'. See J. Stiglitz (2002) 'Transparency in Government', in the World Bank (ed.) *The Right to Tell: The Role of Mass Media in Economic Development*, Washington: World Bank Publications, pp.34–35; J. Stiglitz (1999) 'On Liberty, the Right to Know, and Public Discourse: The Role of Transparency in Public Life', speech delivered at Oxford Amnesty Lecture, Oxford, 27 January. Sociological theories of bureaucracy developed by Weber, Marx and others can also be used to explain the negative administration of FOI. FOI scholars, such as Darch, Underwood and Terrill, have already pointed out this. See Darch and Underwood (2009), op.cit., pp.91–98 and Terrill, op.cit., p.60.

97 Missen, op.cit.,p.42; S. Brown (2000) 'Freedom of Information', paper presented at Seminar on Freedom of Information – A Cultural Perspective, Canberra, 21 February. The Australian Commonwealth Ombudsman found, for instance, that 'a number of agencies were displaying an apparent disregard of, or apathy toward, the provisions of the FOI Act'. See The Australian Commonwealth Ombudsman (1997) *Annual Report 1996–1997*, Canberra: The Australian Commonwealth Ombudsman, p.75.

98 Roberts (2006), op.cit., pp.116–122.

99 J. Herman (2004) 'The Urgent Need for Reform of Freedom of Information in Australia', speech delivered at Conference on Public Right to Know, Sydney, 21 August 2004; K. Chongkittavorn (2001) 'Thai Journalists and Access to Information', paper presented at Conference on Freedom of Information and Civil Society in Asia, Tokyo, 13–14 April; Snell (2002), op.cit., pp.198–199.

100 The practices include long processing time, high fees, wholesale redactions and sweeping exemptions. See S. James (2006) 'The Potential Benefits of Freedom of Information', in R. Chapman and M. Hunt (eds) *Open Government in a Theoretical and Practical Context*, Surrey: Ashgate Publishing, pp.27–28; M. Rosenbaum (2004) 'Open to Question – Journalism and Freedom of Information', *Communications Law*, 9: 131; Lamble, op.cit., pp.100–102.

101 Snell (2006), op.cit., p.300.

102 Snell argues that the type of requesters is a key determinant of government compliance. Aggressive use of FOI legislation by the demand side drivers, journalists in particular, can only lead to a high level of non-compliance. See Snell (2006), op.cit., pp.298–299.

103 H. H. Zhou (2007a) 'Zhengfu xinxi gongkai tiaoli dailai liuda bianhua [FOI Regulations Will Bring about Six Changes]'. *People's Daily*, 14 February, p.13; S. Piotrowski, Y. H. Zhang, W. W. Lin and W. X. Yu (2009) 'Key Issues for Implementation of the Chinese Open Government Information Regulations', *Public Administration Review*, 69: 131.

104 Roberts (2006), op.cit., p.113.

105 Darch and Underwood (2009), op.cit., p.173.

106 P. Sebina (2006) 'Freedom of Information and Records Management: A Learning Curve for Botswana', unpublished thesis, University College London, p.190; R. Snell and P. Sebina (2007) 'Information Flows: The Real Art of Information Management and Freedom of Information', *Archives and Manuscripts*, 35: 73.

107 Roberts (2008), op.cit.

108 Zhou (2007d), op.cit., p.30.

109 Darch and Underwood (2009), op.cit., p.173.

110 Roberts (2008), op.cit.

111 Darch and Underwood (2009), op.cit., p.174.

112 Roberts (2006), op.cit., p.121; R. Callick, (2008) 'Chinese FOI Act Tied by Red Tape'. *The Australian*, 1 May, p.32.

113 Hubbard, op.cit., p.11.
114 Blanton, op.cit., p.7; Ackerman and Sandoval-Ballesteros, op.cit., p.115.
115 Roberts (2006), op.cit., p.110.
116 Hubbard, op.cit., p.5.
117 Horsley (2007a), op.cit.
118 J. Horsley (2003) *China's Pioneering Foray into Open Government: A Tale of Two Cities*, Online. Available HTTP: <http://www.freedominfo.org/news/20030714. htm> (accessed 23 August 2006); J. Horsley (2004) *Shanghai Advances the Cause of Open Government Information in China*, Online. Available HTTP: <http://www. freedominfo.org/news/20040420.htm> (accessed 23 August 2006); J. Horsley (2006) 'Introduction on Open Government Information Implementation', *Government Information Quarterly*, 23: 5–10.
119 There is no general consensus about the coverage of *Zhengwu Gongkai* in China. The coverage has been explained to include all openness practices implemented by any state agency and party apparatus. However, sometimes, the coverage has been interpreted to only include government agencies. See H. C. Lin (2008a) 'Zhengfu xinxi gongkai gaishu [An Overview of FOI]', in Y. C. Mo and H. C. Lin (eds) *Zhengfu xinxi gongkai tiaoli shiyi [Interpretations of China's FOI Regulations]*, Beijing: China Legal Publishing House, pp.35–37. While the coverage could be understood diversely, there is a consensus that *Zhengwu Gongkai* is a non legally-binding proactive way of information disclosure.
120 H. H. Zhou (2008b) 'Xinxi gongkai tiaoli chutai shimo [The Legislative History of FOI Regulations in China]', *E-Government*, 7: 16.
121 S. Wood, when discussing several articles on China's FOI development published by the *Government Information Quarterly*, states that:
China is perhaps not the first place that springs to mind when we think about FOI and Open Government, especially in general terms of freedom of expression and use of the Internet … Though it has to be emphasized that Open Government and Freedom of Information legislation are two different things, the former is more focused upon proactive, discretionary release of information, the latter on a presumptive right to know and right of access to all public information (with some exemptions) enshrined in law.
See S. Wood (2006) *Open Government in China*, Online. Available HTTP: <http:// foia.blogspot.com/2006/06/open-government-in-china-china-is.html> (accessed 21 August 2007).
122 The reason for Wood holding this viewpoint is that the term Open Government or Openness, as noted by Birkinshaw, 'has been used in a pejorative sense in the UK to avoid legal obligations of access to information'. See P. Birkinshaw (2006) 'Freedom of Information and Openness: Fundamental Human Rights', *Administrative Law Review*, 58: 190; D. Heald (2006) 'Varieties of Transparency', in C. Hood and D. Heald (eds) *Transparency: The Key to Better Governance?* Oxford: Oxford University Press, p.26; Freedom of Information Draft Bill, Public Administration Committee, HC 570, 3rd Report Session 1998–1999, HC 570-I, Para 28.
123 Zhou (ed.), op.cit., p.15; Lin, op.cit., p.58.

2 Information flow as an analytical device for FOI research

1 Information flow analysis presented in this book has been jointly developed with Rick Snell, Paul Hubbard and Rhys Stubbs. Their contributions are acknowledged.
2 C. Darch and P. Underwood (2005) 'Freedom of Information Legislation, State Compliance and the Discourse of Knowledge: The South African Experience', *International Information and Library Review*, 37: 80.

3 Darch and Underwood argue that the existing FOI literature is 'largely ... descriptive case studies' and 'relatively little in the way of comparative or theoretical analysis'. See C. Darch and P. Underwood (2009) *Freedom of Information and the Developing World: The Citizen, the State and Models of Openness*, Oxford: Chandos Publishing, p.50.

4 Darch and Underwood (2009), op.cit., p.50; R. Snell (2005) 'Using Comparative Studies to Improve Freedom of Information Analysis: Insights from Australia, Canada and New Zealand', paper presented at Sixth National and Second International Congress on the Right to Information, Mexico, 8–11 November.

5 Van de Donk and Snellen classify theory development into four key phases: concepts as mini theories, statements as prototheories, empirical generalizations as embryonic theories and more or less mature theories. See W. B. H. J. van de Donk and I. Th. M. Snellen (1998) 'Towards a Theory of Public Administration in an Information Age?' in I. Th. M. Snellen and W. B. H. J. van de Donk (eds) *Public Administration in an Information Age: A Handbook*, Fairfax: IOS Press, pp.3–8.

6 Darch and Underwood (2005), op.cit.

7 J. Lewis (2009) *FOIA Blog: Freedom of Information Laws and Policies*, Online. Available HTTP: <http://ww1.huntingdon.edu/jlewis/FOIA/FOIAlog.htm> (accessed 19 August 2009).

8 R. Snell (2006) 'Freedom of Information Practices', *Agenda*, 13: 300.

9 P Hubbard (2008b) *China's Regulations on Open Government Information: Challenges of Nationwide Policy Implementation*, Online. Available HTTP: <http://www.opengovjournal.org/article/viewArticle/2651> (accessed 22 July 2009).

10 D. North (1990) *Institutions, Institutional Change and Economic Performance*, New York: Cambridge University Press, p.vii. North received the Nobel memorial prize in 1993.

11 V. Lenin (1961b) *Lenin Collected Works (Volume 29)*, Moscow: Foreign Language Publishing House, 1961, p.473.

12 Stiglitz applied the theory of information asymmetry to FOI. See J. Stiglitz (2002) 'Transparency in Government', in the World Bank (ed.) *The Right to Tell: The Role of Mass Media in Economic Development*, Washington: World Bank Publications, pp.27–44; J. Stiglitz (1999) 'On Liberty, the Right to Know, and Public Discourse: The Role of Transparency in Public Life', speech delivered at Oxford Amnesty Lecture, Oxford, 27 January.

13 Such as Snell, Sebina and Hubbard. R. Snell and P. Sebina (2007) 'Information Flows: The Real Art of Information Management and Freedom of Information', *Archives and Manuscripts*, 35: 62–68; Snell, op.cit., pp.300–303; P. Hubbard (2004) 'Accountability in the Grey Area: Employing Stiglitz to Tackle Compliance in a World of Structural Pluralism: A Comparative Study', *Freedom of Information Review*, 111: 26–32; P. Hubbard (2005) *Freedom of Information and Security Intelligence: An Economic Analysis in an Australian Context*, Online. Available HTTP: <http://www.opengovjournal.org/article/viewArticle/334> (accessed 21 May 2009).

14 Snell, op.cit., p.300.

15 Ibid.

16 Hubbard (2004), op.cit., pp.26–32.

17 Snell, op.cit., p.300.

18 Ibid, 301.

19 Snell and Sebina, op.cit., pp.62–68; Snell, op.cit., pp. 300–303.

20 Taylor asks the question: '[w]hat is actually happening to the "information asymmetries" that exist between government and the citizen? Are they becoming narrower or wider in a contemporary polity characterized by both freedom *with* and freedom *of* information'. See J. Taylor (2006) 'Freedom *with* Information: Electronic Government, Information Intensity and Challenges to Citizenship' in

R. Chapman and M. Hunt (eds) *Open Government in a Theoretical and Practical Context*, Surrey: Ashgate Publishing, p.136.

21 J. Taylor (2007) 'Rediscovering the Grand Narratives of the Information Polity: Reflections on the Achievement and Potential of the EGPA Study Group on ICT in Public Administration', *Information Polity*, 12: 216; J. Taylor (1998b) 'Informatization as X-ray: What Is Public Administration for the Information Age?' in I. Th. M. Snellen and W. B. H. J. van de Donk (eds) *Public Administration in an Information Age: A Handbook*, Fairfax: IOS Press, p.31.

22 Taylor (2007), op.cit., p.216; Taylor (1998b), op.cit., p.31.

23 Taylor defines various sets of information relationships in the information polity, such as internal relationship in the machinery of government, consumer relationships and citizens relationships. Taylor (1998b), op.cit., pp.27–28.

24 J. Taylor (1998a) 'Governance and Electronic Innovation: Whither the Information Polity?' *Information Communication & Society*, 1: 159. Taylor defines the term information polity in the following two articles. See Taylor (2006), op.cit., p.136; J. Taylor (1999) 'The Information Polity', in W. Dutton (ed.) *Society on the Line: Information Politics in the Digital Age*, New York: Oxford University Press, p.198.

25 Taylor argues that '[t]he information polity encourages x-ray understanding of the body politic ... , enabling new evidence to be examined with new research questions, questions developed from theories and concepts utilized by orthodox studies of public administration'. See Taylor (2006), op.cit., p.136.

26 A. Roberts (2006a), *Blacked Out: Government Secrecy in the Information Age*, New York: Cambridge University Press, pp.116–120; Bookman and Amparan ask that: 'From which government entities are individuals requesting information? Who, exactly, is requesting information? How do people, physically, make requests? These issues are treated serially, with a final section devoted to the successes Mexico can boast of so far, and more importantly, to outstanding challenges to continued implementation.' See Z. Bookman and J. P. G. Amparan (2009) 'Two Steps Forward, One Step Back: Assessing the Implementation of Mexico's Freedom of Information Act', *Mexican Law Review*, 1: 32–49.

27 In particular, their work has been incorporated into government reports in Australia and Canada. See The FOI Independent Review Panel (2008) *The Right to Information: Reviewing Queensland's Freedom of Information Act*, Online. Available HTTP: <http://www.foireview.qld.gov.au/documents_for_download/FOI-review-report-100> (accessed 12 October 2009); The FOI Independent Review Panel (2009) *Enhanced Open and Accountable Government: Review of the Freedom of Information Act 1992*, Online. Available HTTP: <http://www.foireview.qld.gov.au/FOIDiscussionpaper240108.pdf> (accessed 9 January 2011); Tasmanian Department of Justice (2009) *Strengthening Trust in Government ... Everyone's Right to Know*, Online. Available HTTP: <http://www.justice.tas.gov.au/_data/assets/pdf_file/0005/118922/Strengthening-trust-in_Government–everyones_right_to_konw.pdf> (accessed 12 October 2009); The Access to Information Review Task Force (2002) *Access to Information: Making It Work for Canadians*, Online. Available HTTP: <http://www.atirtf-geai.gc.ca/accessReport-e.pdf> (accessed 28 August 2009).

28 Roberts postulates that substantial changes in information and communication technologies to produce and distribute information require new responses and ways of envisaging and managing a more extensive 'pool of digitized "unstructured data" held by government agencies'. See Roberts, op.cit., p.200. In a series of articles and presentations, Snell has followed up several themes and ideas outlined in Roberts' book and contrasted different information environments. See R. Snell (2007) 'Failing the Information Game', *Public Administration Today*, 10: 5–9; R. Snell (2008a) 'Opening up the Mindset Is Key to Change', *The Canberra*

Times, 4 November, pp.10–11; R. Snell (2008b) 'Releasing the Potential of FOI – Making the Transition from FOI Version 1.0 to FOI Version 2.0', speech delivered at the University of Tasmania Law School Staff Seminar, Hobart, 5 November. In Canada and Australia, particularly in the latter, a number of government reports have focused on treating FOI as part of the whole of government information policy, thus approaching information access by addressing capacity on both the supply and demand sides.

29 Snell has contrasted this static and physical conception of information to a more dynamic and multifaceted conception based around digital versions of information. See Snell (2007), op.cit. pp.5–9; Snell (2008a), op.cit. pp.10–11; Snell (2008b), op.cit.

30 The direction of transparency was inspired by Heald's work. Heald classifies directions of transparency into vertical and horizontal transparency. See D. Heald (2006) 'Varieties of Transparency' in C. Hood and D. Heald (eds) *Transparency: The Key to Better Governance?* Oxford: Oxford University Press, p.27.

31 FOI scholars, such as Sebina and Snell, have noticed the causal relationship between FOI and records management. See P. Sebina (2006) 'Freedom of Information and Records Management: A Learning Curve for Botswana', unpublished thesis, University College London; Snell and Sebina, op.cit., pp.54–81.

32 A. Marshall (1920) *Principles of Economics*, 8th edn, London: Macmillan and Co., pp.323–503.

33 M. Anthony (2000) 'The Relationship between Freedom of Expression and Freedom of Information' in J. Beatson and Y. Cripps (eds) *Freedom of Expression and Freedom of Information*, Oxford: Oxford University Press, p.240; L. Neuman and R. Calland (2007) 'Making the Law Work: The Challenges of Implementation', in A. Florini (ed.) *The Right to Know: Transparency for an Open World*, New York: Columbia University Press, p.181.

34 FOI experts like Snell use 'version 1.0' and 'version 2.0' to describe the pull and push models respectively. See Snell (2007), op.cit. pp.5–9; Snell (2008a), op.cit. pp.10–11; Snell (2008b), op.cit.

35 The Tasmanian Directions Paper classifies information disclosure into four levels or types: required, routine, active and assessed disclosure. Assessed disclosure is a type of information disclosure which is used to respond to access requests, and should be considered as a last resort. See Tasmanian Department of Justice, op. cit., pp.33–38.

36 Article 19 (1999) *Right to Know: Principles on Freedom of Information Legislation*, Online. Available HTTP: <http://www.article19.org/pdfs/standards/right-toknow.pdf> (accessed 1 July 2007); Article 19 (2001) *A Model Freedom of Information Law*, Online. Available HTTP: < http://www.article19.org/pdfs/standards/modelfoilaw.pdf> (accessed 18 August 2007).

37 This contrasts with the approach taken by the United Nations Educational Scientific and Cultural Organization, which also aids nations to develop 'effective "infostructures", including information standards and management tools', to facilitate implementation of FOI legislation. The United Nations Educational Scientific and Cultural Organization announces that it assists other states in creating an enabling environment to achieve universal access to information and knowledge.

38 A legalistic approach heavily relies on legal professionals as major advocates and on formal appeal processes to solve disputes, but an administrative approach does not. Guidelines, mediation, negotiation and personal communication may be used to solve a systematic problem or individual disputes. Snell in his comparative administrative law lecture discusses these two different approaches to implementing FOI. He considers that Mexico, New Zealand and Sweden have adopted an administrative approach, but the US has adopted a much more legalistic approach. Australia and the UK have adopted a hybrid of administrative and

legalistic approaches. See R. Snell (2009) 'Constructing a Field: Commonwealth FOI Studies', speech delivered at Comparative Administrative Law Lecture, Hobart, 7 August. Other scholars, like Clark hold a similar view. See D. Clark (1996) 'Open Government in Britain: Discourse and Practice', *Public Money & Management*, 1996, 16: 23.

39 The non-government organization, Involve, produced a paper, titled '*Open Government: Beyond Static Measures*' for Organization for Economic Co-operation and Development in July 2009. K. Gavelin (2009) 'Open Government–Beyond Static Measures Publication'. E-mail (19 August 2009); The Carter Centre developed a concept note, titled '*Access to Information Implementation Assessment Tool*' in August 2009 to lay stress on the government inputs to measure implementation of FOI legislation. L. Neuman (2009) 'The Assessment Indicator System'. E-mail (19 August 2009).

40 For example, T. Mendel (2008) 'Freedom of Information: A Comparative Legal Survey', 2nd edn, Paris: UNESCO.

41 German adopted its FOI legislation on 8 July 2005 and brought it into effect on 1 January 2006.

42 C. Bennett (2001) *Globalization and Access to Information Regimes*, Online. Available HTTP: <http://www.atirtf-geai.gc.ca/paper-globalization1-e.html> (accessed 30 January 2008).

43 See H. Kubicek (2004) 'Third-Generation Freedom of Information in the Context of E-Government: The Case of Bremen, Germany', in G. Aichholzer and H. Burkert (eds) *Public Sector Information in the Digital Age: Between Markets, Public Management and Citizens' Rights*, Cheltenham: Edward Elgar Publishing, p.275.

44 Darch and Underwood (2009), op.cit., p.80.

45 P. Birkinshaw (2006) 'Freedom of Information and Openness: Fundamental Human Rights', *Administrative Law Review*, 2006, 58: 188–190; D. Heald, op.cit., pp.25–26; Bookman and Amparan, op.cit., pp.20–22.

46 M. Hunt and R. Chapman (2006) 'Open Government and Freedom of Information', in R. Chapman and M. Hunt (eds) *Open Government in a Theoretical and Practical Context*, Surrey: Ashgate Publishing, p.1.

3 The improved information environment as a rationale for FOI reform in China

1 Social stability has been regarded by Chinese political leaders as a prerequisite for reform and development since the late 1970s. Chinese political leaders have stated that 'stability is of overriding importance' and 'nothing can be achieved without stability'. See X. P. Deng (1994b) *Deng Xiaoping wenxuan (disan juan) [Selected Works of Xiaoping Deng (Volume III)]*, 2nd edn, Beijing: People's Press, p. 364; Z. M. Jiang (1997) 'Gaoju Deng Xiaoping lilun weida qizhi ba jianshe you zhongguo tese shehuizhuyi shiye quanmian tuixiang ershiyi shiji [Hold High the Great Banner of Deng Xiaoping Theory for an All-round Advancement of the Cause of Building Socialism with Chinese Characteristics to the 21st Century]', speech delivered at the 15th National Congress of the CPC, Beijing, 12 September; J. T. Hu (2007) 'Gaoju zhongguo tese shehuizhuyi weida qizhi wei duoqu quanmian jianshe xiaokang shehui xin shengli er fendou [Hold High the Great Banner of Socialism with Chinese Characteristics and Strive for New Victories in Building a Moderately Prosperous Society in All Respects]', speech delivered at the 17th National Congress of the CPC, Beijing, 24 October.

2 Z. H. Lou (1991) *Renmin de xuanze [The Choice of the People]*, Beijing: China Youth Press, p.129.

3 H. Z. Li, a viceroy in the Qing Dynasty, serves as an example to illustrate this statement. Li was interviewed by a journalist in the *New York Times* in 1896. When asked whether China would introduce a newspaper system similar to that in the Western world, he answered that '[t]here are newspapers in China, but the Chinese editors, unfortunately, do not tell the truth. They do not, as your papers, tell "the truth, the whole truth, and nothing but the truth." The editors in China are great economizers of the truth; they tell only a part of it ... ' See *The New York Times* (1896) 'Li on American Hatred'. 3 September, p.10. In May 1896, Li visited Russia and took part in a coronation ceremony. When he saw many people in the crowd were crushed to death due to massive disorder, he asked Russia's Minister of Finance whether he would report everything he saw to his Emperor or not. The Minister said yes, but Li responded that according to his experience, he would not do the same thing and choose to conceal each bad thing he saw or knew from the emperor in order not to cause the emperor distress. See Q. J. Jia (2004) 'Li Hongzhang de jingyan jieshao [Introduction of Experience in Russia by Hongzhang Li]', *Insight China*, 8: 74.

4 Confucius (2000a) *Verse 18 of Chapter 2 in the Analects of Confucius*, Online. Available   HTTP: <http://www.guoxue.com/jinbu/13jing/lunyu/ly_002.htm> (accessed 10 January 2011).

5 X. Liu (n.d.) *Shuo Yuan (dishi juan)[The Garden of Stories (Chapter 10)]*, Online.   Available   HTTP: <http://www.shuku.net/novels/classic/shuoyuan/shuoyuan10.html> (accessed 10 January 2011).

6 Kong Guang is a good example to illustrate this point. Kong Guang, a former official working in *Shanshu* authority, was known as a very cautious and secretive person who learned from the ideas of his ancestor, Confucius. When one of his friends once asked him about what kinds of trees were planted in front of his office, he ignored this question and changed the subject immediately. *Shanshu* was responsible for delivering official documents between the emperor and senior officials. See G. Ban (2000) *Han shu: kongguang zhuang [The Book of Han: The Biography of Kong Guang]*, Online. Available HTTP: <http://www.guoxue.com/shibu/24shi/hansu/hsuml.htm> (accessed 10 January 2011).

7 Deng, op.cit., p.382.

8 F. Yi (2007) *Buyao wudu le xiaoping tongzhi de duozuo shaoshuo [Don't Misunderstand Deng's Warning on 'Saying Less and Doing More']*, Online. Available HTTP: <http://news.xinhuanet.com/comments/2007–&02/09;/content_5712689.htm> accessed 23 March 2009).

9 Z. C. Li (2003) 'Zhengfu xinxi gongkai yu baozhang zhiqingquan de guanxi [The Relationship between FOI and the Right to Know]', *News Knowledge*, 10: 16.

10 China Central Television (2007b) *Wang guoqing: xinwen fayanren gang jige [Guoqing Wang Talks about the Spokesperson System]*, Online. Available HTTP: <http://news.cctv.com/china/20070713/109210.shtml> (accessed 7 August 2007).

11 The disaster occurred in Nandan on 17 July 2001, causing 81 fatalities. The leadership in Nandan County decided to hide this catastrophe through various methods after they became aware of this disaster. They also reported inaccurate information to the superior government. They considered that the fact of this disaster was impossible to be discovered. The disaster was finally exposed by courageous journalists from *People's Daily*. The major players in this scandal were all punished severely. The Secretary of CPC Nandan County Committee was executed. See X. H. Huang, W. B. Fei and J. Huang (2004) 'Wo shi ge bu zhong bu xiao de ren [I Am an Ungrateful and Disloyal Man]'. *People's Court Daily*, 21 February, p.4; G. Z. Ren. (2002) *Nandai teda kuangnan jiqi jingshi [The Mine Water Leakage Accident in Nandan County and Its Lessons]*, Online. Available HTTP: <http://www.people.com.cn/GB/shehui/212/6048/6320/20020109/644953.html> (accessed 15 April 2008).

12 According to Peterson and Gist, rumour means 'an unverified account or explanation of events, circulating from person to person and pertaining to an object, event or issue of public concern'. See W. Peterson and G. Noel (1951) 'Rumour and Public Opinion', *The American Journal of Sociology*, 57: 159. The term rumour in this book is used to refer unverified explanation for crises that can affect social stability. Allport and Postman argue that the quantity of rumours in circulation depends on two factors: the importance of the news and the ambiguity of the evidence. The secretive and reactive approach contributes to the second factor. See G. Allport and J. Postman (1947) *The Psychology of Rumour*, New York: Russell & Russell Pub., p.34.

13 Zhou argues that 'even a minor rumour can lead to turmoil in the whole society'. See H. H. Zhou (2007c) 'Open Government in China: Practice and Problems', in A. Florini (ed.) *The Right to Know: Transparency for an Open World*, New York: Columbia University Press, p.106.

14 McQuail first argued that one role of the media was as a filter or gatekeeper. See D. McQuail (2005) *McQuail's Mass Communication Theory*, 5th edn, California: Saga Publications Ltd., p.83.

15 L. D. Chen and J. N. Chen (2005) 'Songhuajiang shuiwuran shijian zhong xinxiliu zhangai fenxi [On Impediments to Information Flow during the Crisis of the Songhuajiang River Contamination]', *Press Circles*, 6: 21. This paternalistic approach was also previously favoured by some Western governments. Meijer observes that the Netherlands governments 'were not used to open communication about risks. Before the fireworks factory exploded in the year 2000, many local governments argued that it was better to not actively inform citizens about risks in their direct environment since this could lead to irrational fear in their communities. The general opinion was that governments should take appropriate measures and develop plans to protect citizens against risks, but citizens did not have to know about these risks. The general attitude was a paternalistic one.' See A. J. Meijer (2005) 'Risk Maps on the Internet: Transparency and the Management of Risks', *Information Polity*, 10: 107.

16 The term parent officials was used to call on officials to parent the people they ruled. This is a political heritage of Confucianism with a slight change in today's China.

17 Confucius (2000b) *Verse 9 of Chapter 8 in the Analects of Confucius*, Online. Available HTTP: <http://www.guoxue.com/jinbu/13jing/lunyu/ly_008.htm> (accessed 10 January 2011).

18 Daoism refers to a wide range of Chinese philosophical and religious concepts and had a strong influence on Chinese in ancient China. *Dao* refers to the way. The core concept of Daoism is *Wu Wei*, which means that let nature take its course.

19 Z. Lao (2000) *Daodejing di liushiwu zhang [Chapter 65 in Moral Intelligence]*, Online. Available HTTP: <http://www.guoxue.com/zibu/zibu_zhuziml/laozi.htm> (accessed 10 January 2011).

20 This was the first time for China to make criminal law public. Q. M. Zuo (2000) *Chunqiu zuozhuan zhao gong liu nian [Year 6 of Emperor Zhao in the Commentary on the Spring and Autumn Annals]*, Online. Available HTTP: <http://www.guoxue.com/jinbu/13jing/cqzz/cqzz_010.htm> (accessed 10 January 2011).

21 In November 2005, the Songhuajiang River was contaminated with toxic benzene emitted by explosions at a chemical plant in Jilin Province. This resulted in several days' shutdown of water supplies to the downstream city of Harbin. To conceal the real reason, the Harbin government initially told a white lie to the residents that the shutdown was caused by routine repairs on pipes. Zuoji Zhang, the former Governor of Heilongjiang Province, confessed that one major reason for doing so was the government's worry about low endurance of the public. See X. Gao, K. Y. Li and Y. Yuan (2005) *Zhang Zuoji: wo shi shengzhang ye shi*

baixing [Zuoji Zhang: I am the Governor and Citizen as Well], Online. Available HTTP: <http://politics.people.com.cn/GB/1026/3893203.html> (accessed 20 May 2009).

22 Chen and Chen, op.cit., p.21.

23 D. L. Sheng (2008) 'Xijian mingan shijian buzai wugaizi [It Is Encouraging to Find That the Government Has Not Covered up Sensitive Events]'. *Qilu Evening*, 19 November, p.A2.

24 Y. C. Mo, (2008) 'Quanli ruhe caineng zai yangguang xia liangxing yunxing [How Can Power Be Exercised Well in a Transparent Way]'. *Legal Daily*, 13 February, p.3.

25 Z. D. Mao (1983) *Mao zedong xinwen gongzuo wenxuan [Selected Works of Zedong Mao on Journalism]*, Beijing: Xinhua Publishing, p.193.

26 Ibid.

27 G. M. Yu (2003) 'Baozhang renmin de zhiqingquan shi jiangou guojia xinxi anquan tizhi de genben yuanze [Guaranteeing the People's Right to Know Is the Fundamental Principle for Building the State's Information Security System]', *Practical Journalism*, 6: 27.

28 The death toll of the Tangshan earthquake in 1976 was not disclosed to the public until 17 November 1979, when it was revealed there were over 240,000 fatalities. See X. J. Xu (1979) 'Tangshan dizhen siwang 24 wan duo ren [Death Toll of the Tangshan Earthquake Is More Than 240,000]'. *People's Daily*, 23 November. The death toll of the Tonghai earthquake, which occurred in 1970, was not publicized until 5 January 2000 on its 30th anniversary. The number topped 15,621. See *Digest* (2000) 'Tonghai dadizhen sanshi nianhou jiemi [The Tonghai Earthquake Was Declassified after 30 Years]'. 16 January, p.3. The epidemic of Hepatitis A virus in Shanghai occurred in 1988, infecting 292,301 individuals. The media was not allowed to report it during that period. See M. D. Cheng (2008) *Toushi dangdai zhongguo zhongda tufa shijian [Reflection on Major Crises in Contemporary China]*, Beijing: Chinese Communist Party History Publishing House.

29 Sociologists, such as M. Castells and J. V. Dijk, developed the idea of a 'network society' which refers to 'a society where the key social structures and activities are organized around electronically processed information networks'. See H. Kreisler (2001) Interview with M. Castells (Berkeley, 9 May) and J. V. Dijk (2006) *The Network Society: Social Aspects of New Media*, 2nd edn, California: Sage Publications Ltd., p.20. Castells argues that there is no centre in an ideal network society, which 'works on a binary logic: inclusion/exclusion. All there is in the network is useful and necessary for the existence of the network'. See M. Castells (2000) 'Materials for an Exploratory Theory of the Network Society', *British Journal of Sociology*, 51: 15.

30 The notion of agenda-setting was first formulated in a precise form and tested by Maxwell McCombs and Donald Shaw. See M. McCombs and D. Shaw (1972) 'The Agenda-Setting Function of Mass Media', *Public Opinion Quarterly*, 36: 176–187. Cohen argues that '[t]he press may not be successful much of the time in telling people what to think, but it is stunningly successful in telling its readers what to think about'. See B. Cohen (1963) *The Press and Foreign Policy*, Princeton: Princeton University Press, p.120.

31 The World Bank defines e-government as 'the use by government agencies of information technologies (such as Wide Area Networks, the Internet, and mobile computing) that have the ability to transform relations with citizens, businesses, and other arms of government'. See The World Bank (n.d.) *Definition of E-Government*, Online. Available HTTP : http://web.worldbank.org (accessed 14 September 2009).

32 *Woguo zhengfu xinxi hua de fazhan licheng [The Development of Government Informatization in China]* (2003), Online. Available HTTP: <http://www.china.com.cn/chinese/zhuanti/283258.htm> (accessed 19 May 2008).

33 Golden Bridge is the infrastructure for informatizing the national economy. Golden Customs is used to create an integrated data communications system connecting foreign trade companies, banks, and customs and tax agencies. Golden Card aims at creating a unified payment clearance system to allow the widespread use of credit and debit cards across the whole country. See P. Lovelock and J. Ure (2002) 'Assessing China's Efforts in Constructing an E-Government', in J. H. Zhang and M. Woesler (eds) *China's Digital Dream*, Bochum: European University Press, p.152.

34 The *Guidance on the Leading Group of National Informatization for China's E-Government Construction* No 17 [2002] of the General Office of the CPC Central Committee.

35 Cheng argues that the government online project and the like have caused the government to be more observable, and this has prompted the government to encourage communication and consensus in order to adapt to the changed information environment. See J. Cheng (2002) 'Zouxiang kaifang shehui: zhongguo gonggong xinxi huoqu yu zhengwu gongkai zhidu zhi jiantao [Toward Open Society: Examination on Policies Concerning Access to Public Information and Openness in Government Affairs]', *Tsinghua Forum of Rule of Law*, 3: 473.

36 Taylor argues that information and communication technologies 'bring a *networking logic* into the organizational world'. See J. Taylor (1998b) 'Informatization as X-ray: What Is Public Administration for the Information Age?' in I. Th. M. Snellen and W. B. H. J. van de Donk (eds) *Public Administration in an Information Age: A Handbook*, Fairfax: IOS Press, p.24.

37 Castells defines information networks as 'social networks which process and manage information ... using micro-electronic based technologies'. He argues that information networks are 'the predominant organizational form' and 'the backbone of the network society'. See Castells, op.cit., pp.16–17.

38 W. Z. Wu and X. H. Li (2006) 'Loudong jianguan zhong de muzhi chuanbo [Weak Supervision of the Short Message Communication]', *Journal of Harbin University*, 12: 88.

39 Ren, op.cit. *People's Daily* Online was launched by *People's Daily* in 1997 to disseminate news about China.

40 The video was first posted to Tudou, similar to Youtube. It had roughly 1.8 million hits and was forwarded by international media groups, such as CNN and BTV.

41 D. Bambauer, R. Deibert, J. Palfrey, R. Rohozinski, N. Villeneuve and J. Zittrain (2005) *Internet Filtering in China in 2004–2005: A Country Study*, Online. Available HTTP: <http://cyber.law.harvard.edu/publications/2005/Internet_Filtering_in_China_in_2004_2005> (accessed 6 January 2010). H. Margetts (2006) 'Transparency and Digital Government', in C. Hood and D. Heald (eds) *Transparency: The Key to Better Governance?* Oxford: Oxford University Press, p.199.

42 J. Gittings (2005) *The Changing Face of China: From Mao to Market*, New York: Oxford University Press, pp. 8–9.

43 Ibid.

44 H. X. Zhu, J. C. Hu, and W. T. Sun (2008) '2007 zhongguo hulianwang yuqing fenxi baogao [Analysis Report on Public Opinions on the Internet in China in 2007]', *Today's Mass Media*, 2: 36.

45 Castells argues that '[t]he only way to control the network is not to be into it, and this is a high price to pay for any institution or organization once the network becomes pervasive and channels all kinds of information around the world'. See M. Castells (1996) *The Rise of the Network Society*, Cambridge: Blackwell Publishers, p.352.

46 Castells (2000), op.cit., p.12.

47 The SARS crisis occurred in China between November 2002 and August 2003, causing 5,327 individuals infected with SARS and 349 fatalities. According to the Guangdong Mobile Communication Co., Ltd., there were 40 million text messages on 8 February 2003, with an increase of one million on the next day, and five million on 10 February. Most of these text messages were related to the outbreak of an unidentified fatal flu. See G. Q. Yun and P. Lv (2003) *Yi SARS yiqing weili kan chuanmei yu zhengfu de guanxi [The Relationship between the Media and the Government: Taking the Example of the SARS Incident]*, Online. Available HTTP: <http://www.cuhk.edu.hk/ics/21c/supplem/essay/0304069.htm> (accessed 21 April 2008).
48 Gittings, op.cit., pp.8–9.
49 M. Qiao (2008) 'Shouji duanxin de chuanbo xiaoguo yu zhengzhi yingxiang [The Communication Effect and Political Impact of SMS Messages]', *Contemporary Communications*, 4: 76.
50 L. Lan (2005) 'Open Government and Transparency Policy: China's Experience with SARS', *International Public Management Review*, 6: 63.
51 Ibid.
52 S. Li (2008) 'Zhonghua renmin gongheguo xinxi gongkai tiaoli de zhiding beijing zhuyao neirong ji mulu bianzhi [The Background, Main Contents and Inventory Compilation concerning China's FOI Regulations]', *E-Government*, 5: 22.
53 China Central Television, op.cit.
54 China now has the largest size of netizens since June 2008, reaching 253 million. See China Internet Network Information Centre (2008) *The 22nd Statistical Survey Report on the Internet Development in China*, Online. Available HTTP: <http://www.cnnic.cn/download/2008/CNNIC22threport-en.pdf> (accessed 28 November 2008).
55 W. Crano (1977) 'Primacy versus Recency in Retention of Information and Opinion Change', *Journal of Social Psychology*, 101: 89.
56 Such as QQ, MSN and Bulletin Board System. QQ is the most popular free instant messaging computer program in China. The number of current users is about 340 million.
57 X. Hao (2006) 'Shouji duanxin: diwu meiti de chuanbo qianli yu fazhan wenti [SMS Messages – The Communication Potential and Development Problems of "the Fifth Medium"]', *Southeast Communication*, 1: 15.
58 Castells argues that 'in a society organized around mass media, the existence of messages that are outside the media is restricted to interpersonal networks, thus disappearing from the collective mind'. See Castells (1996), op.cit., p.336.
59 Hao, op.cit., p.15.
60 Y. H. Zhang (2008) 'Shouji duanxin chuangbo zhong de kongzhi queshi yu duice [The Incapability of Controlling the Transmission of SMS Messages and the Solutions]', *News Window*, 1: 105.
61 Qiao, op.cit., p.77.
62 *Southern Daily* (2007) 'Xinxi gongkai shi xiandai gongmin shehui de qianzou [FOI Is the Prelude to Civil Society]'. 15 February, p.A02.
63 The Centre for International Communications Studies of Tsinghua University (2005) 'Zhongguo zhengfu zhizheng nengli yu xinwen fayanren zhidu jianshe [The Ruling Capability of the Chinese Government and the Institutionalization of Spokesperson Systems]', *Today's Mass Media*, 8: 7.
64 The *Decision of the CPC Central Committee on Strengthening the Building of the Party's Ruling Capability* No 18 [2004] of the Central Committee of the CPC. The Chinese government has recognized the importance of guidance of public opinion since the political turmoil of 1989. Jiang states that 'correct guidance of public opinion is good for both the Party and the people'; and incorrect guidance is potentially disastrous for both. See Z. M. Jiang (2006) *Jiang Zemin wenxuan*

(diyi juan) *[Selected Works of Zemin Jiang (Volume I)]*, Beijing: People's Press, p.563. President Hu reiterates this importance, cautioning that 'correct guidance benefits the Party, the nation and the people'; and incorrect guidance, in turn, is prone to injuring all of them. See J. T. Hu, (2008) 'Zai shicha renmin ribaoshe de jianghua [Speech Delivered at the Visit to *People's Daily*]'. *People's Daily*, 20 June, p.4.

65 Li, op.cit., pp.22–23.
66 Hu, op.cit., p.4.
67 W. Cai (2005) Speech delivered at the Fourth National Spokespersons Training Session, Beijing, 2 December.
68 Y. W. Ou (2007) Speech delivered at Seminar on the FOI Regulations, Beijing, 17 March.
69 Such as Professor Hanhua Zhou and Datong Li. Professor Hanhua Zhou, a key member of drafting China's FOI legislation, held this view when he was interviewed by a newspaper reporter of *China Youth Daily*. See Y. J. Wang (2007) 'Zhengfu xinxi gongkai tiaoli shinian pobing [The Breakthrough of Legislating on FOI after a Decade]'. *China Youth Daily*, 25 April, p.3. Datong Li, a Chinese journalist, also held the similar view. See D. T. Li. (2007) *An End to Exclusivity*, Online. Available HTTP: <http://www.opendemocracy.net/node/4585> (accessed 7 March 2009). Darch and Underwood agreed with Li on this. C. Darch and P. Underwood (2009) *Freedom of Information and the Developing World: The Citizen, the State and Models of Openness*, Oxford: Chandos Publishing, p.178.
70 H. H. Zhou (2007e) Speech delivered at Seminar on the FOI Regulations, Beijing, 17 March.
71 *Freedom of Information Regulations 2007*. Art.6.
72 China Central Television, op.cit.
73 Ibid. By 26 September 2006, about 70 ministries and commissions of the State Council and 31 provincial governments had appointed their own spokespersons.
74 B. Song and W. Liu (2008) 'Zhongguo xinwen fayanren zhidu rizhen wanshan [Gradual Perfection of the Spokesperson System in China]'. *People's Daily Overseas Edition*, 7 November, p.1.
75 *Freedom of Information Regulations 2007*. Art.15.
76 Zhou (2007e), op.cit.
77 Lovelock and Ure, op.cit., p.152.
78 The State Council Informatization Office (2006) *Zhongguo xinxihua fazhan baogao [Informatization Development Report in China]*, Online. Available HTTP: <http://www.e-gov.org.cn/ziliaoku/news003/200606/28025.html> (accessed 22 June 2007).
79 China Internet Network Information Centre (2007) *The 19th Statistical Survey Report on the Internet Development in China*, Online. Available HTTP: <http://www.cnnic.net.cn/download/2007/cnnic19threport.pdf> (accessed 7 August 2008).
80 *Overall Framework of National E-Government* No 2 [2006] of the State Council Informatization Office.
81 *Rules on the Scope of State Secrets and Secrecy Levels in the Work of Civil Affairs* No 17 [2000] of the Ministry of Civil Affairs.
82 *Notice on Declassifying Death Tolls from Natural Disasters and the Related Information* No 116 [2005] of the Ministry of Civil Affairs.
83 *Regulations on Preparedness for and Response to Emergent Public Health Hazards 2003*. Art.25.
84 *Prevention and Cure of Infectious Diseases Law 1989*. Art.38.
85 *Criminal Law 1997*. Art.139.
86 H. H. Zhou (2007a) 'Zhengfu xinxi gongkai tiaoli dailai liuda bianhua [FOI Regulations Will Bring about Six Changes]'. *People's Daily*, 14 February, p.13.
87 China Central Television, op.cit.

88 Ibid.
89 H. Qin (2007) Speech delivered at Seminar on the FOI Regulations, Beijing, 17 March.
90 Margetts, op.cit, p.199. Cuillier and Piotrowski also assert that 'reliance on the internet for information was positively associated with support for access to public records'. See D. Cuillier and S. Piotrowski (2009) 'Internet Information-Seeking and Its Relation to Support for Access to Government Records', *Government Information Quarterly*, 26: 441.

4 The improved information environment as a rationale for FOI reform in China

1 H. H. Zhou (2008b) 'Xinxi gongkai tiaoli chutai shimo [The Legislative History of FOI Regulations in China]', *E-Government*, 7: 15.
2 A. Roberts (2008) *Freedom of Information: From Millions to Billions*, Online. Available HTTP: <http://www.sunshineweek.org/sunshineweek/roberts08> (accessed 2 October 2008).
3 Mendel states that '[f]or elections to fulfil their proper function ... the electorate must have access to information'. See T. Mendel (2008) 'Freedom of Information: A Comparative Legal Survey', 2nd edn, Paris: UNESCO, p. 4.
4 C. Darch and P. Underwood (2009) *Freedom of Information and the Developing World: The Citizen, the State and Models of Openness*, Oxford: Chandos Publishing, p.51.
5 See Article 19 of the *Universal Declaration of Human Rights*.
6 Article 19 of the *International Covenant on Civil and Political Rights* and Article 13 (1) of the *American Convention on Human Rights* are alike to the expression found in Articles 19 of the *Universal Declaration of Human Rights*.
7 P. Sebina (2006) 'Freedom of Information and Records Management: A Learning Curve for Botswana', unpublished thesis, University College London, 68.
8 Report of the Special Rapporteur (1998) *Promotion and Protection of the Right to Freedom of Opinion and Expression*, E/CN.4/1998/40, New York: 28 January, Para 14.
9 The Commonwealth Human Rights Initiative (2003) *Open Sesame: Looking for the Right to Information in the Commonwealth*, Online. Available HTTP: <http://www.humanrightsinitiative.org/publications/chogm/chogm_2003/chogm%202003%20report.pdf> (accessed 25 May 2007).
10 Information Clearinghouse Japan (2002) *Breaking down the Walls of Secrecy: The Story of the Citizen's Movement for an Information Disclosure Law*, Online. Available HTTP: <http://www.freedominfo.org/features/20020727.htm> (accessed 26 July 2008).
11 *S.P. Gupta v President of India and others etc.* AIR 1982 SC 149.
12 *Forests Survey Inspection Request* Case, 1 KCCR 176, 88Hun-Ma22, September 4, 1989; *Military Secret Leakage* Case KCCR 64, 89Hun-Ka104, February 25, 1992.
13 Inter-American Court of Human Rights, *Claude Reyes et al v Chile Judgment* of September 19, 2006. The Inter-American Court of Human Rights was 'the first international tribunal to recognise a basic right of access to government information as an element of the right to freedom of expression'. See The Open Society Justice Initiative (2007) *Claude et al v Chile*, Online. Available HTTP: <http://www.justiceinitiative.org/db/resource2?res_id=102628> (accessed 1 March 2009); The European Court of Human Rights followed suit recently in the cases of *Társaság a Szabadságjogokért v Hungary* No 37374/05 § 27, 14.4.2009 and *Kenedi v Hungary* No 31475/05 § 45, 26.5.2009.

14 A. Roberts (2001) 'Structural Pluralism and the Right to Information', *University of Toronto Law Journal*, 51, 259.

15 Sebina, op.cit., p.67.

16 Mason states that '[t]he two freedoms are often mentioned in the same breath, so to speak, as if they are so closely connected or intertwined that one [FOI] is part or counterpart of the other [Freedom of Expression]'. See A. Mason (2000) 'The Relationship between Freedom of Expression and Freedom of Information', in J. Beatson and Y. Cripps (eds) *Freedom of Expression and Freedom of Information*, Oxford: Oxford University Press, 2000, p.225; Sebina, op.cit. The term freedom of information used by Besley and other scholars to analyse the Chinese famine of 1959 and 1961 was synonymous with the idea of a free and independent press. Besley and other scholars observe that 'investigators have pointed to China's lack of democracy and of *freedom of information* [emphasis added] as reasons why it experienced a major famine between 1958 and 1961, with excess mortality figures ranging between 16.5 and 29.5 million'. See T. Besley, R. Burgess, and A. Prat (2002) 'Mass Media and Political Accountability', in the World Bank (ed.) *The Right to Tell: The Role of Mass Media in Economic Development*, Washington: World Bank Publications, p.53.

17 Glasnost, a key term introduced by Gorbachev, could be translated as transparency, but 'the term lends itself to more than one interpretation' because it could 'mean something close to freedom of information and freedom of speech'. Gorbachev said in December 1984 that: '[a]n inalienable component of socialist democracy is glasnost'. See A. Brown (1997) *The Gorbachev Factor*, New York: Oxford University Press, p.125. After Gorbachev became the national leader in 1985, he conducted transparency reform that allowed all information concerning state and government activities to be disclosed and debated in public. See H. Li (2004) 'Zhengzhi gongkaixing: yiyi quexian yu qidi [Political Publicity: Significance, Pitfalls and Inspiration]', *Nanjing Social Science*, 8: 45.

18 H. C. Chen (2003) *Zhengque bawo shenji dingwei tuidong shengji gongzuo xin fazhan [Setting up a Correct Role for Audits to Promote New Development of Audit Work]*, Online. Available HTTP: <http://www.audit.gov.cn/n1057/n1072/n1342/14784.html> (accessed 5 May 2008).

19 Z. L. Huang (2004) 'Jiejian guowai zhizhengdang jingyan jiaoxun jiaqiang dan de zhizheng nengli jianshe [Learning Experiences and Lessons from Ruling Parties in Foreign Countries to Strengthen the Building of Governance Capabilities of the CPC]', *Journal of the Party School of Tianjin Committee of the CPC*, 4: 43; D. C. Cui (2000) 'Eluosi gaige luoru le minzhuhua xianjin (Shang) [The Russian Reform Fell into the Trap of Democratization (Pt 1)]', *China National Conditions and Strength*, 2: 34; T. Y. Li (2002) 'Zai dangdai zhongguo yanjiusuo chunjie zuotanhui shang de jianghua [A Speech at the Spring Festival Forum Held by the Contemporary China Institute]', *Contemporary China History Studies*, 2: 5.

20 Chen, op.cit.

21 Zhou recalled that in 2002 he was invited to assist the editors of China Central Television in reflecting back on their past five years of work for a famous programme – News Probe – to celebrate their achievement. They intended to use the title *You Have the Right to Know* for the retrospective programme, but one leader cancelled the programme without hesitation after he had only glanced at this seemingly sensitive title, and asked one of the editors that 'do you know the reason of the former Soviet Union's collapse?' As a result, the programme did not pass the censoring process. See Zhou (2008b), op.cit.15.

22 H. H. Zhou (ed.) (2003), *Zhengfu xinxi gongkai tiaoli zhuanjia jianyigao [Academic Draft of FOI Regulations]*, Beijing: China Legal Publishing House, pp.22–23; The State Council Informatization Office (2002) *Zhengfu xinxi gongkai tiaoli (cao an) qicao shuoming [Explanation Memorandum of the Draft of*

FOI Regulations 2002], Beijing: The State Council Informatization Office, pp.14–15.

23 L. H. Ju and Y. F. Wang (2005) 'Zhongguo xianshi de zhengwu gongkai yunxing tixi de sida zhizhu [Four Factors of the Operation System of Current China's Openness in Government Affairs]', *Journal of Northeast Normal University*, 6: 43.

24 X. P. Deng (1994a) *Deng Xiaoping wenxuan (dier juan)[Selected Works of Xiaoping Deng (Volume II)]*, 2nd edn, Beijing: People's Press, p.168.

25 Ibid p.285. Deng stated in 1989 that '[d]emoracy is our goal'.

26 Jiang stated in 1997 that '[i]t is our Party's persistent goal to develop socialist democracy'. See Z. M. Jiang (1997) 'Gaoju Deng Xiaoping lilun weida qizhi ba jianshe you zhongguo tese shehuizhuyi shiye quanmian tuixiang ershiyi shiji [Hold High the Great Banner of Deng Xiaoping Theory for an All-round Advancement of the Cause of Building Socialism with Chinese Characteristics to the 21st Century]', speech delivered at the 15th National Congress of the CPC, Beijing, 12 September.

27 President Hu stressed in 2007 that 'to develop socialist democracy is the unswerving goal of the CPC'. See J. T. Hu (2007b) Speech delivered at the Party School of the CPC Central Committee, Beijing, 25 June.

28 Deng, op.cit. p.158; Jiang (1997), op.cit; Hu (2007b), op.cit.

29 F. Bergsten, C. Freeman, N. Lardy and D. Mitchell (2008) China's Rise: Challenges and Opportunities, Washington: Peterson Institute for International Economics, p.58.

30 J. T. Hu (2007a) 'Gaoju zhongguo tese shehuizhuyi weida qizhi wei duoqu quanmian jianshe xiaokang shehui xin shengli er fendou [Hold High the Great Banner of Socialism with Chinese Characteristics and Strive for New Victories in Building a Moderately Prosperous Society in All Respects]', speech delivered at the 17th National Congress of the CPC, Beijing, 24 October; K. P. Yu (2007a) 'Minzhu shi gongheguo de shengming [Democracy Is the Lifeblood of the People's Republic of China]', *People Forum*, 22: 6–8.

31 There is some doubt about China's democratization reform agenda. See J. N. Liu (2007) 'China's Reform: Approaching a Dead End', *China Security*, 3: 90–102; J. Mann (2008) *The China Fantasy: Why Capitalism Will Not Bring Democracy to China*, New York: Penguin, 2008, p.19; J. Grugel (2002) *Democratization: A Critical Introduction*, Hampshire: Palgrave Macmillan, pp.224–226; R. Peerenboom (2007) *China Modernizes: Threats to the West or Model for the Rest?* New York: Oxford University Press, p.280.

32 Premier Wen said in 2007 that: '[w]e never view socialism and democracy as something that are mutually exclusive. As a matter of fact, we see a high degree of democracy and a well developed legal system as inherent requirements of socialism and a key important feature of a mature socialist system'. See J. B. Wen (2007) 'Guanyu shehui zhuyi chuji jieduan de lishi renwu he woguo duiwai zhengce de jige wenti [Our Historical Tasks at the Primary Stage of Socialism and Several Issues concerning China's Foreign Policy]', *People's Daily*, 27 February, p.2.

33 *Opinions on Strengthening the Work of the Chinese People's Political Consultative Conference* No 5 [2006] of the CPC Central Committee. The Chinese People's Political Consultative Conference, a fundamental political structure in China, may not be regarded as a form of deliberative democracy. However, in China, this is considered as a key part of deliberative democracy, but not all. Other universal accepted forms of deliberative democracy, such as consensus conferences and consulting meetings have been held in China at the grassroots level. See B. G. He (2003) 'The Theory and Practice of Chinese Grassroots Governance: Five Models', *Japanese Journal of Political Science*, 4: 303–305; B. G. He (2007) 'Xieshang minzhu he minzhuhua [Deliberative Democracy and Democratization]',

China Institute of Theory on the Chinese People's Political Consultative Conference, 4: 34–35; Bergsten *et al.*, op.cit., p. 63.

34 Many have contributed to the notion of deliberative democracy, such as Joseph Bessette, Jon Elster, Jürgen Habermas, David Held, Joshua Cohen, John Rawls, Amy Gutmann and John Dryzek. Elster argues that the notion of deliberative democracy 'includes collective decision making with the participation of all who will be affected by the decision or their representatives … [and] decision making by means of arguments offered *by* and *to* participants who are committed to the values of rationality and impartiality'. See J. Elster (1998) *Deliberative Democracy*, Cambridge: Cambridge University Press, p.8.

35 Y. X. Lang (2005) 'Shangyishi minzhu yu zhongguo de difang jingyan: zhejiang-sheng wenlingshi de minzhu kentanhui [Deliberative Democracy and Local Experiences in China: A Case Study on the "Democratic Talkfest" in Zhejiang Province]', *Zhejiang Social Science*, 1: 37; R. Stubbs (2008) 'FOI and Democracy in Australia and Beyond', *Australian Journal of Political Science*, 4: 681.

36 He (2007), op.cit., pp.34–35.

37 J. Yan (2009) *Rang minzhu zaofu zhongguo: Yu keping fangtan lu [Make Democracy Benefit China: Dialogue with Professor Keping Yu]*, Beijing: Central Compilation & Translation Press, Preface.

38 *Opinions on Strengthening the Work of the Chinese People's Political Consultative Conference* No 5 [2006] of the CPC Central Committee.

39 Ibid.

40 The State Council Information Office (2007) *The White Paper on China's Political Party System* (15 November, Beijing).

41 K. Marx and F. Engels (1986) *Marx and Engels Collected Works (Volume 22)*, London: Lawrence and Wishart, p.340.

42 Ibid.

43 J. Liu (2005) *Zhiqingquan yu xinxi gongkai fa [The Right to Know and the FOI Act]*, Beijing: Tsinghua University Press, p.245.

44 Lenin argued that: 'Everyone will probably agree that 'the broad democratic principle' presupposes the two following conditions: first, *full publicity* [emphasis added], and secondly, election to all offices. It would be absurd to speak of democracy without publicity, moreover, without a publicity that is not limited to the membership of the organization. We call the German Socialist Party a democratic organization because *all its activities are carried out publicly; even its party congresses are held in public. But no one would call an organization democratic that is hidden from everyone but its members by a veil of secrecy* [emphasis added].' See V. Lenin (1961a) *Lenin Collected Works (Volume 5)*, Moscow: Foreign Language Publishing House, p.477.

45 V. Lenin (1962) *Lenin Collected Works (Volume 10)*, Moscow: Foreign Language Publishing House, p.242.

46 Z. D. Mao (1953) *Mao zedong wen xuan (Di san juan)/[Selected Works of Zedong Mao (Volume III)]*, Beijing: People's Press, p.899.

47 Z. Q. Zhao (2001) 'Zhengwu gongkai fanfubai lunyao [Discussion of Anti-Corruption through Openness in Government Affairs]', *Theory and Modernization*, 6: 52.

48 Jiang (1997), op.cit.

49 Liu, op.cit., p. 245.

50 Mao argued that: '*Our policy must be made known not only to the leaders and to the cadres but also to the broad masses* [emphasis added]. … There are people in our leading organs in some places who think that it is enough for the leaders alone to know the Party's policies and that there is no need to let the masses know them. … This is one of the basic reasons why some of our work cannot be done well. … Subjectively, they too want everyone to take a hand in the work, but

they do not let other people know what is to be done or how to do it. That being the case, how can everyone be expected to get moving and how can anything be done well?' See Z. D. Mao (1961) *Mao zedong quanji (Di si juan)[Collected Works of Zedong Mao (Volume IV)]* 2nd edn, Beijing: People's Press, 1318–1319.

51 E. L. Zhou (1984) *Zhou Enlai wenxuan [Selected Works of Enlai Zhou]*, Beijing: People's Press, p.301.

52 Z. Y. Zhao (1987) 'Yanzhe you zhongguo tese de shehuizhuyi daolu qianjin [Take Strides along the Road to Socialism with Chinese Characteristics]', speech delivered at the 13th National Congress of the CPC, Beijing, 25 October.

53 Ibid.

54 Even Mao, when reflecting on the drawbacks arising from the transparency policy for land reform in 1957, put forward a key principle to guide news reports in China, namely 'the news, old news or no news' (*Xinwen, Jiuwen, Buwen*). See Z. D. Mao (1983) *Mao zedong xinwen gongzuo wenxuan [Selected Works of Zedong Mao on Journalism]*, Beijing: Xinhua Publishing, p.193.

55 J. T. Hu (2002) 'Xianfa wei jianshe xiaokang shehui tigong falv baozhang [Fully Implementing the Constitution to Provide Legal Guarantees for Building a Well-Off Society in All Aspects]', speech delivered at the 20th Anniversary of the Adoption of the Constitution, Beijing, 4 December.

56 J. T. Hu (2004) Speech delivered at the 50th Anniversary of the National People's Congress, Beijing, 15 September.

57 In China, the current Constitution was adopted by the Fifth National People's Congress on 4 December 1982. There are three previous versions of Constitution, including those of 1954, 1975 and 1978, which were repealed. The latest Constitution was revised in 1988, 1993, 1999 and 2004.

58 *Constitution 1982*. Art.1.

59 Hu (2007a), op.cit.

60 Zhou (ed.), op.cit., p.23.

61 Zhou (ed.), op.cit., pp. 22–23; The State Council Informatization Office, op.cit., pp.14–15.

62 Ibid.

63 The State Council Informatization Office, op.cit., p.15.

64 *Constitution 1982*. Art.2.

65 The State Council Informatization Office, op.cit., p.15.

66 Ibid.

67 *Constitution 1982*. Art.27.

68 H. H. Zhou (2007c) 'Open Government in China: Practice and Problems', in A. Florini (ed.) *The Right to Know: Transparency for an Open World*, New York: Columbia University Press, p.105.

69 Zhou. ed., op.cit., pp. 22–23; The State Council Informatization Office, op.cit., pp.14–15; Liu, op.cit., p.89.

70 *Constitution 1982*. Art.41.

71 Zhou. ed., op.cit., pp. 22–23; Y. F. Zhou (2005) 'Woguo zhengfu xinxi gongkai lifa pingxi [Analysis of FOI Law-Making Activities in China]', *Journal of Jinan University*, 6: 56.

72 Y. G. Shang (2005) 'Lun xingzheng gongkai zhidu [Discussion of the System of Administrative Openness]', *The Epochal Tide*, 24: 48.

73 The CPC Central Committee (2008) *Zhongguo gongchandang di shiqijie zhongyang weiyuanhui di er ci quanti huiyi gongbao [Communiqué of the Second Plenary Session of the 17th CPC Central Committee]*, Online. Available HTTP: <http://politics.people.com.cn/GB/1026/6932293.html> (accessed 9 January 2011).

74 K. P. Yu (2007b) Sixiang jiefang yu zhengzhi jinbu [Emancipation of Mind and Political Progress]. *Beijing Daily*, 17 September, p.18.

75 The State Council Information Office (2005) *The White Paper on the Building of Political Democracy in China* (19 October, Beijing).

76 Ibid. The first villagers' committee was established in Guangxi in February 1980. F. Li (2005) 'Xuanju minzhu zai zhongguo de shijian [The Practice of Democratic Elections in China]', *China Reform*, 9: 15.

77 J. Horsley (2007b) 'Toward a More Open China?' in A. Florini (ed.) *The Right to Know: Transparency for an Open World*, New York: Columbia University Press, pp.58–59. The people's commune refers to a collective economic and grassroots regime organization, which was established based on advanced agricultural production cooperatives in 1958. In general, there was one commune per township.

78 *Constitution 1982*. Art.111.

79 Grassroots democracy has been expanded in China through the establishment of four democratic means: democratic election, decision-making, management and supervision. See Jiang (1997), op.cit; *Organic Law of the Villagers' Committee 1998*. Art.2.

80 The Ministry of Civil Affairs (n.d.) *Cunmin zizhi zhuyao chengjiu [The Main Achievements in Villagers' Autonomy]*, Online. Available HTTP: <http://www1.mca.gov.cn/artical/content/WCM_YWJS/20031224145129.htm> (accessed 2 April 2008). The *White Paper on the Building of Political Democracy in China* states that '[t]he villagers supervise the committee's work and the conduct of the village cadres through making village affairs open'. See The State Council Information Office, op.cit.

81 The Ministry of Civil Affairs, op.cit.

82 *Organic Law of the Villagers' Committees (for trial) 1987*. Art.17.

83 The *Notice on Enhancing the Construction of Grassroots Organizations in the Rural Areas* No 10 [1994] of the General Office of the CPC Central Committee.

84 Ibid.

85 The *Notice on Comprehensively Implementing Openness in Village Affairs and Democratic Management* No 9 [1998] of the General Office of the CPC Central Committee.

86 Article 22 under this Law requires villagers' committees to disclose the following matters without delay: matters decided on through discussion by villagers' assemblies as provided for in Article 19 of this Law, and implementation of the decisions; plans for implementing the state policy for family planning; handing out of relief funds and goods; collection of charges for the supply of water and electricity, and other matters that involve villagers' interests and concerns. In terms of financial affairs, this Law mandates its disclosure every six months at least.

87 *Suggestions on Fully Establishing and Enhancing Openness in Village Affairs and Democratic Management* No 17 [2004] of the General Office of the CPC Central Committee.

88 By the end of 2003, more than 95 per cent of villages had fully implemented the policy of openness in village affairs in China. See J. Y. Zhang, S. W. Zou, and C. B. Sun (2003) *Huize baixing de yangguang gongcheng woguo jiji tuixing banshi gongkai zhidu [The 'Sunshine Project' Benefits the Masses: China Actively Promotes Openness in the Process of Administrative Affairs]*, Online. Available HTTP: <http://news.xinhuanet.com/newscenter/2003–12/30/content_1254392.htm> (accessed 10 February 2008).

89 Jiang (1997), op.cit.

90 Ibid.

91 The *Notice on Promoting Openness in Government Affairs around All Government Agencies at the Township Level* No 25 [2000] of the General Office of the CPC Central Committee.

92 Hu (2007a), op.cit.

93 The *Notice on Promoting Openness in Government Affairs around All Government Agencies at the Township Level* No 25 [2000] of the General Office of the CPC Central Committee.

94 The *Notice on Comprehensively Implementing Openness in Village Affairs and Democratic Management* No 9 [1998] of the General Office of the CPC Central Committee.

95 The *Notice on Promoting Openness in Government Affairs around All Government Agencies at the Township Level* No 25 [2000] of the General Office of the CPC Central Committee.

96 The General Office of the Central Commission for Discipline Inspection (2004) *Zhengwu gongkai [Openness in Government Affairs]*, Beijing: Fangzheng Press, p.11.

97 The *Notice on Further Promoting Openness in Government Affairs* No 12 [2005] of the General Office of the CPC Central Committee.

98 Ibid.

99 Jiang (1997), op.cit; Z. M. Jiang (2002) 'Quanmian jianshe xiaokang shehui kaichuang zhongguo tese shehuizhuyi shiye xin jumian [Build a Well-off Society in an All-Round Way and Create a New Situation in Building Socialism with Chinese Characteristics]', speech delivered at the 16th National Congress of the CPC, Beijing, 8 November; Hu (2007a), op.cit.

100 *Organic Law of the Villagers' Committee 1998*, Art.11; *Organic Law of the Urban Residents Committees 1989*, Art.8.

101 According to the State Council Information Office, '[b]y the end of 2004, some 644,000 villagers' committees had been established throughout the country, with most of the provinces, autonomous regions and municipalities directly under the central government having elected their fifth or sixth committees'. See The State Council Information Office, op.cit.

102 The first trial was in two towns in Sichuan Province in 1998. See Y. Cao (2005) 'Jiceng minzhu jiancheng dashi [The Gradual Trend toward Grassroots Democracy]', *People Forum*, 9: 35. In 2004, direct elections were conducted among seven township governments in Shipin County of Yunan Province. See Y. M. Chen (2007) 'Jiceng minzhuhua yu minzhu jicenghua [Grassroots Democratization and Democracy at the Grassroots Level]', *China Reform*, 9: 27.

103 Chen, op.cit., p.27.

104 Article 101 of the *Constitution 1982* confers on local people's congresses at their respective levels, rather than the citizens, to elect and recall governors and deputy governors, mayors and deputy mayors, or heads and deputy heads of counties, districts, townships and towns.

105 W. M. Shi (2005) 'Zhi guibu yi zhi qianli 2000 dao 2005 nian zhongguo jiceng minzhu zhengzhi jianshe huigu [Many a Little Makes a Mickle – An Overview of the Building of Grassroots Democracy in China from 2000 to 2005]', *China Reform*, 9: 18. Chen, op.cit., p.27.

106 Jiang (1997), op.cit.

107 The *Notice on Promoting Openness in Government Affairs around All Government Agencies at the Township Level* No 25 [2000] of the General Office of the CPC Central Committee.

108 The Ministry of Civil Affairs, op.cit.

109 The General Office of the Central Commission for Discipline Inspection, op.cit., p.6.

110 The *Notice on Comprehensively Implementing Openness in Village Affairs and Democratic Management* No 9 [1998] of the General Office of the CPC Central Committee.

111 The General Office of the Central Commission for Discipline Inspection, op.cit., p.11.

112 J. B. Wen (2004b) 'Quanmian tuijin yifa xingzheng nuli jianshe fazhi zhengfu [Pushing forward Administration by Law in an All-Round Way to Build a Government under the Rule of Law]', speech delivered at the National Picturephone Conference on the Work of Law-Based Administration, Beijing, 28 June. The other two major tasks are law-based administration and administrative supervision. The Hu–Wen Administration is a name given to the current Party leader Jintao Hu and Premier Jiabao Wen.
113 Jiang (2002), op.cit.
114 The State Council Information Office, op.cit.
115 Ibid.
116 Ibid.
117 The *Implementation Outline for Pushing Forward Administration by Law in an All-Round Way* No 10 [2004] of the General Office of the State Council.
118 *Working Rules of the State Council* No 14 [2008] of the State Council.
119 *Zhonghua renmin gongheguo guomin jingji he shehui fazhan di shiyi ge wunian guihua gangyao [The 11 Five-Year Plan for National Economy and Social Development]* (2006), Online. Available HTTP: <http://news.xinhuanet.com/misc/2006–03/16/content_4309517_20.htm> (accessed 7 May 2008).
120 Ibid.
121 The *Resolution on Major Issues regarding the Building of a Harmonious Socialist Society* No 19 [2006] of the Central Committee of the CPC.
122 *Zhonghua renmin gongheguo guomin jingji he shehui fazhan di shiyi ge wunian guihua gangyao [The 11 Five-Year Plan for National Economy and Social Development]*, op.cit.
123 Jiang (2002), op.cit.
124 The *Decision of the CPC Central Committee on Strengthening the Building of the Party's Ruling Capability* No 18 [2004] of the Central Committee of the CPC.
125 Hu (2007a), op.cit.
126 The State Council Information Office, op.cit.
127 *Opinions on Strengthening the Work of the Chinese People's Political Consultative Conference* No 5 [2006] of the CPC Central Committee.
128 *Zhonghua renmin gongheguo guomin jingji he shehui fazhan di shiyi ge wunian guihua gangyao [The 11 Five-Year Plan for National Economy and Social Development]*, op.cit; The *Resolution on Major Issues regarding the Building of a Harmonious Socialist Society* No 19 [2006] of the Central Committee of the CPC.
129 Zhou. ed., op.cit., pp.14–15.
130 The State Council Information Office, op.cit; Q. Zhang (2007) *Fazhiban jieshao zhengfu xinxi gongkai tiaoli youguan qingkuang bing dawen [The Legislative Affairs of the State Council Introduces FOI Regulations]*. Press release, 24 April 2007; X. S. Yang (2007) 'Subsidiary Report on Learning FOI Regulations', speech delivered at Conference on Learning FOI Regulations, Beijing, 17 May.
131 Hu (2007a), op.cit.
132 Y. Yin (2007) 'Tan zhengfu xinxi gongkai xingzheng anjian shenli xin silu [New Thoughts on Trying FOI Cases]', *Shanghai Journal of Law*, 5: 52; Zhou (ed.), op.cit., p.57.
133 The *Notice on Further Promoting Openness in Government Affairs* No 12 [2005] of the General Office of the CPC Central Committee.
134 Y. He (2005) *The Leading Group on National Openness in Government Affairs Answered the Questions from Journalists about the Notice on Further Promoting Openness in Government Affairs*. Press release, 27 April 2005.
135 Y. He (2007) 'The Speech of Yong He at the Seventh Meeting of the Leading Group on National Openness in Government Affairs', speech delivered at Beijing, 21 March.

136 Y. S. Gan (2007) 'Speech by Yisheng Gan at the Teleconference on Training in FOI Regulations', speech delivered at Beijing, 17 May; K. T. Cao and Q. Zhang (eds) (2008) *Zhengfu xinxi gongkai tiaoli duben [The Primer on China's FOI Regulations]*, Beijing: China Legal Publishing House, p.37.
137 H. H. Zhou (2008a) Speech delivered at Seminar on the Challenges and Possibilities for Government Information Disclosure, Beijing, 25 June.
138 Ibid.
139 Jiang (2002), op.cit.
140 Hu (2007a), op.cit.
141 The *Notice on Further Promoting Openness in Government Affairs* No 12 [2005] of the General Office of the CPC Central Committee.

5 Law-based administration as a rationale for FOI reform in China

1 R. Vaughn (2000) 'Introduction', in R. Vaughn (ed.) *Freedom of Information*, Burlington: Ashgate, p.xvi.
2 *Federal Register Act* (1935) 44 USC § 1505.
3 *Administrative Procedure Act* (1946) 5 USC § 552 (a) (1) & (2).
4 *Administrative Procedure Act of 1946* (1946) § 3(c), Pub. L. No 79–404, 60 Stat. 238.
5 S. Lamble (2002) 'Computer-Assisted Reporting and Freedom of Information', unpublished thesis, Queensland University, p.127.
6 J. Goldring (1981) 'The Foundations of the "New Administrative Law" in Australia', *Australian Institute of Public Administration*, 40: 86; Susan Streets (2000) *Administrative Law*, 2nd edn, Sydney: Butterworths, p.27.
7 J. McMillan (2002) *Twenty Years of Open Government: What Have We Learnt? Sydney: The Federation Press*, p.6. The *Administrative Appeals Tribunal Act* was adopted in 1975. One year later, the *Ombudsman Act* was passed. The *Administrative Decisions (Judicial Review) Act* was adopted in 1977.
8 X. P. Deng (1994) *Deng Xiaoping wenxuan (dier juan)[Selected Works of Xiaoping Deng (Volume II)]*, 2nd edn, Beijing: People's Press, p.147.
9 The State Council Information Office (2008) *The White Paper on China's Efforts and Achievements in Promoting the Rule of Law* (Beijing, 28 February).
10 *Constitution 1982*. Art.5.
11 Z. M. Jiang (2002) 'Quanmian jianshe xiaokang shehui kaichuang zhongguo tese shehuizhuyi shiye xin jumian [Build a Well-off Society in an All-Round Way and Create a New Situation in Building Socialism with Chinese Characteristics]', speech delivered at the 16th National Congress of the CPC, Beijing, 8 November.
12 The State Council Information Office, op.cit.
13 S. N. Ying (2008) 'Zhongguo xingzhengfa de huigu yu zhanwang [Overview and Expectations of China's Administrative Law]', *The Rule of Law Forum*, 2: 2.
14 Ibid. The other four basic laws are criminal law, civil law, criminal litigation law and civil litigation law.
15 J. B. Wen (2004b) 'Quanmian tuijin yifa xingzheng nuli jianshe fazhi zhengfu [Pushing forward Administration by Law in an All-Round Way to Build a Government under the Rule of Law]', speech delivered at the National Picturephone Conference on the Work of Law-Based Administration, Beijing, 28 June.
16 *Legal Daily* (2008) 'Yifa xingzheng: cong fazhi zhengfu dao fazhi zhengfu [Law-Based Administration: From Government Ruled by Law to Government under the Rule of Law]'. 6 July, p.6.
17 The State Council Information Office, op.cit.
18 The *Decision of Pushing Forward Administration by Law in an All-Round Way* No 23 [1999] of the General Office of the State Council.

19 The *Implementation Outline for Pushing Forward Administration by Law in an All-Round Way* No 10 [2004] of the General Office of the State Council.
20 Peerenboom in his book notes this dismissal by most Western observers, but he suggests that China's efforts to establish rule of law should be taken seriously. See R. Peerenboom (2002) *China's Long March toward Rule of Law*, New York: Cambridge University Press, p.xii. Zimmerman also argues that '[p]rolific legislative activity and increased emphasis on implementation and enforcement are positive steps and indicative that China is serious about the establishment of a genuine legal system based upon the rule of law'. See J. Zimmerman (2005) *China Law Deskbook*, 2nd edn, Chicago: American Bar Association, p.70.
21 During the last three decades, it has seen the fundamental establishment of a socialist legal framework. The National People's Congress and its Standing Committee have enacted 229 laws currently in effect, covering almost all substantive and procedural areas. Apart from this, the State Council has enacted nearly 600 administrative regulations, and local congresses and governments have enacted thousands of local regulations and rules currently in effect. See The State Council Information Office, op.cit.
22 G. L. Xue (2006) *Xingzheng fazhi daolu tanxun: Xue Gangling jiaoshou wenji [Discovering the Roadmap for the Rule of Administrative Law: Combined Works of Professor Xue Gangling]*, Beijing: China Legal Publishing House, p.4. There are other theories, which define the nature of administrative law in China, like theories of administration, service and balance. In particular, the theory of balance, first proposed by Professor Haocai Luo, holds that administrative law should be a law to balance between government powers and citizens' rights. However, this theory 'does not reject the notion of power control'. See J. F. Chen (1999) *Chinese Law: Towards an Understanding of Chinese Law, Its Nature, and Development*, Leiden: Martinus Nijhoff Publishers, pp.135–139.
23 J. Han and J. L. Wang (2006) *Woguo yifa xingzheng de jiben lilun yu shishi [The Basic Theory and Practice of Law-Based Administration in China]*, Chengdu: Southwest University Press, p.42.
24 C. Y. Xin and J. Feng (2005) *WTO yu zhongguo xingzheng fazhi gaige [WTO and China's Administrative Law Reforms]*, Beijing: Social Sciences Academic Press, 2005, p.140.
25 *Constitution 1982.* Art.5.
26 Xin and Feng, op.cit., p.140.
27 *Constitution 1982.* Art.41.
28 Xin and Feng, op.cit., p.140.
29 *Civil Procedure Law 1982.* Art.3. The Article states that the *Civil Procedure Law* is applicable to an administrative lawsuit that courts hear according to the stipulation of the law.
30 Xin and Feng, op.cit., p.142.
31 Ibid.
32 Ibid.
33 Ibid 143.
34 Ying (2008), op.cit., p.2.
35 S. N. Ying (2006) 'Zhongguo xingzhengfa de huigu yu zhanwang [Overview and Expectations of China's Administrative Law]', speech delivered at Zhongshan University, Zhongshan, 6 January.
36 Ibid. China did not establish a similar research group for the introduction of its civil and criminal law. This indicates the difficulty of the adoption of administrative law.
37 Ibid.
38 A. Cheung (2005) 'China's Administrative Litigation Law', *Public Law*, Autumn: 551.

39 Ying (2008), op.cit., p.2.
40 Ibid. Administrative litigation was partly allowed under the *Civil Procedure Law 1982*.
41 Ying (2006), op.cit.
42 Chinese reformers were inspired by the re-establishment of civil law. China adopted its *Civil Procedure Law* four years earlier than that of *Civil Code*. See Ying (2006), op.cit.
43 W. Dun (2003) Interview with Ming'an Jiang, Professor of Peking University (Beijing, 29 September).
44 S. N. Ying (2001) 'Zhongguo xingzhengfa de chuangzhi yu mianlin de wenti [The Establishment of China's Administrative Law and the Problems Encountered]', *Journal of Jianghai Academia*, 1: 61.
45 The law has restrictions. For example, the law only permits courts to review the lawfulness of concrete administrative actions. *Administrative Litigation Law 1989*. Art.2.
46 Cheung, op.cit., p.549; Xin and Feng, op.cit., p.143.
47 *Legal Daily*, op.cit., p.6.
48 Dun, op.cit.
49 P. Potter (1999) 'The Chinese Legal System: Continuing Commitment to the Primacy of State Power', *The China Quarterly*, 159: 674.
50 Xin and Feng, op.cit., p.143.
51 Han and Wang, op.cit., p.42.
52 *Administrative Litigation Law 1989*. Art.5.
53 *Administrative Reconsideration Law 1999*. Art.3. A concrete administrative action refers to an administrative activity of government agencies which aims at specified events or individuals and can only be carried out once, while an abstract administrative action is an activity which aims at the general public and can be repeatedly carried out. These two kinds of actions attract different supervision and control mechanisms and legal remedies. China's *Administrative Litigation Law* allows only a concrete administrative action to be reviewed by courts.
54 *Administrative Reconsideration Law 1999*. Art.7.
55 *Audit Law 1995*. Art.2.
56 The *Administrative Supervision Law* was adopted after the early 1990s, but the debate ran earlier. The book thus includes it in this phase of administrative law reform.
57 *Administrative Supervision Law 1997*. Art.7.
58 Xin and Feng, op.cit., p.143.
59 *Administrative Litigation Law 1989*. Art.67.
60 H. C. Luo (ed.) (2004) *Xiandai xingzheng fazhi de fazhan qushi [The Current Trend in Modern Administrative Law]*. Beijing: China Law Press, p.39.
61 *Zeng Qinghong qiangdiao yao chongfen renshi banbu gongwuyuan fa de zhongyao yiyi [Qinghong Zeng Stresses the Comprehensive Recognition of the Significance of the Passage of the Civil Servant Law]* (2005), Online. Available HTTP: <http://www.gov.cn/zfjs/2005–9/22/content_68644.htm> (accessed 9 February 2008).
62 Han and Wang, op.cit., p.42.
63 Xin and Feng, op.cit., p.144.
64 *Goldberg v Kelly* (1970) 397 US 254, 267–268; Streets, op.cit., pp.157–158; McMillan, op.cit., p.42.
65 Xin and Feng, op.cit., p.145.
66 *Administrative Penalty Law 1996*. Art.42. Some examples of the serious administrative penalties are suspending production and business operations, revoking certificates or business licences and imposing relatively large fines.
67 *Price Law 1997*. Art.23; *Legislation Law 2000*. Arts 34, 58.
68 *Administrative Permission Law 2003*. Art.46.

69 Xin and Feng, op.cit., p.145.
70 J. M. Hu and L. J. Ma (2005) 'Zhengfu guanli yu xinxi gongkai zhi fali jichu [The Legal Foundation for Government Management and FOI]', *Legal Forum*, 4: 16.
71 Y. C. Mo (2008) 'Jing you yangguan zhengfu zouxiang fazhi zhengfu [From Sunshine Government to Government under the Rule of Law]', in Y. C. Mo and H. C. Lin (eds) *Xinxi gongkai tiaoli shiyi [Interpretations of China's FOI Regulations]*, Beijing: China Legal Publishing House, p.2.
72 H. Yan (2008) *Zhengfu xinxi gongkai zhidu yanjiu [Theory and Practice in Government Information Publicity]*, Wuhan: Wuhan University Press, p.41.
73 *Administrative Penalty Law 1996*. Art.4; *Administrative Permission Law 2003*. Art.5.
74 *Legislation Law 2000*. Art.35.
75 D. D. Ye (2008) *Lifa gongkai jinxingshi [Openness in Law-Making Activity Is Underway]*, Online. Available HTTP: <http://www.caijing.com.cn/2008-09-03/110009953.html> (accessed 3 October 2008).
76 J. B. Wen (2008b) 'Shiyi jie renda yici huiyi shang suozuo zhengfu gongzuo baogao [Report on the Work of the Government to the National People's Congress]', speech delivered at the First Session of the 11th National People's Congress, Beijing, 5 March; *Working Rules of the State Council* No 14 [2008] of the State Council.
77 *Administrative Penalty Law 1996*. Art.31.
78 *Administrative Permission Law 2003*. Art.40.
79 P. Li (1993) 'Zai bajie renda yici huiyi shang suo zuo zhengfu gongzuo baogao [Report on the Work of the Government to the National People's Congress]', speech delivered at the First Session of the 8th National People's Congress, Beijing, 15 March.
80 Z. M. Jiang (1997) 'Gaoju Deng Xiaoping lilun weida qizhi ba jianshe you zhongguo tese shehuizhuyi shiye quanmian tuixiang ershiyi shiji [Hold High the Great Banner of Deng Xiaoping Theory for an All-round Advancement of the Cause of Building Socialism with Chinese Characteristics to the 21st Century]', speech delivered at the 15th National Congress of the CPC, Beijing, 12 September.
81 The *Decision of Pushing Forward Administration by Law in an All-Round Way* No 23 [1999] of the General Office of the State Council.
82 The *Implementation Outline for Pushing Forward Administration by Law in an All-Round Way* No 10 [2004] of the General Office of the State Council.
83 Ibid.
84 Ibid.
85 Ibid.

6 Economic growth and anti-corruption efforts

1 C. Darch and P. Underwood (2009) *Freedom of Information and the Developing World: The Citizen, the State and Models of Openness*, Oxford: Chandos Publishing. p.171; J. Horsley (2007a), *China Adopts First Nationwide Open Government Information Regulations*, Online. Available HTTP: <http://www.freedominfo.org/features/20070509.htm> (accessed 28 August 2007); P. Hubbard (2008b) *China's Regulations on Open Government Information: Challenges of Nationwide Policy Implementation*, Online. Available HTTP: <http://www.opengovjournal.org/article/viewArticle/2651> (accessed 22 July 2009).
2 Darch and Underwood, op.cit., p.171; Horsley, op.cit.; Hubbard, op.cit.
3 T. Blanton (2002) 'The Openness Revolution: The Rise of a Global Movement for Freedom of Information', *Development Dialogue*, 1: 16.

4 Ibid.
5 Darch and Underwood, op.cit., n 1; Blanton, op.cit., p.16; G. Sutton and S. Holsen (2006) *China Progresses Information Access and Data Protection Laws*, Online. Available HTTP: <http://www.opengovjournal.org/ article/ view/621/482> (accessed 22 July 2009).
6 Chinese political leaders have taken economic growth as the central task of nation building since the late 1970s. See X. P. Deng (1994b) *Deng Xiaoping wenxuan (disan juan) [Selected Works of Xiaoping Deng (Volume III)]*, 2nd edn, Beijing: People's Press, p.194.
7 The previous mode of economic growth that emphasized the development of heavy industry impaired the development of light and service industries, thus leading to an unreasonable economic structure. Considering this, the central government decided to develop informatization to modify the traditional mode of economic growth. This new mode was first formally confirmed by the Chinese government in 2000, when informatization development was called for to upgrade industrialization. This was reiterated in 2002 at the 16th National Congress of the CPC. See The CPC Central Committee (2000) *Zhongguo gongchandang di shiwu jie zhongyang weiyuanhui di wu ci quanti huiyi gongbao [Communiqué of the Fifth Plenary Session of the 15th CPC Central Committee]*, Online. Available HTTP: <http://cpc.people.com.cn/GB/64162/64168/64568/65401/4429280.html> (accessed 9 January 2011). Z. M. Jiang (2002) 'Quanmian jianshe xiaokang shehui kaichuang zhongguo tese shehuizhuyi shiye xin jumian [Build a Well-off Society in an All-Round Way and Create a New Situation in Building Socialism with Chinese Characteristics]', speech delivered at the 16th National Congress of the CPC, Beijing, 8 November; J. L. Wu (2006) 'Zhongguo yingdang zou shenme yang de gongyehua daolu [Which Path of Industrialization Should China Take?]', *Management World*, 8: 4.
8 The State Council Informatization Office (2002) *Zhengfu xinxi gongkai tiaoli (cao an) qicao shuoming [Explanation Memorandum of the Draft of FOI Regulations 2002]*, Beijing: The State Council Informatization Office, p.14; *Suggestions on Strengthening Exploitation and Use of Information Resources* No 34 [2004] of the General Office of the CPC Central Committee.
9 The State Council Informatization Office (2002). It is argued that government agencies, which hold more than 80 percent of information, should be the main providers of information for reuse.
10 H. H. Zhou (ed.) (2003) *Zhengfu xinxi gongkai tiaoli zhuanjia jianyigao [Academic Draft of FOI Regulations]*, Beijing: China Legal Publishing House, p.19.
11 R. Gellman (2004) 'The Foundation of United States Government Information Dissemination Policy', in G. Aichholzer and H. Burkert (eds) *Public Sector Information in the Digital Age: Between Markets, Public Management and Citizens' Rights*, Cheltenham: Edward Elgar Publishing, p.126.
12 Zhou (ed.), op.cit., pp.19–20; The State Council Informatization Office, op.cit., p.14.
13 Zhou (ed.), op.cit., pp.19–20.
14 The EU Commission's *Green Paper on Public Sector Information* was published in 1998. It largely dealt with problems impeding exploitation of public sector information. The EU Commission (1998), *Green Paper on Public Sector Information* Com(1998)585.
15 The *Comprehensive Assessment of Public Information Dissemination*, which was published in 2001, focused on issues arising from dissemination and emphasised that public information was a strategic national resource. See The US National Commission Libraries and Information Science (2001) *The Comprehensive Assessment of Public Information Dissemination*, Online. Available HTTP: <http://www.nclis.gov/govt/assess/assess.execsum.pdf> (accessed 27 March 2008).

16 Zhou (ed.), op.cit., pp.19–20.
17 For example Australia. The Australian Attorney-General's Department and the Ombudsman's annual reports on FOI have repeatedly mentioned these problems.
18 This is the case in Australia. R. McLeod (2000) 'Freedom of Information', paper presented at the Seminar on Freedom of Information – A Current Perspective, 21 February.
19 Ibid.
20 S. Lamble (2004) 'Media Use of FOI Surveyed: New Zealand Puts Australia and Canada to Shame', *Freedom of Information Review*, 109: 5; M. Paterson (2004) 'Transparency in the Modern State Happy Birthday FOI! or Commiserations?', *Alterative Law Journal*, 29: 10.
21 The Australian Attorney-General's Department (1987) *Freedom of Information Act 1982 Annual report 1986–1987*, Canberra: The Australian Attorney-General's Department, p.iii; The Australian Attorney-General's Department (1988) *Freedom of Information Act 1982 Annual report 1987–1988*, Canberra: The Australian Attorney-General's Department, p.iv.
22 G. Terrill (2000a) 'Individualism and Freedom of Information Legislation', *Freedom of Information Review*, 87: 31; Finn observes that the current commercial-in-confidence exemption is overprotected as Australia's FOI legislation only mandates a test of causing individual disadvantage, rather than inhibiting the competition process. See C. Finn (2003) 'Rethinking Commercial Confidentiality in the Decade of Competition Policy', *Freedom of Information Review*, 106: 66.
23 Australian Commonwealth (1981b) *Parliamentary Debates,* House of Representatives, Canberra: 2 April 1981, p.1059 (Senator Durack, the Attorney-General of Western Australia).
24 McLeod, op.cit.
25 Ibid.
26 Y. Volman (2004) 'Exploitation of Public Sector Information in the Context of the *eEurope* Action Plan', in G. Aichholzer and H. Burkert (eds) *Public Sector Information in the Digital Age: Between Markets, Public Management and Citizens' Rights*, Cheltenham: Edward Elgar Publishing, p.95.
27 Ibid.
28 Gellman, op.cit., p.124.
29 *Copyright Act* (1994) 17 USC § 105.
30 These four dissemination practices are: 1. establishing an exclusive, restricted, or other distribution arrangement that interferes with timely and equitable availability of public information to the public; 2. restricting or regulating the use, resale, or redissemination of public information by the public; 3. charging fees or royalties for resale or redissemination of public information; and 4. establishing user fees for public information that exceed the cost of dissemination. *Paperwork Reduction Act* (1995) 44 USC § 3506 (d) (4).
31 The UK Advisory Panel on Public Sector Information (2006) *Public Sector Information Policy in Australia*, Online. Available HTTP: <http://www.appsi.gov.uk/reports/policy-australia.pdf> (accessed 5 January 2008).
32 The Australian Attorney-General's Department states that: 'As a general principle, no fees are charged where the reproduced material is being provided free-of-charge to the public. Where permission is sought to use Commonwealth copyright material for advertizing or commercial purposes to generate a financial return, the Commonwealth may set an appropriate payment or requires an equitable share of the revenue. Additional service fees are applicable for the commercial use of the Commonwealth added value, for example the typesetting, graphic design or electronic formatting, which provides savings in cost and time.' See The Australian Attorney-General's Department (2006) *Commonwealth Copyright*, Online. Available HTTP: <http://www.ag.gov.au/www/agd/agd.nsf/Page/

Copyright_CommonwealthCopyrightAdministration_Commonwealthcopyright>
(accessed 4 May 2008).

33 P. Weiss (2004) 'Borders in Cyberspace: Conflicting Public Sector Information
Policies and Their Economic Impacts', in G. Aichholzer and H. Burkert (eds)
*Public Sector Information in the Digital Age: Between Markets, Public Manage-
ment and Citizens' Rights*, Cheltenham: Edward Elgar Publishing, p.138.

34 *Directive (EC) No 98/2003 of 17 November 2003 on the Re-use of Public Sector
Information* [2003] OJ L 345/90.

35 Weiss, op.cit., p.148.

36 Zhou (ed.), op.cit., p.57.

37 The *Notice on Suggestions for Enforcing 2006's Legislation Work and 2006's
Legislative Plan* No 2 [2006] of the General Office of the State Council.

38 H. H. Zhou (2007b) *Zhengfu jianguan yu xingzheng fa [Government Governance
and Administrative Law]*, Beijing: Beijing University Press, Preface.

39 H. H. Zhou (2008b) 'Xinxi gongkai tiaoli chutai shimo [The Legislative History
of FOI Regulations in China]', *E-Government*, 7, 16.

40 Ibid.

41 J. Becker (2001) 'Comrade Jiang Zemin Does Indeed Seem a Proper Choice.'
London Review of Books, 24 May, p.12; Darch and Underwood, op.cit., p.175.

42 Zhou (2008b), op.cit.

43 Zhou recalled that in 1997, he was honoured to be invited by the State Secrecy
Bureau to take part in the work of revising the *Law on the Protection of State
Secrets*. He refused this invitation at first for fear that he would become privy to
state secrets. Jianwen Zong, a deputy director working in the State Secrecy
Bureau, explained to Zhou that the Bureau was only engaged in legislation, and
did not involve any state secrets. More importantly, Zong mentioned that the
revision of the *Law on the Protection of State Secrets* would include consideration
of the relationship between maintaining secrecy and disclosing information, and
said that administrative law scholars should have more interest in information
disclosure. Zong's persistence persuaded Zhou, and he decided to involve himself
in this revision work. His research visit to Oslo University in Norway in late 1998
was the beginning of his FOI research and the introduction of the idea of FOI
into China. See Zhou (2007b), op.cit.

44 H. H. Zhou (2007d) 'Woguo tuixing xinxi gongkai zhidu de yiyi yu tedian [Sig-
nificance and Features of Introducing FOI Legislation in China]', *China Today
Forum*, 6: 29.

45 Ibid.

46 Some will raise the question, 'how is it possible to improve secrecy through
transparency?' Given the fact that a myriad of general documents have been
classified into state secrets and there are scarce resources for the maintenance of
state secrets, it is reasonable to say that increasing transparency can assist in uti-
lizing the scarce resources more effectively and efficiently. See Zhou (2008b),
op.cit.

47 Ibid. Zhou indicated that he could do FOI research and share research results
with the State Secrecy Bureau.

48 Y. J. Wang (2007) 'Zhengfu xinxi gongkai tiaoli shinian pobing [The Breakthrough of Legislating on FOI after a Decade]'. *China Youth Daily*, 25 April, p.3.

49 In December 1999, the Leading Group on National Informatization was formed,
with the former Vice Premier Bangguo Wu as the head. To further strengthen this
leadership, former Premier Rongji Zhu became the head of the Leading Group of
National Informatization in August 2001, and Premier Jiabao Wen has been the
head since 2003. The State Council Informatization Office was also established as
the General Office of the Leading Group. See *Woguo Zhengfu Xinxihua de fazhan
licheng [A Historical Overview of Development of Informatization in China]*

(2007), Online. Available HTTP: <http://e-gov.nsa.gov.cn/digest.asp?articleid=335> (accessed 5 April 2008); *Zhengfu xinxihua dashi ji [A Chronicle of Significant Events in Government Informatization]* (2003), Online. Available HTTP: <http://www.china.com.cn/chinese/zhuanti/283818.htm> (accessed 19 May 2008).

50 Zhou (2007b), op.cit.
51 Wu, op.cit., p.4.
52 Zhou (2007b), op.cit.
53 The Advisory Committee for State Informatization has been reorganized three times. Zhou has kept his membership since 2001.
54 The State Council Informatization Office, op.cit., p.22.
55 The *Guidance on Building E-Government* No 17 [2002] of the General Office of the CPC Central Committee.
56 Ibid.
57 H. H. Zhou (2007f) 'Xinxi gongkai tiaoli chutai shimo [The Legislative History of FOI Regulations in China]', speech delivered at the Second Summit on E-Government, Beijing, 28 June.
58 The State Council Informatization Office, op.cit., p.23.
59 For more information about entrepreneurship policy, see D. Hart (2003) 'Entrepreneurship Policy: What It Is and Where It Came from', in D. Hart (ed.) *The Emergence of Entrepreneurship Policy: Governance, Start-ups, and Growth in the U.S. Knowledge Economy*, Cambridge: Cambridge University Press, pp. 3–19.
60 In China's WTO access protocol, China agreed that 'laws, regulations and other measures pertaining to or affecting trade' could only be enforced after they had been 'published and readily available to other WTO Members, individuals and enterprises'; an official journal should be established or designated for 'the publication of all laws, regulations and other measures pertaining to or affecting trade'; an enquiry point should be established or designated for facilitating access to the disclosed information from any individual, enterprise or WTO Member; and replies to application for this information should be provided in strict timeframes. See World Trade Organization (2001) *Protocol on the Accession of the People's Republic of China*, (WT/L/432) 23 November, Part I, C (1).
61 J. Horsley (2007b) 'Toward a More Open China?', in A. Florini (ed.) *The Right to Know: Transparency for an Open World*, New York: Columbia University Press, p.62; H. Liu (2004) *Zhengfu xinxi gongkai zhidu [FOI Legal Systems]*, Beijing: China Social Sciences Press, 2004, p.16; M. J. Zhang (2003) *Kaifang de zhengfu: zhengfu xinxi gongkai falv zhidu yanjiu [Open Government: Research on FOI Laws]*, Beijing: China Law Press, 2003, p.208.
62 The State Council Informatization Office, op.cit., p.18.
63 Liu, op.cit., p.237.
64 A. Roberts (2006a), *Blacked Out: Government Secrecy in the Information Age*, New York: Cambridge University Press, p.110.
65 Z. Q. Zhao (2001) 'Zhengwu gongkai fanfubai lunyao [Discussion of Anti-Corruption through Openness in Government Affairs]', *Theory and Modernization*, 6: 54; Roberts, op.cit., p.110; Blanton, op.cit., p.16.
66 Mendel, op.cit.; Sutton and Holsen, op.cit.
67 Roberts agrees with an analyst that FOI legislation in China is used to enlist 'ordinary people to serve as watchdogs on behalf of the centre'. See A. Roberts (2008) *Freedom of Information: From Millions to Billions*, Online. Available HTTP: <http://www.sunshineweek.org/sunshineweek/roberts08> (accessed 2 October 2008).
68 Z. Y. Zhao (1987)'Yanzhe you zhongguo tese de shehuizhuyi daolu qianjin [Take Strides along the Road to Socialism with Chinese Characteristics]', speech delivered at the 13th National Congress of the CPC, Beijing, 25 October; Z. M. Jiang

(1992) 'Jiakuai gaige kaifang he xiandaihua jianshe bufa tuoqu you zhongguo tese shehui zhuyi shiye de gengda shengli [Accelerate Strides toward Reform and Opening up and Modernism, Strive for Greater Victories in Building Socialism with Chinese Characteristics]', speech delivered at the 14th National Congress of the CPC, Beijing, 12 October.

69 Y. B. Hu (1982) 'Quanmian kaichuang shehuizhuyi xiandaihua jianshe de xin jumian [Comprehensively Create a New Situation in Building Socialism with Chinese Characteristics]', speech delivered at the 12th National Congress of the CPC, Beijing, 1 September.

70 Jiang (2002), op.cit.

71 A. Loong-Yu (2006) 'Alter-Globo in Hong Kong', *New Left Review*, 42: 125.

72 J. Stiglitz (2002) 'Transparency in Government', in the World Bank (ed.) *The Right to Tell: The Role of Mass Media in Economic Development*, Washington: World Bank Publications, p.35.

73 The National Congress of the CPC called on leading agencies to improve the openness of their activities, and let the people know about and discuss important matters. See Zhao, op.cit.

74 Zhang, op.cit., p.207; Zhou (ed.), op.cit., p.26.

75 Jiang (2002), op.cit.

76 *Zhongguo zhengfu qian lianheguo fubai gongyue ti sitiao jianyi [The Chinese Government Signed the United Nations Convention against Corruption and Put up Four Recommendations]* (2003), Online. Available HTTP: <http://news.xinhuanet. com/world/2003–12/11/content_1224815.htm> (accessed 5 April 2008).

77 The *Notice on Enforcement Outline for the Establishment and Improvement of a Corruption Punishing and Prevention System with Equal Attention Paid to Educa-tion, Institutions and Supervision* No 3 [2005] of the Central Committee of the CPC.

78 *Zhongguo guojia yufang fubaiju zhengshi jiepai shouren juzhang mawen jianghua [The National Corruption Prevention Bureau Established: Speech by the First Head Ma Wen]* (2007), Online. Available HTTP: <http://www.chinanews.com.cn/ gn/news/2007/09–13/1025663.shtml> (accessed 13 September 2007).

79 The National Corruption Prevention Bureau (2007) *Guojia yufang fubaiju ban-gongshi neishe jigou yu zhize [Departments and Responsibilities of the National Corruption Prevention Bureau]*, Online. Available HTTP: <http://yfj.mos.gov.cn/ yfj/news.jsp?mid=20071109026298> (accessed 5 February 2008).

80 A. G. Hu (2002) 'Public Exposure of Economic Losses Resulting from Corruption', *China & World Economy*, 4: 44.

81 The State Council Informatization Office, op.cit., p.15. Zhou argues that the establishment of an access regime in China would be cheap. See Zhou (ed.), op. cit., p.23. This is different from other countries, such as Australia and Germany. The affordability of this expensive mechanism is a major concern in these two countries. See The Australian Senate Standing Committee on Constitutional and Legal Affairs, Parliament of Commonwealth (1979) *Freedom of Information Bill 1978, and Related Aspects of Archives Bill 1978*, Canberra: Commonwealth of Australia, 1979, p.[6.5–6.25]; B. Candler (1984) 'The Australian Freedom of Information Act: A Personal View', in R. Gregory (ed.) *The Official Information Act: A Beginning*, Wellington: New Zealand Institute of Public Administration, p.24; H. Kubicek (2004) 'Third-Generation Freedom of Information in the Con-text of E-Government: The Case of Bremen, Germany', in G. Aichholzer and H. Burkert (eds) *Public Sector Information in the Digital Age: Between Markets, Public Management and Citizens' Rights*, Cheltenham: Edward Elgar Publishing, p.275.

82 Zhou (ed.), op.cit., p.26; Q. Zhang (2007) *Fazhiban jieshao zhengfu xinxi gongkai tiaoli youguan qingkuang bing dawen [The Legislative Affairs of the State Council Introduces FOI Regulations]*. Press release, 24 April.

83 Y. W. Ou (2007) Speech delivered at Seminar on the FOI Regulations, Beijing, 17 March.

84 H. H. Zhou (2007c) 'Open Government in China: Practice and Problems', in A. Florini (ed.) *The Right to Know: Transparency for an Open World*, New York: Columbia University Press, p.106.

85 In 2005, an official in Hunan Province recalled that he had difficulty in photo-copying a central government document, *Opinions of the CPC Central Committee and the State Council concerning Some Policies on Promoting the Increase of Farmers' Income*, for a friend. This document was marked with the label, confidential, the lowest secrecy level set out in the *Law on the Protection of State Secrets 1988*. See C. P. Luo and J. Feng (2005) 'Zhongguo baomi zhidu chongzhi dixian [The Classification System Rectified].' *The Beijing News*, 20 September, p.A22–23.

86 In 2000, the Editorial Department of the Commentaries for Rural Development published a booklet *The Work Manual on Reducing Farmers' Burden*, used to assist farmers to familiarize themselves with the central policy documents. There were 12,000 copies were sold to farmers within Jiangxi Province in two weeks, but the Editorial Department was then prevented from selling this booklet. The copies of the booklet that had already been sold were recalled through various methods. The recalling agencies adopted the slogan that 'the adverse effects must be eliminated wherever the copies of the booklet are sold'. See China Central Television (2000) *The Booklet on the Reduction of the Farmers' Burden Was Forbidden to Be Distributed in Jiangxi Province*, Online. Available HTTP: <http://www.cctv.com/financial/jingji/sanji/zhoume/0102_22/z22_17.html> (accessed 22 March 2008).

87 Zhou (2007c), op.cit., p.113.

88 X. P. Deng (1994a) *Deng Xiaoping wenxuan (dier juan)[Selected Works of Xiaoping Deng (Volume II)]*, 2nd edn, Beijing: People's Press, p.333.

89 The General Office of the Central Commission for Discipline Inspection (2004) *Zhengwu gongkai [Openness in Government Affairs]*, Beijing: Fangzheng Press, pp.6–17.

90 The *Implementation Outline for Pushing Forward Administration by Law in an All-Round Way* No 10 [2004] of the General Office of the State Council.

91 Y. He (2004) 'The Speech of Yong He at the Second Meeting of the Leading Group on National Openness in Government Affairs', speech delivered at Beijing, 29 April.

92 Roberts (2006a), op.cit., p.110.

93 Y. He (2007) 'The Speech of Yong He at the Seventh Meeting of the Leading Group on National Openness in Government Affairs', speech delivered at Beijing, 21 March.

94 H. Qin (2007) Speech delivered at Seminar on the FOI Regulations, Beijing, 17 March.

95 Roberts argues that the effectiveness of the access mechanism as an anti-corruption tool is 'largely unknown'. Roberts (2006a), op.cit., p.121; Mendel points out that 'the right to information is [not] a strategy for exposing individual acts of wrongdoing'. See Mendel, op.cit. Their concern has been partly demonstrated in practice. Cheng observes that there was no FOI case connected with the fight against corruption in the process of implementing local FOI Rules in China. See J. Cheng (2008) 'Difang zhengfu xinxi gongkai guiding shishi qingkuang diaoyan baogao: zhengfu xinxi gongkai tiaoli shishi, women keyi qidai shenme? [Investigation Report on Implementation of Sub-National FOI Rules: What Can We Expect Now That FOI Regulations Are in Effect?]'. *Legal Daily*, 11 May, p.3; Bookman and Guerrero Amparan argue that 'the impact of transparency and the right to know on corruption has been unimpressive' in Mexico. See Z. Bookman

and J. P. G. Amparan (2009) 'Two Steps Forward, One Step Back: Assessing the Implementation of Mexico's Freedom of Information Act', *Mexican Law Review*, 1: 49.

7 Gradual legislative process for FOI reform in China

1 Z. Y. Zhao (1987) 'Yanzhe you zhongguo tese de shehuizhuyi daolu qianjin [Take Strides along the Road to Socialism with Chinese Characteristics]', speech delivered at the 13th National Congress of the CPC, Beijing, 25 October.
2 The *Notice on Promoting Openness in Government Affairs around All Government Agencies at the Township Level* No 25 [2000] of the General Office of the CPC Central Committee.
3 The *Notice on Further Promoting Openness in Government Affairs* No 12 [2005] of the General Office of the CPC Central Committee.
4 Zhao, op.cit.
5 Ibid.
6 The General Office of the Central Commission for Discipline Inspection (2004) *Zhengwu gongkai [Openness in Government Affairs]*, Beijing: Fangzheng Press, p.7.
7 Ibid.
8 Ibid.
9 Ibid.
10 The *Notice on Comprehensively Implementing Openness in Village Affairs and Democratic Management* No 9 [1998] of the General Office of the CPC Central Committee.
11 The *Notice on Promoting Openness in Government Affairs around All Government Agencies at the Township Level* No 25 [2000] of the General Office of the CPC Central Committee.
12 The General Office of the Central Commission for Discipline Inspection, op.cit., p.16.
13 Ibid 11.
14 Z. M. Jiang (2002) 'Quanmian jianshe xiaokang shehui kaichuang zhongguo tese shehuizhuyi shiye xin jumian [Build a Well-off Society in an All-Round Way and Create a New Situation in Building Socialism with Chinese Characteristics]', speech delivered at the 16th National Congress of the CPC, Beijing, 8 November.
15 Local regulations, which are passed by the local people's congresses, have a higher legal status than administrative rules.
16 All these three cities adopted its *Openness in Government Affairs Rules* in 2003.
17 Article 44 under the *Police Law 1995* requires that the rules and regulations formulated by the police agencies which have a direct bearing on the interests of the public shall be made known to the public.
18 The *Notice on Implementing Openness in Police Affairs in All Public Securities Agencies* No 43 [1999] of the Ministry of Public Security.
19 The *Notice on Further Promoting Openness in Government Affairs in All Administration by Industry and Commerce Agencies* No 154 [2000] of the General Office of the State Administration for Industry and Commerce.
20 The *Notice on Suggestions for Further Implementing 'Eight Openness Items' concerning Civilized Tax Collection in All Tax Agencies* No 144 [2000] of the State Administration of Taxation; *Suggestions on Further Promoting Openness in Government Affairs* No 69 [2006] of the State Administration of Taxation.
21 Article 19 of the *Archives Law 1987* requires state archives centres to generally disclose archives upon the expiration of 30 years from the date of their generation. The Ministry of Foreign Affairs did not give much respect to this requirement

before. However, in 2004, the Ministry established a special library for these archives and declassified its archives from between 1949 and 1955. In 2006, it declassified the archives from between 1956 and 1960, and decided to do similar work every two years. See *Woguo kaifang 1956 dao 1960 nianjian jiemi waijiao dangan [Declassified Foreign Affairs Archives from between 1956 to 1960 Were Accessible in China]* (2006), Online. Available HTTP: <http://news.xinhuanet. com/banyt/2006-7/19/content_4852638.htm> (accessed 29 March 2008).

22 Y. J. Li and Q. Zhang (2006) *Muqian quanguo sanshiyi ge shengqushi zhengfu jianli zhengwu gongkai guanli zhidu [Thirty-One Provincial Governments Adopted Rules on Openness in Government Affairs]*, Online. Available HTTP: <http://news. xinhuanet.com/politics/2006-12/10/content_5463360.htm> (accessed 19 May 2008).

23 Normative documents provide rules, guidelines or characteristics for government activities.

24 S. Y. Zhu (2003) 'Woguo zhengfu xinxi gongkai de xianzhuang fenxi yu sikao [Analysis of and Thoughts on the Current Situation of FOI in China]', *Expanding Horizons*, 3: 31.

25 This website only provides access to the Gazette of the State Council published later than 1999. The website also provides a link to access gazettes of local governments.

26 The *Notice on Further Promoting Openness in Government Affairs* No 12 [2005] of the General Office of the CPC Central Committee.

27 Ibid.

28 Ibid.

29 Ibid.

30 J. Liu (2005) *Zhiqingquan yu xinxi gongkai fa [The Right to Know and the FOI Act]*, Beijing: Tsinghua University Press, p.282. According to the *Legislation Law 2000*, the *Constitution*, which is adopted and amended by the National People's Congress, enjoys the highest level of legal authority. An act or law, which is adopted and amended by the National People's Congress or the standing committee of the National People's Congress, is at the second level of legal authority. Regulations, which are divided into administrative regulations, local regulations, autonomous regulations and separate regulations, are at the third level of legal authority and are issued by the State Council or local people's congresses and cannot override a law. The FOI Regulations are administrative regulations, which were adopted by the State Council. Administrative rules are at the fourth level of legal authority, and are passed by state organs, provincial governments, or governments in comparatively larger cities. Many local FOI Rules, which were adopted by provincial governments and comparatively larger cities, are at this level.

31 A comparatively larger city refers to a city where a provincial or autonomous regional people's government is located or where a special economic zone is located, or a city approved as such by the State Council.

32 *Legislation Law 2000*. Art.73.

33 By the end of 2006, about 28 cities passed their normative documents about FOI.

34 J. Cheng (2008) 'Difang zhengfu xinxi gongkai guiding shishi qingkuang diaoyan baogao: zhengfu xinxi gongkai tiaoli shishi, women keyi qidai shenme? [Investigation Report on Implementation of Sub-National FOI Rules: What Can We Expect Now That FOI Regulations Are in Effect?]'. *Legal Daily*, 11 May, p.3; J. Cheng (2008) 'Zhengfu xinxi gongkai tiaoli yu gonggong tushuguan de shijian [FOI Regulations and Public Libraries]', *Information and Documentation Services*, 4: 17.

35 *Wuhan shouli zhengfu xinxi gongkai an shenjie laodongju beipan weigui [The Trial of the First FOI Case in Wuhan City Was Completed with the Judgment of the*

    Labor Bureau Violating Wuhan FOI Interim Rules] (2004), Online. Available
    HTTP: <http://www.qtfz.gov.cn:8080/show.jsp?id=3303> (accessed 7 May 2008).
36 D. H. Li and J. D. Li (2006) 'Yangguang zhengfu weihe zaoyu bolimeng [Why Is
    There the Effect of Glass Door Happening to Sunshine Government]'. *Henan
    Daily*, 22 June, p.12.
37 Liu, op.cit., p.282.
38 H. H. Zhou (2007e) Speech delivered at Seminar on the FOI Regulations, Beijing,
    17 March.
39 Pearlman argues that:'[S]ub-national Freedom of Information laws ... provide
    perhaps the best foundation from which to build a successful national Freedom of
    Information regime. They are the functional equivalents of laboratory micro-
    cosms that can be moulded and adapted to fit even the most unusual political,
    bureaucratic, social and economic cultures in which they must operate.' See
    M. Pearlman (2008) *The Importance of Freedom of Information at the Sub-National
    Level*, Online. Available HTTP: <http://www.state.ct.us/FOI/Articles/Sun-National_
    Artic.htm> (accessed 3 October 2008).
40 J. Horsley (2004) *Shanghai Advances the Cause of Open Government Information
    in China*, Online. Available HTTP: <http://www.freedominfo.org/news/20040420.
    htm> (accessed 19 September 2008).
41 Ibid.
42 The Shanghai Legislative Affairs Office and the Shanghai Institute for Adminis-
    trative Law Studies (2007) '2006 nian fazhiban gongzuo zongjie ji 2007 nian
    gongzuo yaodian [Work Review for 2006 and Work Outline for 2007 of the
    Shanghai Legislative Affairs Office]', *The Brief Report on the Shanghai Government
    Rule of Law*, 4.
43 Ibid.
44 S. Li (2008) 'Zhonghua renmin gongheguo xinxi gongkai tiaoli de zhiding beijing
    zhuyao neirong ji mulu bianzhi [The Background, Main Contents and Inventory
    Compilation concerning China's FOI Regulations]', *E-Government*, 5: 22.
45 The State Council Informatization Office (2002) *Zhengfu xinxi gongkai tiaoli (cao
    an) qicao shuoming [Explanation Memorandum of the Draft of FOI Regulations
    2002]*, Beijing: The State Council Informatization Office, p.13.
46 Ibid p.23.
47 Y. He (2004) 'The Speech of Yong He at the Second Meeting of the Leading
    Group on National Openness in Government Affairs', speech delivered at Beijing,
    29 April.
48 H. H. Zhou (ed.) (2003), *Zhengfu xinxi gongkai tiaoli zhuanjia jianyigao [Aca-
    demic Draft of FOI Regulations]*, Beijing: China Legal Publishing House, p.18;
    M. J. Zhang (2003) *Kaifang de zhengfu: zhengfu xinxi gongkai falv zhidu yanjiu
    [Open Government: Research on FOI Laws]*, Beijing: China Law Press, p.218.
49 The effectiveness of local FOI Rules was undermined by other conflicting regula-
    tions and laws as they have higher levels of legal authority than FOI Rules. See
    S. H. Huang (2007) 'Guanzhu lianghui [Pay Attention to the Sessions of the Chinese
    People's Political Consultative Conference and the National People's Congress]'.
    Fujian Daily, 12 March, p.2; Z. B. Liao and X. Z. Cheng (2003) 'Jujiao lianghui
    [Focus on the Sessions of the Chinese People's Political Consultative Conference
    and the National People's Congress]'. *Information Times*, 4 March, p.A3.
50 The Standing Committee of the 10th National People's Congress published its
    legislative plan in 2003. The plan has been classified into two categories. Fifty-
    nine bills and amendments fell into the priority category and amendments which
    should be reviewed in the 10th National People's Congress, while 17 bills and
    amendments that fell into the secondary priority were required to carry out
    research and draft. Whether these 17 bills and amendments can be reviewed or
    not depended on the real situation.

51 The National People's Congress (2003) *Shi jie quanguo renda changweihui lifa guihua [The Legislative Plan of the 10th Standing Committee of the National People's Congress]*, Online. Available HTTP: <http://www.npc.gov.cn/npc/xinwen/rdyw/wj/2004–02/23/content_328577.htm> (accessed 31 May 2008).
52 The Internal and Judicial Affairs Committee of the National People's Congress (2004) *Quanguo renda neiwu sifa weiyuanhui guanyu di shi jie quanguo renmin daibiao dahui di er ci huiyi zhuxi tuan jiaofu shenyi de daibiao tichu de yian shenyi jieguo de baogao [The Report on the Review Results of the Proposals from the Deputies of the Second Plenary Session of the 10th National People's Congress by the Internal and Judicial Affairs Committee of the National People's Congress]*, Online. Available HTTP: <http://www.npc.gov.cn/was40/detail?record=1&channelid=20179& searchword = %20(%20%D5%FE%B8%AE%D0%C5%CF%A2%B9%AB%BF%AA%B7%A8+%29+and+%28+IDS%3D%27337520'%20)> (accessed 12 January 2009).
53 Ibid.
54 Zhou (ed.), op.cit., p.17.
55 Ibid. *Administrative Litigation Law 1989.* Art.52.
56 Zhou (ed.), op.cit., p.17; Zhang, op.cit., p.219.
57 Zhou (ed.), op.cit., p.17.
58 Zhang, op.cit., p.219.
59 The State Council Informatization Office, op.cit., p.23.
60 The *Guidance on Building E-Government* No 17 [2002] of the General Office of the CPC Central Committee.
61 The State Council Informatization Office, op.cit., p.23.
62 Ibid. This draft proposed by experts and academics was published in August 2003.
63 The State Council Informatization Office, op.cit., p.24; H. H. Zhou (2008b) 'Xinxi gongkai tiaoli chutai shimo [The Legislative History of FOI Regulations in China]', *E-Government*, 7: 17.
64 Zhou (2007e), op.cit.
65 He (2004), op.cit.
66 Ibid.
67 Y. He (2005b) 'The Speech of Yong He at the Fourth Meeting of the Leading Group on National Openness in Government Affairs', speech delivered at Beijing, 25 March.
68 The *Notice on Promoting Openness in Government Affairs around All Government Agencies at the Township Level* No 25 [2000] of the General Office of the CPC Central Committee.
69 Y. He (2005a) *The Leading Group on National Openness in Government Affairs Answered the Questions from Journalists about the Notice on Further Promoting Openness in Government Affairs.* Press release, 27 April.
70 The *Notice on Promoting Openness in Government Affairs around All Government Agencies at the Township Level* No 25 [2000] of the General Office of the CPC Central Committee.
71 Y. He (2006) 'The Speech of Yong He at the Sixth Meeting of the Leading Group on National Openness in Government Affairs', speech delivered at Beijing, 31 March; Y. He (2007) 'The Speech of Yong He at the Seventh Meeting of the Leading Group on National Openness in Government Affairs', speech delivered at Beijing, 21 March.
72 X. S. Yang (2007) 'Subsidiary Report on Learning FOI Regulations', speech delivered at Conference on Learning FOI Regulations, Beijing, 17 May.
73 J. B. Wen (2004) 'Shijie renda erci huiyi shang suozuo zhengfu gongzuo baogao [Report on the Work of the Government to the National People's Congress]', speech delivered at the Second Session of the 10th National People's Congress, Beijing, 16 March.

74 The *Implementation Outline for Pushing Forward Administration by Law in an All-Round Way* No 10 [2004] of the General Office of the State Council.
75 Ibid.
76 The *Notice on Promoting Openness in Government Affairs around All Government Agencies at the Township Level* No 25 [2000] of the General Office of the CPC Central Committee.
77 H. H. Zhou (2005) 'Regulation on Government Information Publication in China: Practice, Problems and Prospect', speech delivered at Conference on China Policy Dialogue 2005, Columbia, 1 June.
78 The Journalist in the China Legislative Information Network System (2007) Interview with a Leader in the State Council Legislative Affairs Office (Beijing, 25 April).
79 Ibid.
80 H. H. Zhou (2007d) 'Woguo tuixing xinxi gongkai zhidu de yiyi yu tedian [Significance and Features of Introducing FOI Legislation in China]', *China Today Forum*, 6: 30.
81 The *Notice on Suggestions for Enforcing 2006's Legislation Work and 2006's Legislative Plan* No 2 [2006] of the General Office of the State Council.
82 *New Regulation Approved to Boost Government Transparency* (2007), Online. Available HTTP: <http://english.gov.cn/2007–01/17/content_499497.htm> (accessed 12 March 2007).

8 China's limited push model of FOI legislation

1 The idea and practice of New Public Management emerged in the 1980s in the UK to reform public administration and public service according to a citizen-as-customer view. Many counties followed suit in the 1990s due to the promotion by international institutions, such as the World Bank. See C. Hood (1991) 'A Public Management for All Seasons', *Public Administration*, 69: 3–19; M. Barzelay (2001) 'Origins of the New Public Management: An International View from Public Administration/Political Science', in K. McLaughlin and S. Osborne (eds) *New Public Management: Current Trends and Future Prospects*, London: Routledge, p.15.
2 D. W. Schartum (2004) 'Information Access Legislation for the Future? Possibilities according to a Norwegian Experience', in G. Aichholzer and H. Burkert (eds) *Public Sector Information in the Digital Age: Between Markets, Public Management and Citizens' Rights*, Cheltenham: Edward Elgar Publishing, p.76; M. Craglia and M. Blakemore (2004) 'Access Models for Public Sector Information: The Spatial Data Context', in G. Aichholzer and H. Burkert (eds) *Public Sector Information in the Digital Age: Between Markets, Public Management and Citizens' Rights*, Cheltenham: Edward Elgar Publishing, p.187.
3 The FOI Independent Review Panel (2008) *The Right to Information: Reviewing Queensland's Freedom of Information Act*, Online. Available HTTP: <http://www.foireview.qld.gov.au/documents_for_download/FOI-review-report-10062008.pdf> (accessed 9 January 2011); Tasmanian Department of Justice (2009) *Strengthening Trust in Government ... Everyone's Right to Know*, Online. Available HTTP: <http://www.justice.tas.gov.au/_data/assets/pdf_file/0005/118922/Strengthening-trust-in_Government–everyones_right_to_konw.pdf> (accessed 12 October 2009); The Department of Premier and Cabinet in New South Wales states that '[t]he new legislation shifts the focus toward greater proactive disclosure'. The Department of Premier and Cabinet in New South Wales (2009) *Open Government Information: FOI Reform in New South Wales*, Online. Available HTTP: <http://www.dpc.nsw.gov.au/prem/foi_reform–open_government_information> (accessed

12 October 2009). The New South Wales Parliament passed new FOI legislation on 26 June 2009. One objective of the new FOI legislation is 'authorizing and encouraging the proactive public release of government information by agencies'. *Government Information (Public Access) Act 2009*. Art 3.

4 H. Kubicek (2004) 'Third-Generation Freedom of Information in the Context of E-Government: The Case of Bremen, Germany', in G. Aichholzer and H. Burkert (eds) *Public Sector Information in the Digital Age: Between Markets, Public Management and Citizens' Rights*, Cheltenham: Edward Elgar Publishing, p.280; M. Paterson (2005) *Freedom of Information and Privacy in Australia*, Sydney: LexisNexis Butterworths, p.498.

5 A. Roberts (2006a) *Blacked Out: Government Secrecy in the Information Age*, New York: Cambridge University Press, pp.199–227; A. Roberts (2006b) 'Dashed Expectations: Governmental Adaptation to Transparency Rules', in C. Hood and D. Heald (eds) *Transparency: The Key to Better Governance?* Oxford: Oxford University Press, pp.114–115; A. Roberts (2007) 'Future Challenges for the RTI Movement', speech delivered at the 5th International Conference of Information Commissioners, Wellington, 26–29 November.

6 Schartum, op.cit., p.76.

7 G. Terrill (2000) 'Individualism and Freedom of Information Legislation', *Freedom of Information Review*, 87: 30.

8 Schartum, op.cit., p.76.

9 Schedler and Proeller argue that one key element of new public management is customer orientation or quality management, which can be exemplified by one-stop shops, service level agreements and e-government. See K. Schedler and I. Proeller (2001) 'The New Public Management: A Perspective from Mainland Europe', in K. McLaughlin and S. Osborne (eds) *New Public Management: Current Trends and Future Prospects*, London: Routledge, p.165.

10 Craglia and Blakemore, op.cit., p.187.

11 Schartum, op.cit., pp.76–77.

12 A. Roberts (2001) 'Structural Pluralism and the Right to Information', *University of Toronto Law Journal*, 51: 244.

13 Schartum, op.cit., p.77; R. Gellman (2004) 'The Foundation of United States Government Information Dissemination Policy', in G. Aichholzer and H. Burkert (eds) *Public Sector Information in the Digital Age: Between Markets, Public Management and Citizens' Rights*, Cheltenham: Edward Elgar Publishing, p.126.

14 R. Snell (2008a) 'Opening up the Mindset Is Key to Change.' *The Canberra Times*, 4 November, pp.10–11; Paterson also calls for the improvement of FOI legislation by establishing 'an obligation for agencies to anticipate requests and to use information technology to make broad categories of information immediately available in a readily accessible form'. See Paterson, op.cit., p.498.

15 Gellman, op.cit., p.126; M. Tankersley (1998) 'How the Electronic Freedom of Information Act Amendments of 1996 Update Public Access for the Information Age', *Administrative Law Review*, 50: 422.

16 *Freedom of Information Act 2000*. Arts 19, 20.

17 *Federal Transparency and Access to Public Government Information Law 2002*. Arts 7, 9.

18 The FOI Independent Review Panel, op.cit; Tasmanian Department of Justice, op.cit; The Department of Premier and Cabinet in New South Wales, op.cit.

19 X. S. Yang (2007) 'Subsidiary Report on Learning FOI Regulations', speech delivered at Conference on Learning FOI Regulations, Beijing, 17 May.

20 H. H. Zhou (2007a) 'Zhengfu xinxi gongkai tiaoli dailai liuda bianhua [FOI Regulations Will Bring about Six Changes]. *People's Daily*, 14 February, p.13.

21 The *Notice on Further Promoting Openness in Government Affairs* No 12 [2005] of the General Office of the CPC Central Committee.

22 Yang, op.cit.

23 The Hunan Government (2008) *Freedom of Information Regulations 2007 Annual Report 2008,* Hunan: The Hunan Government.

24 Y. J. Wang (2007) 'Zhengfu xinxi gongkai tiaoli shinian pobing [The Break-through of Legislating on FOI after a Decade]'. *China Youth Daily,* 25 April, p.3.

25 *Freedom of Information Regulations 2007.* Art.10. Article 10 requires government agencies at or above the county level to put emphasis on proactive disclosure of the following government information: 1. Administrative regulations, rules, and normative documents; 2. Plans for national economic and social development, plans for specific projects, plans for regional development and related policies; 3. Statistical information on national economic and social development; 4. Reports on financial budgets and final accounts; 5. Items subject to an administrative fee and the legal basis and standards therefor; 6. Catalogues of the government's centralized procurement projects, their standards and their implementation; 7. Matters subject to administrative permission and their legal bases, conditions, quantities, procedures and deadlines and catalogues of all the materials that need to be submitted when applying for the administrative permission, and the hand-ling thereof; 8. Information on the approval and implementation of major con-struction projects; 9. Policies and measures on such matters as poverty assistance, education, medical care, social security and job creation and their actual imple-mentation; 10. Emergency plans for, early warning information concerning, and counter measures against sudden public events; and 11. Information on the supervision and inspection of environmental protection, public health, safe production, food and drugs, and product quality.

26 *Freedom of Information Regulations 2007.* Art.11. Article 11 adds four extra categories of information for government agencies at the county level to dis-seminate: 1. Important and major matters in urban and rural construction and management; 2. Information on operation of social and public interest business; 3. Information on land requisition or land appropriation, household demolition and resettlement, and the distribution and use of compensation or subsidy funds relating thereto; and 4. Information on the management, usage and distribution of social donations in funds and in kind for emergency and disaster relief, special care for families of martyrs and military service personnel, and assistance to poverty stricken and low income families.

27 *Freedom of Information Regulations 2007.* Art.12. Article 12 requires township government agencies to lay stress on disseminating the following information: 1. Information on implementation of rural work policies of the state; 2. Information on fiscal income and expenses and the management and use of various specialized funds; 3. Overall township (town) land use plans and information on the ver-ification of land to be used by farmers for their primary residences; 4. Informa-tion on land requisition or land appropriation, household demolition and resettlement, and the distribution and use of compensation or subsidy funds; 5. Information on township (town) credits and debts, fund raising and labor levies; 6. Information on the distribution of social donations in funds and in kind for emergency and disaster relief, special care for families of martyrs and military service personnel, and assistance to poverty stricken and low income families; 7. Information on contracting, leasing and auctioning of township and town collec-tively owned enterprises and other township and town economic entities; and 8. Information on implementation of the family planning policy.

28 *Freedom of Information Regulations 2007.* Art.9.

29 Article 15 requires government agencies to proactively disclose government information through government bulletins, government websites, press con-ferences, newspapers and periodicals, radio, television or any other means easy for the general public to access.

30 The *Notice on Preparing for the Implementation of FOI Regulations* No 54 [2007] the General Office of the State Council.
31 Ibid.
32 *Freedom of Information Regulations 2007*.Art.16.
33 *Freedom of Information Regulations 2007*.Art.16.
34 In 2000, the Shenzhen archives became the pioneer in receiving current documents from all local government agencies and providing them to the public on request. These new government information services were expanded to other localities rapidly. In 2003, the number of the centres rose to 220 around the country. See S. Guan (2004) 'Fazhan kuai fanwei guang, xingshi duo: yi gongkai xianxing wenjian liyong gongzuo shuping [Rapid Development, Broad Coverage and Various Methods: Discussion of the Use of Current Documents]', *China Archives*, 2: 7.
35 W. B. Xiao (2008c; 2008f) Interview with Librarians (Interview in person, 22 June; 8 July). In the past, only very limited categories of government information, such as official bulletins, were subscribed to by public libraries. Since 2003 libraries cannot subscribe to even these documents as the central government prevented government agencies from undertaking pressured subscription for official publications. This means that any official documents without an ISBN or ISSN cannot be available for subscription. See *Notice on Further Governing the Abusive Distribution of Party and Official Publications by Taking Advantage of Their Position and Power to Alleviate Primary Levels and Farmers' Burden* No 19 [2003] of the General Office of the CPC Central Committee.
36 *Freedom of Information Regulations 2007*. Art.19.
37 *Freedom of Information Regulations 2007*. Art.19.
38 Tankersley, op.cit., p.423.
39 *Freedom of Information Regulations 2007*. Art.19.
40 *Freedom of Information Regulations 2007*. Art.19.
41 Snell and Sebina argue that 'if governments are unable to maintain and operate good records management programs, it is unlikely that they will be transparent and accountable'. See R. Snell and P. Sebina (2007) 'Information Flows: The Real Art of Information Management and Freedom of Information', *Archives and Manuscripts*, 35: 73.
42 Tankersley, op.cit., p.424.
43 *Freedom of Information Regulations 2007*. Art.18.
44 *Freedom of Information Regulations 2007*. Art.33.
45 *Freedom of Information Regulations 2007*. Art.35.
46 Q. Zhang (2007) *Fazhiban jieshao zhengfu xinxi gongkai tiaoli youguan qingkuang bing dawen [The Legislative Affairs of the State Council Introduces FOI Regulations]*. Press release, 24 April.
47 Y. F. Zhou (2005) 'Woguo zhengfu xinxi gongkai lifa pingxi [Analysis of FOI Law-Making Activities in China]', *Journal of Jinan University*, 6: 57.
48 H. H. Zhou (ed.) (2003), *Zhengfu xinxi gongkai tiaoli zhuanjia jianyigao [Academic Draft of FOI Regulations]*, Beijing: China Legal Publishing House, p.16.
49 The State Council Informatization Office (2002) *Zhengfu xinxi gongkai tiaoli (cao an) qicao shuoming [Explanation Memorandum of the Draft of FOI Regulations 2002]*, Beijing: The State Council Informatization Office, p.25.
50 The Open Society Justice Initiative (2006) *Transparency & Silence: A Survey of Access to Information Laws and Practices in 14 Countries*, Online. Available HTTP: <http://www.soros.org/resources/articles_publications/publications/transparency_20060928/transparency_20060928.pdf> (accessed 12 November 2006); V. Iyer (2000) *Freedom of Information: Principles for Legislation*, Online. Available HTTP: <http://unpan1.un.org/intradoc/groups/public/documents/APCITY/UNPAN 002177.pdf> (accessed 13 July 2007).

51 *Freedom of Information Regulations 2007*. Art.13.
52 W. B. Xiao (2008a) Interview with a Chinese Government Official (Interview in person, 16 June).
53 J. Horsley (2007a) *China Adopts First Nationwide Open Government Information Regulations*, Online. Available HTTP: <http://www.freedominfo.org/features/20070509.htm> (accessed 12 May 2007).
54 *Several Suggestions on the Implementation of the FOI Regulations* No 36 [2008] of the General Office of the State Council.
55 Article 19 (1999) *Right to Know: Principles on Freedom of Information Legislation*, Online. Available HTTP: <http://www.article19.org/pdfs/standards/right-toknow.pdf> (accessed 1 July 2007).
56 *Freedom of Information Regulations 2007*. Art.14.
57 B. K. Lim and S. P. Guo (2007) *China Vows Government Transparency, within Limits*, Online. Available HTTP: <http://www.reuters.com/article/idUS-PEK7649220070424> (accessed 22 September 2008); F. Geoffrey and J. Y. Qin (2007) China Moves to Boost Transparency, But Much Is Kept Hidden. *Wall Street Journal*, 25 April, p.A6.
58 *Several Suggestions on the Implementation of the FOI Regulations* No 36 [2008] of the General Office of the State Council.
59 Iyer, op.cit.; Article 19, op.cit.
60 Article 19, op.cit.
61 *Freedom of Information Regulations 2007*. Art.8.
62 Horsley, op.cit.
63 Zhou (ed.), op.cit., p.113.
64 Horsley, op.cit.; L. Zheng (2007) 'Enacting and Implementing Open Government Information Regulations in China: Motivations and Barriers', paper presented at the First International Conference on Theory and Practice of Electronic Governance, Macao, 10–13 December.
65 Trade secrets refers to any technology information or business operation information which is unknown to the public, can bring about economic benefits to the obligee, has practical utility and about which the obligee has adopted secret-keeping measures. *Anti-trust Law 1993*. Art.10.
66 Iyer, op.cit.
67 M. Frankel (2001) *Freedom of Information: Some International Characteristics*, Online. Available HTTP: <http://www.cfoi.org.uk/pdf/amsterdam.pdf> (accessed 13 November 2006).
68 *Freedom of Information Regulations 2007*. Art.14.
69 T. Hart (2005) *Freedom of Information/Access to Government Information Checklist: Minimum Requirements for a Freedom of Information Act (FOIA) and Its Implementation*. Beijing: EU-China Information Society Project.
70 M. McDonagh (1998) *Freedom of Information in Ireland*, Dublin: Round Hall Sweet & Maxwell, p.84.
71 Article 19, op.cit.
72 McDonagh, op.cit., p.84.
73 Mclsaac classifies a public interest test into two categories: a general and special test. See B. Mclsaac (2001) *The Nature and Structure of Exempting Provisions and the Use of the Concept of a Public Interest Override*, Online. Available HTTP: <http://www.atirtf-geai.gc.ca/paper-nature1-e.html> (accessed 15 April 2008).
74 A special public interest test is found in FOI legislation of Australia, Ireland, Canada and the United Kingdom. A general public interest test is found in FOI legislation of New Zealand, India and South Africa.
75 D. Banisar (2005) *Effective Open Government: Improving Public Access to Government Information*, Online. Available HTTP: <http://www.olis.oecd.org/

olis/2005doc.nsf/0/cb40b8eb18975d01c1256fd300582d2d/$FILE/JT00181243.PDF>
(accessed 11 August 2007).
76 *Freedom of Information Regulations 2007*. Art.14.
77 Article 19, op.cit.
78 The Open Society Justice Initiative, op.cit.
79 FOI Rules in Hebei, Hubei, Jiangsu and Liaoning Provinces provided for this principle.
80 J. B. Wen (2008) 'Renzhen guanche dang de shiqida jingshen dali tuijin lianzheng jianshe he fanfubai gongzuo [Seriously Adhere to the Spirits of the 17th National Congress of the CPC to Promote Vigorously the Work of Incorruptibility Construction and Anti-Corruption]', *Qiushi*, 9: 6.
81 F. Z. Chen (2008) 'Guangyu zhengfu xinxi gongkai tiaoli de jige wenti [Several Issues in Relation to FOI Regulations (Pt 2)]', *China Public Administration*, 1: 22.
82 Yang, op.cit.

9 Compliance with proactive disclosure requirements in practice

1 P. Hubbard (2008b) *China's Regulations on Open Government Information: Challenges of Nationwide Policy Implementation*, Online. Available HTTP: <http://www.opengovjournal.org/article/viewArticle/2651> (accessed 22 July 2009).
2 J. T. Hu (2007a) 'Gaoju zhongguo tese shehuizhuyi weida qizhi wei duoqu quanmian jianshe xiaokang shehui xin shengli er fendou [Hold High the Great Banner of Socialism with Chinese Characteristics and Strive for New Victories in Building a Moderately Prosperous Society in All Respects]', speech delivered at the 17th National Congress of the CPC, Beijing, 24 October.
3 J. T. Hu (2008) 'Zai shicha renmin ribaoshe de jianghua [Speech Delivered at the Visit to *People's Daily*]'. *People's Daily*, 20 June, p.4.
4 Premier Wen committed in March 2004 to establishing a government information disclosure system for the first time. See J. B. Wen (2004a) 'Shijie renda erci huiyi shang suozuo zhengfu gongzuo baogao [Report on the Work of the Government to the National People's Congress]', speech delivered at the Second Session of the 10th National People's Congress, Beijing, 16 March.
5 J. B. Wen (2008b) 'Shiyi jie renda yici huiyi shang suozuo zhengfu gongzuo baogao [Report on the Work of the Government to the National People's Congress]', speech delivered at the First Session of the 11th National People's Congress, Beijing, 5 March.
6 J. B. Wen (2009) 'R Shiyi jie renda erci huiyi shang suozuo zhengfu gongzuo baogao [Report on the Work of the Government to the National People's Congress]', speech delivered at the Second Session of the 11th National People's Congress, Beijing, 5 March.
7 J. B. Wen (2008c) 'Renzhen guanche dang de shiqida jingshen dali tuijin lianzheng jianshe he fanfubai gongzuo [Seriously Adhere to the Spirits of the 17th National Congress of the CPC to Promote Vigorously the Work of Incorruptibility Construction and Anti-Corruption]', *Qiushi*, 9: 6. This article was based on Wen's speech at the first incorruptibility conference of the State Council on 25 March 2008 and published on 1 May 2008, the date on which the FOI Regulations took effect.
8 *Working Rules of the State Council* No 14 [2008] of the State Council.
9 *Freedom of Information Regulations 2007*. Art.3.
10 C. H. Hu (2008) 'Zhengfu xinxi gongkai de tizhi [The FOI Mechanism]', in Y. C. Mo and H. C. Lin (eds) *Zhengfu xinxi gongkai tiaoli shiyi [Interpretations of the FOI Regulations in China]*, Beijing: China Legal Publishing House, p.95; X. S. Yang (2007) 'Subsidiary Report on Learning FOI Regulations', speech delivered at

Conference on Learning FOI Regulations, Beijing, 17 May; It is common to see FOI offices 'set up in ministers' offices to oversee implementation and to be a nodal point in the administration' of FOI in order to ensure compliance with FOI legislation. See Oslo Governance Centre (2006) *UNDP and the Right to Information*, Online. Available HTTP: <http://www.freedominfo.org/documents/Seminar_Report – UNDP_and_the_Right_to_Information.pdf> (accessed 5 September 2008).

11 The *Notice on Rules on Major Responsibilities, Divisions and Personnel Quotas of the General Office of the State Council* No 60 [2008] of the General Office of the State Council.

12 The *Notice on Preparing for the Implementation of FOI Regulations* No 54 [2007] of the General Office of the State Council; *Several Suggestions on the Implementation of the FOI Regulations* No 36 [2008] of the General Office of the State Council.

13 R. Snell (2001) 'Administrative Compliance – Evaluating the Effectiveness of Freedom of Information', *Freedom of Information Review*, 93: 29.

14 A. Roberts (2008) *Freedom of Information: From Millions to Billions*, Online. Available HTTP: <http://www.sunshineweek.org/sunshineweek/roberts08> (accessed 31 May 2008); Hubbard, op.cit., p.11.

15 Roberts, op.cit.

16 H. H. Zhou (2007d) 'Woguo tuixing xinxi gongkai zhidu de yiyi yu tedian [Significance and Features of Introducing FOI Legislation in China]', *China Today Forum*, 6: 30.

17 *People's Daily* (2008) 'Xin yi lun guowuyuan jigou gaige qingdong [The Plan for Restructuring the State Council]'. 16 March, p.5.

18 The informatization agencies had commissioned China Software Testing Centre and China Centre for Informatization Performance Assessment to evaluate the performance of government websites for four years (2005–2008). However, they would not directly commission any agencies to assess the performance of government websites in the future, only providing a key indicator system for other assessment agencies to make reference. See X. S. Yang (2009) Speech delivered at the Press Conference on the Seventh Assessment of the Performance of China's Government Websites, Beijing, 11 January.

19 Other indicators include online business, public participation, web design and maintenance. See *Zhongguo zhengfu wangzhan jixiao pinggu zhibiao tixi (2008) [The Indicator System for Assessing the Performance of Government Websites in 2008]* (2008), Online. Available HTTP: <http://xxhs.miit.gov.cn/n11293472/n11295327/n11297217/11746784.html> (accessed 17 March 2009).

20 The *Notice on Preparing for the Implementation of FOI Regulations* No 54 [2007] of the General Office of the State Council; *Several Suggestions on the Implementation of the FOI Regulations* No 36 [2008] of the General Office of the State Council.

21 Y. L. Li and S. W. Wang (2007) 'Zuohao 2007 nian zhengwu gongkai gongzuo yingjie shiqida zhao kai [Fully Implementing the Work of Openness in Government Affairs in 2007 to Support the Opening of the 17th National Congress of the Communist Party of China]'. *Discipline Inspection Daily*, 23 March, p.1.

22 Y. He (2008) 'The Speech of Yong He at the Eighth Meeting of the Leading Group on National Openness in Government Affairs', speech delivered at Beijing, 24 March.

23 Y. J. Li (2007a) *Guanyu biaozhang quanguo zhengwu gongkai gongzuo xianjin danwei de jueding yinfa [The Decision on Awarding Agencies for Their Excellent Work on Openness in Government Affairs Issued]*, Online. Available HTTP: <http://news.xinhuanet.com/newscenter/2007-9/03/content_6657106.htm> (accessed 6 April 2008).

24 Y. J. Li. (2007b) *Guanyu mingming quanguo zhengwu gongkai shifandian de jueding yinfa [The Decision on Nominating National Models of Openness in Government Affairs Issued]*, Online. Available HTTP: <http://news.xinhuanet.com/newscenter/2007–9/03/content_6657023.htm> (accessed 6 April 2008).

25 *China Discipline Inspection Daily* (2007) 'Sangongkai jilu minzhu fazhi jianshe licheng [Three Kinds of Openness Record the Historical Development of Democracy and Legal Systems]'. 3 September, p.1.

26 The National Corruption Prevention Bureau (2007) *Guojia yufang fubaiju bangongshi neishe jigou yu zhize [Departments and Responsibilities of the National Corruption Prevention Bureau]*, Online. Available HTTP: <http://yfj.mos.gov.cn/yfj/news.jsp?mid=20071109026298> (accessed 5 February 2008).

27 *Fayanren zhidu 25 nian huigu [The Retrospective of the 25-Year Spokesperson System]* (2008), Online. Available HTTP: <http://www.51fayan.com/fyrzd25/> (accessed 8 December 2008).

28 C. Wang (2008) *Present a Real China to the World in a More Transparent Way*. Press release, 30 December.

29 Ibid.

30 Audit storms refer to 'an ongoing auditing campaign' run by the Audit Office through making audit results public and exposing misuse or wrongful appropriation of public funds in China. See X. Chen and J. C. Guo (2005) 'Lessons from "Audit Storm" in China', *Chinese Business Review*, 4: 1–3; J. Horsley (2007b) 'Toward a More Open China?', in A. Florini (ed.) *The Right to Know: Transparency for an Open World*, New York: Columbia University Press, p.66.

31 S. X. Liu (2004) 'Shenji bu zai gua fengbao gongkai touming jiang zhubu zhiduhua jingchanghua [Disclosure of Audit Results Will Be Institutionalized and Regularly in China Which Will Not Become Storms Any More]'. *China Youth Daily*, 4 November.

32 *Guangzhou Daily* (2008) 'Tiemian li jinhua xieren shenji fengbao jixu gua [Upright Jinhua Li Left the Office with Audit Storms Still Going on]'. 18 March, p.A4.

33 S. X. Liu (2006) 'Pan Yue: fengbao bing meiyou rang huanbao bumen geng qiangshi [Yue Pan: Environmental Protection Storms Have Not Yet Made Environmental Agencies More Powerful]'. *China Youth Daily*, 6 April, p.7.

34 L. Ma (2007) 'Shangye mimi dangbuliao chaobiao paiwu de dangjianpai [Trade Secrets Cannot Become the Excuse for Standard-Exceeding Emission]'. *The Beijing News*, 23 May, p.A19.

35 H. H. Zhou (2008b) 'Xinxi gongkai tiaoli chutai shimo [The Legislative History of FOI Regulations in China]', *E-Government*, 7: 17.

36 F. Y. Xi (2008) 'Baomifa xiugai yi mojian shiernian jiang suoxiao guojia mimi fanwei [12-Year Consideration of Revising the *Law on the Protection of State Secret*]'. *Legal Daily*, 22 July, p.4.

37 J. Cheng (2008) 'Zhengfu xinxi gongkai tiaoli yu gonggong tushuguan de shijian [FOI Regulations and Public Libraries]', *Information and Documentation Services*, 4, 17; Doty argues that: 'Part of the success of FOIA … stems from the existence of trained librarians, archivists, information resource managers, and other information professionals both external and internal to government. These important intermediaries, and their professional associations, are essential to distributing government information, helping private citizens, journalists, and businesses use such information successfully, and pressuring government to be more open and responsive to the needs of the people.' See P. Doty (2000) *Freedom of Information in the United States: Historical Foundations and Current Trends*, Online. Available HTTP: <http://www.utexas.edu/research/tipi/reports2/foia_doty.pdf.> (accessed 8 September 2006).

38 W. B. Xiao (2008p) Interview with Archivists (Interview in person, 1 August).

39 H. Liu (2007) 'Dangan fa xiuding gongzuo yi qidong [The Revision of the *Archives Law* Initiated]'. *Legal Daily*, 1 May, p.4.
40 Ibid.
41 Beijing TRS Information Technology Co., Ltd. (2009) Interview with Zhigeng Wang, Director of the Digital Resource and Service Department of the National Library (Beijing, 6 February).
42 W. B. Xiao (2008l; 2008n) Interview with Archivists (Interview in person, 22 July, 23 July). The participants said that all library resources were openly accessed, and this made government agencies feel uncomfortable about providing government information to libraries.
43 Beijing TRS Information Technology Co., Ltd., op.cit.
44 Z. Cheng (2009) *Jianli zhengfu xinxi gongkai chuangbo de zhuanyong tongdao [Call for Establishing a Private Channel for Releasing Government Information]*, Online. Available HTTP: <http://www.chinalawlib.org.cn/LunwenShow.aspx?CID=20081224141625700185&AID=20090223195302737037& FID = 20081224141208467131> (accessed 4 May 2009).
45 The National People's Congress (2008) *Shiyi jie quanguo renda changweihui lifa guihua [The Legislative Plan of the 11th Standing Committee of the National People's Congress]*, Online. Available HTTP: <http://www.npc.gov.cn/npc/xinwen/syxw/2008–10/29/content_1455985.htm> (accessed 31 October 2008).
46 The Shanghai Government (2008) *Freedom of Information Rules 2004 Annual Report 2008*, Shanghai: The Shanghai Government.
47 Hubbard, op.cit., p.19; W. B. Xiao (2008e; 2008m) Interview with Chinese Government Officials (Interview in person, 24 June, 23 July).
48 The General Office of the State Council (2008b) *Sichuang kaizhan zhengfu xinxi gongkai tiaoli shixing zhunbei gongzuo zuoyou chengxiao [Preparation for Implementation of FOI Regulations in Sichuan Was Tremendously Effective]*, Online. Available HTTP: <http://www.gov.cn/zfjs/2007–9/18/content_753799.htm> (accessed 19 March 2009).
49 *Suggestions on Strengthening Exploitation and Use of Information Resources* No 34 [2004] of the General Office of the CPC Central Committee.
50 Ibid.
51 Ibid.
52 Sebina argues that new FOI adopters should consider records management as 'an integral part of the access regime rather than an afterthought or an optional extra'. See P. Sebina (2006) 'Freedom of Information and Records Management: A Learning Curve for Botswana', unpublished thesis, University College London, p.185.
53 Y. W. Ou (2007) Speech delivered at Seminar on the FOI Regulations, Beijing, 17 March.
54 H. Qin (2007) Speech delivered at Seminar on the FOI Regulations, Beijing, 17 March.
55 The General Office of the State Council, 2008a) *Freedom of Information Regulations 2007 Annual Report 2008*, Beijing: The General Office of the State Council.
56 P. Hubbard (2008a) 'Discussion of China's FOI Reform' (18 May).
57 Y. He (2008) 'The Speech of Yong He at the Eighth Meeting of the Leading Group on National Openness in Government Affairs', speech delivered at Beijing, 24 March.
58 *Working Rules of the State Council* No 14 [2008] of the State Council; *Decision of the State Council on Strengthening Administration by Law in the Municipal and County Governments* No 17 [2008] of the State Council.
59 *Working Rules of the State Council* No 14 [2008] of the State Council.
60 Such as *Regulations on the Work of Selecting and Appointing Leading Party and Government Cadres 2002*, *Provisional Regulations on the Open Selection of*

Leading Cadres of the Party and Government 2004, Interim Rules on the Tenure System of Leading Cadres of the Party and Government 2006, Rules on the Inter-communication System of Leading Cadres of the Party and Government 2006.

61 Between 1996 and 2003, more than 40,000 civil servants, accounting for about 0.8 per cent, resigned or were dismissed. See *Guojia gongwuyuan cizhi citui gongzuo zongshu [A Summary of the Work of Civil Servants' Resignation and Dismissal]* (2003), Online. Available HTTP: <http://www.china.com.cn/chinese/zhuanti/gwy/385982.htm> (accessed 11 March 2009).

62 The idea belongs to John McMillan, the Australian Commonwealth Ombudsman. See J. McMillan (2002) *Twenty Years of Open Government: What Have We Learnt?* Sydney: The Federation Press, pp.7–8.

63 Deng argued in 1980 that 'we should see to it that our cadres are younger on the average, better educated and better qualified professionally'. See X. P. Deng (1994a) *Deng Xiaoping wenxuan (dier juan) [Selected Works of Xiaoping Deng (Volume II)]*, 2nd edn, Beijing: People's Press, p.326.

64 *Renshibu pandian ganbu renshi zhidu gaige 30nian huigu san jieduan [Thirty-Year Reform of the Cadre of Personnel System Overviewed by the Ministry of Personnel with Three Phases]* (2008), Online. Available HTTP: <http://www.china.com.cn/news/txt/2008–04/11/content_14937807.htm> (accessed 14 April 2008). The percentage in 1977 was only 18 per cent.

65 R. W. Sheng (2003) Interview with the Ministry of Personnel (Beijing, 12 August).

66 The *Notice on Training Sessions for FOI Regulations* [2007] of the Legislative Affairs Office of the State Council.

67 The *Notice on Preparing for the Implementation of FOI Regulations* No 54 [2007] the General Office of the State Council. It required local governments to list FOI as a training course for civil servants.

68 *Freedom of Information Regulations 2007.* Art.9.

69 *Freedom of Information Regulations 2007.* Art.9.

70 Wang, op.cit.

71 In January 2008, the south of China experienced snowstorms that resulted in millions of people being unable to return home to celebrate the traditional Chinese New Year. Many cities suffered blackouts and water shortages for a week. The government promised that it would disclose prompt information to win public support. See *Zhongguo shi shengqu zao hanjian xuezai yi chixu ban yue 3287 wan ren shouzai [Rare Snow Storms in China's 10 Provinces and Has Lasted for Half a Month with 32.87 Million People Being Caught up]* (2008), Online. Available HTTP: <http://www.chinanews.com.cn/gn/news/2008/01–26/1146727.shtml> (accessed 15 April 2008).

72 On 12 May 2008, a magnitude 8.0 earthquake took place in Sichuan Province. The death toll amounted to 69,000, with another 18,000 missing. The government allowed national and international media groups to report this disaster extensively and rapidly. The death toll was updated and disclosed to the public regularly. The National Earthquake Bureau released the information on this massive earthquake to the public only 18 minutes after the outbreak. China Central Television and some local TV stations provided 24-hour coverage of the disaster to give live reports. See Z. J. Ma and P. J. Shi (2008) *Issues on May 12 Wenchuan Earthquake and Damage Evaluation.* Press release, 4 September; H. Han (2008) 'Dizhen xinxi touming chengle zhixu de wendingqi [Transparency in Earthquake Information as a Tool for Maintaining Social Order]'. *The Economic View*, 15 May, p.A04.

73 P. Ford (2008) 'This Time, Beijing's Disaster Response Is Open, Sensitive'. *Christian Science Monitor*, 4 February, p.6.

74 A CNN journalist states that '[t]oday's more open, quick and aggressive reporting is a stark departure from China's poor performance in recent years'. J. FlorCruz (2008) *China's Government Gives Rare Transparent Look at Disaster*, Online.

Available HTTP: <http://www.cnn.com/2008/WORLD/asiapcf/05/15/florcruz. china/> (accessed 22 May 2008); George Yeo, the Foreign Minister of Singapore, argues that the transparent way in which China released the information on the earthquake is 'novel' and 'incredible'. See S. C. Yin (2008) *China's Handling of Quake News 'Novel'*, Online. Available HTTP: <http://www.straitstimes.com/Free/ Story/STIStory_238121.html> (accessed 17 May 2008).

75 J. B. Wen (2008a) *Jiabao Wen Meets with UN Secretary-General Ban Ki-moon in the Quake-Hit Area*. Press release, 24 May 2008.

76 After about 8000 taxi drivers in Chongqing went out strike in the morning of 3 November 2008, the media released this information at noon. The Chongqing government held four press conferences about this strike during the next two days. On 6 November, the Party Secretary Xilai Bo and other government officials arranged an open discussion with taxi drivers, citizens and other representatives, which was allowed to broadcast live by the media. See W. A. Li and H. Deng (2008) *Chaotic Taxi Strike Pays off in Chongqing*, Online. Available HTTP: <http://english.caijing.com.cn/2008-11-15/110028781.html> (accessed 2 December 2008).

77 On 17 November 2008, up to 2000 residents attacked the party headquarters of the city of Longnan in Gansu Province in protest against a government resettlement plan. The Party newspaper, *Gansu Daily*, released this news in the morning of 18 November. The Longnan Government held a press conference on this riot the same day. See *Gansu Daily* (2008) 'Longnanshi wuduqu fasheng quntixing shangfang shijian [A Massive Incident Occurred in the Wudu District of the Longnan City]'. 18 November, p.1.

78 Li and Deng, op.cit.

79 Ibid.

80 In the morning of 28 April 2008, China's worst rail disaster in a decade occurred in Shandong Province which resulted in 72 fatalities and 416 injuries. This accident was caused by the derailment of railway train T195 and collision with another train. The earliest news report was publicized only 4.5 hours after the crash. The death toll was reported at noon and the reason for this accident was released in the afternoon. See *Jiaoji tielu huoche xiangzhuang shigu queren yunanzhe 72 ren [There Were 72 Killed in Train Collision in Shandong]*(2008), Online. Available HTTP: <http://news.163.com/08/0503/00/4AVRQBG40001124J. html> (accessed 3 May 2008).

81 A subway tunnel collapse occurred in the city of Hangzhou in Zhejiang Province on 15 November 2008, causing 17 deaths and 4 missing. The Hangzhou government held a press conference to release the information on this crisis the same day. More than 70 media groups were allowed to air this accident live. The Hangzhou government made a commitment that it would disclose this accident in an open, true and timely manner. See S. Yuan and Y. Jiang (2008) *Hangzhou ditie taxian: hangzhou shiwei shuji tichu bage zhua yaoqiu [The Hangzhou Subway Collapse: The Party Secretary Calls for Eight Requirements]*, Online. Available HTTP: <http://www.chinanews.com.cn/gn/news/2008/11–16/1451030.shtml> (accessed 3 December 2008).

82 In January 2007, the Beijing government noticed a rumour spreading through SMS text messages that said 'don't eat pork! Pork in Beijing has been contaminated by a virus that can cause pyogenic encephalitis'. The Bureaus of Health, Agriculture and Public Security immediately released the accurate information to deny this rumour. See *Pork Meat Disease Outbreak in Beijing: Health Official* (2007), Online. Available HTTP: <http://english.peopledaily.com.cn/ 200701/14/eng20070114_341068.html> (accessed 2 August 2008).

83 After the rumour saying that bananas grown on Hainan contained viruses similar to SARS spread around China by text messages in May 2007, the Ministry of

Agriculture countered this rumour, stating that 'it is purely a rumour and it is impossible for bananas to contain SARS-like viruses'. See China Central Television (2007a) '*Nongyebu: hainan xiaojiao hanyou leisi SARS bingdu [The Ministry of Agriculture Denied the Rumour Saying That Bananas Had Viruses Similar to SARS]*', Online. Available HTTP: <http://vsearch.cctv.com/plgs_play.php?ref=cctvcomprog_20070523_1506487> (accessed 2 December 2008).

84 In September 2008, the company Sanlu, which was based in the city of Shijiazhuang, was found to produce baby milk powder contaminated by melamine. The Shijiazhuang government undertook a secretive and reactive approach to respond to this crisis, and tried to conceal this contamination and sent a late report to the superior government. This approach caused the government the loss of valuable time to deal with the crisis. See *Nanjing Daily* (2008) 'Shijiazhuangshi zhengfu jiu sanlu naifen shijian daoqian [The Shijiangzhuang Government Apologized for the Sanlu Milk Power Scandal]'. 1 October, p.A01.

85 Changjiang Li (the Minister of the General Administration of Quality Supervision, Inspection and Quarantine) resigned over this contamination scandal. Xianguo Wu (the Party Secretary of the CPC Shijiazhuang Municipal Committee) was dismissed. Mayor Chuntang Ji and Vice Mayor Fawang Zhang as well as three other responsible city officials were sacked.

86 R. Q. Zhang (2008) 'Jiaqiang yulun yindao tigao zhizheng nengli [Strengthening Guidance of Public Opinion to Improve the Ruling Capability]'. *Yanzhao Evening*, 15 December, p.A3.

87 *Freedom of Information Regulations 2007*. Art.9.

88 *Interim Measures for Public Participation in Environmental Impact Assessment 2005*. Art.7.

89 *Freedom of Information Regulations 2007*. Art.9.

90 The Xiamen Paraxylene plant project was not subject to the *Interim Measures for Public Participation in Environmental Impact Assessment* as the project was approved before the Measures became effective. However, Xiamen citizens pressured the government, arguing that this project contributed to pollution and was potentially dangerous. Under pressure, the Xiamen government agreed to release the environmental assessment information and seek public comments. After extensive interactive communications with the citizens via an online survey and two public hearings, the government found that about 90 per cent of the citizens resisted this project. As a result, the Xiamen government planned to move this controversial project to another more suitable city. See H. J. Zhu (2007a) 'Gongzhong canyu beihou de zhengfu kaoliang [The Xiamen Government's Consideration of Public Participation]. *Southern Weekend*, 20 December, p.A01; H. J. Zhu (2007b) 'Wo shisi hanwei ni shuohua de quanli [I Will Fight to Death for Your Right to Say It]'. *Southern Weekend*, 20 December, p.A02.

91 In late 2007, a proposed Maglev train route and an environmental impact assessment of the Maglev construction project were posted on government websites to seek public comments. This information was also released to concerned residents after they questioned the convenience of accessing it. Residents worried that the new Maglev train would bring about noise pollution and possibly dangerous radiation. They thus took part in a harmonious walk to oppose this project. This event resulted in the suspension of the Maglev construction. See K. Zhou (2008) 'Shanghai cixuanfu youhua fangan tingqu gefang yijian [The Proposed Shanghai Maglev Construction Project Available for Public Opinion]'. *China Youth Daily*, 14 January, p.7; W. J. Zhang (2008) *Introduction on Shanghai Major Construction Projects in 2008*. Press release, 19 March.

92 In March 2008, after the central government approved a $5 billion oil refinery project in Guangdong province, senior officials in this province were also committed to disclosing the environmental impact assessment of this project and

seeking public comments on it. See S. Y. Tian and H. Xin (2008) 'Nansha xiangmu huo juxing tingzhenghui [Public Hearings will be Held for the Guangdong Oil Refinery Project]'. *Southern Metropolis Daily*, 11 March, p.A09.

93 On 9 November 2007, the National Development and Reform Commission released its proposed readjustment of public holidays and conducted its online survey through the most widely known websites in China, including sina.com, sohu.com and people.com. About 1.55 million netizens took part in this survey, and more than 80 per cent of them showed their support for this readjustment. The State Council adopted new rules on public holidays on 14 December 2007 after considering public comments. See W. Liu (2007) 'Bacheng wangmin zhichi tiaozheng jiejiari [Eighty Per cent of Netizens Support the Readjustment of Public Holidays]'. *Beijing Times*, 16 November, p.2.

94 The Chinese government released its draft plan for health care reform to collect public comments between 14 October and 14 November 2008. This reform aims at providing universal medical service to all Chinese people. 27,892 comments were left on the National Development and Reform Commission website after public debates were completed. See The National Development and Reform Commission (2008a) *Guanyu shenhua yiyao weisheng tizhi gaige de yijian (zhengqiu yijian gao) gongkai zhengqiu yijian de gonggao [Public Notice on Openly Soliciting Comments on 'Opinions about Deepening China's Healthcare Reform (Draft for Input)]'*, Online. Available HTTP: <http://shs.ndrc.gov.cn/yg/qianyan/t20080401_202368.htm> (accessed 15 December 2008).

95 The National Development and Reform Commission and three other authorities publicized a draft scheme on fuel taxation and reform of the refined oil pricing mechanism to solicit public comments between 5 December and 12 December 2008. See The National Development and Reform Commission (2008b) *Guojia fazhan gaige deng bumen gongbu chengpin youjia shuifei gaige fangan gongkai zhengqiu yijian [The National Development and Reform Commission and other Authorities Publicized the Draft Scheme on Fuel Taxation and Reform of the Refined Oil Pricing Mechanism to Seek Public Comments]*, Online. Available HTTP: <http://www.ndrc.gov.cn/xwfb/t20081205_250290.htm> (accessed 8 December 2008).

96 The State Council Legislative Affairs Office first launched this online system in 2007. T. Hou, X. Q. Kong, G. Y.Yan and Z. Z. Sun (2008) 'Xingzheng lifa caoan yijian zhengji guanli xinxi xitong jianshe yanjiu [On the Construction of an Online Information System for Seeking Public Opinions on Drafts of Administrative Rules]', *E-Government*, 7: 90–93. Other legislative affairs offices, such as Shanghai and Shandong, followed suit.

97 *Freedom of Information Regulations 2007*. Art.9.

98 In late November 2008, a netizen learnt from the official website of the Tielin government in Liaoning Province that this local government, only responsible for about 3.04 million citizens, had 9 deputy mayors and 20 deputy secretary-generals. He then posted this fact to the Internet. See J. J. Guo and W. Liu (2008) 'Tielingshi zhengfu she ershi ge fu mishuzhang yin zhengyi [Twenty Deputy Secretary-Generals in the Tielin Government Sparked Heated Discussion]'. *Chengdu Business Daily*, 27 November, p.7. A netizen revealed that there were 11 deputy mayors and 16 deputy secretary-generals in the Xinxiang government in Henan Province. See K. C. Li and Y. R. Wu (2008) 'Xinxiang: fushizhang zhiyou san ming meiyou chaobian [Eight Deputy Mayors in Xinxiang Did not Exceed Personnel Quotas]'. *Oriental Morning Post*, 3 December, p.A20. A netizen revealed that the Pingjiang government in Hunan Province had 10 vice county magistrates and 4 magistrate assistants. Pingjiang is a national poverty county. See Y. F. Deng (2008) 'Hunan pingjiang she shige fuxianzhang [Ten County Deputy Mayors in the Pingjiang County of Hunan Province]'. *New Express Daily*, 4 December, p.A26.

99 The *Notice on Standardizing the Quotas of Assistants and Deputy Secretary-Generals at the Local Level* No 3 [2009] of the Organization Department of the CPC Central Committee.

100 In early 2006, Shuwei Chen, a consumer rights activist, sent his requests to 37 government agencies in the city of Shenzhen in Guangdong Province for information that is required to be proactively disclosed, such as details of major leaders and the allocation and use of special financial funds. Many government agencies did not reply to Chen. He then submitted 37 applications for administrative reconsideration. The Shenzhen Legislative Affairs Office consulted with Chen after noticing Chen's series of applications, and it finally persuaded him to withdraw all his applications. Although Chen did not get the information requested, he prompted local government agencies to reconsider their transparency policies. The Office said that the *Chen* case taught a lesson to Shenzhen government agencies, and forced them to become more transparent. Chen also submitted his requests to several government agencies in the city of Zhuhai in Guangdong Province for similar proactively disclosed information. Although his requests were refused, he won support from the administrative reconsideration agency – the Zhuhai government. See The Guangdong Legislative Affairs Office (2006) *Guangdong sheng: zhengwugongkai yinfa xingzheng fuyi xilie an de xindongxiang zhide gaodu guanzhu [Guangdong Province: Series of Administrative Reconsideration Cases Related to FOI Deserved More Attention]*, Online. Available HTTP: <http://www. fazhi.com.cn/article/dfxx/zffzdt/200603/20060300053093.shtml> (accessed 7 June 2009); *Decision of Administrative Reconsideration Made by the Zhuhai People's Government* No 8 [2006] of the Zhuhai People's Government.

101 After the city of Wuhan brought its FOI Rules into effect in 2004, Zhihong Huang, a foremost combatant against deceptive advertising, sent 16 applications in 2005 to government agencies demanding that they should publicize FOI inventories on their official websites. After he had not received any reply from 10 agencies, he filed administrative reconsideration against them. His administrative reconsideration attracted the attention of the Wuhan Legislative Affairs Office which called on these agencies to comply with their proactive disclosure duty. These agencies finally disclosed their FOI inventories on their websites. See L. Yang (2005) *Yi shimin xiang shi bumen yifa suoqu zhiqingquan zai wuhaishi fazhiban zhichi xia huode chenggong [A Citizen Requested Government Information from 10 Agencies and Achieved Success with the Support of the Wuhan Legislative Affairs Office]*, Online. Available HTTP: <http://www.whfzb.gov.cn/Article,868. html> (accessed 21 October 2008).

102 J. X. Wang (2008a) 'Zhejiang yuyao 68 ming cunmin gaoying shizhengfu [Sixty-Eight Villagers in Yuyao City of Zhejiang Province Won Their FOI Lawsuit]'. *China Youth Daily*, 10 October, p.6.

103 The *Notice on the Pilot Project for Developing the Administrative Reconsideration Committee in Several Provinces and Special Municipalities* No 71 [2008] of the Legislative Affairs Office of the State Council.

104 Between 1 May 2008 and 31 December 2008, 881 applications were made for administrative reconsideration of agency decisions on access requests in 17 provinces. The total number is greater than this. The number is likely to increase in the future.

105 Jianguo Xu, a Beijing lawyer, filed a request dated 1 May 2008 to the Huangzhou District Bureau of Transport for some proactively disclosed information concerning this Bureau's structure, function and working procedures. The Bureau did not answer Xu's request. Xu thus brought the Bureau to court on 2 June. His action won support from the court. See D. D. Tian (2008) 'Zhengfu bumen shouci baisu [The Government Agency Lost Its FOI Lawsuit for the First Time]'. *People's Daily*, 10 October, p.10.

106 C. X. Chu (2008) 'Hubei tongbao xinxi gongkai baisu diyian [The Hubei Government Issued a Bulletin on the Government's First Failure in Relation to FOI Lawsuits]'. *The Beijing News*, 11 October, p.A13.

107 Ibid.

108 On 4 May 2008, Zhou, the head of a relocated household, filed a request to the Rugao Construction Bureau of Jiangsu Province for a building dismantlement licence and other necessary legal documents, which were in the category of proactively disclosed information set out in the FOI Regulations. The government did not answer his request until he took it to court. See The Rugao Propaganda Department (2008) *Nantong shouli zhengfu xinxi gongkai lei xingzheng anjian jiean [The First FOI Lawsuit in Nantong City Was Finalized]*, Online. Available HTTP: <http://www.chinacourt.org/html/article/200808/05/315763.shtml> (accessed 1 January 2011).

109 Xie, a farmer, applied to the Xuchang Development and Reform Commission for policy documents regarding subsidies for breeding pigs on 16 June 2008. Xie took the Commission to court for its mute refusal. The court supported Xie's action, and held that the Commission had the duty to disclose the policy documents sought. The Commission finally gave these documents to Xie after the court actively mediated in this dispute. See Z. He and J. L. Pu (2008) 'Henan shouli zhengfu xinxi gongkai xingzheng susong an tingwai hejie [The First FOI Lawsuit in Henan Province Reached out of Court Settlement]'. *Workers' Daily*, 28 August, p.6.

110 Professor Hanhua Zhou, in an interview with *Southern Weekend* journalists, said that an administrative lawsuit or reconsideration might not be better than a report or complaint to remedy access requests. See Y. T. Su and M. Z. Cai (2008) 'Shishi xinxi gongkai xinfa zaoyu kaitou nan [Implementation of FOI Regulations Challenged at the Beginning]'. *Southern Weekend*, 10 July, p.A05.

111 On 1 May 2008, Puzheng Han, a Hebei lawyer, reported several central government agencies' failure to disclose national standards to the State Council. He said that the General Administration of Quality Supervision, Inspection and Quarantine failed to proactively disclose the national standards of security requirements for students' stationery. He also mentioned that the Ministry of Health released its national standards for food safety and occupation health on its website, but it did not consider the online version as official. In addition, he found that the Ministry of Housing and Urban-Rural Development had sold national standards of urban development. See Y. X. Wu (2008) 'Cangzhou lvshi tousu duo buwei xinxi bu gongkai [A Cangzhou Lawyer Complained to Several State Agencies about the Failure to Disclose Information]'. *Yanzhao City Daily*, 6 May, p.5.

112 S. P. Liu (2008) 'Cangzhou lvshi jianyan huo guowuyuan zhongshi [The Suggestions of a Cangzhou Lawyer Attracted the Attention of the State Council]'. *Yanzhao City Daily*, 5 August, p.5.

113 Ibid.

114 J. Horsley (2007a) *China Adopts First Nationwide Open Government Information Regulations*, Online. Available HTTP: <http://www.freedominfo.org/features/20070509.htm> (accessed 28 August 2007); P. Hubbard (2008b) *China's Regulations on Open Government Information: Challenges of Nationwide Policy Implementation*, Online. Available HTTP: <http://www.opengovjournal.org/article/viewArticle/265> (accessed 22 July 2009).

115 W. B. Xiao (2008c) Interview with Government Officials (Interview in person, 20 June).

116 Y. W. Ou and Y. B. Lv (2006) 'Zhengfu xinxi gongkai zhidu yu woguo de zhengfu xinxi gongkai lifa [FOI System and Legislation of FOI in China]', *Journal of Guangxi Administrative Cadre Institute of Politics and Law*, 6: 18.

117 H. Q. Dun and D. D. Ye (2007) *Xinxi gongkai tuikai mengfeng [The Beginning of FOI Work]*, Online. Available HTTP: <http://www.caijing.com.cn/newcn/ruleof-law/other/2007-04-30/18768.shtml> (accessed 31 August 2007).
118 The Guangdong Legislative Affairs Office, op.cit.
119 Yang, op.cit.
120 Tian, op.cit., p.10
121 Wu, op.cit., p.5.
122 H. J. Li (2008) *Qinghua xuezhe shenqing gongkai wenchuan dizhen liedu xinxi [A Tisunghua Academic Requested Information on Seismic Intensity Distribution Map]*, Online. Available HTTP: <http://www.caijing.com.cn/2008-06-13/100069541.html> (accessed 22 October 2008).
123 *Wenchuan 8.0 ji dizhen liedu fenbutu [The M8.0 Earthquake Intensity Distribution Map in Wenchuan]* (2008), Online. Available HTTP: <http://www.cea.gov.cn/manage/html/8a8587881632fa5c0116674a018300cf/_content/0809/01/1220238314350.html> (accessed 22 October 2008).
124 Wang, op.cit., p.6.
125 The Rugao Propaganda Department, op.cit.
126 He and Pu, op.cit.

10 Non-compliance with reactive disclosure requirements in practice

1 Cheng argues that government agencies have used the scope of government information, FOI exemptions and conflicts of law and regulations as grounds to refuse access requests. See J. Cheng (2009) 'Zheng fu xinxi gongkai de falv shiyong wenti yanjiu [Research on the Application of Law to Government Information Disclosure]', *Political Science and Law*, 3: 29.
2 *Several Suggestions on the Implementation of FOI Regulations* No 36 [2008] of the General Office of the State Council.
3 The General Office of the Inner-Mongolia Autonomous Region (2008) *Nei-menggu zizhiqu bangongting zhengfu xinxi gongkai zhinan [The General Office's FOI Guide]*, Online. Available HTTP: <http://zfxxgk.nmg.gov.cn/default/modules/gkzn/znmx.jsp?columnid=iroot19001&articleid=15160> (accessed 10 October 2008).
4 The General Office of the Inner-Mongolia Autonomous Region (n.d.) *Neimenggu zizhiqu bangongting zhengfu xinxi gongkai zhinan [The General Office's FOI Guide]*, Online. Available HTTP: <http://www.nmg.gov.cn/gkml/> (accessed 8 February 2011).
5 *Freedom of Information Rules of the Commission of National Defence and Science Industry* (2007). Art.2.
6 F. M. Ma (2008) *Zhonghua renmin gongheguo zhengfu xinxi gongkai tiaoli zhuyao falv guifan jiedu [Explanations of Major Clauses in FOI Regulations]*, Online. Available HTTP: <http://www.henan.gov.cn/ztzl/system/2008/02/29/010059943.shtml> (accessed 12 March 2008); J. L. Wu (2009) 'Zhengfu xinxi gongkai xingzheng susong youguan wenti de sikao [Issues Related to FOI Lawsuits]', *E-Government*, 4: 39.
7 The Shanghai Legislative Affairs Office and the Shanghai Institute for Adminis-trative Law Studies (2008a), 'Zhengfu xinxi gongkai de dafu xingshi [The Methods of Replying to Access Requests]', *The Brief Report on the Shanghai Government Rule of Law*, 16.
8 Ibid.
9 W. M. Zhao (2008) 'Toushi zhengfu xinxi gongkai tiaoli shishi hou diyi an [Reflecting on the First Lawsuit after FOI Regulations Took Effect]', *Legal Daily* (Beijing) 6 May, 8; B. X. Jiang and G. Y. Li (2009) 'Zhengfu xinxi gongkai

xingzheng susong ruogan wenti tantao [Discussion of Issues Related to FOI Lawsuits]', *Political Science and Law*, 3: 18.

10 Ibid.

11 Y. Q. Xie (2008) 'Cunmin liangzhi suzhuang gao zhen zhengfu [Villagers Filed Two Lawsuits against the Township Government]', *Huashang Newspaper*, 16 October, p.A14.

12 G. Y. Li (2008) 'Zhengfu xinxi gongkai de jige huise didai [Several Intangible Areas Related to FOI]', *People's Court Daily*, 15 August, p.6.

13 H. Liu (2008) 'Lun zhengfu xinxi gongnkai de ruogan falv wenti [Several Legal Issues Related to FOI]', *Political Science and Law*, 6: 70.

14 X. Y. Sun (2008) 'Zhengfu xinxi gongkai diyi an jiangchi chenzhou [The First FOI Case Suspended in Chenzhou]', *The Beijing News*, 13 May, p.A21.

15 F. Z. Chen (2007) 'Guangyu zhengfu xinxi gongkai tiaoli de jige wenti [Several Issues in Relation to FOI Regulations (Pt 1)]', *China Public Administration*, 2007, 11: 21.

16 *Lian v The General Team of Transportation Police* (2005) 165 The Shanghai No 2 Intermediary People's Court (The Second Instance).

17 X. Zhang (2005) *Su mou yaoqiu renshi guanli jiguan gongkai zhengfu xinxi shangsu an [Su Sued against the Personnel Management Bureau for Not Disclosing Government Information]*, Online. Available HTTP: <http://www.shezfy.com/spyj/alpx_view.aspx?id=2905> (accessed 11 May 2008).

18 G. Li (2008) *Shanghaihai shi zhengfu jujue gongkai gongwuyuan shang MBA xuefei qingkuang bei qisu [The Legal Action against the Shanghai Government for Refusing to Disclose Information on Tuition Fees Paid for Civil Servants' Executive Master of Business Administration Training Courses]*, Online. Available HTTP: <http://www.pil.org.cn/article_view.asp?uid=964> (accessed 10 October 2008).

19 *Su v Shanghai Huangpu District Personnel Bureau* (2005) 72 The Shanghai No 2 Intermediary People's Court (The Second Instance).

20 *Archives Law 1987.* Art.19.

21 J. Cheng (2008) 'Zhengfu xinxi gongkai tiaoli yu gonggong tushuguan de shijian [FOI Regulations and Public Libraries]', *Information and Documentation Services*, 4: 17.

22 *Freedom of Information Rules 2004.* Art.35.

23 Li, op.cit., p.6.

24 Liu, op.cit., p.69.

25 M. Chen (2007) 'Hanhua Zhou: tiaoli de yaohai shi ba xinxi gongkai biancheng zhengfu de fading yiwu [Hanhua Zhou: The Key of FOI Regulations Is to Make FOI Become the Duty of the Government]', *21st Century Business Herald*, 27 April, p.1.

26 Ibid.

27 Liu, op.cit., p.70.

28 Ibid.

29 L. Jie and X. Y. Sun (2008) 'Ershiliu shimin zhuanggao guangzhoushi laobaoju [Twenty Six Guangzhou Citizens Took the Guangzhou Labor Bureau to Court]', *China Youth Daily*, 7 January, p.7.

30 Ibid.

31 X. D. Qin (2008) *Xinxi gongkai xingzheng susong anjian kaiting anhuisheng zhengfu cheng beigao [An FOI Lawsuit Was Tried with the Anhui Government Being Sued]*, Online. Available HTTP: <http://www.caijing.com.cn/2008-10-09/110018705.html> (accessed 10 October 2008).

32 Zhao, op.cit., p.8.

33 L. Zhao and Y. T. Su (2008) 'Zhengfu xinxi yidian rengduo [Many Doubts about Government Information Disclosure]', *Southern Weekend*, 8 May, p.A04.

34 Ibid.
35 W. B. Xiao (2008) Interview with a Chinese Government Official (Interview in person, 9 July).
36 The Shanghai Legislative Affairs Office and the Shanghai Institute for Administrative Law Studies (2008b) 'Zhengfu xinxi gongkai yu xinfang shixiang guanxi bianxi [Analysis of Discrimination between Access Requests and Petitions]', *The Brief Report on the Shanghai Government Rule of Law*, 5.
37 X. D. Zeng (2008) *Guojia zhijian gongju bei lianmin yaoqiu gongkai zhengzhou tapu zhaji diaocha baogao [The General Administration of Quality Supervision, Inspection and Quarantine Was Asked to Disclose the Investigation Report on the Quality of the Mills Produced by a Top Company in Zhengzhou]*, Online. Available HTTP: <http://www.cnr.cn/news/200810/t20081017_505126016.html> (accessed 18 November 2008). The quality of the mills has been questioned by businesses and National People's Congress deputies in recent years.
38 *Freedom of Information Rules of the Ministry of Education* (2008). Art.14.
39 *Freedom of Information Rules of the National Bureau of Tax* (2008). Art.13.
40 *Freedom of Information Interim Rules of the Archives Bureau* (2008). Art.9.
41 *Freedom of Information Rules* (2004). Art.10.
42 Li, op.cit., p.6.
43 Y. Yin and Y. Ding (2007) 'Zhengfu xinxi gongkai xingzheng anjian de falv sikao [On Legal Issues of FOI Lawsuits]', *Shanghai Journal of Law*, 1: 40.
44 *Jordan v United States Dept of Justice* (1978) 591 F 2d 753, 772–773.
45 *Interim Rules on Freedom of Information on the Government Website of the Commission of National Defence and Science Industry* (2007). Art.2.
46 *Interim Rules on Freedom of Information of the Bureau of Intellectual Property* (2008). Art.7.
47 The city of Zhengzhou in Henan Province brought its FOI Rules into effect in 2005. In 2006, Ren requested the information on planning and licence arrangements for the installation of parking-meter mechanisms. However, his request was refused for the reason that the information sought was marked as a confidential state secret. While the government admitted that the classification of parking planning as secret was unreasonable, they still held that some of the information sought concerning high-precision topographic maps fell into the category of state secrets. See D. H. Li and J. D. Li (2006) 'Yangguang zhengfu weihe zaoyu bolimeng [Why Is There the Effect of Glass Door Happening to Sunshine Government]'. *Henan Daily*, 22 June, p.12.
48 Y. Wu (2008) 'Xinxi gongkai hai xu zai chai bolimen [The Glass Door Effect Need to be Broken by FOI]', *People's Daily*, 9 May, p.11.
49 X. D. Qin and Z. X. L. Chen (2008b) 'Yangguang zhengfu panshan qibu [Slowly Move toward Sunshine Government]', *Caijing*, 9: 138.
50 X. M. Li and W. Le (2008) 'Yaoqiu xinxi gongkai lei anjian de sifa shencha [Judicial Review of FOI Lawsuits]'. *People's Court Daily*, 10 October, p.6.
51 Y. Y. Lu and L. Yang (2008) 'Zhengfu xinxi gongkai tiaoli bendi kake [Non-Compliance with FOI Regulations Found at the Sub-National Level]'. *Henan Business Daily*, 12 June, p.A10.
52 Wu, op.cit., p.11.
53 *Yiwei gongmin shenqing zhengfu xinxi gongkai zhi lu [A Citizen's Story about Access to Government Information]* (2008), Online. Available HTTP: <http://www.jsia.gov.cn/Browse/noinfocontent.aspx?id=1991&tablename=tnoinfo> (accessed 10 October 2008).
54 *Several Suggestions on the Implementation of FOI Regulations* No 36 [2008] of the General Office of the State Council.
55 *Working Procedures for Access to Government Information of the Bureau of Foreign Currencies* (2008). Art.14.

56 Z. Z. He (2008) 'Zhengfu xinxi gongkai: haiyou yiduan lu yaozou [FOI Still Has a Long Way to Go]', *21st Century Business Herald*, 8 July, p.8.
57 J. X. Wang (2008a) 'Yi lvshi pilu zhengfu xinxi gongkai zhi guai xianzhuang [A Lawyer Discussed Various Strange Phenomena regarding FOI]', *China Youth Daily*, 10 May, p.3.
58 H. S. Yang (2008) *Gebie difang zhengfu xinxi xianru bugongkai kunjing [Non-Disclosure Problems for Several Local Governments]*, Online. Available HTTP: <http://news.xinhuanet.com/politics/2008–07/30/content_8851290.htm> (accessed 10 March 2009).
59 Wang, op.cit., p.3.
60 The Shanghai Science and Technology Commission (2005) *Freedom of Information Rules 2004 Annual Report 2005,* Shanghai: The Shanghai Science and Technology Commission; Wu, op.cit., p.40.
61 *Administrative Litigation Law* (1989). Art.33.
62 R. Snell (2001) 'Administrative Compliance – Evaluating the Effectiveness of Freedom of Information', *Freedom of Information Review*, 93: 28.
63 The Shanghai Government (2008) *Freedom of Information Rules 2004 Annual Report 2008*, Shanghai: The Shanghai Government.
64 H. Q. Dun and D. D. Ye (2007) *Xinxi gongkai tuikai mengfeng [The Beginning of FOI Work]*, Online. Available HTTP: <http://www.caijing.com.cn/newcn/ruleof-law/other/2007-04-30/18768.shtml> (accessed 31 August 2007).
65 *Gao v Ninghai County People's Government* (2006) 3 The People's Court of Fenghua City (The First Instance).
66 J. Horsley (2007a) *China Adopts First Nationwide Open Government Information Regulations*, Online. Available HTTP: <http://www.freedominfo.org/features/20070509.htm> (accessed 28 August 2007); P. Hubbard (2008b) *China's Regulations on Open Government Information: Challenges of Nationwide Policy Implementation*, Online. Available HTTP: <http://www.opengovjournal.org/article/viewArticle/265> (accessed 22 July 2009).
67 G. Y. Li (2009) 'Zhengfu xinxi gongkai xingzheng susong de dangshiren [Parties to FOI Lawsuits]', *E-Government*, 4: 44; G. Y. Li (2007) 'Zhengfu xinxi gongkai xingzheng susong de shouli wenti (Shang) [Several Issues concerning the Acceptance of FOI Lawsuits (Pt 1)]', *People's Court Daily*, 31 May, p.6.
68 Ibid.
69 Yin and Ding, op.cit., p.41.
70 *Freedom of Information Regulations* (2007). Art.33.
71 *Administrative Litigation Law* (1989). Art.11.
72 Li and Li, op.cit., p.12.
73 *Administrative Litigation Law* (1989). Art.41. This Article stipulates that the following conditions shall be met when a suit is brought: the plaintiff must be a citizen, a legal person or any other organization that considers a concrete administrative action to have infringed upon his or its lawful rights and interests; there must be a specific defendant or defendants; there must be a specific claim and a corresponding factual basis for the suit; and the suit must fall within the scope of cases acceptable to the court and the specific jurisdiction of the court where it is filed.
74 X. D. Qin and Z. X. L. Chen (2008a) *Gongmin shenqing xinxi gongkai cuxing yangguang zhengfu [Citizens Applied for Government Information to Promote 'Sunshine Government']*, Online. Available HTTP: <http://www.caijing.com.cn/20080504/59254.shtml> (accessed 17 May 2008).
75 *Yuhua Chen v The Beijing Municipal Public Security Bureau* (2008) 155 The Dongcheng District People's Court of Beijing (The First Instance).
76 *Liying Gao v The Beijing Sijiqing Township Government* (2008) 201 The Haidian District People's Court of Beijing (The First Instance).

77 Jiang and Li, op.cit., p.12; Li, op.cit., p.6.

78 The *Supreme Court's Explanation on Several Questions Related to the Implementation of the Administrative Litigation Law* (1989).Art.1.

79 Li, op.cit., p.6.

80 J. Ma, Y. L. Deng, X. J. Wang and F. Xu (2008) 'Xinxi gongkai tiaoli wu yue yi ri shishi shitan zhengfu xinxi gongkai [FOI Regulations Came into Force on 1 May: Obtaining a Real Picture of FOI]', *Youth Weekend*, 15 May, p.A08.

81 *Jinsong Hao v The Shaanxi Forestry Department* (2008) 1 The Lianhu District People's Court of Xi'an.

82 Ibid.

83 Zhao, op.cit., p.8.

84 W. J. Wang and J. M. Yu (2008) 'Xinxi gongkai zhengfu bumen shiying ma? [Are Government Agencies Getting Used to FOI?]', *People's Daily*, 8 May, p.10. The Supreme Court circulated *Several Issues Related to the Trial of Civil Dispute Cases Related to Restructuring of Enterprises Provisions* in 2003. Article 3 stipulates that courts shall not accept civil actions regarding disputes occurring in the course of administrative adjustment or transfer of an enterprise's state-owned assets by a competent government department. This Article became the basis for the court rejecting the FOI lawsuit lodged by Huang and others.

85 S. J. Lin (2008) 'Xinxi gongkai shenqing kaitounan xuezhe cheng xiang xingwei yishu [FOI Requests Encounter Difficulties at the Beginning, Similar to Action Art]', *Procuratorial Daily*, 23 July, p.5.

86 Article 20 of the *Supreme Court's Explanation on Several Questions Related to Implementation of the Administrative Litigation Law 1989* only allows the government agency, rather than its instrumentalities, to be the defending party, even if its instrumentalities make a concrete administrative action.

87 Lin, op.cit., p.5.

88 Public Interest Litigation (2005) *Luwanqu fayuan jujue shouli jinhufei zhiqingquan anjian de budangxing [Inappropriateness of the Rejection of an FOI Lawsuit by the Shanghai Luwan District Court]*, Online. Available HTTP: <http://www.pil.org.cn/article_view.asp?uid=175> (accessed 5 September 2007).

89 The Supreme Court allows courts to accept a lawsuit regarding a government agency which does not perform its statutory duty within 60 days. The *Supreme Court's Explanation on Several Questions Related to the Implementation of the Administrative Litigation Law* (1989). Art.39.

90 Zhao, op.cit., p.8.

91 Article 42 of the *Administrative Litigation Law* stipulates that when a court receives a bill of complaint, it shall, upon examination, file a case within seven days or decide to reject the complaint.

92 Zhao, op.cit., p.8.

93 Lin, op.cit., p.5.

94 In 2004, Lian submitted his request to the General Team of Transportation Police of the Shanghai Municipal Public Security Bureau (Transportation Police) for the following two documents: 1. suggestions about the trial on compensation arising from injuries; 2. references concerning compensation occurring traffic accidents. The Transportation Police replied that it did not hold the information requested. Lian brought a lawsuit to the Shanghai Huangpu District Court. The Court rejected Lian's claim as it held that the information sought fell outside the scope of information that is defined under the Shanghai FOI Rules. Lian then filed a lawsuit to the Shanghai No 2 Intermediate Court. The Court upheld the judgment made by the Shanghai Huangpu District. It considered that the defendant had no duty to disclose such information as the information generated by the defendant was a category of internal working materials which did not fall within the scope of the information defined under the Shanghai FOI Rules. See *Lian v*

The General Team of Transportation Police (2005) 165 The Shanghai No 2 Intermediary People's Court (The Second Instance).

95 In 2004, Su submitted his request to the Shanghai Huangpu District Personnel Bureau for the notice concerning the reform of salaries issued by this Bureau, the Shanghai Personnel Bureau's explanation for this reform and the Shanghai Municipal Staff Quota Office's notice on this reform. The Bureau replied that it had no duty to disclose the last two pieces of information as they fell outside the scope of the information defined under the Shanghai FOI Rules. Su applied for external review by the Shanghai Huangpu District Court. The Court considered that the information requested was communicated orally, and thus did not meet the definition of government information under the Shanghai FOI Rules. As a result, the Shanghai Huangpu District Court rejected Su's claim. The Shanghai No 2 Intermediary Court upheld the judgement made by the Shanghai Huangpu District Court. See *Su v Shanghai Huangpu District Personnel Bureau* (2005) 72 The Shanghai No 2 Intermediary People's Court (The Second Instance).

96 Ibid.

97 Y. Yin (2007) 'Tan zhengfu xinxi gongkai xingzheng anjian shenli xin silu [New Thoughts on Trying FOI Cases]', *Shanghai Journal of Law*, 5: 52.

98 Qin and Chen, op.cit., p.138.

99 Qin, op.cit.

100 *Supreme Court's Explanation on Several Questions Related to Implementation of the Administrative Litigation Law* (1989). Art.12.

101 Li, op.cit., p.6.

102 Lin, op.cit., p.5.

103 *Administrative Litigation Law* (1989). Art.32.

104 Yin and Ding, op.cit., p.43; Wu, op.cit., p. 40.

105 The first challenge to an FOI decision in Shanghai occurred only 10 days after the city brought its FOI Rules into effect. On 10 May 2004, Dong submitted a request to the Shanghai Xuhui District Real Estate Bureau for registration information concerning her father's purchase of a house and the government's takeover of the house from 1 September 1947 to 16 July 1968. After the Real Estate Bureau refused to disclose the information, Dong brought an appeal to the Shanghai No 1 Intermediate Court, but the Court considered that there was no longer a need to decide whether it should be disclosed or not as the Real Estate Bureau argued that the information sought did not exist, and so it rejected Dong's appeal. See D. Q. Li and X. Q. Wang (2004) 'Shanghai yi shimin shou su zhengfu xinxi bu gongkai [A Shanghaiese Lodged the First FOI Lawsuit]', *Oriental Morning Post*, 14 June, p.A1; *Oriental Outlook* (2005) '70 sui laoren baisu zhengfu xinxi gongkai diyi an bu liao liao zhi [A 70-Year-Old Woman Lost Her Case Which Was the First FOI Case That Was Closed without Ending]', 19 August.

106 S. X. Liu and C. Wang (2008) 'Gongmin jie xinxi gongkai tiaoli tiwen zhengfu [Citizens Challenge the Government through FOI Regulations]', *China Youth Daily*, 6 May, p.7; H. H. Zhou (2007e) Speech delivered at Seminar on the FOI Regulations, Beijing, 17 March.

107 A. Roberts (2006a) *Blacked Out: Government Secrecy in the Information Age*, New York: Cambridge University Press, pp.116–117.

108 C. Darch and P. Underwood (2009) *Freedom of Information and the Developing World: The Citizen, the State and Models of Openness*, Oxford: Chandos Publishing, p.173.

109 F. Y. Liu and C. H. Wang (2005) *Duo wei shijiao xia de zhengfu xinxi gongkai [Evaluating FOI from Different Perspectives]*, Beijing: China Remin University Press, p.15.

110 Ibid.

111 *Constitution* (1982). Art.33.
112 *Constitution* (1982). Art.13.
113 *Property Law* (2007). Art.4.
114 L. Y. Niu (2003) 'Sunzhigang shijian yu weixian shencha zhidu [Scrutinization of the Constitutional Review System following the Sun Incident]', *Outlook Weekly*, 22: 50–51. Zhigang Sun was treated as a vagrant and detained in a repatriation centre in Guangzhou in March 2003. He was beaten to death by inmates a few days later.
115 *Measures for the Administration of Relief for Vagrants and Beggars without Assured Living Sources in Cities* (2003).
116 Xianzhu Zhang first sued a personnel bureau for its refusal of recruiting him due to his positive Hepatitis B virus status. In 2004, many Chinese citizens petitioned the Standing Committee of the National People's Congress to review discriminatory employment against Hepatitis B virus carriers. See China Law and Governance Review (2006) *Voices against Discrimination: An Update of Recent Cases and Developments*, Online. Available HTTP: <http://www.chinareview.info/pages/case.htm> (accessed 24 April 2008).
117 *General Standards on Physical Examinations concerning the Employment of Civil Servants (for Trial)* (2005). Art.7.
118 In China, a general retirement age for females is 55, but 60 for males.
119 Xianghua Zhou sued against the unconstitutionality of retirement age requirements in 2005 in China for the first time, but she lost her action. See Z. H. Niu (2006) 'Pingdingshan nannv tongling tuixiu an you xin jinzhan dangshiren tiqi weixian shencha jianyi [The Latest Developments in the Case regarding Different Retirement Age for Males and Females in Pingdingshan: Review of the Constitution Recommended]', *Dahe Daily*, 24 July, p.A09.
120 L. Li, J. Feng, M. Y. Wang and Y. Z. Wu (eds) (2006) *Zhongguo fazhi fazhan baogao [The Development Report of Rule of Law in China]*, Beijing: Social Sciences Academic Press, 2006, p.72.
121 In 1998, Lifa Yao became the forerunner who was elected as a deputy of the fourth people's congress of Qianjiang City by a method of self-nomination. In 2003, Lian Wang won a deputy election in Futian District of Shenzhen City as an independent candidate. In the same year, Zhiyong Xu and Hailian Lie also secured their self-nomination and won their deputy election in their own election districts in Beijing.
122 For example, Youjian Huang and his colleagues applied for a survey report on the restructure of a water supply company. The government refused their request. The court did not accept their legal action. See W. M. Zhao (2008) 'Toushi zhengfu xinxi gongkai tiaoli shishi hou diyi an [Reflecting on the First Lawsuit after FOI Regulations Took Effect]', *Legal Daily*, 6 May, p.8; Zhou filed a request for a building dismantlement licence and other necessary legal documents. The government did not answer his request until he filed a lawsuit in the court. See The Rugao Propaganda Department (2008) *Nantong shouli zhengfu xinxi gongkai lei xingzheng anjian jiean [The First FOI Lawsuit in Nantong City Was Finalized]*, Online. Available HTTP: <http://www.chinacourt.org/html/article/200808/05/315763.shtml> (accessed 1 January 2011); Yaofang Xu and 67 other villagers filed a request to the Yuyao Government of Zhejiang Province for information on land transfer. The government rejected their request, but the administrative reconsideration agency supported their application. See J. X. Wang (2008b) 'Zhejiang yuyao 68 ming cunmin gaoying shizhengfu [Sixty-Eight Villagers in Yuyao City of Zhejiang Province Won Their FOI Lawsuit]', *China Youth Daily*, 10 October, p.6; Tianlin Liu requested information on his village's household demolition, resettlement and compensation in 2000. The government refused his request on the ground that the information sought did not exist. See H. Zhang and

S. P. Song (2008) 'Tiaoli shishi hou benshi shouqi gongmin yaoqiu zhengfu xinxi gongkai de anli [The First FOI Case in Zhengzhou after Implementation of FOI Regulations]'. *Zhengzhou Evening*, 7 August, p.A12.

123 For example, Mingxin Zhu lodged her request to the Beijing Municipal Public Security Bureau for information on the progress of her daughter's criminal case. Mingxin Zhu is the mother of Ling Zhu who became the victim of an unsolved 1995 thallium poisoning case. The government has not yet given her any response. Family members of the victims of Baotou air crash in 2004 applied to the Civil Aviation Administration of China for information on the survey of this crash. The government rejected their request. See J. Ma, Y. L. Deng, X. J. Wang and F. Xu (2008) 'Xinxi gongkai tiaoli wu yue yi ri shishi shitan zhengfu xinxi gongkai [FOI Regulations Came into Force on 1 May: Obtaining a Real Picture of FOI]', *Youth Weekend*, 15 May, p.A08.

124 Bin Qiao requested information on the Shenzhen Justice Bureau's processing of his complaint about a public notary office's rejection of his notary application. The government replied to him in an unofficial way. See L. Zhong (2008) *Siren youxiang chongdang zhengwu gongkai pingtai shenzhen sifaju beisu [The Shenzhen Justice Bureau Was Sued for Replying to an FOI Request via a Private Email]*, Online. Available HTTP: <http://www.21cbh.com/HTML/2008/8/26/HTML_X87778CRQ1PG.html> (accessed 22 October 2008).

125 For example, Jin submitted a request to the Dongcheng District Housing Management Bureau for information on the registration records concerning over 50 houses which were purchased by her father and subsequently taken over by the government. The government refused her request. See J. J. Chen (2008) 'Beijingshi fayuan xitong shouli diyiqi sheji zhengfu xinxi gongkai anjian [The Beijing Court Accepted the First FOI Lawsuit]', *The Beijing News*, 19 June, p.A22.

126 Yang filed a request to a personnel department for information on how his pension was calculated. The government rejected his request, but the administrative reconsideration agency supported the request. See G. S. Lv (2008) 'Woshi shou xian shimin yong xinxi gongkai tiaoli weiquan geli [The First FOI Request Lodged in Taiyuan City for Protecting the Access Right]', *Taiyuan Daily*, 14 November, p.3. After the FOI Regulations took effect, veterans and former government officials requested their personnel files stored at the archives in order to claim benefits provided by the government. On many occasions, government agencies replied that the information sought did not exist. W. B. Xiao (2008k; 2008o) Interview with Archivists (Interview in person, 21 July; 30 July).

127 W. B. Xiao (2008i) Interviews with Chinese Citizens (Interview in person, 17 June).

128 W. B. Xiao (2008j) Interviews with Chinese Citizens (Interview in person, 19 June); Q. C. Huang (2008) 'Shenqing xinxi gongkai zaoyu bolimen [FOI Requests Confronted Difficulties]'. *People's Daily*, 12 Nov., p.13.

129 W. B. Xiao (2008h) Interviews with Chinese Academics (Interview in person, 12 July 2008); C. Yuan (2008) 'Haidianqu: zhengfu xinxi gongkai zhihou [After the Implementation of FOI Regulations in Haidian District]'. *China Business News*, 11 June, p.A06.

130 W. B. Xiao (2008b; 2008m) Interview with Chinese Government Officials (Interview in person, 18 June; 23 July).

131 H. C. Lin (2008a) 'Zhengfu xinxi gongkai de susong zhilu duzai hechu [What Factors Impede FOI Lawsuits]'. *Legal Daily*, 4 December, p.3.

132 Ibid.

133 Roberts, op.cit., p.121.

134 R. Callick (2008) 'Chinese FOI Act Tied by Red Tape', *The Australian*, 1 May, p.32.

135 Hachten and Scotton assert that '[w]hen the Communist leaders told government newspapers they had to start paying their own way, Chinese editors got much

more freedom to publish material that would attract readers'. The publication of evening tabloids have prepared the ground for editors to 'publish almost anything they think will attract readers'. See W. Hachten and J. Scotton (2006) *The World News Prism: Global Information in a Satellite Age*, 7th edn, New Jersey: Wiley-Blackwell, p.104.

136 In an interview with a Chinese government official, she said that several journalists went to her office and raised a similar question, 'is that true that you will answer our requests?', after the FOI Regulations took effect. W. B. Xiao (2008q) Interviews with a Chinese Government Official (Interview in person, 1 August).

137 S. James (2006) 'The Potential Benefits of Freedom of Information', in R. Chapman and M. Hunt (eds) *Open Government in a Theoretical and Practical Context*, Surrey: Ashgate Publishing, pp.27–28; M. Rosenbaum (2004) 'Open to Question – Journalism and Freedom of Information', *Communications Law*, 9: 131; S. Lamble (2002) 'Computer-Assisted Reporting and Freedom of Information', unpublished thesis, Queensland University.

138 J. Herman (2004) 'The Urgent Need for Reform of Freedom of Information in Australia', speech delivered at Conference on Public Right to Know, Sydney, 21 August; K. Chongkittavorn (2001) 'Thai Journalists and Access to Information', paper presented at Conference on Freedom of Information and Civil Society in Asia, Tokyo, 13–14 April; R. Snell (2002) 'FOI and the Delivery of Diminishing Returns, or How Spin-Doctors and Journalists Have Mistreated a Volatile Reform', *The Drawing Board: An Australian Review of Public Affairs*, 3: 198–199.

139 S. M. Li (2008) *Beida san jiaoshou dingshang shoudu jichang gaosulu [Three Professors at Beijing University Watched Closely on the Tolls of Beijing Airport Expressway]*, Online. Available HTTP: <http://big5.xinhuanet.com/gate/big5/news.xinhuanet.com/legal/2008–06/18/content_8389725.htm> (accessed 20 October 2008).

140 X. B. Wang (2008) 'Dongbei shouli guanzhu zhengfu zhangmu shenqing zuo dijiao [The First FOI Request for Government Financial Accounts in Northeast China Submitted]'. *Commercial Times*, 25 October, p.A03.

Bibliography

References

Ackerman, J. and Sandoval-Ballesteros, I. (2006) 'The Global Explosion of Freedom of Information Laws', *Administrative Law Review*, 58: 85–130.

Aitken, J. (1998) 'Open Government in New Zealand', in McDonald, A. and Terrill, G. (eds) *Open Government: Freedom of Information and Privacy*, London: Macmillan Press Ltd., pp.117–142.

Ali, M. A. (2003) *Freedom of Information in South Asia: Comparative Perspectives on Civil Society Initiative*, Online. Available HTTP: <http://www.jdhr.org/publications/papers/Mukhtar%20A%20Ali-Media%20panel-0Edited%2027.4.pdf> (accessed 25 February 2009).

Allport, G. and Postman, J. (1947) *The Psychology of Rumour*, New York: Russell & Russell Pub.

Article 19 (1999) *Right to Know: Principles on Freedom of Information Legislation*, Online. Available HTTP: <http://www.article19.org/pdfs/standards/righttoknow.pdf> (accessed 1 July 2007).

——(2001) *A Model Freedom of Information Law*, Online. Available HTTP: <http://www.article19.org/pdfs/standards/modelfoilaw.pdf> (accessed 18 August 2007).

——(2002) *Promoting Practical Access to Democracy: A Survey of Freedom of Information in Central and Eastern Europe*, Online. Available HTTP: <http://www.article19.org/pdfs/publications/freedom-of-information-survey-of-central-and-e.pdf> (accessed 25 February 2009).

Australian Commonwealth (1981) *Parliamentary Debates*, House of Representatives, Canberra: 8 April, p.1232 (Senator Evans).

Bambauer, D., Deibert, R., Palfrey, J., Rohozinski, R., Villeneuve, N. and Zittrain, J. (2005) *Internet Filtering in China in 2004–2005: A Country Study*, Online. Available HTTP: <http://cyber.law.harvard.edu/publications/2005/Internet_Filtering_in_China_in_2004_2005> (accessed 6 January 2010).

Ban, G. (2000) *Han shu: kongguang zhuang [The Book of Han: The Biography of Kong Guang]*, Online. Available HTTP: <http://www.guoxue.com/shibu/24shi/hansu/hsuml.htm> (accessed 10 January 2011).

Banisar, D. (2005) *Effective Open Government: Improving Public Access to Government Information*, Online. Available HTTP: <http://www.olis.oecd.org/olis/2005doc.nsf/0/cb40b8eb18975d01c1256fd300582d2d/$FILE/JT00181243.PDF> (accessed 11 August 2007).

——(2006) *Freedom of Information around the World 2006: A Global Survey of Access to Government Information Laws*, Online. Available HTTP: <http://www.freedom info.org/documents/global_survey2006.pdf> (accessed 9 November 2006).

Barzelay, M. (2001) 'Origins of the New Public Management: An International View from Public Administration/Political Science', in McLaughlin, K. and Osborne, S. (eds) *New Public Management: Current Trends and Future Prospects*, London: Routledge.

Bayne, P. (1984) *Freedom of Information: An Analysis of the Freedom of Information Act 1982 (Cth) and a Synopsis of the Freedom of Information Act 1982 (Vic)*, Sydney: Law Book Co.

Becker, J. (2001) Comrade Jiang Zemin Does Indeed Seem a Proper Choice. *London Review of Books*, 24 May, p.12.

Beijing TRS Information Technology Co., Ltd. (2009) Interview with Zhigeng Wang, Director of the Digital Resource and Service Department of the National Library (Beijing, 6 February).

Bennett, C. (1991) 'Review Article: What Is Policy Convergence and What Causes It?', *British Journal of Political Science*, 21: 215–233.

——(1997) 'Understanding Ripple Effects: The Cross-National Adoption of Policy Instruments for Bureaucratic Accountability', *Governance: An International Journal of Policy and Administration*, 10: 213–233.

——(2001) *Globalization and Access to Information Regimes*, Online. Available HTTP: <http://www.atirtf-geai.gc.ca/paper-globalization1-e.html> (accessed 30 January 2008).

Bergsten, F., Freeman, C., Lardy, N. and Mitchell, D. (2008) *China's Rise: Challenges and Opportunities*, Washington: Peterson Institute for International Economics.

Besley, T., Burgess, R. and Prat, A. (2002) 'Mass Media and Political Accountability', in the World Bank (ed.) *The Right to Tell: The Role of Mass Media in Economic Development*, Washington: World Bank Publications, pp. 45–60.

Birkinshaw, P. (2006) 'Freedom of Information and Openness: Fundamental Human Rights', *Administrative Law Review*, 58: 177–218.

Blanton, T. (2002) 'The Openness Revolution: The Rise of a Global Movement for Freedom of Information', *Development Dialogue*, 1: 16.

Bookman, Z. and Amparan, J. P. G. (2009) 'Two Steps forward, One Step Back: Assessing the Implementation of Mexico's Freedom of Information Act', *Mexican Law Review*, 1: 3–51.

Brown, A. (1997) *The Gorbachev Factor*, New York: Oxford University Press.

Brown, S. (2000) 'Freedom of Information', paper presented at Seminar on Freedom of Information – A Cultural Perspective, Canberra, 21 February.

Cai, W. (2005) Speech delivered at the Fourth National Spokespersons Training Session, Beijing, 2 December.

Callick, R. (2008) 'Chinese FOI Act Tied by Red Tape', *The Australian*, 1 May, p.32.

Candler, B. (1984) 'The Australian Freedom of Information Act: A Personal View', in Gregory, R. (ed.) *The Official Information Act: A Beginning*, Wellington: New Zealand Institute of Public Administration, pp.16–30.

Cao, K. T. and Zhang, Q. (eds) (2008) *Zhengfu xinxi gongkai tiaoli duben [The Primer on China's FOI Regulations]*, Beijing: China Legal Publishing House.

Cao, Y. (2005) 'Jiceng minzhu jiancheng dashi [The Gradual Trend toward Grassroots Democracy]', *People Forum*, 9: 34–35.

Castells, M. (1996) *The Rise of the Network Society*, Cambridge: Blackwell Publishers.

——(2000) 'Materials for an Exploratory Theory of the Network Society', *British Journal of Sociology*, 51: 5–24.

Chen, F. Z. (2007) 'Guangyu zhengfu xinxi gongkai tiaoli de jige wenti [Several Issues in Relation to FOI Regulations (Pt 1)]', *China Public Administration*, 11: 21–23.

——(2008) 'Guangyu zhengfu xinxi gongkai tiaoli de jige wenti [Several Issues in Relation to FOI Regulations (Pt 2)]', *China Public Administration*, 1: 21–23.

Chen, H. C. (2003) *Zhengque bawo shenji dingwei tuidong shengji gongzuo xin fazhan [Setting up a Correct Role for Audits to Promote New Development of Audit Work]*, Online. Available HTTP: <http://www.audit.gov.cn/n1057/n1072/n1342/14784.html> (accessed 5 May 2008).

Chen, J. F. (1999) *Chinese Law: Towards an Understanding of Chinese Law, Its Nature, and Development*, Leiden: Martinus Nijhoff Publishers.

Chen, J. J. (2008) 'Beijingshi fayuan xitong shouli diyiqi sheji zhengfu xinxi gongkai anjian [The Beijing Court Accepted the First FOI Lawsuit]', *The Beijing News*, 19 June, p. A22.

Chen, L. D. and Chen, J. N. (2005) 'Songhuajiang shuiwuran shijian zhong xinxiliu zhangai fenxi [On Impediments to Information Flow during the Crisis of the Songhuajiang River Contamination]', *Press Circles*, 6: 19–22.

Chen, M. (2007) 'Hanhua Zhou: tiaoli de yaohai shi ba xinxi gongkai biancheng zhengfu de fading yiwu [Hanhua Zhou: The Key of FOI Regulations Is to Make FOI Become the Duty of the Government]', *21st Century Business Herald*, 27 April, p.1.

Chen, X. and Guo, J. C. (2005) 'Lessons from "Audit Storm" in China', *Chinese Business Review*, 4: 1–7.

Chen, Y. M. (2007) 'Jiceng minzhuhua yu minzhu jicenghua [Grassroots Democratization and Democracy at the Grassroots Level]', *China Reform*, 9: 27–30.

Cheng, J. (2002) 'Zouxiang kaifang shehui: zhongguo gonggong xinxi huoqu yu zhengwu gongkai zhidu zhi jiantao [Toward Open Society: Examination on Policies Concerning Access to Public Information and Openness in Government Affairs]', *Tsinghua Forum of Rule of Law*, 3: 460–476.

——(2008a) 'Zhengfu xinxi gongkai tiaoli yu gonggong tushuguan de shijian [FOI Regulations and Public Libraries]', *Information and Documentation Services*, 4: 16–18.

——(2008b) 'Difang zhengfu xinxi gongkai guiding shishi qingkuang diaoyan baogao: zhengfu xinxi gongkai tiaoli shishi, women keyi qidai shenme? [Investigation Report on Implementation of Sub-National FOI Rules: What Can We Expect Now That FOI Regulations Are in Effect?]', *Legal Daily*, 11 May, p.3.

——(2009) 'Zheng fu xinxi gongkai de falv shiyong wenti yanjiu [Research on the Application of Law to Government Information Disclosure]', *Political Science and Law*, 3: 28–36.

Cheng, M. D. (2008) *Toushi dangdai zhongguo zhongda tufa shijian [Reflection on Major Crises in Contemporary China]*, Beijing: Chinese Communist Party History Publishing House.

Cheng, Z. (2009) *Jianli zhengfu xinxi gongkai chuangbo de zhuanyong tongdao [Call for Establishing a Private Channel for Releasing Government Information]*, Online. Available HTTP: <http://www.chinalawlib.org.cn/LunwenShow.aspx?CID=20081224 141625700185&AID=20090223195302737037& FID = 20081224141208467131> (accessed 4 May 2009).

Cheung, A. (2005) 'China's Administrative Litigation Law', *Public Law*, Autumn: 549–570.

China Central Television (2000) *Jiangxi: Chajin nongmin jianfu shouce [The Booklet on the Reduction of the Farmers' Burden Was Forbidden to Be Distributed in Jiangxi Province]*, Online. Available HTTP: <http://www.cctv.com/financial/jingji/sanji/zhoume/0102_22/z22_17.html> (accessed 22 March 2008).

——(2007a) *Nongyebu: hainan xiaojiao hanyou leisi SARS bingdu [The Ministry of Agriculture Denied the Rumour Saying That Bananas Had Viruses Similar to SARS]*, Online. Available HTTP: <http://vsearch.cctv.com/plgs_play.php?ref=cctvcomprog_20070523_1506487> (accessed 2 December 2008).

——(2007b) *Wang guoqing: xinwen fayanren gang jige [Guoqing Wang Talks about the Spokesperson System]*, Online. Available HTTP: <http://news.cctv.com/china/20070713/109210.shtml> (accessed 7 August 2007).

China Discipline Inspection Daily (2007) *Sangongkai jilu minzhu fazhi jianshe licheng [Three Kinds of Openness Record the Historical Development of Democracy and Legal Systems]*, 3 September, p.1.

China Internet Network Information Centre (2007) *The 19th Statistical Survey Report on the Internet Development in China*, Online. Available HTTP: <http://www.cnnic.net.cn/download/2007/cnnic19threport.pdf> (accessed 7 August 2008).

——(2008) *The 22nd Statistical Survey Report on the Internet Development in China*, Online. Available HTTP: <http://www.cnnic.cn/download/2008/CNNIC22threport-en.pdf> (accessed 28 November 2008).

China Law and Governance Review (2006) *Voices against Discrimination: An Update of Recent Cases and Developments*, Online. Available HTTP: <http://www.chinareview.info/pages/case.htm> (accessed 24 April 2008).

Chongkittavorn, K. (2001) 'Thai Journalists and Access to Information', paper presented at Conference on Freedom of Information and Civil Society in Asia, Tokyo, 13–14 April.

Chu, C. X. (2008) '*Hubei tongbao xinxi gongkai baisu diyian [The Hubei Government Issued a Bulletin on the Government's First Failure in Relation to FOI Lawsuits]*', *The Beijing News*, 11 October, p.A13.

Clark, D. (1996) 'Open Government in Britain: Discourse and Practice', *Public Money & Management*, 16: 23–30.

Cohen, B. (1963) *The Press and Foreign Policy*, Princeton: Princeton University Press.

Commonwealth (1981) *Parliamentary Debates*, House of Representatives, Canberra: 2 April, p.1059 (Senator Durack, the Attorney-General of Western Australia).

Confucius (2000a), *Verse 18 of Chapter 2 in the Analects of Confucius*, Online. Available HTTP: <http://www.guoxue.com/jinbu/13jing/lunyu/ly_002.htm> (accessed 10 January 2011).

——(2000b), *Verse 9 of Chapter 8 in the Analects of Confucius*, Online. Available HTTP: <http://www.guoxue.com/jinbu/13jing/lunyu/ly_008.htm> (accessed 10 January 2011).

Craglia, M. and Blakemore, M. (2004) 'Access Models for Public Sector Information: The Spatial Data Context', in Aichholzer, G. and Burkert, H. (eds) *Public Sector Information in the Digital Age: Between Markets, Public Management and Citizens' Rights*, Cheltenham: Edward Elgar Publishing, p.187.

Crano, W. (1977) 'Primacy versus Recency in Retention of Information and Opinion Change', *Journal of Social Psychology*, 101: 87–96.

Cui, D. C. (2000)'*Eluosi gaige luoru le minzhuhua xianjin (Shang) [The Russian Reform Fell into the Trap of Democratization (Pt 1)]*', *China National Conditions and Strength*, 2: 34–35.

Cuillier, D. and Piotrowski, S. (2009) 'Internet Information-Seeking and Its Relation to Support for Access to Government Records', *Government Information Quarterly*, 26: 441–449.

Darch, C. and Underwood, P. (2005) 'Freedom of Information Legislation, State Compliance and the Discourse of Knowledge: The South African Experience', *International Information and Library Review*, 37: 77–86.

——(2009) *Freedom of Information and the Developing World: The Citizen, the State and Models of Openness*, Oxford: Chandos Publishing.

Delagrave, A. (2001) *Creating a Culture of Openness & Transparency*, Online. Available HTTP: <http://www.atirtf-geai.gc.ca/speeches/london01-e.html> (accessed 18 August 2009).

Deng, X. P. (1994a) *Deng Xiaoping wenxuan (dier juan) [Selected Works of Xiaoping Deng (Volume II)]*, 2nd edn, Beijing: People's Press.

——(1994b) *Deng Xiaoping wenxuan (disan juan) [Selected Works of Xiaoping Deng (Volume III)]*, 2nd edn, Beijing: People's Press.

Deng, Y. F. (2008) 'Hunan pingjiang she shige fuxianzhang [Ten County Deputy Mayors in the Pingjiang County of Hunan Province]', *New Express Daily*, 4 December, p.A26.

Digest (2000) 'Tonghai dadizhen sanshi nianhou jiemi [The Tonghai Earthquake Was Declassified after 30 Years]', 16 January, p.3.

Dijk, J. V. (2006) *The Network Society: Social Aspects of New Media*, 2nd edn, California: Sage Publications Ltd.

Donk, W. B. H. J. van de and Snellen, I. Th. M. (1998) 'Towards a Theory of Public Administration in an Information Age?' in Snellen, I. Th. M. and Donk, W. B. H. J. van de (eds) *Public Administration in an Information Age: A Handbook*, Fairfax: IOS Press, pp.3–8.

Doty, P. (2000) *Freedom of Information in the United States: Historical Foundations and Current Trends*, Online. Available HTTP: <http://www.utexas.edu/research/tipi/reports2/foia_doty.pdf.> (accessed 8 September 2006).

Dun, H. Q. and Ye, D. D. (2007) *Xinxi gongkai tuikai mengfeng [The Beginning of FOI Work]*, Online. Available HTTP: <http://www.caijing.com.cn/newcn/ruleoflaw/other/2007-04-30/18768.shtml> (accessed 31 August 2007).

Dun, W. (2003) Interview with Ming'an Jiang, Professor of Peking University (Beijing, 29 September).

Eagles, I., Taggart, M. and Liddell, G. (1992) *Freedom of Information in New Zealand*, Auckland: Oxford University Press.

Elster, J. (1998) *Deliberative Democracy*, Cambridge: Cambridge University Press.

Fayanren zhidu 25 nian huigu [The Retrospective of the 25-Year Spokesperson System] (2008), Online. Available HTTP: <http://www.51fayan.com/fyrzd25/> (accessed 8 December 2008).

Finn, C. (2003) 'Rethinking Commercial Confidentiality in the Decade of Competition Policy', *Freedom of Information Review*, 106, 60–67.

FlorCruz, J. (2008) *China's Government Gives Rare Transparent Look at Disaster*, Online. Available HTTP: <http://www.cnn.com/2008/WORLD/asiapcf/05/15/flor-cruz.china/> (accessed 22 May 2008).

Foerstel, H. (2000) *Freedom of Information and the Right to Know: The Origins and Applications of the Freedom of Information Act*, London: Greenwood Press.

Ford, P. (2008) *This Time, Beijing's Disaster Response Is Open, Sensitive*, Christian Science Monitor, 4 February, p.6.

Frankel, M. (2001) *Freedom of Information: Some International Characteristics*, Online. Available HTTP: <http://www.cfoi.org.uk/pdf/amsterdam.pdf> (accessed 13 November 2006).

Freedom of Information Draft Bill Public Administration Committee, HC 570, 3rd Report Session 1998–1999, HC 570-I.

Gan, Y. S. (2007) 'Speech by Yisheng Gan at the Teleconference on Training in FOI Regulations', speech delivered at Beijing, 17 May.

Gansu Daily (2008) *Longnanshi wuduqu fasheng quntixing shangfang shijian [A Massive Incident Occurred in the Wudu District of the Longnan City]*, 18 November, p.1.

Gao, X., Li, K. Y. and Yuan, Y. (2005) *Zhang Zuoji: wo shi shengzhang ye shi baixing [Zuoji Zhang: I am the Governor and Citizen as Well]*, Online. Available HTTP: <http://politics.people.com.cn/GB/1026/3893203.html> (accessed 20 May 2009).

Gavelin, K. (2009) 'Open Government–Beyond Static Measures Publication'. E-mail (19 August).

Gellman, R. (2004) 'The Foundation of United States Government Information Dissemination Policy', in Aichholzer, G. and Burkert, H. (eds) *Public Sector Information in the Digital Age: Between Markets, Public Management and Citizens' Rights*, Cheltenham: Edward Elgar Publishing, pp.123–135.

Geoffrey, F. and Qin, J. Y. (2007) 'China Moves to Boost Transparency, But Much Is Kept Hidden', *Wall Street Journal*, 25 April, p.A6.

Gillis, R. (1998) 'Freedom of Information and Open Government in Canada', in McDonald, A. and Terrill, G. (eds) *Open Government: Freedom of Information and Privacy*, London: Macmillan Press Ltd., pp.143–166.

Gittings, J. (2005) *The Changing Face of China: From Mao to Market*, New York: Oxford University Press.

Goldring, J. (1981) 'The Foundations of the "New Administrative Law" in Australia', *Australian Institute of Public Administration*, 40, 79–102.

Grugel, J. (2002) *Democratization: A Critical Introduction*, Hampshire: Palgrave Macmillan.

Guan, S. (2004) 'Fazhan kuai fanwei guang, xingshi duo: yi gongkai xianxing wenjian liyong gongzuo shuping [Rapid Development, Broad Coverage and Various Methods: Discussion of the Use of Current Documents]', *China Archives*, 2: 7–9.

Guangzhou Daily (2008) 'Tiemian li jinhua xieren shenji fengbao jixu gua [Upright Jinhua Li Left the Office with Audit Storms Still Going on]', 18 March, p.A4.

Guo, J. J. and Liu, W. (2008) 'Tielingshi zhengfu she ershi ge fu mishuzhang yin zhengyi [Twenty Deputy Secretary-Generals in the Tielin Government Sparked Heated Discussion]', *Chengdu Business Daily*, 27 November, p.7.

Guojia gongwuyuan cizhi citui gongzuo zongshu [A Summary of the Work of Civil Servants' Resignation and Dismissal] (2003), Online. Available HTTP: <http://www.china.com.cn/chinese/zhuanti/gwy/385982.htm> (accessed 11 March 2009).

Hachten, W. and Scotton, J. (2006) *The World News Prism: Global Information in a Satellite Age*, 7th edn, New Jersey: Wiley-Blackwell.

Han, H. (2008) 'Dizhen xinxi touming chengle zhixu de wendingqi [Transparency in Earthquake Information as a Tool for Maintaining Social Order]', *The Economic View*, 15 May, p.A04.

Han, J. and Wang, J. L. (2006) *Woguo yifa xingzheng de jiben lilun yu shishi [The Basic Theory and Practice of Law-Based Administration in China]*, Chengdu: Southwest University Press.

Hao, X. (2006) 'Shouji duanxin: diwu meiti de chuanbo qianli yu fazhan wenti [SMS Messages – The Communication Potential and Development Problems of "the Fifth Medium"]', *Southeast Communication*, 1: 15–16.

Hart, D. (2003) 'Entrepreneurship Policy: What It Is and Where It Came from', in Hart, D. (ed.) *The Emergence of Entrepreneurship Policy: Governance, Start-ups, and Growth in the U.S. Knowledge Economy*, Cambridge: Cambridge University Press, pp.3–19.

Hart, T. (2005) *Freedom of Information/Access to Government Information Checklist: Minimum Requirements for a Freedom of Information Act (FOIA) and Its Implementation*. Beijing: EU-China Information Society Project.

He, B. G. (2003) 'The Theory and Practice of Chinese Grassroots Governance: Five Models', *Japanese Journal of Political Science*, 4, 293–314.

——(2007) 'Xieshang minzhu he minzhuhua [Deliberative Democracy and Democratization]', *China Institute of Theory on the Chinese People's Political Consultative Conference*, 4: 34–39.

He, Y. (2004) 'The Speech of Yong He at the Second Meeting of the Leading Group on National Openness in Government Affairs', speech delivered at Beijing, 29 April.

——(2005a) *The Leading Group on National Openness in Government Affairs Answered the Questions from Journalists about the Notice on Further Promoting Openness in Government Affairs*. Press release, 27 April.

——(2005b) 'The Speech of Yong He at the Fourth Meeting of the Leading Group on National Openness in Government Affairs', speech delivered at Beijing, 25 March.

——(2006) 'The Speech of Yong He at the Sixth Meeting of the Leading Group on National Openness in Government Affairs', speech delivered at Beijing, 31 March.

——(2007) 'The Speech of Yong He at the Seventh Meeting of the Leading Group on National Openness in Government Affairs', speech delivered at Beijing, 21 March.

——(2008) 'The Speech of Yong He at the Eighth Meeting of the Leading Group on National Openness in Government Affairs', speech delivered at Beijing, 24 March.

He, Z. and Pu, J. L. (2008) 'Henan shouli zhengfu xinxi gongkai xingzheng susong an tingwai hejie [The First FOI Lawsuit in Henan Province Reached out of Court Settlement]', *Workers' Daily*, 28 August, p.6.

He, Z. Z. (2008) 'Zhengfu xinxi gongkai: haiyou yiduan lu yaozou [FOI Still Has a Long Way to Go]', *21st Century Business Herald*, 8 July, p.8.

Heald, D. (2006) 'Varieties of Transparency', in Hood, C. and Heald, D. (eds) *Transparency: The Key to Better Governance?* Oxford: Oxford University Press, pp.25–43.

Herman, J. (2004) 'The Urgent Need for Reform of Freedom of Information in Australia', speech delivered at Conference on Public Right to Know, Sydney, 21 August.

Hood, C. (1991) 'A Public Management for All Seasons', *Public Administration*, 69: 3–19.

Horsley, J. (2003) *China's Pioneering Foray into Open Government: A Tale of Two Cities*, Online. Available HTTP: <http://www.freedominfo.org/news/20030714.htm> (accessed 23 August 2006).

——(2004) *Shanghai Advances the Cause of Open Government Information in China*, Online. Available HTTP: <http://www.freedominfo.org/news/20040420.htm> (accessed 23 August 2006).

——(2006) 'Introduction on Open Government Information Implementation', *Government Information Quarterly*, 23: 5–10.

——(2007a) *China Adopts First Nationwide Open Government Information Regulations*, Online. Available HTTP: <http://www.freedominfo.org/features/20070509. htm> (accessed 28 August 2007).

——(2007b) 'Toward a More Open China?' in Florini, A. (ed.) *The Right to Know: Transparency for an Open World*, New York: Columbia University Press, pp. 54–91.

——(2009) 'Weibing's Draft for Comments' (6 May).

Hou, T., Kong, X. Q., Yan, G. Y. and Sun, Z. Z. (2008) 'Xingzheng lifa caoan yijian zhengji guanli xinxi xitong jianshe yanjiu [On the Construction of an Online Information System for Seeking Public Opinions on Drafts of Administrative Rules]', *E-Government*, 7: 90–93.

Hu, A. G. (2002) 'Public Exposure of Economic Losses Resulting from Corruption', *China & World Economy*, 4: 44–49.

Hu, C. H. (2008) 'Zhengfu xinxi gongkai de tizhi [The FOI Mechanism]', in Mo, Y. C. and Lin, H. C. (eds) *Zhengfu xinxi gongkai tiaoli shiyi [Interpretations of the FOI Regulations in China]*, Beijing: China Legal Publishing House, pp. 89–118.

Hu, J. M. and Ma, L. J. (2005) 'Zhengfu guanli yu xinxi gongkai zhi fali jichu [The Legal Foundation for Government Management and FOI]', *Legal Forum*, 4: 13–20.

Hu, J. T. (2002) 'Xianfa wei jianshe xiaokang shehui tigong falv baozhang [Fully Implementing the Constitution to Provide Legal Guarantees for Building a Well-Off Society in All Aspects]', speech delivered at the 20th Anniversary of the Adoption of the Constitution, Beijing, 4 December.

——(2004) Speech delivered at the 50th Anniversary of the National People's Congress, Beijing, 15 September.

——(2007a) 'Gaoju zhongguo tese shehuizhuyi weida qizhi wei duoqu quanmian jianshe xiaokang shehui xin shengli er fendou [Hold High the Great Banner of Socialism with Chinese Characteristics and Strive for New Victories in Building a Moderately Prosperous Society in All Respects]', speech delivered at the 17th National Congress of the CPC, Beijing, 24 October.

——(2007b) Speech delivered at the Party School of the CPC Central Committee, Beijing, 25 June.

——(2008) 'Zai shicha renmin ribaoshe de jianghua [Speech Delivered at the Visit to People's Daily]', *People's Daily*, 20 June, p. 4.

Hu, Y. B. (1982) 'Quanmian kaichuang shehuizhuyi xiandaihua jianshe de xin jumian [Comprehensively Create a New Situation in Building Socialism with Chinese Characteristics]', speech delivered at the 12th National Congress of the CPC, Beijing, 1 September.

Huang, Q. C. (2008) 'Shenqing xinxi gongkai zaoyu bolimen [FOI Requests Confronted Difficulties]', *People's Daily*, 12 November, p. 13.

Huang, S. H. (2007) 'Guanzhu lianghui [Pay Attention to the Sessions of the Chinese People's Political Consultative Conference and the National People's Congress]', *Fujian Daily*, 12 March, p. 2.

Huang, X. H., Fei, W. B., and Huang, J. (2004) 'Wo shi ge bu zhong bu xiao de ren [I Am an Ungrateful and Disloyal Man]', *People's Court Daily*, 21 February, p. 4.

Huang, Z. L. (2004) 'Jiejian guowai zhizhengdang jingyan jiaoxun jiaqiang dan de zhizheng nengli jianshe [Learning Experiences and Lessons from Ruling Parties in Foreign Countries to Strengthen the Building of Governance Capabilities of the CPC]', *Journal of the Party School of Tianjin Committee of the CPC*, 4: 41–49.

Hubbard, P. (2004) 'Accountability in the Grey Area: Employing Stiglitz to Tackle Compliance in a World of Structural Pluralism: A Comparative Study', *Freedom of Information Review*, 111: 26–32.

——(2005) *Freedom of Information and Security Intelligence: An Economic Analysis in an Australian Context*, Online. Available HTTP: <http://www.opengovjournal.org/article/viewArticle/334> (accessed 21 May 2009).

——(2008a) 'Discussion of China's FOI Reform' (18 May 2008).

——(2008b) *China's Regulations on Open Government Information: Challenges of Nationwide Policy Implementation*, Online. Available HTTP: <http://www.open govjournal.org/article/viewArticle/2651> (accessed 22 July 2009).

Hunt, M. and Chapman, R. (2006) 'Open Government and Freedom of Information', in Chapman, R. and Hunt, M. (eds) *Open Government in a Theoretical and Practical Context*, Surrey: Ashgate Publishing.

Information Clearinghouse Japan (2002) *Breaking down the Walls of Secrecy: The Story of the Citizen's Movement for an Information Disclosure Law*, Online. Available HTTP: <http://www.freedominfo.org/features/20020727.htm> (accessed 26 July 2008).

Iyer, V. (2000) *Freedom of Information: Principles for Legislation*, Online. Available HTTP: <http://unpan1.un.org/intradoc/groups/public/documents/APCITY/UNPAN002177. pdf> (accessed 13 July 2007).

James, S. (2006) 'The Potential Benefits of Freedom of Information', in Chapman, R. and Hunt, M. (eds) *Open Government in a Theoretical and Practical Context*, Surrey: Ashgate Publishing, pp.27–32.

Jia, Q. J. (2004) 'Li Hongzhang de jingyan jieshao [Introduction of Experience in Russia by Hongzhang Li]', *Insight China*, 8: 73–75.

Jiang, B. X. and Li, G. Y. (2009) 'Zhengfu xinxi gongkai xingzheng susong ruogan wenti tantao [Discussion of Issues Related to FOI Lawsuits]', *Political Science and Law*, 3: 12–26.

Jiang, Z. M. (1992) 'Jiakuai gaige kaifang he xiandaihua jianshe bufa tuoqu you zhongguo tese shehui zhuyi shiye de gengda shengli [Accelerate Strides toward Reform and Opening up and Modernism, Strive for Greater Victories in Building Socialism with Chinese Characteristics]', speech delivered at the 14th National Congress of the CPC, Beijing, 12 October.

——(1997) 'Gaoju Deng Xiaoping lilun weida qizhi ba jianshe you zhongguo tese shehuizhuyi shiye quanmian tuixiang ershiyi shiji [Hold High the Great Banner of Deng Xiaoping Theory for an All-round Advancement of the Cause of Building Socialism with Chinese Characteristics to the 21st Century]', speech delivered at the 15th National Congress of the CPC, Beijing, 12 September.

——(2002) 'Quanmian jianshe xiaokang shehui kaichuang zhongguo tese shehuizhuyi shiye xin jumian [Build a Well-off Society in an All-Round Way and Create a New Situation in Building Socialism with Chinese Characteristics]', speech delivered at the 16th National Congress of the CPC, Beijing, 8 November.

——(2006)*Jiang Zemin wenxuan (diyi juan) [Selected Works of Zemin Jiang (Volume I)]*, Beijing: People's Press.

Jiaoji tielu huoche xiangzhuang shigu queren yunanzhe 72 ren [There Were 72 Killed in Train Collision in Shandong] (2008), Online. Available HTTP: <http://news.163. com/08/0503/00/4AVRQBG40001124J.html> (accessed 3 May 2008).

Jie, L. and Sun, X. Y. (2008) 'Ershiliu shimin zhuanggao guangzhoushi laobaoju [Twenty-Six Guangzhou Citizens Took the Guangzhou Labor Bureau to Court]', *China Youth Daily*, 7 January, p.7.

Ju, L. H. and Wang, Y. F. (2005) 'Zhongguo xianshi de zhengwu gongkai yunxing tixi de sida zhizhu [Four Factors of the Operation System of Current China's Openness in Government Affairs]', *Journal of Northeast Normal University*, 6: 43–47.

Kolhammar, J. (2008) *The Challenge to Implement the Open Government Information Regulation in China*, Online. Available HTTP: <http://en.chinaelections.org/newsinfo.asp?newsid=17891> (accessed 2 October 2008).

Kreisler, H. (2001) Interview with M. Castells (Berkeley, 9 May).

Kubicek, H. (2004) 'Third-Generation Freedom of Information in the Context of E-Government: The Case of Bremen, Germany', in Aichholzer, G. and Burkert, H. (eds) *Public Sector Information in the Digital Age: Between Markets, Public Management and Citizens' Rights*, Cheltenham: Edward Elgar Publishing, pp. 275–286.

Lamble, S. (2002) 'Computer-Assisted Reporting and Freedom of Information', unpublished thesis, Queensland University.

——(2003) 'FOI as a United States' Foreign Policy Tool: A Carrot and Stick Approach', *Freedom of Information Review*, 105: 38–43.

——(2004) 'Media Use of FOI Surveyed: New Zealand Puts Australia and Canada to Shame', *Freedom of Information Review*, 109: 5–9.

Lan, L. (2005) 'Open Government and Transparency Policy: China's Experience with SARS', *International Public Management Review*, 6: 60–75.

Lang, Y. X. (2005) 'Shangyishi minzhu yu zhongguo de difang jingyan: zhejiangsheng wenlingshi de minzhu kentanhui [Deliberative Democracy and Local Experiences in China: A Case Study on the "Democratic Talkfest" in Zhejiang Province]', *Zhejiang Social Science*, 1, 33–38.

Lao, Z. (2000), *Daodejing di liushiwu zhang [Chapter 65 in Moral Intelligence]*, Online. Available HTTP: <http://www.guoxue.com/zibu/zibu_zhuziml/laozi.htm> (accessed 10 January 2011).

Legal Daily (2008) 'Yifa xingzheng: cong fazhi zhengfu dao fazhi zhengfu [Law-Based Administration: From Government Ruled by Law to Government under the Rule of Law]', 6 July, p. 6.

Lenin, V. (1961a) *Lenin Collected Works (Volume 5)*, Moscow: Foreign Language Publishing House.

——(1961b) *Lenin Collected Works (Volume 29)*, Moscow: Foreign Language Publishing House.

——(1962) *Lenin Collected Works (Volume 10)*, Moscow: Foreign Language Publishing House.

Lewis, J. (2009) *FOIA Blog: Freedom of Information Laws and Policies*, Online. Available HTTP: <http://ww1.huntingdon.edu/jlewis/FOIA/FOIAlog.htm> (accessed 19 August 2009).

Li, D. H. and Li, J. D. (2006) 'Yangguang zhengfu weihe zaoyu bolimeng [Why Is There the Effect of Glass Door Happening to Sunshine Government]', *Henan Daily*, 22 June, p. 12.

Li, D. Q. and Wang, X. Q. (2004) 'Shanghai yi shimin shou su zhengfu xinxi bu gongkai [A Shanghaiese Lodged the First FOI Lawsuit]', *Oriental Morning Post*, 14 June, p. A1.

Li, D. T. (2007) *An End to Exclusivity*, Online. Available HTTP: <http://www.open democracy.net/node/4585> (accessed 7 March 2009).

Li, F. (2005) 'Xuanju minzhu zai zhongguo de shijian [The Practice of Democratic Elections in China]', *China Reform*, 9: 15–21.

Li, G. (2008) *Shanghaihai shi zhengfu jujue gongkai gongwuyuan shang MBA xuefei qingkuang bei qisu [The Legal Action against the Shanghai Government for Refusing to Disclose Information on Tuition Fees Paid for Civil Servants' Executive Master of*

Business Administration Training Courses], Online. Available HTTP: <http://www.
pil.org.cn/ article_view.asp?uid = 964> (accessed 10 October 2008).

Li, G. Y. (2007) 'Zhengfu xinxi gongkai xingzheng susong de shouli wenti (Shang)
[Several Issues concerning the Acceptance of FOI Lawsuits (Pt 1)]', *People's Court
Daily*, 31 May, p. 6.

——(2008) 'Zhengfu xinxi gongkai de jige huise didai [Several Intangible Areas Related
to FOI]', *People's Court Daily*, 15 August, p.6.

——(2009) 'Zhengfu xinxi gongkai xingzheng susong de dangshiren [Parties to FOI
Lawsuits]', *E-Government*, 4: 43–51.

Li, H. (2004) 'Zhengzhi gongkaixing: yiyi quexian yu qidi [Political Publicity:
Significance, Pitfalls and Inspiration]', *Nanjing Social Science*, 8: 44–53.

Li, H. J. (2008) *Qinghua xuezhe shenqing gongkai wenchuan dizhen liedu xinxi [A
Tisunghua Academic Requested Information on Seismic Intensity Distribution Map]*,
Online. Available HTTP: <http://www.caijing.com.cn/2008-06-13/100069541.html>
(accessed 22 October 2008).

Li, K. C. and Wu,Y. R. (2008) 'Xinxiang: fushizhang zhiyou san ming meiyou chaobian [Eight Deputy Mayors in Xinxiang Did not Exceed Personnel Quotas]',
Oriental Morning Post, 3 December, p. A20.

Li, L., Feng, J., Wang, M. Y. and Wu, Y. Z. (eds) (2006) *Zhongguo fazhi fazhan
baogao [The Development Report of Rule of Law in China]*, Beijing: Social Sciences
Academic Press.

Li, P. (1993) 'Zai bajie renda yici huiyi shang suo zuo zhengfu gongzuo baogao [Report
on the Work of the Government to the National People's Congress]', speech delivered
at the First Session of the 8th National People's Congress, Beijing, 15 March.

Li, S. (2008) 'Zhonghua renmin gongheguo xinxi gongkai tiaoli de zhiding beijing
zhuyao neirong ji mulu bianzhi [The Background, Main Contents and Inventory
Compilation concerning China's FOI Regulations]', *E-Government*, 5: 21–26.

Li, S. M. (2008) *Beida san jiaoshou dingshang shoudu jichang gaosulu [Three Professors at Beijing University Watched Closely on the Tolls of Beijing Airport
Expressway]*, Online. Available HTTP: <http://big5.xinhuanet.com/gate/big5/news.
xinhuanet.com/legal/2008–06/18/content_8389725.htm> (accessed 20 October 2008).

Li, T. Y. (2002) 'Zai dangdai zhongguo yanjiusuo chunjie zuotanhui shang de jianghua
[A Speech at the Spring Festival Forum Held by the Contemporary China Insti-
tute]', *Contemporary China History Studies*, 2: 4–8.

Li, W. A. and Deng, H. (2008) *Chaotic Taxi Strike Pays off in Chongqing*, Online.
Available   HTTP: <http://english.caijing.com.cn/2008-11-15/110028781.html>
(accessed 2 December 2008).

Li, X. M. and Le, W. (2008) 'Yaoqiu xinxi gongkai lei anjian de sifa shencha [Judicial
Review of FOI Lawsuits]', *People's Court Daily*, 10 October, p.6.

Li, Y. J. (2007a) *Guanyu biaozhang quanguo zhengwu gongkai gongzuo xianjin danwei
de jueding yinfa [The Decision on Awarding Agencies for Their Excellent Work on
Openness in Government Affairs Issued]*, Online. Available HTTP: <http://news.xin
huanet.com/newscenter/2007–9/03/content_6657106.htm> (accessed 6 April 2008).

——(2007b) *Guanyu mingming quanguo zhengwu gongkai shifandian de jueding yinfa
[The Decision on Nominating National Models of Openness in Government Affairs
Issued]*, Online. Available HTTP: <http://news.xinhuanet.com/newscenter/2007–9/
03/content_6657023.htm> (accessed 6 April 2008).

Li, Y. L. and Wang, S. W. (2007) 'Zuohao 2007 nian zhengwu gongkai gongzuo
yingjie shiqida zhao kai [Fully Implementing the Work of Openness in Government

Affairs in 2007 to Support the Opening of the 17th National Congress of the Communist Party of China]', *Discipline Inspection Daily*, 23 March, p.1.

Li, Y. J. and Zhang, Q. (2006) *Muqian quanguo sanshiyi ge shengqushi zhengfu jianli zhengwu gongkai guanli zhidu [Thirty-One Provincial Governments Adopted Rules on Openness in Government Affairs]*, Online. Available HTTP: <http://news.xinhuanet.com/politics/2006–12/10/content_5463360.htm> (accessed 19 May 2008).

Li, Z. C. (2003) 'Zhengfu xinxi gongkai yu baozhang zhiqingquan de guanxi [The Relationship between FOI and the Right to Know]', *News Knowledge*, 10: 16–17.

Liao, Z. B. and Cheng, X. Z. (2003) 'Jujiao lianghui [Focus on the Sessions of the Chinese People's Political Consultative Conference and the National People's Congress]', *Information Times*, 4 March, p. A3.

Lim, B. K. and Guo, S. P. (2007) *China Vows Government Transparency, within Limits*, Online. Available HTTP: <http://www.reuters.com/article/idUSPEK7649220070424> (accessed 22 September 2008).

Lin, H. C. (2008a) 'Zhengfu xinxi gongkai gaishu [An Overview of FOI]', in Mo, Y. C. and Lin, H. C. (eds) *Zhengfu xinxi gongkai tiaoli shiyi [Interpretations of China's FOI Regulations]*, Beijing: China Legal Publishing House, pp.27–57.

——(2008b) 'Zhengfu xinxi gongkai de susong zhilu duzai hechu [What Factors Impede FOI Lawsuits]', *Legal Daily*, 4 December, p.3.

Lin, S. J. (2008) 'Xinxi gongkai shenqing kaitounan xuezhe cheng xiang xingwei yishu [FOI Requests Encounter Difficulties at the Beginning, Similar to Action Art]', *Procuratorial Daily*, 23 July, p.5.

Liu, S. X. (2004) 'Shenji bu zai gua fengbao gongkai touming jiang zhubu zhiduhua jingchanghua [Disclosure of Audit Results Will Be Institutionalized and Regularly in China Which Will Not Become Storms Any More]', *China Youth Daily*, 4 November.

Liu, F. Y. and Wang, C. H. (2005)*Duo wei shijiao xia de zhengfu xinxi gongkai [Evaluating FOI from Different Perspectives]*, Beijing: China Remin University Press.

Liu, Hong (2007) 'Dangan fa xiuding gongzuo yi qidong [The Revision of the *Archives Law* Initiated]', *Legal Daily*, 1 May, p.4.

Liu, Hua (2008) 'Lun zhengfu xinxi gongnkai de ruogan falv wenti [Several Legal Issues Related to FOI]', *Political Science and Law*, 6, 66–71.

Liu, Heng (2004) *Zhengfu xinxi gongkai zhidu [FOI Legal Systems]*, Beijing: China Social Sciences Press.

Liu, J. N. (2007) 'China's Reform: Approaching a Dead End', *China Security*, 3: 90–102.

Liu, J. (2005)*Zhiqingquan yu xinxi gongkai fa [The Right to Know and the FOI Act]*, Beijing: Tsinghua University Press.

Liu, S. P. (2008) 'Cangzhou lvshi jianyan huo guowuyuan zhongshi [The Suggestions of a Cangzhou Lawyer Attracted the Attention of the State Council]', *Yanzhao City Daily*, 5 August, p.5.

Liu, S. X. (2006) 'Pan Yue: fengbao bing meiyou rang huanbao bumen geng qiangshi [Yue Pan: Environmental Protection Storms Have Not Yet Made Environmental Agencies More Powerful]', *China Youth Daily*, 6 April, p.7.

Liu, S. X. and Wang, C. (2008) 'Gongmin jie xinxi gongkai tiaoli tiwen zhengfu [Citizens Challenge the Government through FOI Regulations]', *China Youth Daily*, 6 May, p. 7.

Liu, W. (2007) 'Bacheng wangmin zhichi tiaozheng jiejiari [Eighty Per cent of Netizens Support the Readjustment of Public Holidays]', *Beijing Times*, 16 November, p. 2.

Liu, X. (n.d.) *Shuo Yuan (dishi juan) [The Garden of Stories (Chapter 10)]*, Online. Available HTTP: <http://www.shuku.net/novels/classic/shuoyuan/shuoyuan10.html> (accessed 10 January 2011).

Loong-Yu, A. (2006) 'Alter-Globo in Hong Kong', *New Left Review*, 42: 117–130.

Lou, Z. H. (1991) *Renmin de xuanze [The Choice of the People]*, Beijing: China Youth Press.

Lovelock, P. and Ure, J. (2002) 'Assessing China's Efforts in Constructing an E-Government', in Zhang, J. H. and Woesler, M. (eds) *China's Digital Dream*, Bochum: European University Press.

Lu, Y. Y. and Yang, L. (2008) 'Zhengfu xinxi gongkai tiaoli bendi kake [Non-Compliance with FOI Regulations Found at the Sub-National Level]', *Henan Business Daily*, 12 June, p.A10.

Luo, C. P. and Feng, J. (2005) 'Zhongguo baomi zhidu chongzhi dixian [The Classification System Rectified]', *The Beijing News*, 20 September, p.A22–23.

Luo, H. C. (ed.) (2004) *Xiandai xingzheng fazhi de fazhan qushi [The Current Trend in Modern Administrative Law]*. Beijing: China Law Press.

Lv, G. S. (2008) 'Woshi shou xian shimin yong xinxi gongkai tiaoli weiquan geli [The First FOI Request Lodged in Taiyuan City for Protecting the Access Right]', *Taiyuan Daily*, 14 November, p.3.

Ma, F. M. (2008) *Zhonghua renmin gongheguo zhengfu xinxi gongkai tiaoli zhuyao falv guifan jiedu [Explanations of Major Clauses in FOI Regulations]*, Online. Available HTTP: <http://www.henan.gov.cn/ztzl/system/2008/02/29/010059943.shtml> (accessed 12 March 2008).

Ma, J., Deng, Y. L., Wang, X. J. and Xu, F. (2008) 'Xinxi gongkai tiaoli wu yue yi ri shishi shitan zhengfu xinxi gongkai [FOI Regulations Came into Force on 1 May: Obtaining a Real Picture of FOI]', *Youth Weekend*, 15 May, p.A08.

Ma, L. (2007) 'Shangye mimi dangbuliao chaobiao paiwu de dangjianpai [Trade Secrets Cannot Become the Excuse for Standard-Exceeding Emission]', *The Beijing News*, 23 May, p.A19.

Ma, Z. J. and Shi, P. J. (2008) *Issues on May 12 Wenchuan Earthquake and Damage Evaluation*. Press release, 4 September.

Mann, J. (2008) *The China Fantasy: Why Capitalism Will Not Bring Democracy to China*, New York: Penguin.

Mao, Z. D. (1953) *Mao zedong wen xuan (Di san juan) [Selected Works of Zedong Mao (Volume III)]*, Beijing: People's Press.

——(1983) *Mao zedong xinwen gongzuo wenxuan [Selected Works of Zedong Mao on Journalism]*, Beijing: Xinhua Publishing.

——(1991) *Mao zedong quanji (Di si juan) [Collected Works of Zedong Mao (Volume IV)]*, 2nd edn, Beijing: People's Press.

Margetts, H. (2006) 'Transparency and Digital Government', in Hood, C. and Heald, D. (eds) *Transparency: The Key to Better Governance?* Oxford: Oxford University Press, pp.197–207.

Marshall, A. (1920) *Principles of Economics*, 8th edn, London: Macmillan and Co.

Marx, K. and Engels, F. (1986) *Marx and Engels Collected Works (Volume 22)*, London: Lawrence and Wishart.

Mason, A. (2000) 'The Relationship between Freedom of Expression and Freedom of Information' in Beatson, J. and Cripps, Y. (eds) *Freedom of Expression and Freedom of Information*, Oxford: Oxford University Press, pp.225–348.

McCombs, M. and Shaw, D. (1972) 'The Agenda-Setting Function of Mass Media', *Public Opinion Quarterly*, 36: 176–187.

McCrann, G. E. (2007) *An Examination of the Conditions Surrounding the Passage of the 1966 US Freedom of Information Act*, Online. Available HTTP: <http://www.opengovjournal.org/article/viewArticle/995> (accessed 22 July 2009).

McDonagh, M. (1998) *Freedom of Information in Ireland*, Dublin: Round Hall Sweet & Maxwell.

McLeod, R. (2000) 'Freedom of Information', paper presented at the Seminar on Freedom of Information – A Current Perspective, 21 February.

McIsaac, B. (2001) *The Nature and Structure of Exempting Provisions and the Use of the Concept of a Public Interest Override*, Online. Available HTTP: <http://www.atirtf-geai.gc.ca/paper-nature1-e.html> (accessed 15 April 2008).

McMillan, J. (2002) *Twenty Years of Open Government: What Have We Learnt?* Sydney: The Federation Press.

McQuail, D. (2005) *McQuail's Mass Communication Theory*, 5th edn, California: Saga Publications Ltd.

Meijer, A. J. (2005) 'Risk Maps on the Internet: Transparency and the Management of Risks', *Information Polity*, 10: 105–113.

Mendel, T. (2008) 'Freedom of information: A Comparative Legal Survey', 2nd edn, Paris: UNESCO.

Missen, A. (2002) 'Freedom of Information – The Australian Experience', *Freedom of Information Review*, 100: 42–46.

Mo, Y. C. (2008) 'Jing you yangguan zhengfu zouxiang fazhi zhengfu [From Sunshine Government to Government under the Rule of Law]', in Mo, Y. C. and Lin, H. C. (eds) *Xinxi gongkai tiaoli shiyi [Interpretations of China's FOI Regulations]*, Beijing: China Legal Publishing House.

——(2008) 'Quanli ruhe caineng zai yangguang xia liangxing yunxing [How Can Power Be Exercised Well in a Transparent Way]', *Legal Daily*, 13 February, p.3.

Nanjing Daily (2008) 'Shijiazhuangshi zhengfu jiu sanlu naifen shijian daoqian [The Shijiangzhuang Government Apologized for the Sanlu Milk Power Scandal]', 1 October, p.A01.

Neuman, L. (2009) 'The Assessment Indicator System'. E-mail (19 August).

Neuman, L. and Calland, R. (2007) 'Making the Law Work: The Challenges of Implementation', in Florini, A. (ed.) *The Right to Know: Transparency for an Open World*, New York: Columbia University Press.

New Regulation Approved to Boost Government Transparency (2007) Online. Available HTTP: <http://english.gov.cn/2007–01/17/content_499497.htm> (accessed 12 March 2007).

Niu, L. Y. (2003) 'Sunzhigang shijian yu weixian shencha zhidu [Scrutinization of the Constitutional Review System following the Sun Incident]', *Outlook Weekly*, 22: 50–52.

Niu, Z. H. (2006) 'Pingdingshan nannv tongling tuixiu an you xin jinzhan dangshiren tiqi weixian shencha jianyi [The Latest Developments in the Case regarding Different Retirement Age for Males and Females in Pingdingshan: Review of the Constitution Recommended]', *Dahe Daily*, 24 July, p.A09.

North, D. (1990) *Institutions, Institutional Change and Economic Performance*, New York: Cambridge University Press.

Oriental Outlook (2005) '70 sui laoren baisu zhengfu xinxi gongkai diyi an bu liao liao zhi [A 70-Year-Old Woman Lost Her Case Which Was the First FOI Case That Was Closed without Ending]', 19 August.

Oslo Governance Centre (2006) *UNDP and the Right to Information*, Online. Available HTTP: <http://www.freedominfo.org/documents/Seminar_Report–UNDP_and_the_Right_to_Information.pdf> (accessed 5 September 2008).

Ou, Y. W. (2007) Speech delivered at Seminar on the FOI Regulations, Beijing, 17 March.

Ou, Y. W. and Lv, Y. B. (2006) 'Zhengfu xinxi gongkai zhidu yu woguo de zhengfu xinxi gongkai lifa [FOI System and Legislation of FOI in China]', *Journal of Guangxi Administrative Cadre Institute of Politics and Law*, 6: 14–19.

Pasquier, M. and Vileneuve, J. P. (2006) 'The Totally Transparent Administration: Radical Change or Bureaucratic Illusion?', paper presented at Conference on Public Managers under Pressure between Politics, Professionalism and Civil Society, Milan, 6 September.

Paterson, M. (2004) 'Transparency in the Modern State Happy Birthday FOI! or Commiserations?', *Alterative Law Journal*, 29: 10–14.

——(2005) *Freedom of Information and Privacy in Australia*, Sydney: LexisNexis Butterworths.

Pearlman, M. (2008) *The Importance of Freedom of Information at the Sub-National Level*, Online. Available HTTP: <http://www.state.ct.us/FOI/Articles/Sun-National_Artic.htm> (accessed 3 October 2008).

Peerenboom, R. (2002) *China's Long March toward Rule of Law*, New York: Cambridge University Press.

——(2007) *China Modernizes: Threats to the West or Model for the Rest?* New York: Oxford University Press.

People's Daily (2008) 'Xin yi lun guowuyuan jigou gaige qingdong [The Plan for Restructuring the State Council]', 16 March, p.5.

Peterson, W. and Noel, G. (1951) 'Rumour and Public Opinion', *The American Journal of Sociology*, 57: 159–167.

Piotrowski, S., Zhang, Y. H., Lin, W.W. and Yu, W.X. (2009) 'Key Issues for Implementation of the Chinese Open Government Information Regulations', *Public Administration Review*, 69, 129–135.

Pork Meat Disease Outbreak in Beijing: Health Official (2007), Online. Available HTTP: <http://english.peopledaily.com.cn/200701/14/eng20070114_341068.html> (accessed 2 August 2008).

Potter, P. (1999) 'The Chinese Legal System: Continuing Commitment to the Primacy of State Power', *The China Quarterly*, 159: 673–683.

Public Interest Litigation (2005) *Luwanqu fayuan jujue shouli jinhufei zhiqingquan anjian de budangxing [Inappropriateness of the Rejection of an FOI Lawsuit by the Shanghai Luwan District Court]*, Online. Available HTTP: <http://www.pil.org.cn/article_view.asp?uid=175> (accessed 5 September 2007).

Qiao, M. (2008) 'Shouji duanxin de chuanbo xiaoguo yu zhengzhi yingxiang [The Communication Effect and Political Impact of SMS Messages]', *Contemporary Communications*, 4: 76–77.

Qin, H. (2007) Speech delivered at Seminar on the FOI Regulations, Beijing, 17 March.

Qin, X. D. (2008) *Xinxi gongkai xingzheng susong anjian kaiting anhuisheng zhengfu cheng beigao [An FOI Lawsuit Was Tried with the Anhui Government Being Sued]*, Online. Available HTTP: <http://www.caijing.com.cn/2008-10-09/110018705.html> (accessed 10 October 2008).

Qin, X. D. and Chen, Z. X. L. (2008a) *Gongmin shenqing xinxi gongkai cuxing yang-guang zhengfu [Citizens Applied for Government Information to Promote 'Sunshine*

Government'], Online. Available HTTP: <http://www.caijing.com.cn/20080504/59254.shtml> (accessed 17 May 2008).

——(2008b) 'Yangguang zhengfu panshan qibu [Slowly Move toward Sunshine Government]', *Caijing*, 9: 132–138.

Ren, G. Z. (2002) *Nandai teda kuangnan jiqi jingshi [The Mine Water Leakage Accident in Nandan County and Its Lessons]*, Online. Available HTTP: <http://www.people.com.cn/GB/shehui/212/6048/6320/20020109/644953.html> (accessed 15 April 2008).

Renshibu pandian ganbu renshi zhidu gaige 30nian huigu san jieduan [Thirty-Year Reform of the Cadre of Personnel System Overviewed by the Ministry of Personnel with Three Phases] (2008), Online. Available HTTP: <http://www.china.com.cn/news/txt/2008–04/11/content_14937807.htm> (accessed 14 April 2008).

Report of the Special Rapporteur (1998) *Promotion and Protection of the Right to Freedom of Opinion and Expression*, E/CN.4/1998/40, New York: 28 January, Para 14.

Roberts, A. (1998) *Limited Access: Assessing the Health of Canada's Freedom of Information Laws*, Online. Available HTTP: <http://www.cna-acj.ca/Client/CNA/cna.nsf/object/LimitedAccess/$file/limitedaccess.pdf> (accessed 17 November 2006).

——(2001)'Structural Pluralism and the Right to Information', *University of Toronto Law Journal*, 51: 243–271.

——(2002) 'New Strategies for Enforcement of the Access to Information Act', *Queen's Law Journal*, 27, 647–682.

——(2006a) *Blacked Out: Government Secrecy in the Information Age*, New York: Cambridge University Press.

——(2006b) 'Dashed Expectations: Governmental Adaptation to Transparency Rules', in Hood, C. and Heald, D. (eds) *Transparency: The Key to Better Governance?* Oxford: Oxford University Press, pp.107–125.

——(2007) 'Future Challenges for the RTI Movement', speech delivered at the 5th International Conference of Information Commissioners, Wellington, 26–29 November.

——(2008) *Freedom of Information: From Millions to Billions*, Online. Available HTTP: <http://www.sunshineweek.org/sunshineweek/roberts08> (accessed 2 October 2008).

Rosenbaum, M. (2004) 'Open to Question – Journalism and Freedom of Information', *Communications Law*, 9: 126–135.

Schartum, D. W. (2004) 'Information Access Legislation for the Future? Possibilities according to a Norwegian Experience', in Aichholzer, G. and Burkert, H. (eds) *Public Sector Information in the Digital Age: Between Markets, Public Management and Citizens' Rights*, Cheltenham: Edward Elgar Publishing, pp. 69–90.

Schedler, K. and Proeller, I. (2001) 'The New Public Management: A Perspective from Mainland Europe', in McLaughlin, K. and Osborne, S. (eds) *New Public Management: Current Trends and Future Prospects*, London: Routledge, pp.163–180.

Sebina, P. (2006) 'Freedom of Information and Records Management: A Learning Curve for Botswana', unpublished thesis, University College London.

Shang, Y. G. (2005) 'Lun xingzheng gongkai zhidu [Discussion of the System of Administrative Openness]', *The Epochal Tide*, 24, 48–49.

Sheng, D. L. (2008) 'Xijian mingan shijian buzai wugaizi [It Is Encouraging to Find That the Government Has Not Covered up Sensitive Events]', *Qilu Evening*, 19 November, p. A2.

Sheng, R. W. (2003) Interview with the Ministry of Personnel (Beijing, 12 August).

Shi, W. M. (2005) 'Zhi guibu yi zhi qianli 2000 dao 2005 nian zhongguo jiceng minzhu zhengzhi jianshe huigu [Many a Little Makes a Mickle – An Overview of the Building of Grassroots Democracy in China from 2000 to 2005]', *China Reform*, 9: 15–21.

Snell, R. (1999) 'Administrative Compliance and Freedom of Information in Three Jurisdictions: Australia, Canada and New Zealand', paper presented at Conference on Freedom of Information: One Year on, Dublin, 23 April.

——(2000) 'The Kiwi Paradox – A Comparison of Freedom of Information in Australia and New Zealand', *Federal Law Review*, 28: 575–616.

——(2001) 'Administrative Compliance – Evaluating the Effectiveness of Freedom of Information', *Freedom of Information Review*, 93: 26–32.

——(2002) 'FOI and the Delivery of Diminishing Returns, or How Spin-Doctors and Journalists Have Mistreated a Volatile Reform', *The Drawing Board: An Australian Review of Public Affairs*, 3: 187–207.

——(2005) 'Using Comparative Studies to Improve Freedom of Information Analysis: Insights from Australia, Canada and New Zealand', paper presented at Sixth National and Second International Congress on the Right to Information, Mexico, 8–11 November.

——(2006) 'Freedom of Information Practices', *Agenda*, 13: 291–307.

——(2007) 'Failing the Information Game', *Public Administration Today*, 10: 5–9.

——(2008a) 'Opening up the Mindset Is Key to Change', *The Canberra Times*, 4 November, pp.10–11.

——(2008b) 'Releasing the Potential of FOI – Making the Transition from FOI Version 1.0 to FOI Version 2.0', speech delivered at the University of Tasmania Law School Staff Seminar, Hobart, 5 November.

——(2009) 'Constructing a Field: Commonwealth FOI Studies', speech delivered at Comparative Administrative Law Lecture, Hobart, 7 August.

Snell, R. and Sebina, P. (2007) 'Information Flows: The Real Art of Information Management and Freedom of Information', *Archives and Manuscripts*, 35: 54–81.

Snell, R. and Xiao, W. (2007) 'Freedom of Information Returns to China', *Public Administration Today*, 10: 44–47.

Song, B. and Liu, W. (2008) 'Zhongguo xinwen fayanren zhidu rizhen wanshan [Gradual Perfection of the Spokesperson System in China]', *People's Daily Overseas Edition*, 7 November, p.1.

Southern Daily (2007) 'Xinxi gongkai shi xiandai gongmin shehui de qianzou [FOI Is the Prelude to Civil Society]', 15 February, p.A02.

Stiglitz, J. (1999) 'On Liberty, the Right to Know, and Public Discourse: The Role of Transparency in Public Life', speech delivered at Oxford Amnesty Lecture, Oxford, 27 January.

——(2002) 'Transparency in Government', in the World Bank (ed.) *The Right to Tell: The Role of Mass Media in Economic Development*, Washington: World Bank Publications, pp.27–44.

Stubbs, R. (2008) 'FOI and Democracy in Australia and Beyond', *Australian Journal of Political Science*, 4: 667–684.

Streets, S. (2000) *Administrative Law*, 2nd edn, Sydney: Butterworths, pp.79–102.

Su, Y. T. and Cai, M. Z. (2008) 'Shishi xinxi gongkai xinfa zaoyu kaitou nan [Implementation of FOI Regulations Challenged at the Beginning]', *Southern Weekend*, 10 July, p.A05.

Sun, X. Y. (2008) 'Zhengfu xinxi gongkai diyi an jiangchi chenzhou [The First FOI Case Suspended in Chenzhou]', *The Beijing News*, 13 May, p.A21.

Suominen, K. (2003) 'Access to Information in Latin America and the Caribbean', *Comparative Media Law Journal*, 2: 30–68.

Sutton, G. and Holsen, S. (2006) *China Progresses Information Access and Data Protection Laws*, Online. Available HTTP: <http://www.opengovjournal.org/article/view/621/482> (accessed 22 July 2009).

Tankersley, M. (1998) 'How the Electronic Freedom of Information Act Amendments of 1996 Update Public Access for the Information Age', *Administrative Law Review*, 50: 421–457.

Tasmanian Department of Justice (2009) *Strengthening Trust in Government ... Everyone's Right to Know*, Online. Available HTTP: <http://www.justice.tas.gov.au/_data/assets/pdf_file/0005/118922/Strengthening-trust-in_Government–everyones_right_to_konw.pdf> (accessed 12 October 2009)

Taylor, J. (1998a) 'Governance and Electronic Innovation: Whither the Information Polity?' *Information Communication & Society*, 1: 144–62.

——(1998b) 'Informatization as X-ray: What Is Public Administration for the Information Age?' in Snellen, I. Th. M. and Donk, W. B. H. J. van de (eds) *Public Administration in an Information Age: A Handbook*, Fairfax: IOS Press, pp. 21–32.

——(1999) 'The Information Polity', in Dutton, W. (ed.) *Society on the Line: Information Politics in the Digital Age*, New York: Oxford University Press, pp.197–198.

——(2006) 'Freedom *with* Information: Electronic Government, Information Intensity and Challenges to Citizenship' in Chapman, R. and Hunt, M. (eds) *Open Government in a Theoretical and Practical Context*, Surrey: Ashgate Publishing.

——(2007) 'Rediscovering the Grand Narratives of the Information Polity: Reflections on the Achievement and Potential of the EGPA Study Group on ICT in Public Administration', *Information Polity*, 12: 213–217.

Terrill, G. (1998) 'The Rise and Decline of Freedom of Information in Australia', in McDonald, A. and Terrill, G. (eds) *Open Government: Freedom of Information and Privacy*, London: Macmillan Press Ltd., pp. 89–115.

——(2000a) 'Individualism and Freedom of Information Legislation', *Freedom of Information Review*, 87: 30–32.

——(2000b)*Secrecy and Openness: The Federal Government from Menzies to Whitlam and beyond*, Melbourne: Melbourne University Publishing.

The Access to Information Review Task Force (2002) *Access to Information: Making It Work for Canadians*, Online. Available HTTP: <http://www.atirtf-geai.gc.ca/accessReport-e.pdf> (accessed 28 August 2009).

The Australian Attorney-General's Department (1974) *Proposed Freedom of Information Legislation: Report of Interdepartmental Committee*, Canberra: Australian Government Publishing Service.

——(1983) *Freedom of Information Act 1982 Annual Report 1982–1983*, Canberra: Australian Attorney-General's Department.

——(1987) *Freedom of Information Act 1982 Annual Report 1986–1987*, Canberra: Australian Attorney-General's Department.

——(1988) *Freedom of Information Act 1982 Annual Report 1987–1988*, Canberra: Australian Attorney-General's Department.

——(2006) *Commonwealth Copyright*, Online. Available HTTP: <http://www.ag.gov.au/www/agd/agd.nsf/Page/Copyright_CommonwealthCopyrightAdministration_Commonwealthcopyright> (accessed 4 May 2008).

The Australian Commonwealth Ombudsman (1997) *Annual Report 1996–1997*, Canberra: Australian Commonwealth Ombudsman.

The Australian Senate Standing Committee on Constitutional and Legal Affairs, Parliament of Commonwealth (1979) *Freedom of Information Bill 1978, and Related Aspects of Archives Bill 1978*, Canberra: Commonwealth of Australia.

The Centre for International Communications Studies of Tsinghua University (2005) 'Zhongguo zhengfu zhizheng nengli yu xinwen fayanren zhidu jianshe [The Ruling Capability of the Chinese Government and the Institutionalization of Spokesperson Systems]', *Today's Mass Media*, 8: 7–9.

Zhongguo zhengfu qian lianheguo fubai gongyue ti sitiao jianyi [The Chinese Government Signed the United Nations Convention against Corruption and Put up Four Recommendations] (2003), Online. Available HTTP: <http://news.xinhuanet.com/world/2003–12/11/content_1224815.htm> (accessed 5 April 2008).

The Commonwealth Human Rights Initiative (2003) *Open Sesame: Looking for the Right to Information in the Commonwealth*, Online. Available HTTP: <http://www.humanrightsinitiative.org/publications/chogm/chogm_2003/chogm%202003%20report.pdf> (accessed 25 May 2007).

The CPC Central Committee (2000) *Zhongguo gongchandang di shiwu jie zhongyang weiyuanhui di wu ci quanti huiyi gongbao [Communiqué of the Fifth Plenary Session of the 15th CPC Central Committee]*, Online. Available HTTP: <http://cpc.people.com.cn/GB/64162/64168/64568/65404/4429268.html> (accessed 9 January 2011).

——(2008) *Zhongguo gongchandang di shiqijie zhongyang weiyuanhui di er ci quanti huiyi gongbao [Communiqué of the Second Plenary Session of the 17th CPC Central Committee]*, Online. Available HTTP: <http://politics.people.com.cn/GB/1026/6932293.html> (accessed 9 January 2011).

The Department of Premier and Cabinet in New South Wales (2009) *Open Government Information: FOI Reform in New South Wales*, Online. Available HTTP: <http://www.dpc.nsw.gov.au/prem/foi_reform–open_government_information> (accessed 12 October 2009).

The EU Commission (1998) *Green Paper on Public Sector Information*, 585.

The FOI Independent Review Panel (2008) *The Right to Information: Reviewing Queensland's Freedom of Information Act*, Online. Available HTTP: <http://www.foireview.qld.gov.au/documents_for_download/FOI-review-report-10062008.pdf> (accessed 9 January 2011).

——(2009) *Enhanced Open and Accountable Government: Review of the Freedom of Information Act 1992*, Online. Available HTTP: <http://www.foireview.qld.gov.au/FOIDiscussionpaper240108.pdf> (accessed 9 January 2011).

The General Office of the Central Commission for Discipline Inspection (2004) *Zhengwu gongkai [Openness in Government Affairs]*, Beijing: Fangzheng Press.

The General Office of the Inner-Mongolia Autonomous Region (2008) *Neimenggu zizhiqu bangongting zhengfu xinxi gongkai zhinan [The General Office's FOI Guide]*, Online. Available HTTP: <http://zfxxgk.nmg.gov.cn/default/modules/gkzn/znmx.jsp?columnid=iroot19001&articleid=15160> (accessed 10 October 2008).

The General Office of the Inner-Mongolia Autonomous Region (n.d.) *Neimenggu zizhiqu bangongting zhengfu xinxi gongkai zhinan [The General Office's FOI Guide]*, Online. Available HTTP: <http://www.nmg.gov.cn/gkml/> (accessed 8 February 2011).

The General Office of the State Council (2008a) *Freedom of Information Regulations 2007 Annual Report 2008*, Beijing: The General Office of the State Council.

——(2008b) *Sichuang kaizhan zhengfu xinxi gongkai tiaoli shixing zhunbei gongzuo zuoyou chengxiao [Preparation for Implementation of FOI Regulations in Sichuan Was Tremendously Effective]*, Online. Available HTTP: <http://www.gov.cn/zfjs/2007–9/18/content_753799.htm> (accessed 19 March 2009).

The Guangdong Legislative Affairs Office (2006) *Guangdong sheng: zhengwugongkai yinfa xingzheng fuyi xilie an de xindongxiang zhide gaodu guanzhu [Guangdong Province: Series of Administrative Reconsideration Cases Related to FOI Deserved More Attention]*, Online. Available HTTP: <http://www.fazhi.com.cn/article/dfxx/zffzdt/200603/20060300053093.shtml> (accessed 7 June 2009).

The Hunan Government (2008) *Freedom of Information Regulations 2007 Annual Report 2008*, Hunan: The Hunan Government.

The Internal and Judicial Affairs Committee of the National People's Congress (2004) *Quanguo renda neiwu sifa weiyuanhui guanyu di shi jie quanguo renmin daibiao dahui di er ci huiyi zhuxi tuan jiaofu shenyi de daibiao tichu de yian shenyi jieguo de baogao [The Report on the Review Results of the Proposals from the Deputies of the Second Plenary Session of the 10th National People's Congress by the Internal and Judicial Affairs Committee of the National People's Congress]*, Online. Available HTTP: <http://www.npc.gov.cn/was40/detail?record=1&channelid=20179& searchword = % 20(%20%D5%FE%B8%AE%D0%C5%CF%A2%B9%AB%BF%AA%B7%A8+%29 +and+%28+IDS%3D%27337520'%20)> (accessed 12 January 2009).

The Journalist in the China Legislative Information Network System (2007) Interview with a Leader in the State Council Legislative Affairs Office (Beijing, 25 April).

The Ministry of Civil Affairs (n.d.) *Cunmin zizhi zhuyao chengjiu [The Main Achievements in Villagers' Autonomy]*, Online. Available HTTP: <http://www1.mca.gov.cn/artical/content/WCM_YWJS/20031224145129.htm> (accessed 2 April 2008).

The National Corruption Prevention Bureau (2007) *Guojia yufang fubaiju bangongshi neishe jigou yu zhize [Departments and Responsibilities of the National Corruption Prevention Bureau]*, Online. Available HTTP: <http://yfj.mos.gov.cn/yfj/news.jsp?mid=20071109026298> (accessed 5 February 2008).

The National Development and Reform Commission (2008a) *Guanyu shenhua yiyao weisheng tizhi gaige de yijian (zhengqiu yijian gao) gongkai zhengqiu yijian de gonggao [Public Notice on Openly Soliciting Comments on 'Opinions about Deepening China's Healthcare Reform (Draft for Input)]'*, Online. Available HTTP: <http://shs.ndrc.gov.cn/yg/qianyan/t20080401_202368.htm> (accessed 15 December 2008).

——(2008b) *Guojia fazhan gaige deng bumen gongbu chengpin youjia shuifei gaige fangan gongkai zhengqiu yijian [The National Development and Reform Commission and other Authorities Publicized the Draft Scheme on Fuel Taxation and Reform of the Refined Oil Pricing Mechanism to Seek Public Comments]*, Online. Available HTTP: <http://www.ndrc.gov.cn/xwfb/t20081205_250290.htm> (accessed 8 December 2008).

The National People's Congress (2003) *Shijie quanguo renda changweihui lifa guihua [The Legislative Plan of the 10th Standing Committee of the National People's Congress]*, Online. Available HTTP: <http://www.npc.gov.cn/npc/xinwen/rdyw/wj/2004–02/23/content_328577.htm> (accessed 31 May 2008).

——(2008) *Shiyi jie quanguo renda changweihui lifa guihua [The Legislative Plan of the 11th Standing Committee of the National People's Congress]*, Online. Available HTTP: <http://www.npc.gov.cn/npc/xinwen/syxw/2008–10/29/content_1455985.htm> (accessed 31 October 2008).

The New York Times (1896) *Li on American Hatred*, 3 September, p.10.

The New Zealand Committee on Official Information (1980) *Towards Open Government: General Report*, Online. Available HTTP: <http://www.ombudsmen.parliament.nz/imagelibrary/100168.pdf> (accessed 31 May 2008).

The Open Society Justice Initiative (2006) *Transparency & Silence: A Survey of Access to Information Laws and Practices in 14 Countries*, Online. Available HTTP: <http://www.soros.org/resources/articles_publications/publications/transparency_20060928/transparency_20060928.pdf> (accessed 12 November 2006).

——(2007) *Claude et al v Chile*, Online. Available HTTP: <http://www.justiceinitiative.org/db/resource2?res_id=102628> (accessed 1 March 2009).

The Rugao Propaganda Department (2008) *Nantong shouli zhengfu xinxi gongkai lei xingzheng anjian jiean [The First FOI Lawsuit in Nantong City Was Finalized]*, Online. Available HTTP: <http://www.chinacourt.org/html/article/200808/05/315763.shtml> (accessed 1 January 2011).

The Shanghai Government (2008) *Freedom of Information Rules 2004 Annual Report 2008*, Shanghai: The Shanghai Government.

The Shanghai Legislative Affairs Office and the Shanghai Institute for Administrative Law Studies (2007) '2006 nian fazhiban gongzuo zongjie ji 2007 nian gongzuo yaodian [Work Review for 2006 and Work Outline for 2007 of the Shanghai Legislative Affairs Office]', *The Brief Report on the Shanghai Government Rule of Law*, 4.

——(2008a) 'Zhengfu xinxi gongkai de dafu xingshi [The Methods of Replying to Access Requests]', *The Brief Report on the Shanghai Government Rule of Law*, 16.

——(2008b) 'Zhengfu xinxi gongkai yu xinfang shixiang guanxi bianxi [Analysis of Discrimination between Access Requests and Petitions]', *The Brief Report on the Shanghai Government Rule of Law*, 5.

The Shanghai Science and Technology Commission (2005) *Freedom of Information Rules 2004 Annual Report 2005*, Shanghai: The Shanghai Science and Technology Commission.

The State Council Information Office (2005) *The White Paper on the Building of Political Democracy in China* (Beijing, 19 October).

——(2007) *The White Paper on China's Political Party System* (Beijing, 15 November).

——(2008) *The White Paper on China's Efforts and Achievements in Promoting the Rule of Law* (Beijing, 28 February).

The State Council Informatization Office (2002) *Zhengfu xinxi gongkai tiaoli (cao an) qicao shuoming [Explanation Memorandum of the Draft of FOI Regulations 2002]*, Beijing: The Informatization Office of the State Council.

——(2006) *Zhongguo xinxihua fazhan baogao [Informatization Development Report in China]*, Online. Available HTTP: <http://www.e-gov.org.cn/ziliaoku/news003/200606/28025.html> (accessed 22 June 2007).

The UK Advisory Panel on Public Sector Information (2006) *Public Sector Information Policy in Australia*, Online. Available HTTP: <http://www.appsi.gov.uk/reports/policy-australia.pdf> (accessed 5 January 2008).

The US National Commission Libraries and Information Science (2001) *The Comprehensive Assessment of Public Information Dissemination*, Online. Available HTTP: <http://www.nclis.gov/govt/assess/assess.execsum.pdf> (accessed 27 March 2008).

The World Bank (n.d.) *Definition of E-Government*, Online. Available HTTP: <http://web.worldbank.org/ AUTHOR CONFIRM (accessed 14 September 2009).

Tian, D. D. (2008) 'Zhengfu bumen shouci baisu [The Government Agency Lost Its FOI Lawsuit for the First Time]', *People's Daily*, 10 October, p.10.

Tian, S. Y. and Xin, H. (2008) 'Nansha xiangmu huo juxing tingzhenghui [Public Hearings will be Held for the Guangdong Oil Refinery Project]', *Southern Metropolis Daily*, 11 March, p.A09.

Vaughn, R. (2000) 'Introduction', in Vaughn, R. (ed.) *Freedom of Information*, Burlington: Ashgate.

Vleugels, R. (2006) *Overview of FOIA Countries Worldwide – February 1 2006*, Online. Available HTTP: <http://www.statewatch.org/news/2006/feb/foia-feb-2006.pdf> (accessed 3 October 2008).

Volman, Y. (2004) 'Exploitation of Public Sector Information in the Context of the *eEurope* Action Plan', in Aichholzer, G. and Burkert, H.(eds) *Public Sector Information in the Digital Age: Between Markets, Public Management and Citizens' Rights*, Cheltenham: Edward Elgar Publishing.

Wang, C. (2008) *Present a Real China to the World in a More Transparent Way*, press release, 30 December.

Wang, J. X. (2008a) 'Yi lvshi pilu zhengfu xinxi gongkai zhi guai xianzhuang [A Lawyer Discussed Various Strange Phenomena regarding FOI]', *China Youth Daily*, 10 May, p.3.

——(2008b) 'Zhejiang yuyao 68 ming cunmin gaoying shizhengfu [Sixty-Eight Villagers in Yuyao City of Zhejiang Province Won Their FOI Lawsuit]', *China Youth Daily*, 10 October, p.6.

Wang, W. J. and Yu, J. M. (2008) 'Xinxi gongkai zhengfu bumen shiying ma? [Are Government Agencies Getting Used to FOI?]', *People's Daily*, 8 May, p.10.

Wang, X. B. (2008) 'Dongbei shouli guanzhu zhengfu zhangmu shenqing zuo dijiao [The First FOI Request for Government Financial Accounts in Northeast China Submitted]', *Commercial Times*, 25 October, p.A03.

Wang, Y. J. (2007) 'Zhengfu xinxi gongkai tiaoli shinian pobing [The Breakthrough of Legislating on FOI after a Decade]', *China Youth Daily*, 25 April, p.3.

Weiss, P. (2004) 'Borders in Cyberspace: Conflicting Public Sector Information Policies and Their Economic Impacts', in Aichholzer, G. and Burkert, H. (eds) *Public Sector Information in the Digital Age: Between Markets, Public Management and Citizens' Rights*, Cheltenham: Edward Elgar Publishing, pp.137–159.

Wen, J. B. (2004a) 'Shijie renda erci huiyi shang suozuo zhengfu gongzuo baogao [Report on the Work of the Government to the National People's Congress]', speech delivered at the Second Session of the 10th National People's Congress, Beijing, 16 March.

——(2004b) 'Quanmian tuijin yifa xingzheng nuli jianshe fazhi zhengfu [Pushing forward Administration by Law in an All-Round Way to Build a Government under the Rule of Law]', speech delivered at the National Picturephone Conference on the Work of Law-Based Administration, Beijing, 28 June.

——(2007) 'Guanyu shehui zhuyi chuji jieduan de lishi renwu he woguo duiwai zhengce de jige wenti [Our Historical Tasks at the Primary Stage of Socialism and Several Issues concerning China's Foreign Policy]', *People's Daily*, 27 February, p. 2.

——(2008a) *Jiabao Wen Meets with UN Secretary-General Ban Ki-moon in the Quake-Hit Area*. Press release, 24 May.

——(2008b) 'Shiyi jie renda yici huiyi shang suozuo zhengfu gongzuo baogao [Report on the Work of the Government to the National People's Congress]', speech delivered at the First Session of the 11th National People's Congress, Beijing, 5 March.

——(2008c) 'Renzhen guanche dang de shiqida jingshen dali tuijin lianzheng jianshe he fanfubai gongzuo [Seriously Adhere to the Spirits of the 17th National Congress of the CPC to Promote Vigorously the Work of Incorruptibility Construction and Anti-Corruption]', *Qiushi*, 9: 3–8.

——(2009) 'Shiyi jie renda erci huiyi shang suozuo zhengfu gongzuo baogao [Report on the Work of the Government to the National People's Congress]', speech delivered at the Second Session of the 11th National People's Congress, Beijing, 5 March.

Wen, W. P. (2008) *Chinese Scholars Hail Government Information Transparency Regulations*, Online. Available HTTP: <http://en.chinaelections.org/newsinfo.asp?newsid=17678> (accessed 2 October 2008).

Wenchuan 8.0 ji dizhen liedu fenbutu [The M8.0 Earthquake Intensity Distribution Map in Wenchuan] (2008), Online. Available HTTP: <http://www.cea.gov.cn/manage/html/8a8587881632fa5c0116674a018300cf/_content/0809/01/1220238314350.html> (accessed 22 October 2008).

Whitlam, G. (1972) 'It Is Time for Leadership', speech delivered at the Blacktown Civic Centre, Sydney, 13 November.

Woguo kaifang 1956 dao 1960 nianjian jiemi waijiao dangan [Declassified Foreign Affairs Archives from between 1956 to 1960 Were Accessible in China] (2006), Online. Available HTTP: <http://news.xinhuanet.com/banyt/2006–7/19/content_4852638.htm> (accessed 29 March 2008).

Woguo zhengfu xinxi hua de fazhan licheng [The Development of Government Informatization in China] (2003), Online. Available HTTP: <http://www.china.com.cn/chinese/zhuanti/283258.htm> (accessed 19 May 2008).

Woguo Zhengfu Xinxihua de fazhan licheng [A Historical Overview of Development of Informatization in China] (2007), Online. Available HTTP: <http://e-gov.nsa.gov.cn/digest.asp?articleid=335> (accessed 5 April 2008).

Wood, S. (2006) *Open Government in China*, Online. Available HTTP: <http://foia.blogspot.com/2006/06/open-government-in-china-china-is.html> (accessed 21 August 2007).

World Trade Organization (2001) *Protocol on the Accession of the People's Republic of China*, (WT/L/432) 23 November, Part I, C (1).

Wu, Jie Lin (2009) 'Zhengfu xinxi gongkai xingzheng susong youguan wenti de sikao [Issues Related to FOI Lawsuits]', *E-Government*, 4, 39–42.

Wu, Jin Lian (2006) 'Zhongguo yingdang zou shenme yang de gongyehua daolu [Which Path of Industrialization Should China Take?]', *Management World*, 8, 1–7.

Wu, W. Z. and Li, X. H. (2006) 'Loudong jianguan zhong de muzhi chuanbo [Weak Supervision of the Short Message Communication]', *Journal of Harbin University*, 12, 85–88.

Wu, Y. (2008) 'Xinxi gongkai hai xu zai chai bolimen [The Glass Door Effect Need to be Broken by FOI]', *People's Daily*, 9 May, p.11.

Wu, Y. X. (2008) 'Cangzhou lvshi tousu duo buwei xinxi bu gongkai [A Cangzhou Lawyer Complained to Several State Agencies about the Failure to Disclose Information]', *Yanzhao City Daily*, 6 May, p.5.

Wuhan shouli zhengfu xinxi gongkai an shenjie laodongju beipan weigui [The Trial of the First FOI Case in Wuhan City Was Completed with the Judgment of the Labor Bureau Violating Wuhan FOI Interim Rules] (2004), Online. Available HTTP: <http://www.qtfz.gov.cn:8080/show.jsp?id=3303> (accessed 7 May 2008).

Xi, F. Y. (2008) 'Baomifa xiugai yi mojian shiernian jiang suoxiao guojia mimi fanwei [12-Year Consideration of Revising the Law *on the Protection of State Secret*]', *Legal Daily*, 22 July, p.4.

Xiao, W. B. (2008a) Interview with a Chinese Government Official (Interview in person, 16 June).

——(2008b) Interview with Chinese Government Officials (Interview in person, 18 June).

——(2008c) Interview with Government Officials (Interview in person, 20 June).

——(2008d) Interview with Librarians (Interview in person, 22 June).

——(2008e) Interview with Chinese Government Officials (Interview in person, 24 June).

——(2008f) Interview with Librarians (Interview in person, 8 July).

——(2008g) Interview with a Chinese Government Official (Interview in person, 9 July).

——(2008h) Interviews with Chinese Academics (Interview in person, 12 July).

——(2008i) Interviews with Chinese Citizens (Interview in person, 17 June).

——(2008j) Interviews with Chinese Citizens (Interview in person, 19 June).

——(2008k) Interview with Archivists (Interview in person, 21 July).

——(2008l) Interview with Archivists (Interview in person, 22 July).

——(2008m) Interview with Archivists (Interview in person, 23 July).

——(2008n) Interview with Chinese Government Officials (Interview in person, 23 July).

——(2008o) Interview with Archivists (Interview in person, 30 July).

——(2008p) Interview with Archivists (Interview in person, 1 August).

——(2008q) Interviews with a Chinese Government Official (Interview in person, 1 August).

——(2008r) Interviews with a Chinese Government Official (Interview in person, 1 August).

Xie, Y. Q. (2008) 'Cunmin liangzhi suzhuang gao zhen zhengfu [Villagers Filed Two Lawsuits against the Township Government]', *Huashang Newspaper*, 16 October, p. A14.

Xin, C. Y. and Feng, J. (2005) *WTO yu zhongguo xingzheng fazhi gaige [WTO and China's Administrative Law Reforms]*, Beijing: Social Sciences Academic Press.

Xu, X. J. (1979) 'Tangshan dizhen siwang 24 wan duo ren [Death Toll of the Tangshan Earthquake Is More Than 240,000]', *People's Daily*, 23 November.

Xue, G. L. (2006) *Xingzheng fazhi daolu tanxun: Xue Gangling jiaoshou wenji [Discovering the Roadmap for the Rule of Administrative Law: Combined Works of Professor Xue Gangling]*, Beijing: China Legal Publishing House.

Yan, H. (2008) *Zhengfu xinxi gongkai zhidu yanjiu [Theory and Practice in Government Information Publicity]*, Wuhan: Wuhan University Press.

Yan, J. (2009) *Rang minzhu zaofu zhongguo: Yu keping fangtan lu [Make Democracy Benefit China: Dialogue with Professor Keping Yu]*, Beijing: Central Compilation & Translation Press.

Yang, H. S. (2008) *Gebie difang zhengfu xinxi xianru bugongkai kunjing [Non-Disclosure Problems for Several Local Governments]*, Online. Available HTTP: <http://news.xinhuanet.com/politics/2008–07/30/content_8851290.htm> (accessed 10 March 2009).

Yang, L. (2005) *Yi shimin xiang shi bumen yifa suoqu zhiqingquan zai wuhaishi fazhiban zhichi xia huode chenggong [A Citizen Requested Government Information from*

10 Agencies and Achieved Success with the Support of the Wuhan Legislative Affairs Office], Online. Available HTTP: <http://www.whfzb.gov.cn/Article,868.html> (accessed 21 October 2008).

Yang, X. S. (2007) 'Subsidiary Report on Learning FOI Regulations', speech delivered at Conference on Learning FOI Regulations, Beijing, 17 May.

——(2009) Speech delivered at the Press Conference on the Seventh Assessment of the Performance of China's Government Websites, Beijing, 11 January.

Ye, D. D. (2008) *Lifa gongkai jinxingshi [Openness in Law-Making Activity Is Underway]*, Online. Available HTTP: <http://www.caijing.com.cn/2008-09-03/110009953.html> (accessed 3 October 2008).

Yi, F. (2007) *Buyao wudu le xiaoping tongzhi de duozuo shaoshuo [Don't Misunderstand Deng's Warning on 'Saying Less and Doing More']*, Online. Available HTTP: <http://news.xinhuanet.com/comments/2007–02/0f9/content_5712689.htm>accessed 23 March 2009).

Yin, S. C. (2008) *China's Handling of Quake News 'Novel'*, Online. Available HTTP: <http://www.straitstimes.com/Free/Story/STIStory_238121.html> (accessed 17 May 2008).

Yin, Y. (2007) 'Tan zhengfu xinxi gongkai xingzheng anjian shenli xin silu [New Thoughts on Trying FOI Cases]', *Shanghai Journal of Law*, 5: 51–52.

Yin, Y. and Ding, Y. (2007) 'Zhengfu xinxi gongkai xingzheng anjian de falv sikao [On Legal Issues of FOI Lawsuits]', *Shanghai Journal of Law*, 1: 40–43.

Ying, S. N. (2001) 'Zhongguo xingzhengfa de chuangzhi yu mianlin de wenti [The Establishment of China's Administrative Law and the Problems Encountered]', *Journal of Jianghai Academia*, 1: 60–64.

——(2006) 'Zhongguo xingzhengfa de huigu yu zhanwang [Overview and Expectations of China's Administrative Law]', speech delivered at Zhongshan University, Zhongshan, 6 January.

——(2008) 'Zhongguo xingzhengfa de huigu yu zhanwang [Overview and Expectations of China's Administrative Law]', *The Rule of Law Forum*, 2: 1–8.

Yiwei gongmin shenqing zhengfu xinxi gongkai zhi lu [A Citizen's Story about Access to Government Information] (2008), Online. Available HTTP: <http://www.jsia.gov.cn/Browse/noinfocontent.aspx?id=1991&tablename=tnoinfo> (accessed 10 October 2008).

Yu, G. M. (2003) 'Baozhang renmin de zhiqingquan shi jiangou guojia xinxi anquan tizhi de genben yuanze [Guaranteeing the People's Right to Know Is the Fundamental Principle for Building the State's Information Security System]', *Practical Journalism*, 6: 27–28.

Yu, K. P. (2007a) 'Minzhu shi gongheguo de shengming [Democracy Is the Lifeblood of the People's Republic of China]', *People Forum*, 22: 6–8.

——(2007b) 'Sixiang jiefang yu zhengzhi jinbu [Emancipation of Mind and Political Progress]', *Beijing Daily*, 17 September, p.18.

Yuan, C. (2008) 'Haidianqu: zhengfu xinxi gongkai zhihou [After the Implementation of FOI Regulations in Haidian District]', *China Business News*, 11 June, p. A06.

Yuan, S. and Jiang, Y. (2008) *Hangzhou ditie taxian: hangzhou shiwei shuji tichu bage zhua yaoqiu [The Hangzhou Subway Collapse: The Party Secretary Calls for Eight Requirements]*, Online. Available HTTP: <http://www.chinanews.com.cn/gn/news/2008/11–16/1451030.shtml> (accessed 3 December 2008).

Yun, G. Q. and Lv, P. (2003) *Yi SARS yiqing weili kan chuanmei yu zhengfu de guanxi [The Relationship between the Media and the Government: Taking the Example of the SARS Incident]*, Online. Available HTTP: <http://www.cuhk.edu.hk/ics/21c/supplem/essay/0304069.htm> (accessed 21 April 2008).

Zeng Qinghong qiangdiao yao chongfen renshi banbu gongwuyuan fa de zhongyao yiyi [Qinghong Zeng Stresses the Comprehensive Recognition of the Significance of the Passage of the Civil Servant Law] (2005), Online. Available HTTP: <http://www.gov.cn/zfjs/2005–9/22/content_68644.htm> (accessed 9 February 2008).

Zeng, X. D. (2008) *Guojia zhijian gongju bei lianmin yaoqiu gongkai zhengzhou tapu zhaji diaocha baogao [The General Administration of Quality Supervision, Inspection and Quarantine Was Asked to Disclose the Investigation Report on the Quality of the Mills Produced by a Top Company in Zhengzhou]*, Online. Available HTTP: <http://www.cnr.cn/news/200810/t20081017_505126016.html> (accessed 18 November 2008).

Zhang, H. and Song, S. P. (2008) 'Tiaoli shishi hou benshi shouqi gongmin yaoqiu zhengfu xinxi gongkai de anli [The First FOI Case in Zhengzhou after Implementation of FOI Regulations]', *Zhengzhou Evening*, 7 August, p.A12.

Zhang, J. Y., Zou, S. W. and Sun, C. B. (2003) *Huize baixing de yangguang gongcheng woguo jiji tuixing banshi gongkai zhidu [The 'Sunshine Project' Benefits the Masses: China Actively Promotes Openness in the Process of Administrative Affairs]*, Online. Available HTTP: <http://news.xinhuanet.com/newscenter/2003–12/30/content_1254392.htm> (accessed 10 February 2008).

Zhang, M. J. (2003) *Kaifang de zhengfu: zhengfu xinxi gongkai falv zhidu yanjiu [Open Government: Research on FOI Laws]*, Beijing: China Law Press.

Zhang, Q. (2007) *Fazhiban jieshao zhengfu xinxi gongkai tiaoli youguan qingkuang bing dawen [The Legislative Affairs of the State Council Introduces FOI Regulations]*. Press release, 24 April.

Zhang, R. Q. (2008) 'Jiaqiang yulun yindao tigao zhizheng nengli [Strengthening Guidance of Public Opinion to Improve the Ruling Capability]', *Yanzhao Evening*, 15 December, p.A3.

Zhang, W. J. (2008) *Introduction on Shanghai Major Construction Projects in 2008*. Press release, 19 March.

Zhang, X. (2005) *Su mou yaoqiu renshi guanli jiguan gongkai zhengfu xinxi shangsu an [Su Sued against the Personnel Management Bureau for Not Disclosing Government Information]*, Online. Available HTTP: <http://www.shezfy.com/spyj/alpx_view.aspx?id=2905> (accessed 11 May 2008).

Zhang, Y. H. (2008) 'Shouji duanxin chuangbo zhong de kongzhi queshi yu duice [The Incapability of Controlling the Transmission of SMS Messages and the Solutions]', *News Window*, 1: 104–106.

Zhao, L. and Su, Y. T. (2008) 'Zhengfu xinxi yidian rengduo [Many Doubts about Government Information Disclosure]', *Southern Weekend*, 8 May, p.A04.

Zhao, W. M. (2008) 'Toushi zhengfu xinxi gongkai tiaoli shishi hou diyi an [Reflecting on the First Lawsuit after FOI Regulations Took Effect]', *Legal Daily* (Beijing), 6 May, 8.

Zhao, Z. Q. (2001) 'Zhengwu gongkai fanfubai lunyao [Discussion of Anti-Corruption through Openness in Government Affairs]', *Theory and Modernization*, 6: 51–56.

Zhao, Z. Y. (1987) 'Yanzhe you zhongguo tese de shehuizhuyi daolu qianjin [Take Strides along the Road to Socialism with Chinese Characteristics]', speech delivered at the 13th National Congress of the CPC, Beijing, 25 October.

Zhengfu xinxihua dashi ji [A Chronicle of Significant Events in Government Informatization] (2003), Online. Available HTTP: <http://www.china.com.cn/chinese/zhuanti/283818.htm> (accessed 19 May 2008).

Zheng, L. (2007) 'Enacting and Implementing Open Government Information Regulations in China: Motivations and Barriers', paper presented at the First International Conference on Theory and Practice of Electronic Governance, Macao, 10–13 December.

Zhong, L. (2008) *Siren youxiang chongdang zhengwu gongkai pingtai shenzhen sifaju beisu [The Shenzhen Justice Bureau Was Sued for Replying to an FOI Request via a Private Email]*, Online. Available HTTP: <http://www.21cbh.com/HTML/2008/8/26/HTML_X87778CRQ1PG.html> (accessed 22 October 2008).

Zhongguo guojia yufang fubaiju zhengshi jiepai shouren juzhang mawen jianghua [The National Corruption Prevention Bureau Established: Speech by the First Head Ma Wen] (2007), Online. Available HTTP: <http://www.chinanews.com.cn/gn/news/2007/09–13/1025663.shtml> (accessed 13 September 2007).

Zhongguo shi shengqu zao hanjian xuezai yi chixu ban yue 3287 wan ren shouzai [Rare Snow Storms in China's 10 Provinces and Has Lasted for Half a Month with 32.87 Million People Being Caught up] (2008), Online. Available HTTP: <http://www.chinanews.com.cn/gn/news/2008/01–26/1146727.shtml> (accessed 15 April 2008).

Zhongguo zhengfu wangzhan jixiao pinggu zhibiao tixi (2008)[The Indicator System for Assessing the Performance of Government Websites in 2008] (2008), Online. Available HTTP: <http://xxhs.miit.gov.cn/n11293472/n11295327/n11297217/11746784.html> (accessed 17 March 2009).

Zhonghua renmin gongheguo guomin jingji he shehui fazhan di shiyi ge wunian guihua gangyao [The 11 Five-Year Plan for National Economy and Social Development] (2006), Online. Available HTTP: <http://news.xinhuanet.com/misc/2006–03/16/content_4309517_20.htm> (accessed 7 May 2008).

Zhou, E. L. (1984) *Zhou Enlai wenxuan [Selected Works of Enlai Zhou]*, Beijing: People's Press.

Zhou, H. H. (ed.) (2003) *Zhengfu xinxi gongkai tiaoli zhuanjia jianyigao [Academic Draft of FOI Regulations]*, Beijing: China Legal Publishing House.

——(2005) 'Regulation on Government Information Publication in China: Practice, Problems and Prospect', speech delivered at Conference on China Policy Dialogue, Columbia, 1 June.

——(2007a) 'Zhengfu xinxi gongkai tiaoli dailai liuda bianhua [FOI Regulations Will Bring about Six Changes]', *People's Daily*, 14 February, p.13.

——(2007b) *Zhengfu jianguan yu xingzheng fa [Government Governance and Administrative Law]*, Beijing: Beijing University Press.

——(2007c) 'Open Government in China: Practice and Problems', in Florini, A. (ed.) *The Right to Know: Transparency for an Open World*, New York: Columbia University Press.

——(2007d) 'Woguo tuixing xinxi gongkai zhidu de yiyi yu tedian [Significance and Features of Introducing FOI Legislation in China]', *China Today Forum*, 6: 29–30.

——(2007e) Speech delivered at Seminar on the FOI Regulations, Beijing, 17 March.

——(2007f) 'Xinxi gongkai tiaoli chutai shimo [The Legislative History of FOI Regulations in China]', speech delivered at the Second Summit on E-Government, Beijing, 28 June.

——(2008a) Speech delivered at Seminar on the Challenges and Possibilities for Government Information Disclosure, Beijing, 25 June.

——(2008b) 'Xinxi gongkai tiaoli chutai shimo [The Legislative History of FOI Regulations in China]', *E-Government*, 7, 15–17.

Zhou, K. (2008) 'Shanghai cixuanfu youhua fangan tingqu gefang yijian [The Proposed Shanghai Maglev Construction Project Available for Public Opinion]', *China Youth Daily*, 14 January, p.7.

Zhou, Y. F. (2005) 'Woguo zhengfu xinxi gongkai lifa pingxi [Analysis of FOI Law-Making Activities in China]', *Journal of Jinan University*, 6: 54–61.

Zhu, H. J. (2007a) 'Gongzhong canyu beihou de zhengfu kaoliang [The Xiamen Government's Consideration of Public Participation]', *Southern Weekend*, 20 December, p.A01.

——(2007b) 'Wo shisi hanwei ni shuohua de quanli [I Will Fight to Death for Your Right to Say It]', *Southern Weekend*, 20 December, p.A02.

Zhu, H. X., Hu, J. C., and Sun, W. T. (2008) '2007 zhongguo hulianwang yuqing fenxi baogao [Analysis Report on Public Opinions on the Internet in China in 2007]', *Today's Mass Media*, 2: 31–40.

Zhu, S. Y. (2003) 'Woguo zhengfu xinxi gongkai de xianzhuang fenxi yu sikao [Analysis of and Thoughts on the Current Situation of FOI in China]', *Expanding Horizons*, 3: 31–33.

Zimmerman, J. (2005) *China Law Deskbook*, 2nd edn, Chicago: American Bar Association.

Zuo, Q. M. (2000), *Chunqiu zuozhuan zhao gong liu nian [Year 6 of Emperor Zhao in the Commentary on the Spring and Autumn Annals]*, Online. Available HTTP: <http://www.guoxue.com/jinbu/13jing/cqzz/cqzz_010.htm> (accessed 10 January 2011).

Cases

Forests Survey Inspection Request Case (1989) 1 KCCR 176, 88 Hun-Ma 22, September 4.

Gao v Ninghai County People's Government (2006) 3 The People's Court of Fenghua City (The First Instance).

Goldberg v Kelly (1970)397 US 254, 267–68.

Inter-American Court of Human Rights (2006) *Claude Reyes et al v Chile Judgment* of September 19.

Jinsong Hao v The Shaanxi Forestry Department (2008) 1 The Lianhu District People's Court of Xi'an.

Jordan v United States Dept of Justice (1978) 591 F 2d 753, 772–73.

Kenedi v Hungary (2009) No 31475/05, 26.5.2009.

Lian v The General Team of Transportation Police (2005) 165 The Shanghai No 2 Intermediary People's Court (The Second Instance).

Liying Gao v The Beijing Sijiqing Township Government (2008) 201 The Haidian District People's Court of Beijing (The First Instance).

Military Secret Leakage (1992) Case KCCR 64, 89Hun-Ka104, February 25.

S.P. Gupta v President of India and others etc. (1982) AIR 1982 SC 149.

Su v Shanghai Huangpu District Personnel Bureau (2005) 72 The Shanghai No 2 Intermediary People's Court (The Second Instance).

Társaság a Szabadságjogokért v Hungary (2009) No 37374/05, 14.4.2009.

Yuhua Chen v The Beijing Municipal Public Security Bureau (2008) 155 The Dongcheng District People's Court of Beijing (The First Instance).

Legislation

Administrative Appeals Tribunal Act (1975).
Administrative Decisions (Judicial Review) *Act* (1977).
Administrative Litigation Law (1989).
Administrative Penalty Law (1996).
Administrative Permission Law (2003).
Administrative Procedure Act of 1946 (1946) Pub. L. No 79–404, 60 Stat. 238.
Administrative Procedure Act (1946) 5 USC.
Administrative Reconsideration Law (1999).
Administrative Supervision Law (1997).
American Convention on Human Rights Anti-trust Law (1993).
Archives Law (1987).
Audit Law (1995).
Civil Procedure Law (1982).
Civil Servant Law (2005).
Constitution (1982).
Copyright Act (1994) 17 USC.
Criminal Law (1997)
Criminal Litigation Law (1996).
Directive (EC) No 98/2003 of 17 November 2003 on the Re-use of Public Sector Information (2003) OJ L 345/90.
Federal Register Act (1935) 44 USC.
Federal Transparency and Access to Public Government Information Law (2002).
Freedom of Information Act (2000).
Freedom of Information Interim Rules of the Archives Bureau (2008)
Freedom of Information Regulations (2007).
Freedom of Information Rules (2004).
Freedom of Information Rules of the Archives Bureau (2008).
Freedom of Information Rules of the Commission of National Defence and Science Industry (2007).
Freedom of Information Rules of the Ministry of Education (2008).
Freedom of Information Rules of the National Bureau of Tax (2008).
General Standards on Physical Examinations concerning the Employment of Civil Servants (for Trial) (2005).
Government Information (Public Access) *Act* (2009).
Green Paper on Public Sector Information Com (1998) 585.
Interim Measures for Public Participation in Environmental Impact Assessment (2006).
Interim Measures on Freedom of Environmental Information (2007).
Interim Regulations on National Civil Servants (1993).
Interim Rules on Freedom of Information of the Bureau of Intellectual Property (2008).
Interim Rules on Freedom of Information on the Government Website of the Commission of National Defence and Science Industry (2007).
Interim Rules on the Tenure System of Leading Cadres of the Party and Government (2006).
Law on Administrative Penalties for Public Security (2005).
Law on the Prevention and Cure of Infectious Diseases (1989).

Law on the Protection of State Secrets (1988).
Legislation Law (2000).
Measures for the Administration of Relief for Vagrants and Beggars without Assured Living Sources in Cities (2003).
Ombudsman Act (1976).
Organic Law of the Urban Residents Committees (1989).
Organic Law of the Villagers' Committee (1998).
Organic Law of the Villagers' Committees (for trial) (1987).
Paperwork Reduction Act (1995) 44 USC.
Police Law (1995).
Prevention and Cure of Infectious Diseases Law (1989).
Price Law (1997).
Property Law (2007).
Provisional Regulations on the Open Selection of Leading Cadres of the Party and Government (2004).
Regulations on Preparedness for and Response to Emergent Public Health Hazards (2003).
Regulations on the Work of Selecting and Appointing Leading Party and Government Cadres (2002).
Rules for the Implementation of the Provisions on the Public Security Agency's Handling of Cases Involving the Crime of Injury (2006).
Rules on the Intercommunication System of Leading Cadres of the Party and Government (2006).
Supreme Court's Explanation on Several Questions Related to the Implementation of the Administrative Litigation Law (1989).
Supreme Court's Several Issues Related to the Trial of Civil Dispute Cases Related to Restructuring of Enterprises Provisions (2003).
Working Procedures for Access to Government Information of the Bureau of Foreign Currencies (2008).

Policy documents

Decision of Administrative Reconsideration Made by the Zhuhai People's Government No 8 (2006) of the Zhuhai People's Government.
Decision of Pushing forward Administration by Law in an All-Round Way No 23 (1999) of the General Office of the State Council.
Decision of the CPC Central Committee on Strengthening the Building of the Party's Ruling Capability No 18 (2004) of the Central Committee of the CPC.
Decision of the State Council on Strengthening Administration by Law in the Municipal and County Governments No 17 (2008) of the State Council.
Guidance on Building E-Government No 17 (2002) of the General Office of the CPC Central Committee.
Guidance on the Leading Group of National Informatization for China's E-Government Construction No 17 (2002) of the General Office of the CPC Central Committee.
Implementation Outline for Pushing forward Administration by Law in an All-Round Way No 10 (2004) of the General Office of the State Council.
Notice on Comprehensively Implementing Openness in Village Affairs and Democratic Management No 9 (1998) of the General Office of the CPC Central Committee.

Notice on Declassifying Death Tolls from Natural Disasters and the Related Information No 116 (2005) of the Ministry of Civil Affairs.

Notice on Disclosure of Death Tolls and Related Natural Disasters Information (2005).

Notice on Enforcement Outline for the Establishment and Improvement of a Corruption Punishing and Prevention System with Equal Attention Paid to Education, Institutions and Supervision No 3 (2005) of the Central Committee of the CPC.

Notice on Enhancing the Construction of Grassroots Organizations in the Rural Areas No 10 (1994) of the General Office of the CPC Central Committee.

Notice on Further Governing the Abusive Distribution of Party and Official Publications by Taking Advantage of Their Position and Power to Alleviate Primary Levels and Farmers' Burden No 19 (2003) of the General Office of the CPC Central Committee.

Notice on Further Promoting Openness in Government Affairs in All Administration by Industry and Commerce Agencies No 154 (2000) of the General Office of the State Administration for Industry and Commerce.

Notice on Further Promoting Openness in Government Affairs No 12 (2005) of the General Office of the CPC Central Committee.

Notice on Implementing Openness in Police Affairs in All Public Securities Agencies No 43 (1999) of the Ministry of Public Security.

Notice on Preparing for the Implementation of FOI Regulations No 54 (2007) of the General Office of the State Council.

Notice on Promoting Openness in Government Affairs around All Government Agencies at the Township Level No 25 (2000) of the General Office of the CPC Central Committee.

Notice on Rules on Major Responsibilities, Divisions and Personnel Quotas of the General Office of the State Council No 60 (2008) of the General Office of the State Council.

Notice on Standardizing the Quotas of Assistants and Deputy Secretary-Generals at the Local Level No 3 (2009) of the Organization Department of the CPC Central Committee.

Notice on Suggestions for Enforcing 2006's Legislation Work and 2006's Legislative Plan No 2 (2006) of the General Office of the State Council.

Notice on Suggestions for Further Implementing 'Eight Openness Items' concerning Civilised Tax Collection in All Tax Agencies No 144 (2000) of the State Administration of Taxation.

Notice on the Pilot Project for Developing the Administrative Reconsideration Committee in Several Provinces and Special Municipalities No 71 (2008) of the Legislative Affairs Office of the State Council.

Notice on Training Sessions for FOI Regulations (2007) of the Legislative Affairs Office of the State Council.

Opinions on Strengthening the Work of the Chinese People's Political Consultative Conference No 5 (2006) of the CPC Central Committee.

Overall Framework of National E-Government No 2 (2006) of the State Council Informatization Office.

Resolution on Certain Questions in the History of Our Party since the Founding of the People's Republic of China (1981).

Resolution on Major Issues regarding the Building of a Harmonious Socialist Society No 19 (2006) of the Central Committee of the CPC.

Rules on the Scope of State Secrets and Secrecy Levels in the Work of Civil Affairs No 17 (2000) of the Ministry of Civil Affairs.

Several Suggestions on the Implementation of China's FOI Regulations No 36 (2008) of the General Office of the State Council.

Suggestions on Fully Establishing and Enhancing Openness in Village Affairs and Democratic Management No 17 (2004) of the General Office of the CPC Central Committee.

Suggestions on Further Promoting Openness in Government Affairs No 69 (2006) of the State Administration of Taxation.

Suggestions on Strengthening Exploitation and Use of Information Resources No 34 (2004) of the General Office of the CPC Central Committee.

Working Rules of the State Council No 14 (2008) of the State Council.

Index

access mechanism 8, 15, 46, 48–50, 58, 66, 68–9, 85, 105, 119, 121; citizen-initiated access 10, 80–1; *see also* access to information

access to information 5, 24–5, 39, 48–9, 52, 73, 84, 109, 113, 118–20

accountability deficit 1–3, 7, 21, 24, 81, 122; erosion of government accountability 2; expansion of bureaucratic power 2; FOI reform in the US, Australia and Canada 14; growth of government 2; liberal democracies 1, 4, 6, 11, 24, 76, 81

administrative law reforms 9, 17, 51–9, 96, 112; administrative lawsuit 56, 101–2, 113, 116–17; administrative reconsideration 14, 56, 77, 100–3, 109, 112–13; administrative transparency 10, 57, 59; *Implementation Outline for pushing forward Administration by Law in an All-Round Way* 47, 58, 68, 78; procedural due process 56–9; rule of law package 51–2

anti-corruption efforts 8, 17, 37, 49–50, 59–69, 123; anti-corruption agencies 9, 47, 68–9, 76–7; Central Commission for Discipline Inspection 49, 66, 77; corruption prevention 66–8, 92; prevent corruption 67

archivists 93; increasing interest in FOI legislation 93; provide professional support for better records management 93

Article 19 3, 5, 24, 39; *American Convention on Human Rights* 39; European Court of Human Rights 39; Inter-American Court of Human Rights 39; *International Covenant on*

Civil and Political Rights 39; United Nations Special Rapporteur 39; to seek, receive 39; *Universal Declaration of Human Rights* 39

authoritarian state 6; such as China 6

availability of information for access 13

beneficial policies 67–8; not well known to the masses 67; those for improving farmers' income or reducing farmers' burden 67

beneficiary 8, 22, 26–7, 36, 124–5; and then a contributor to the Chinese information environment 124; transformation of the Chinese information environment 26

best practice 86; anyone should be able to exercise the access right 86; the scope of exemptions under the FOI Regulation is inconsistent with 86

Blanton 3, 6

broad and vague exemptions 11, 80, 86, 108; arguably been weakened by 86; to refuse access requests 108

burden of proof 117; to dismiss FOI legal actions 127

bureaucratic control 15, 51

capacity and willingness 11–12, 20, 121, 124; to different levels of government compliance and non-compliance 12; factor of government capacity and willingness 11; to request public information 121

central political commitment 14, 40, 89–90, 104, 124; democratization reform agenda 17, 38; preconditions for FOI reform 40

Chen 40, 76, 100, 103, 112–14